THE SUCCESSFUL LAW STUDENT

THE
SUCCESSFUL
LAW
STUDENT

AN INSIDER'S GUIDE
TO STUDYING LAW

**IMOGEN MOORE
CRAIG NEWBERY-JONES**

OXFORD
UNIVERSITY PRESS

OXFORD

UNIVERSITY PRESS

Great Clarendon Street, Oxford, OX2 6DP,
United Kingdom

Oxford University Press is a department of the University of Oxford.
It furthers the University's objective of excellence in research, scholarship,
and education by publishing worldwide. Oxford is a registered trade mark of
Oxford University Press in the UK and in certain other countries

© Oxford University Press 2018

The moral rights of the authors have been asserted

Impression: 1

Public sector information reproduced under Open Government Licence v3.0
(http://www.nationalarchives.gov.uk/doc/open-government-licence/open-government-licence.htm)

Published in the United States of America by Oxford University Press
198 Madison Avenue, New York, NY 10016, United States of America

British Library Cataloguing in Publication Data
Data available

Library of Congress Control Number: 2017957218

ISBN 978–0–19–875708–5

Printed in Great Britain by
Bell & Bain Ltd., Glasgow

Links to third party websites are provided by Oxford in good faith and
for information only. Oxford disclaims any responsibility for the materials
contained in any third party website referenced in this work.

For Kate and Eliza

For Lena

PREFACE

We took our own first steps in law a good few years ago now—rather more years for one of us than the other. But we can still recall that those steps were not easy. Learning the law, and being a law student, can undoubtedly be challenging. But it is also rewarding, and we are glad we persevered despite the doubts we both had at times.

Our reward is that we now get to spend our working lives teaching, supporting, guiding and learning from new generations of law students, while watching the progress of our former students with pride and admiration. We genuinely feel pretty lucky most of the time.

But what qualifies us to write this book? Perhaps disappointingly, we wouldn't necessarily class ourselves as having been 'successful law students'. Looking back, we could both have spent our time far more wisely and had an even more rewarding educational experience—one of us by spending a little less time in the pub, and the other by spending a little less time in the library. (We'll let you guess which one is which.)

We've learned a lot since then. Between us we have had very different educational experiences, worked in very different environments and have taught law in five different universities with friends in many more. We've taught literally thousands of law students, answered even more questions and dealt with just about every concern going.

We understand that support is essential throughout your legal journey. Law and studying law at university can be strange at times, with new words, experiences, expectations and challenges. We are still grateful to all those who have supported us through our own journeys—from our personal tutors at university, to mentors, friends and colleagues throughout our careers (far too many to name, sorry, we hope you know we are referring to you), and of course, our families.

Every law student will find valuable sources of support. You will too. We hope that this book will be a welcome addition to your own support network. We want you to succeed.

Imogen Moore
Craig Newbery-Jones

ACKNOWLEDGEMENTS

We are enormously grateful to our many friends and colleagues who have encouraged and/or tolerated us through the production of this book. Even when you weren't quite sure what on earth we were doing, or what we were doing it for, you didn't tell us too often. Thank you. Thank you too to our families—whether long-established or newly-welcomed—for giving us the time and space to write.

We must also thank OUP for taking on this project with such enthusiasm, and in particular Lucy Read and Lucy Hyde—absolute masters of patience, tolerance and artful persuasion.

We are grateful for permission to use a variety of quotes in this book, with acknowledgements as follows:

Chapter 1: Excerpt from *Stranger in a Strange Land* by Robert A. Heinlein, copyright © 1961 by Robert A. Heinlein; copyright renewed © 1989 by Virginia Heinlein; copyright © 1991 by Virginia Heinlein. Used by permission of Berkley, an imprint of Penguin Publishing Group, a division of Penguin Random House LLC. All rights reserved. Published in the UK by permission of The Robert A. and Virginia Heinlein Prize Trust c/o The Lotts Agency, Ltd.

Chapter 2: Excerpt from *Tiger at the Gates* by Jean Giraudoux, translated by Christopher Fry. Reprinted with the kind permission of Tam Fry.

Chapter 3: Excerpt from *Danny, the Champion of the World* by Roald Dahl, copyright © 1975 by Roald Dahl Nominee Limited. Used by permission of Penguin Random House LLC. All rights reserved. Reprinted in the UK with permission of David Higham Associates.

Chapter 5: Excerpt from an interview with Jay-Z, taken from 'Not a Businessman—a Business, Man,' by Anthony Decurtis, *Men's Health*, October 5, 2010. Reprinted with permission of Wright's Media.

Chapter 7: Excerpt from *A Game of Thrones: A Song of Ice and Fire: Book One* by George R.R. Martin, copyright © 1996 by George R.R. Martin. Used by permission of Bantam Books, an imprint of Random House, a division of Penguin Random House LLC. All rights reserved. Published in the U.K. by permission of George R.R. Martin c/o The Lotts Agency, Ltd.

Chapter 8: Excerpt from *The Phantom Tollbooth*, text copyright © 1961 by Norton Juster, renewed 1989 by Norton Juster. Illustrations copyright © 1961 by Jules Feiffer, renewed 1989 by Jules Feiffer. Used by permission of Brandt & Hochman Literary Agents, Inc.

Chapter 11: Excerpt from *Harry Potter and the Order of the Phoenix*: Copyright © 2003 J.K. Rowling.

Chapter 13: Excerpt from *Thanks for the Feedback: The Science and Art of Receiving Feedback Well* by Douglas Stone and Sheila Heen, copyright © 2014 by Douglas Stone and Sheila Heen. Used by permission of Viking Books, an imprint of Penguin Publishing Group, a division of Penguin Random House LLC. All rights reserved.

Chapter 14: Excerpt from *With Hemingway: A Year in Key West and Cuba* by Arnold Samuelson. Copyright © 1984 by Arnold Samuelson. Reprinted by arrangement with Dian Darby and The Barbara Hogenson Agency, Inc. All rights reserved.

Chapter 15: Excerpt from *1066 and All That: A Memorable History of England* by W.C. Sellar, R.J. Yeatman, Copyright © 2010 Methuen Publishing Ltd. Reprinted with permission.

Chapter 16: Excerpt from *A Hat Full of Sky* by Terry Pratchett. Used by permission of HarperCollins Publishers.

Chapter 20: Excerpt from *Harry Potter and the Deathly Hallows*: Copyright © 2007 J.K. Rowling.

This book could not have been written without our students— whether from Bristol, Plymouth, Reading, Exeter or Birmingham. We are proud to have taught you all, and delighted to have shared in your achievements.

The book has undoubtedly benefited from the helpful advice and comments of student and lecturer reviewers during the writing process. Thank you. We are particularly grateful to those law students and graduates who offered us their thoughts on the law student experience, many of which appear throughout the book. We would also like to thank the alumni offices at the following universities who put us in touch with their graduates: Canterbury Christ Church University, Coventry University, Lancaster University, London School of Economics, Northumbria University, Staffordshire University, University of East London, University of Hertfordshire, and University of Sunderland. All those who have contributed in any way (other than those who wish to remain anonymous) are listed below, followed by a little more about some of the students behind the voices.

Adam Hill, First year LLB student, University of York

Dr Alexander Murray, Senior Lecturer in Law, Anglia Law School, Anglia Ruskin University

Alexandra Townsley, Third year student, Law and American Law LLB, University of Nottingham

Alice Munnelly, Third year student, Law with European Legal Studies, King's College London

Amy Bristol, First year LLB student, University of Warwick

Andrea Garvey, Second year LLB (Hons) student, Swansea University

Anna Vigars QC, Barrister, Guildhall Chambers

Annie Dutton, University of Oxford Careers Service

Anthony Poole, Second year LLB student, Swansea University

Bronagh Finnegan, Communications Officer

Charlie Shepherd, Company Director

Caroline Strevens, SFHEA Reader in Legal Education and Head of Portsmouth Law School

Catey Thomas, Teaching Fellow in Law, University of Bristol Law School

Chantelle Gardner, Third year MLaw student, University of Central Lancashire

Dr Charlotte Bishop, Lecturer, University of Exeter Law School

Charlotte Brown, Third year LLB student, Bournemouth University

Dr Chloe Wallace, Associate Professor, School of Law, University of Leeds

Chris Yates, Partner, Clifford Chance LLP

Clare Doolan, University of Birmingham Careers Service

Damien Seddon, Paralegal, Woodfines

Daniel Olugbola, Second year LLB student, University of Keele

Danny Smith, Solicitor-Advocate, PCB Solicitors

David McCormick, Barrister, Exchange Chambers

David Willingham, Retired, formerly Head of Risk Financing at Save the Children

Dawn Farrow, University of Law Careers Service

Dr Dawn Watkins, Associate Professor, Leicester Law School, University of Leicester

Edward Burtonshaw-Gunn, PhD Student and Land Law Tutor, University of Bristol

Emma-Jane Darley, University of Central Lancashire, MLAW, Year 2

Emily Barrett, Fourth year student, Law with Study in Continental Europe, University of Bristol

Ffion Haf Llewelyn, Lecturer, Aberystwyth Law School, University of Aberystwyth

Fiona Lin, Third year student, Law, University of Cambridge

Frances Easton, Third year student, Law, University of Birmingham

Gabrielle Bargas, Second year student, LLB Law with French Law, University College London

Dr Gary Betts, Associate Head of School, School of Law, Coventry University

Gavin Teasdale, Solicitor, PGS Law LLP

Geoffrey Main, Teacher of A Level Law, Thomas Bennett Community College

George Dick, Second year student, LLB Scots Law, University of Dundee

Glen Joel Sylvester, Third year LLB (Hons) student, Bournemouth University

Godwin Tan, Third year LLB student, University College London

Hazel Stones, Retired secretary/PA

Isabel Anderson, Third year LLB student, Aberystwyth University

James Mohajer, Postgraduate student, London School of Economics

Jamie Hill, Barrister

Jane Alice Murray, Legal Assistant, Local Authority

Jenny Keaveney, University of Kent Careers and Employability Service

Jessica Allen, Fourth year student, Law with French and French Law, University of Nottingham

Jonathan Brew, Senior Partner, Harrison Clark Rickerbys

Julia Davenport, Third year LLB student, University of Manchester

Juliet Tomlinson, University of Oxford Careers Service

Karina Rooney, Progress Tutor, Queen Elizabeth Sixth Form College

Kate Briden, Director, Royal Courts of Justice Group

Katie Sandercock, Third year student, LLB with Placement Year, University of the West of England

Kenneth Roberts, Second year student, LLB Hons Accelerated Route, University of South Wales

Lali Wiratunga, National Manager Davidson Institute at Westpac Banking Corporation, Australia

Dr Laura Bennett, Associate Professor of Law and Director of UG Programmes, University of Reading

Lita Aguimoy Jones, Second year LLB student, Staffordshire University

Liz MacDonald, Trainee Solicitor, Whatley Weston & Fox

Dr Luke Price, Lecturer, University of Exeter Law School

Lul Sheikh-Salah, Third year LLB student, BPP University

Madeleine Burrell, Third year student, Law with German Law, University of Oxford

Monica Chen, Second year LLB student, University College London

Natasha Bellinger, Barrister, Magdalen Chambers

Nina Ali, Administrator at Coventry University and People Manager at Jake Restaurants Ltd T/A McDonalds

Octavia Knapper, Second year LLB student, Lancaster University Law School

Panashe Musabayana, Second year student, LLB Law with Criminology, Keele University

Peter Bailey, In-house Author at Sweet & Maxwell, and part-time teacher in Law at Reading Law School

Dr Piyel Haldar, Senior Lecturer in Law, Birkbeck College, University of London

Polly Metcalfe, University of Oxford Careers Service

Quynh Anh Thi Le, Second year student, LLB with study abroad, University of Warwick

Rebecca Agliolo, Fourth year student, Law, University of Cambridge

Rebecca Little, Second year LLB student, Nottingham Trent University

Dr Richard Bowyer, Senior Lecturer, University of Exeter

Richard Costidell, PhD Student and Assistant Teacher, University of Bristol

Roger Taylor, retired Solicitor, now in business development, charity work and a practising Notary Public

Ross McKirdy, First year LLB student, Robert Gordon University

Salauoddin Asghar, Strategy and Performance Manager, London Borough of Barking and Dagenham

Sammee Hart, Second year LLB student, University of East London

Sarah Kinsella

Seema Kandelia, Senior Lecturer, Westminster Law School, University of
Westminster

Shahrzad Atai Ahari, Head of Middle East Desk, Child & Child

Shuang Zhang, Senior Associate, Burkardt and Partners, Shanghai, China

Shubreet Kaur, Advocate, Punjab and Haryana High Court, India

Simon Brooman, Senior Lecturer, School of Law, Liverpool John Moores
University

Sophie McCrory-Crowther, First year LLB student, University of Keele

Staci-Louise Quinn, Third year LLB student, Liverpool John Moores
University

Steph Potter, Second year LLB student, University of York

Theresa Wilson, Fourth year student, part-time LLB, Edinburgh Napier
University

Thomas Staunton, University of Derby Careers Service

Dr Tom Webb, Lecturer, Lancaster University Law School

Dr Tracey Elliott, Lecturer, Leicester Law School, University of Leicester

Tracey Innes, University of Aberdeen Careers Service

Valentin Van de Walle, First year student, LLB in English and French Law,
King's College London

Victoria Chan, Third year student, LLB Distance Learning, Nottingham Trent
University

William Hibberd, Year 12 student, Birkenhead Sixth Form College

Zoe Lindsey, Postgraduate student, University of Nottingham

STUDENT VOICES IN 'THE SUCCESSFUL LAW STUDENT'

More than 30 law students and 30 graduates, now working in many different roles, provided their insights and experiences of studying law during the writing of this book. Some of them tell you a bit more about themselves and their experiences below:

 'I chose to study law because of the versatility of a law degree and to fulfil a lifelong dream. As a full-time mature student, prioritising my law studies and juggling family-life can sometimes be extremely challenging but is also very rewarding in terms of the variety of skills one gains. The greatest challenge I have encountered in my legal studies thus far was planning for my dissertation. The sheer amount of research and words involved made it seem like a daunting task; nevertheless, my determination, persistence, optimism and belief pulled me through. I now look forward to graduating next year.'

Glen Joel Sylvester,
Third year LLB (Hons) student, Bournemouth University

 'As an international student from Vietnam, I have always been curious about Britain's culture and its social setting, especially how law facilitates individuals' interaction and behaviour at the micro-level. Learning about the study of law from open days and public lectures prompted me to pursue a full-time law degree at the University of Warwick. Currently commencing my third year in Australia, I have found that the most challenging aspect in my studies has been setting aside my time for independent study. With work commitment and extra-curricular activities, finding time to properly prepare for seminars can be difficult.'

Quynh Anh Thi Le, Second year student,
LLB with study abroad, University of Warwick

'I chose to study law because I wanted to make a difference. As it turned out, my contribution to law this far hasn't been in the field of human rights, but legal technology. In my third year, I became aware of the growing significance of legal technology, and its undeniable impact on the legal profession. (If you haven't read Richard Susskind, I strongly recommend it!) Myself and other Cambridge law students started a legal technology company called 'Elexirr' during my final year at university; the greatest challenge I have faced as a law student is attempting to 'educate the educators' about the need for legal technology education in law school.'

Rebecca Agliolo, Fourth year law student,
University of Cambridge

'I found out I loved law by accident. I was a single mother on jobseeker's allowance with no qualifications and the Jobcentre had placed me on a course to help me seek work in which we were put on a work placement for a week. I landed a position in a solicitor's office in Canary Wharf for my placement and from there I knew it was what I wanted to do. I went back to college, completed the relevant qualifications to get into university, and started studying a law degree. My greatest challenges so far have been adjusting from college to university in the first year, and trying to catch up after unplanned absences due to being unwell. Trying to juggle university and home is difficult too sometimes.'

Sammee Hart, Second year LLB student,
University of East London

CONTENTS

CONTENTS

PART 1
A SUCCESSFUL START

1

INTRODUCING *THE SUCCESSFUL LAW STUDENT*

*'Straining at gnats and
swallowing camels is a
required course in
all law schools.'*

ROBERT A. HEINLEIN,
Stranger in a Strange Land

WELCOME

Welcome to *The Successful Law Student*! The aim of this book is to give you the best possible chance of success when studying law at university—whether you are about to start your studies or are already underway. This book is for you if you are:

- Applying for or have just accepted a place to study law at university;
- About to start a law degree;
- Studying law at university;
- Thinking about whether to study law at university.

Our aim is to guide you, honestly and supportively, through the law student experience from before you start your studies to graduation and beyond, and with just about everything in between.

We're not here to convince you to study law—nor to try to put you off. We won't be attempting to teach you the law. Nor will we be trying to teach you specific legal skills. There are lots of other books that do those things. And, as different universities take different approaches to both legal content and skills, we'll let your own tutors guide you to suitable texts for their approach at the appropriate time.

So, what *will* we be doing? We will touch on some of the law, and on some legal skills. But our focus is on the things that might just make a big difference to your experience, from how to get the most out of lectures, to how to approach law exams; and from starting university to finding a rewarding career. We'll also look beyond the learning process to equally important things such as balancing your time effectively, and managing the pressures of legal study at university. We'll hopefully answer some questions you might have about studying law, including perhaps some you wouldn't like to ask, or hadn't realised you should be asking. (And if your first question is about the 'gnats and camels' quote that opened this book, we'll explain that at the end of this chapter.)

A LEARNING PARTNERSHIP

This book is based on our experiences teaching and supporting law students over many years in several different universities. But we're not here to tell you exactly what to do, or when to do it. Life, and legal study, is not that simple. There is nearly always more than one way of approaching something, and there are always choices to be made.

Learning law is a partnership—and you will need to be an active part of that learning process. That starts here. There'll be lots to think about through the course of this book, and we won't be making decisions for you, although we'll try to help you make them for yourself.

So, we won't be looking to impose our own way of thinking or one particular approach to study on you. Even if we both had the same way of thinking or approach (we don't!), our experience has shown us that the diversity of students, institutions and law programmes means that one size will never fit all. Our aim is to guide and support you on your own journey. To provide you with the information and tools that will help you to find a route through the law student experience that works for you.

To make sure you don't just get our view on what matters, we are helped throughout the book by two important further sources of advice:

'I wish I'd known . . .'

An important feature of this book is the advice provided by real law students. A panel of students at different universities, studying different law programmes and with different backgrounds, have kindly offered us their take on a wide range of issues. Often what they say supports or illustrates our advice; sometimes they provide a different perspective.

We hope you find their insight helpful—we certainly have. At the very least you will see that you are not alone in the exciting, stimulating, but undoubtedly challenging, journey of a successful law student.

'Insider knowledge'

We are also delighted to have input from those looking at the law student experience from the other direction. We've included advice, tips and nuggets of experience from those within legal practice (including solicitors and barristers), those within legal education and law graduates who have gone on to succeed in a range of other careers.

Their advice and experience is invaluable—we're sure you'll find it instructive. You may also be inspired by the range of careers and experiences open to the successful law student.

SUCCESS AND THE LAW STUDENT

This book is all about succeeding as a law student. Success means different things to different people. It isn't just about marks and careers, however important they are. It is also about finding a balance between work, life and study, achieving your goals, and finding fulfilment in what you do.

I WISH I'D KNOWN . . .

- -

'Success is however you define it. Success might mean money and an amazing city career to some. Others might not be attracted by external validation and materialism. Success means finding out what you want to get from life and working to achieve it.'

Monica Chen, University College London, LLB, Year 2

In this book our aim is to help you achieve success as a law student, however you might define that. We'll look more closely at 'success' in Chapter 3, and help you to think about what succeeding as a law student means for you.

INSIDER KNOWLEDGE

'Success used to mean how much reward you could get from a job. Now it means how happy I am with my career.'

Damien Seddon, Paralegal, Woodfines

WHAT'S IN THIS FOR ME?

We've split this book into six broad sections, covering different aspects of your time as a law student. You can read this book from start to finish, taking a roughly chronological path through the law student experience. Or you might choose to focus on specific areas that are particularly relevant to you right now.

- Part One: A Successful Start

  - This part provides guidance if you are still thinking about whether or not to study law, and possibly reassurance if you've just made this decision. It looks at what 'success' means, and attributes and activities that might help you to achieve success as a law student. It also covers the transition to university legal study, whatever your starting point.

- Part Two: Successful Legal Study

  - In order to ensure you are in the best position to achieve success as a law student, Part Two looks at different aspects of studying law at university. This section covers what you'll study in terms of both knowledge and skills, and finding and using legal resources.

- Part Three: Successful Learning: Making the Most of Teaching and Learning in Law

  - In Part Three we discuss teaching methods in law, what to expect and how to get the best out of the learning opportunities available to you. These range from formal timetabled classes to more informal opportunities. This part also looks at key skills such as reading and research, and critical legal thinking.

- **Part Four: Successful Assessment: Making the Most of Assignments, Assessments and Feedback**
  - Part Four explores assessment in law, including exams, essays, research projects and other less common types of assessment. It looks at how you can do your best in all law assessments, looking both at general skills and those specific to particular assessments. It also considers the feedback you will get on your work, and what to do with it.

- **Part Five: Success Outside the Classroom: Making the Most of Other Opportunities**
  - Success as a law student isn't just about doing well in class and exams; there are loads of other opportunities out there that you will need to engage with. This part looks at everything from studying abroad, to extracurricular activities whether law-based or not, including mooting, negotiation, volunteering and paid work.

- **Part Six: Ensuring a Successful Future**
  - This part looks towards life after legal studies. But you'll need to think about these things while you are a law student, or even before. Part Six covers career choices and pathways (both legal and non-legal), and what you need to do and think about to be ready to move on successfully.

Even if you read this book from cover to cover, you'll need to return to particular points later on, as they become directly relevant to particular stages in your studies. We've included cross-references throughout the book so you can easily follow up connected topics covered in different chapters if you are just dipping in from time to time.

GNATS AND CAMELS

Before we go any further, we'll briefly return to the quote that starts this chapter. You may not immediately associate the law and legal study with gnats or camels. We don't blame you. But the quote is a telling one.

The quote refers to an old saying: 'to strain out gnats, but swallow camels'. (The saying is actually based on a biblical verse criticising law makers.) Someone who 'strains gnats but swallows camels' is someone who focuses on the small, relatively unimportant things but misses the big picture. In law that might mean concentrating on the minutiae of regulations, but ignoring the broader requirements of justice or fairness.

Does studying law at university really encourage this as the quote suggests? We don't think so. One of the many joys of studying law is the broad and complex picture it provides of society and justice in myriad forms. But the quote does reveal a common problem for those studying law. Such are the complexities of the law—and the pressures of studying and assessment—that there can be an understandable tendency to get hung up on minor points.

That doesn't mean detail, precision and accuracy aren't important for success as a law student. Of course they are. And this book will help you to get the most from your studies so you can indeed demonstrate your detailed understanding of the law.

But more generally, one of the aims of this book is to help you to see the bigger picture throughout your legal studies. To keep a sense of perspective, and to understand what you need to focus on. That way, you'll be much better equipped for success as a law student. And as a reminder of that bigger picture—of both law and success—you'll find a camel accompanying you on every page.

I WISH I'D KNOWN . . .

'Treat this stage of your life as a marathon. It is not a quick and easy route. There are lots of bends and sometimes you may pass the same building twice, but know that eventually, if you really push hard enough, you will cross that finish line!'

James Mohajer, Postgraduate student, London School of Economics

2

THINKING ABOUT STUDYING LAW

*'There is no better way
of exercising the
imagination than
the study of law.'*

JEAN GIRAUDOUX,
Tiger at the Gates

INTRODUCTION

If you have already made the decision to study law at university then you can skip this chapter. But if you haven't yet made up your mind about whether to study law, or are reviewing or questioning your plans, then this chapter may help you to reach a firm decision.

Making the decision to undertake a law degree may not be easy. You may be wondering what studying law at university will be like, or where a law degree might lead. You might be unsure about what options there are: studying law is not limited to single-honours law degrees. You may be questioning whether a law degree is worthwhile if you have no desire to become a lawyer.

Conversely, even if your ultimate aim is to become a lawyer, you may be unsure whether you must, or should, complete a law degree. Or perhaps your concerns are more about whether you are suited to studying law, or whether you'd find it sufficiently interesting and challenging (or even too challenging). In this chapter we will consider these issues, giving you some things to think about when deciding whether studying law is for you.

STUDYING LAW—WHAT IS IT?

Deciding to study law can be a bit of a step into the unknown. It might feel a less safe option than choosing a subject like history or biology that you've already studied. Most law students have not studied A-level law, and in any event, A-level law is very different from studying law at university. (We'll discuss the benefits and drawbacks of having studied A-level law in a bit.)

I WISH I'D KNOWN . . .

'Don't worry about having no prior knowledge; the majority of students have no experience of legal studies and tutors expect to be starting with blank slates.'

Madeleine Burrell, University of Oxford, Law with German Law, Year 3

Don't be put off by unfamiliarity with the subject. Studying law can be hugely rewarding. It is a fascinating look into society at all levels, is intellectually stimulating, develops a broad range of skills and covers everything from critical thinking and legal theories to pragmatic decision making. It exercises the imagination by requiring engagement with difficult issues and demanding constructive problem solving. And from a career perspective a law degree offers myriad opportunities.

What is law?

What is law? This question has kept some of the best academic minds in business for years. You may be relieved to hear that this chapter is not the place for such deep discussions. Instead we ask, what is law from the perspective of someone looking to study law at university?

Law encompasses many areas and concepts, and overlaps with other subjects. Whether your interests lie in community, commerce, history, science or politics, there is likely to be something in law for you. You are probably already aware that laws can be complex, imprecise and even malleable, and law as a concept or an academic subject is just as hard to pin down because of its scope and variety.

It doesn't help that law has no easy classification such as a 'science' or an 'art', which might help you to link it to your other interests. Law is often included within the 'social sciences' faculty in universities, but this is not universal, and law is quite different from other social sciences. Perhaps the difficulty of classification in itself reveals the diversity and intriguing nature of legal study.

An initial temptation is to think of law as being about crime. Criminal law is usually the most visible part of law, and might appear to affect us most directly. In fact criminal law makes up only a very small portion of the law to which we are subject and which you will study at university. The more you get to know about law, the more you will see the importance of other legal areas. The great reach of law is neatly summed up by Raymond Wacks in 'Law: A Very Short Introduction' (2015):

> Your job, your home, your relationships, your very life—and your death—all, and more, are managed, controlled and directed by the law. It lies at the heart of every society, protecting rights, imposing duties, and establishing a framework for the conduct of almost all social, political, and economic activity. Punishing offenders, compensating the injured, and enforcing agreements are merely some of the tasks of a modern legal system. In addition, it strives to achieve justice, promote freedom, uphold the rule of law, and protect security.

What will I learn?

Law is a vast subject. A law degree does not pretend to teach you all the law there is, or might ever need to know, any more than a history degree would attempt to teach you all of history. When you study law, you study particular areas of law, just as you have studied particular aspects of any other subject you've studied. These could range from contract law to medical law, and from constitutional law to legal history.

Even more importantly, you study how the law works, how to approach the law and how to think in a legal way. Studying law at university equips the successful law student not just with knowledge of the law and the ability to apply it to resolve problems, but also a wide range of valuable skills, attributes and experiences. Particular skills that a law degree typically develops are:

- Comprehension;
- Logical reasoning;
- Analysis;
- Flexible thinking;
- Communication in different formats;
- Independent working;
- Personal responsibility and motivation;
- Team working;
- Research skills.

Such varied skills, combined with the range and variety of subjects studied, make law a particularly stimulating academic experience. They also make law graduates highly employable.

WHERE WILL LAW TAKE ME?

Law is not a purely vocational subject, simply training those who want to be lawyers. A law degree is very useful for those who do want to become lawyers, but the academic study of law is much more than this. In many vocational degree courses, such as Medicine, Accounting or Education, nearly all students taking the course are heading for a specific profession (or group of professions). Law is different. The skills a law degree develops are valued in a very wide range of careers, and it attracts a hugely diverse range of students. A large proportion of law students do not actually go on to practise as lawyers, but instead use their highly employable skills in other areas.

So law graduates may go on to join the legal professions, for example becoming a solicitor or a barrister. They may also go into other 'legal' jobs, such as the courts and tribunals service, lecturers, research associates, legal publishing, the police service, and legal departments in business or the civil service. Chapter 20 provides more information on the legal professions and other career pathways.

There are also many careers that don't require legal knowledge as such, but which value the skills developed by a law degree as well as the clear intellectual ability and determination evidenced by gaining that degree. For example law graduates are welcomed in business, management, finance, journalism, human resources, publishing, the voluntary sector, the armed forces, teaching and beyond. Many students we have taught have become lawyers, whether solicitors, barristers, legal executives or 'in-house' lawyers. But our law students have also gone on to be accountants, managers, lecturers, editors, civil servants, teachers, youth workers, police officers, pilots and politicians.

INSIDER KNOWLEDGE

'I am amazed at the varying careers that those I studied law with have ended up doing. Makes being a barrister seem a bit dull in comparison! The important point to note is a law degree is a fantastic springboard onto other careers; not just into the legal profession.'

Natasha Bellinger, Barrister, Magdalen Chambers

STUDYING LAW—THE LAW DEGREE

There are many different degree programmes containing law: we'll look at these in a moment. For now we'll focus on straightforward single-honours undergraduate law degrees as we discuss typical/common features. These degrees usually last for three years full-time, four years in Scotland. They usually result in the qualification 'LLB' (Bachelor of Laws), but you may also come across 'BA Law'.

A law degree is not simply, or even mainly, about transferring knowledge about the law to you. So what does a law degree teach you? We'll consider this from two angles—what you will study, and how you will study.

What will I study?

A law degree will offer a range of legal and law-related subjects, usually organised in 'modules', 'units' or 'courses'. (The name depends on the institution: 'module' is most common.) Some modules will be compulsory, others will be optional. Some will focus on particular areas of law, others more on skills or particular legal activities.

The qualifying law degree and core modules

The number and content of compulsory modules you take is likely to depend on whether the programme leads to a 'qualifying law degree', or QLD. That is because a 'QLD' requires certain core modules to be passed, so these are made compulsory and are often clustered in the first and second years of the law programme.

A QLD satisfies the academic stage of training to become a barrister or solicitor in England and Wales. A graduate with a non-QLD (even if called a law degree) currently has to take an additional law degree or diploma or add on additional elements of further study to satisfy the academic stage of training for the legal professions. (There are further requirements to qualification, including additional vocational training, and a job as a lawyer is far from guaranteed. More information on the legal professions and qualifying routes is provided in Chapter 20, which also considers key differences between qualification in England/Wales and Scotland.)

As many law students either want to work in the legal profession or want to keep their options open, many universities' standard law degrees are QLDs. However, the importance of a QLD is changing because the solicitors' profession in England and Wales will soon no longer require one for qualification. (We'll discuss the forthcoming changes to training further in Chapter 20.) Even so, it is likely that the QLD will remain important to the content and organisation of most law degree programmes, although more flexibility and variety may emerge.

A QLD must cover the 'foundations of legal knowledge' required by the legal professions. Even after the forthcoming changes to qualification for the solicitors' professions these subjects will continue to be important to professional training and practice. The foundation subjects in England and Wales (they differ slightly in Scotland) are:

- Contract Law;
- Tort Law;
- Criminal Law;
- Land (or Property) Law;

- Equity and Trusts;
- Public (or Constitutional and Administrative) Law;
- EU Law.

We'll explain more about these subjects in Chapter 5. As well as these 'core' subjects you are likely to have other compulsory modules, usually at least one covering the legal system and legal skills. The rest of your study will be made up of further optional modules.

I WISH I'D KNOWN . . .

'Don't be put off by your preconceived ideas about a core module. If you have a good lecturer or tutor then they will be able to make you enjoy the subject regardless of how dull you thought it might be. Don't write off a core module until you've tried it!'

Emily Barrett, University of Bristol, Law with Study in Continental Europe, Year 4

Optional modules

The number and variety of optional modules vary between institutions, depending on the approach of the law school and the expertise available. Common optional modules include:

- Family Law;
- Company Law;
- International Law;
- Human Rights Law;
- Commercial Law;
- Medical Law;
- Employment Law;
- Law and Ethics.

Different institutions will also offer a variety of other interesting specialist subjects ranging from Refugee Law to Insolvency Law, and from Gender, Sexuality and Law to Finance Law. You may also have the option of taking more skills-based modules, such as Advocacy, Dispute Resolution or Negotiation. There will also be research-based modules such as Dissertations or Research Projects, and practice-focused modules, such as Law Clinic, Work-Based Learning or Pro Bono Project modules.

Optional modules allow you to focus on subjects you are most interested in, are particularly relevant to your career plans, or are taught or assessed in ways that play to your strengths. Your choice of options in any particular year will depend on the institution and usually your choices increase as the degree progresses. You may also get the chance to study a subject outside the law school, such as a language or business module.

Credits and choices

The number of modules you study each year, and the number of options you can choose, will depend on how the particular law programme is arranged. Most universities follow a modular structure that assigns a number of credits to each module with a certain number of credits to be completed per year. This means programmes may have fewer larger modules, or more smaller modules. More modules will usually give you more options. But that also means more subjects to get to grips with, and possibly more assessments.

So while programme structures differ, they all offer both advantages and disadvantages. And the 'credit' basis of modules ensures that universities can offer a great deal of choice and flexibility, while providing a level playing field between institutions and degree programmes in terms of how much work you will be expected to do.

How will I study?

Law degree programmes also vary in the way they are taught. Traditionally law has been taught by large group lectures, supplemented with smaller tutorials or seminars. Even within the basic teaching format there is a great deal of variety, and the standard terminology of 'lectures', 'tutorials' and 'seminars' can disguise some really innovative and exciting classes.

Some law schools have moved away from the traditional lecture/tutorial teaching format. Some may favour exclusively large group teaching, perhaps breaking the large group into smaller units for parts of the session. Others may have much reduced (or even no) lecture time with greater emphasis on student-led learning through structured workbooks and classes led by fellow students. Some programmes favour individual work, while others favour group work, and some take a 'problem-based' or more practice-orientated approach. The majority combine elements of more than one approach. More information on teaching and learning in law is provided later, particularly in Chapter 9.

Whatever the structure and teaching methods employed, at the heart of a law programme is 'learning the law': knowing and understanding what the law is, critiquing, evaluating and commenting upon it, and applying it to issues and problems. That means locating and understanding the substantive law, such as land law, or employment law, but also understanding how the law works, and how to think 'legally' in analysing and applying law to new problems.

You will engage closely with legal resources—legal cases, statutes, books, articles and more. Chapter 7 provides more detail on legal resources. You will be expected to find information for yourself, but don't worry, you'll be given guidance on what the law is, and where to find it—whether that guidance is given in lectures, seminars, worksheets, online materials, reading lists or guided workbooks. Depending on the law programme and individual lecturers, you may get highly detailed and structured materials, or you may just get guidance on what you should read (or watch) with greater expectation of individual problem solving or teamwork. You'll practise and develop your skills of applying the law to problems and analysing and contextualising the law.

What is certain is that you will be expected to read, and read some more . . . and then read a bit more. You will absorb, synthesise and question the material you read, think about what it means, and learn to comment and criticise, reason by induction and deduction, apply and advise. It is these skills that make a law graduate so very employable.

IS LAW FOR ME?

We obviously think that studying law is an excellent way to spend your time. But we are not out to convince you of that. Instead we are going to give you some things to think about, so that you can decide whether or not law is for you.

Your interests and aptitudes

Law is not reserved for people with very specific interests or qualities. Regardless of what you have studied before, you can be a successful law student. The fact you have previously favoured, for example, science-based subjects such as chemistry or maths, makes you no less suited to law than someone who has favoured more traditionally discursive subjects such as English or history.

That isn't to say though that everyone will enjoy studying law at university; it isn't to everyone's taste. What might make it more likely that you are suited to and will enjoy studying law?

Words

Law involves words, lots of them. If you enjoy language and deciphering meaning then law can be a very fulfilling subject to study. Legal language can be complex, so a keenly enquiring mind and perseverance are huge advantages.

But don't be put off by the common misconception that legal language is completely indecipherable or requires expertise in Latin. It isn't and it doesn't. As with all specialist subjects, you may have to learn some specialist terms, but the best lawyers and judges commonly write and speak in commendably clear and plain English. It won't be simple, but it can be plainly expressed.

Reading

Inevitably law involves a lot of reading, from varied sources. Many students are surprised by just how much reading they have to do. It will help enormously if you don't find extensive reading off-putting.

Legal study will also require you to research topics, following trails of material and sifting for relevant information. If you dread picking up a textbook, or reading something that requires a bit of thought, or researching for something in the library or in online resources, then law is probably not for you.

I WISH I'D KNOWN . . .

'I wish I'd known how much reading was involved. Students are expected to read in full at least the important cases ... After reading the cases, students must read long chapters of the recommended textbook. Finally, if time remains, students can go on to read further reading to deepen their understanding and earn extra marks on the exam.'

Gabrielle Bargas, University College London, LLB Law with French Law, Year 2

Writing

A lot of the work you will do as a law student will involve writing. If you get no satisfaction from constructing written work in different forms, then you may not enjoy legal study.

As a law student you will spend plenty of time making notes and writing essays, so you should be prepared for this. Some law degrees still make very heavy use of essay writing. But this isn't the whole picture—you may also be drafting legal advice to clients, producing information leaflets, writing notes on cases, advising law reform bodies, reflecting on learning processes, or even creating posters or blogs. You will need to have, or be prepared to develop, good skills in clear and precise writing, directed appropriately to particular tasks.

Speaking

Because legal dramas often focus on barristers in court, it is tempting to think that a love of public speaking is a necessary attribute to be a law student. That really isn't true. It isn't even necessary in order to be a lawyer, let alone a law student.

However, the successful law student will need to do some speaking. You will need to be prepared to formulate your thoughts orally, at least in small group situations or when speaking to tutors. That is something that you won't be able to avoid in any academic environment, whatever the subject, and you will swiftly develop skills and confidence in this area. If you enjoy oral communication then you may well love the law, with plenty of additional opportunities such as advocacy courses, mooting competitions, debates etc. Of course you'll also need to be prepared to listen to and engage with the views of others.

INSIDER KNOWLEDGE

'Law chose me. I love arguing, debating and advocacy. I was fascinated by law and the prospect of making it my livelihood.'

David McCormick, Barrister, Exchange Chambers

Broad interests

Law aids or intrudes upon everything. From the most personal and intimate such as parental rights, assault or housing, to the most global such as refugees, mineral rights and space law. If you have an interest in the world about you, in the working of society and the rights and interests of the people and other entities within it, then law is an endlessly fascinating subject.

If on the other hand, you have little interest in reading a newspaper or watching the news, and struggle to care about what is right or wrong in the world around you, then you may find it difficult to sustain a sufficient interest in law to be a successful law student.

Practical work

Law is very practical because it is relevant to everything around you. You will find it interesting if you like seeing and questioning how things work, and resolving problems. If you are interested in working as a lawyer, you will enjoy seeing how law (and lawyers) work in practice.

But law isn't a practical subject in the sense that you will be doing experiments and getting your hands dirty. As a student you won't commonly be attending court or speaking to real clients, although there are opportunities for this. If you prefer to spend your time outside or in a laboratory, then law is probably not the place for you.

Figure 2.1 represents particular interests and aptitudes that might make you better suited to studying law at university.

FIGURE 2.1: Interests and aptitudes for studying law

Do I want to be a law student?

The factors we've looked at above provide a glimpse of the law student experience. What else distinguishes the law degree from some other areas of study, and might influence your decision to study law?

- Comparatively little of your time will be spent in the classroom. That doesn't mean you have little work to do. You will have regular but relatively few classes but will do a lot of self-guided study and preparation.

- You will spend a lot of your time reading, making notes and thinking. A lot of this reading will be interesting, but you'll need to be prepared to work through some that isn't. The library may come to feel like a second home!

- Lecturers/tutors will be helpful and supportive, but will expect you to take responsibility for your own learning. You will need to learn to manage your time and motivate yourself.

- You will be expected to work hard from the start, and should not expect to find the work easy. Law students sometimes report that they seem to work harder than students in some other degree courses, particularly in the first year.

- You are unlikely to find all legal subjects equally interesting, but you might be surprised at what you find most rewarding.

- Wherever you are, the legal learning community (staff and fellow students) will be diverse and interesting.

- You will be continually stretched, challenged and stimulated.

- On graduation you will find yourself in possession of a highly regarded academic achievement.

I WISH I'D KNOWN . . .

'I wish I'd known how intense it was going to be. It feels like it goes from zero to 100 in seconds.'

Emma-Jane Darley, University of Central Lancashire, MLAW, Year 2

Course requirements

Law is a demanding and popular academic subject. The number of places available on law programmes has increased in recent years, but getting on to a law degree programme remains highly competitive.

Entry tariffs

Institutions typically have high academic entry tariffs for law programmes. For the top universities you can expect to be asked for three A grades at A-level, or equivalent, and many other universities set their tariffs at the equivalent of AAB or ABB. Don't give up immediately if you don't obtain the results you were hoping for though—universities may accept lower grades if they really want you, or have some spaces left in clearing.

Other universities will accept students with less stellar A-level results. But law is academically challenging and you need to show clear academic ability and/or promise to get onto a law programme. Your grades at A-level or equivalent may also be relevant if you subsequently seek highly competitive positions in the legal profession.

The majority of law schools do not require applicants to have studied any particular subjects. So as long as you get the grades, it doesn't matter if these are in physics, maths and biology, or French, history and English, or media studies, psychology and law. However many universities do not include general studies or critical thinking within their tariff.

Some institutions do require, or favour, particular A-level (or equivalent) subjects. These are usually the universities with very high entry tariffs. Where this is the case, the tendency is to prefer 'traditional' subjects (such as geography, chemistry or Spanish) rather than 'modern' subjects (such as theatre studies or sociology). If you have a particular institution in mind then check what their requirements are. If you are about to choose your A-level subjects explore this now to keep your options open.

What about A-level law?

You might think that if you want to study law at university, studying law at A-level would put you in a stronger position than other applicants. Perhaps surprisingly that isn't the case for a number of reasons.

To begin with, as we've just mentioned, some law schools require applicants to have studied subjects (or at least two subjects) within a preferred subjects list. These lists don't necessarily include law. Accordingly if you have law as one of your A-levels you may not satisfy the entry requirements of the university you have set your heart on. Don't worry though, this approach is not common, and there will be plenty of other excellent universities that will be happy to take you with the right grades.

Views differ on whether A-level law benefits a prospective law student. Overall, it does not appear to offer any benefit compared to other A-levels, and so your application is not treated differently whether or not you have studied A-level law. Law schools start with the assumption that students have no prior legal knowledge and teach accordingly. And programmes very quickly move on from the basic concepts of legal systems, criminal law and contract law typically covered at A-level.

So while some of the initial information in a few modules may be more familiar if you have taken A-level law, this advantage does not last long, and is unlikely to make a difference to your overall degree result. But it may help you to feel more comfortable in the early days which is undoubtedly a benefit—just don't allow that to lull you into thinking you don't need to work hard!

Our advice is that if you want to study law at A-level because you think you will enjoy it, then do so. But if you have your heart set on a particular university law programme, first check their requirements so you don't limit your options. If you are already studying law at A-level, then continue to enjoy it. You can enjoy the benefit of knowing that that you are interested in the subject that you are hoping to study at university, and you may find your first weeks of study a bit easier.

Conversely, if you are not studying or do not want to study law at A-level, then don't worry about this at all—you will not be disadvantaged. Tutors will not expect you to have any knowledge or familiarity with even basic legal concepts, and as a true novice you can enjoy coming to the subject fresh without having to 'unlearn' material taught at a different level.

The Law National Admissions Test (LNAT)

University entry requirements are most commonly based on A-level or equivalent grades, but some universities also require their applicants to take the LNAT (the Law National Admissions Test). Some other universities don't require applicants to take the LNAT, but will have regard to it as part of an application. This may boost your chances of acceptance should your grades (or predicted grades) not quite be at the level required by the institution. Many other universities do not use the LNAT at all within the application process. Use of the LNAT is not an indicator of the quality of the law programme or institution you are applying to.

The LNAT doesn't test legal knowledge, so there is no advantage to someone studying A-level law, or who comes from a legal background. It tests things like verbal reasoning and analytical skills that are important for the study of law. If you do need to take the LNAT as part of your application there is nothing specifically to study for but it is sensible to access sample questions and find out more about what is being tested before you take the test.

The LNAT website provides lots of helpful information: http://www.lnat.ac.uk/. The website also has an up-to-date list of the institutions and courses that require the LNAT. Other institutions will be able to advise on their attitude to the LNAT, so you can decide whether to take the test.

Career goals

Your choice of degree course may be influenced by your career plans. If you envisage a career in law then a law degree is an obvious choice, and is usually the quickest route to professional legal qualification. It isn't essential though—many people who ultimately become professional lawyers graduate in other subjects, and then take an additional shorter law degree or Graduate Diploma in Law (GDL). We'll look at the GDL later in this chapter.

While a law degree is not essential to go into legal practice it can reassure you that the law genuinely interests you and enables you to obtain a broader appreciation of the law than a shorter further degree or diploma permits. It will engage you with many more areas of law and may reveal an area of law in which you'd like to specialise.

If you have other clear career goals—perhaps the civil service, voluntary sector, management or finance—you may also be interested in studying law. As we've seen, the skills and attributes developed by a law degree are very well suited to a wide variety of professional and other roles. And if you don't yet know what you want to do, a law degree keeps a large number of doors open, from accounting and the armed forces to education and politics. But there are limits—we have to accept that a law degree is not an ideal place from which to launch a career in maths, medicine or zoology.

INSIDER KNOWLEDGE

'I was attracted to law because of the challenge I knew it would bring. I also knew very early on that it was unlikely I would practice law, and my decision to study it was based on the sound level of communication, analytical and critical thinking skills that I would gain, that would stand me well in many professions. I was not wrong.'

Bronagh Finnegan, Communications Officer

SELECTING A LAW PROGRAMME

When it comes to selecting a law programme there are numerous options. If your goal (or a possible goal) is to become a lawyer, remember too the relevance of the qualifying law degree (QLD, explained earlier in this chapter).

Duration

So far we've focused on the standard undergraduate law (LLB) degree, which typically lasts for a three-year period, full-time. However there are shorter and longer programmes of study available.

In Scotland, four years is the standard undergraduate degree length. Law schools elsewhere in the UK also sometimes offer four-year law programmes. These may combine both academic and vocational parts of legal study in a single package rather than as two separate programmes.

This might be of interest if you know you want to go into legal practice, or want a programme with more practice-based content than a typical law degree. Law degrees with additional study (such as a language) are also often four years in length.

Two-year intensive undergraduate law degrees are also available, covering much the same material as a three-year degree. These programmes are not currently very common, although recent government pronouncements suggest they may become more common in future. They help you to complete your studies in as short a time as possible, but are obviously more intensive than a conventional degree, and may reduce your opportunities for extra-curricular activities.

A more common form of two-year law degree is normally on offer only to graduates with a degree in a non-law subject. This may be an 'accelerated LLB' or Masters programme that covers all the foundations of legal knowledge and a limited choice of options. These offer a degree-level alternative to a GDL. These programmes are generally reserved for graduate students because of the intensive nature of the study.

Type

A full law programme—such as that offered by a standard LLB or BA Law—allows you to focus exclusively (or almost exclusively) on the law, and obtain broad and deep understanding of a wide range of legal subjects. You have the convenience of being based in one department, and the skills you develop are easily transferable across modules. The majority of law students opt for a full law programme through a standard law degree.

However not all students want to limit their study options to law, and so other programmes offer the chance to study law alongside other subjects, or with other experiences. There can be benefits from the broader perspective obtained from studying other subjects. You may also develop different skills and learn new approaches to study. Combined programmes may keep different career options open, or stop you getting bored with a particular subject. But they also may limit your law option choices, and you may have to deal with more than one university department.

Figure 2.2 shows a simplified representation of law programmes. The range of options is even more extensive in practice.

FIGURE 2.2: Choosing a law programme

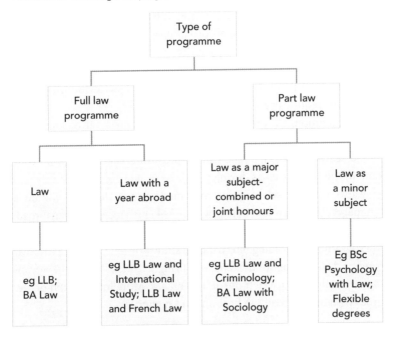

Combined (or joint) honours degrees

There are numerous combination honours degree programmes allowing a variety of subjects to be studied alongside law. You could for example study law jointly with another subject, such as LLB Law and Politics. Or with law as a major subject with other minor subjects, for example LLB Law with Criminology and Criminal Justice Studies, or BA Law with Psychology. Some combined/joint programmes lead to a QLD, depending on the subjects studied, while others don't.

Law can also be studied as a minor subject, for example BSc Criminology and Criminal Justice Studies with Law, BA Politics with Law. Although unlikely to be a QLD, a programme of this kind may provide some exemptions from study if you decide to pursue legal practice. These programmes can be a good option if you unsure whether to immerse yourself in law: they give you a flavour of legal study and develop some legal skills, while enabling you to pursue other academic interests.

Degrees with a year abroad

Many universities offer students the possibility of a year studying abroad. Some law schools offer a year abroad as part of a law programme structure. For example, programmes such as Law with International Study or Law with European Study usually provide a qualifying law degree, with additional experience of studying in another legal jurisdiction. These do not usually require particular language expertise.

Less commonly, a programme may offer some level of joint legal expertise or dual legal qualification. For example Law with French Law would see you studying French and aspects of French law during your time in the UK as well as during your year in France. Alternatively you may also be able to select a joint/combined honours degree of law and a language, eg LLB Law and Italian, which is likely to include a year abroad. These degrees require good language skills, usually an A or B at A-level.

Programmes including international study normally add an extra year to your degree programme, and will bring extra costs, but the advantages usually far outweigh the disadvantages. More information on degrees with time abroad can be found in Chapter 16.

Flexible degrees

More unusually, you may be able to study elements of law within a flexible degree. A flexible degree allows students to choose modules from a range of different programmes. They are not common, but enable you to gain academic skills and experience while exploring multiple subjects.

However, studying bits of law within a fully flexible degree can be difficult; it is not easy to grasp legal concepts without the familiarity of regular legal study. On the other hand you benefit from exposure to legal thinking and individual legal subjects, while gaining a broad academic perspective and diverse experiences. You also develop important interdisciplinary skills (the ability to think and work outside and across conventional academic boundaries).

Delivery of the law programme

When selecting a law programme, consider how the course is organised and taught. There is no 'right' or 'wrong' way to teach law, just different ways. Your experience will be very different depending on where you study, so spend some time thinking about what might suit you best.

Classes and assessments

Many law schools have expanded significantly in recent years. Large law schools may take up to about 500 students per year across their programmes; while smaller schools may take only seventy to 200. You might like the idea of a large law school: you will meet lots of new people, and a larger staff body usually means more choice of optional modules. Or you may prefer a smaller law school for a more personal experience and the chance to get to know your colleagues and lecturers better.

You should also consider the size of classes. Teaching sessions may range from only a few students to the full cohort of 400 or more, but there will usually be a range of different class sizes.

It is also worth considering how teaching is organised. Do you think you will get on best with conventional lectures, seminars and tutorials, or with more self-guided learning and peer-led classes? Do you want a traditional academic focus, or a problem-based learning approach? More information on different approaches to teaching law is provided in Chapter 9 if you want to explore further.

Methods of assessment also vary between law schools, and are discussed in Chapter 12. Some institutions rely heavily on traditional exams; others have a lot of coursework; and many use a variety of different assessments depending on the subject being studied. Some spread assessment over each academic year; others rely on final assessments. Think about what might suit you best, and how important this is to you.

I WISH I'D KNOWN . . .

'I wish I'd known that not every law degree course out there is the same. For example, I found out [the] law degree via Open University is very much assignment based whereas, the law degree I am undertaking is 50/50 coursework and exam. Other unis are more exam based. So it varies from uni to uni.'

Anonymous, 3rd year LLB student

Resources, support and other activities

Your experience as a law student will also be influenced by the resources available, the support offered and the opportunities open to you within or outside the curriculum.

Make sure you check out obvious resources such as the library and course materials. Think about other important (often extra-curricular) opportunities. What additional experiences are offered and how are they organised? Consider activities such as mooting, negotiation, debating or working in a law clinic—there is more information in Chapters 17–18. And what support will you be offered on a personal basis to help your study and enhance your experience? Most law schools offer a personal tutoring system to support you (see Chapter 4), as well as lots of other centrally run student support, but these will differ between institutions.

Finding out

When you explore these questions, you can find a lot of information from brochures and university websites. Remember though that marketing information inevitably aims to give the best possible impression. Explore claims further, and check things out at open day. Use open days to ask questions, not just of those presenting, but of students too.

Questions to consider at open day

- Is the law degree a qualifying law degree or does it otherwise meet the requirements of the legal professions? Is this true of all the different law programmes you offer? Can I change to other law programmes during the degree?

- Do you offer the chance of a year abroad? If so, where? Do I need to select this on application, or can I add it in after I've started studying?

- Are there any particular subjects/qualifications you require or favour of applicants? Why?

- How can I best prepare for a law degree?

- How many undergraduate students take law programmes each year? Is that just the LLB, or all the law programmes combined?

- How much contact time with a member of staff will I have each week? What form does that contact take?

- As an undergraduate who will I be taught by? (Ideally you will see professors and senior staff as well as part-time/sessional staff and postgraduate student teachers.)

- What optional law modules do you offer? When will I get to choose these? Can I take non-law modules if I want to?

- What jobs have your recent graduates secured; can you give me some examples? What is your employability rate into graduate-level positions?

- What careers support do you offer?

- How does your personal tutoring system work? How many personal tutees does each member of staff have? How often will I meet with my personal tutor?

- What additional opportunities are there for developing my skills and experience? Are these part of the course, or optional extras? Are they open to all students or are numbers limited?

Internet forums like The Student Room can be helpful if you have specific queries about a law school or programme. Forums like this may give you quite polarised views though so don't be too influenced by one person's experience.

Choosing a university

Your choice of university is a big decision whatever degree programme you aim for. While it is sometimes possible to move between universities after you've started your studies, this is rarely easy to arrange and you may find yourself having to repeat a year of study or take additional classes. It may also lead to further expense. So take your time making the best decision you can.

As a prospective law student, remember that you will spend most of your time in or around the law school and with law tutors and students. If you don't like the law school, its attitude and atmosphere, or aren't happy with its facilities or opportunities, then think twice about applying to that particular university. Similarly make sure that the university offers a law programme of the type you want, narrowing down your choices to programmes that suit your interests, learning style and goals.

I WISH I'D KNOWN . . .

Before going to university, I didn't really think about the course I was choosing but the institution that provided it. What I realised quite soon after was that the course structure is just as important. For example, at my university, the core modules are weighted as 30 credits per year, with optional modules valued at 15 credits per semester. However, many other universities accord all modules a value of 20 credits per semester. . . . This means you can choose more optional modules that you're more likely to enjoy and excel in! The optional modules on offer can also vary significantly from institution to institution based on the expertise of the lecturers based there.

Jessica Allen, University of Nottingham, Law with French and French Law, Year 4

Your choice of university may be comparatively easy if you need or want to attend a university close to where you live. Or you may have a very wide range of institutions to consider, particularly if you have no strong preferences about the particular law programme you will follow. Whether your choices are wide or narrow, undertake plenty of research to find out as much as you can about possible institutions.

Location

'Education, Education, Education' obviously trumps 'Location, Location, Location'. It is better to have a good educational experience in an unappealing location, than a poor one in a beautiful city. But location can still help to narrow down your choices, whether you want to stay close to home, or move away. Is there a place that enables you to pursue your hobbies and interests, or puts you in a better place to further your career plans? You will probably be spending three or more years there, so look for somewhere you feel comfortable living and studying. Think about:

• What makes you favour this location? Have you already visited? If not, do so as soon as possible.

- How easy or difficult is it to get to? How will you get there (and back)?
- Is it a city or campus university? Which do you like the feel of better? If outside town, is it still easy to get to? Are there good public transport links?
- What accommodation is there? Are any halls of residence close to the campus/main university area?
- Does the location have an active legal centre? Interaction between the law school and courts and legal practitioners can enhance your studies.
- Can you continue to enjoy your interests—perhaps live music, a top-class sports team, or good surfing beaches?

Resources/facilities

Although you'll spend much of your time within the law school, wider university resources and facilities are also important. You can expect as a minimum a reasonable library and access to electronic resources. Some universities do provide more for their students—but don't be too swayed by 'freebies'. You might check though whether, for example, course materials are provided free of charge or at a discounted rate, or whether there is access to free or discounted bus travel.

If you have a disability make sure you find out what support will be available to you while you study, and to assist you when attending open days for example. All universities will make reasonable adjustments for students with disabilities or other learning needs including dyslexia and dyspraxia. Find out what arrangements will be made and how you can access support.

You should also investigate the services provided by the university, such as student accommodation, food and drink outlets, clubs and societies (a wide range shows a diverse and engaged student community), student union/guild/association, financial support, well-being services and so on. Open days give you the chance to investigate and compare these facilities and services, and check out the atmosphere of the university. These opportunities, and any follow-up or 'offer-holder' days, will help you to make your decision.

Part-time and distance learning

Most law students attend university in person and full-time, whether or not moving home permanently or temporarily. But not all students will choose, or be able, to uproot and/or stop working but still want to pursue their dream of studying law. Studying part-time, and/or from a distance may enable this.

Part-time learning, where offered, usually offers the same (or almost the same) range of compulsory and optional modules as for full-time students, but over a longer period of time. It still requires a great deal of commitment on your part, perhaps more, as you will need to retain your motivation over many years. But it allows you to fit your studies around work or home commitments, or cope with health issues. Many universities will be prepared to discuss your particular needs to make sure you can attend all compulsory classes and access materials.

Distance learning usually involves taking a programme online with limited formal contact time, and little or no requirement to attend at a physical location. The Open University is probably the most famous provider of distance learning, but is not the only one. If you are considering studying for a law degree through distance learning, you should still consider much of the advice already given. Look into the structure of the programme, the types of teaching resources used, the opportunities and resources available to you and the contact time and arrangements with lecturers and instructors.

THE GRADUATE DIPLOMA IN LAW (GDL)

What is the GDL?

The Graduate Diploma in Law (GDL) is also known as the Common Professional Examination (CPE) or the 'conversion course'. It allows non-law graduates (or occasionally those with career experience equivalent to an undergraduate degree) to fulfil the academic stage of legal training without undertaking a full law degree.

Because a qualifying law degree (QLD) will soon no longer be needed for entry to the solicitors' profession (see earlier, and Chapter 20) the GDL may become much less popular. However, law firms—and other legal employers—are still likely to want applicants to have had some legal academic training. So the GDL may continue to be valued, and two-year postgraduate law degrees (see earlier) may also grow in popularity. It should be noted that the GDL is not an option for those studying and qualifying in Scotland in any event.

The GDL is an intensive programme that over one year covers the seven subjects that make up the 'foundations of legal knowledge' (see earlier in this chapter, and Chapter 5), legal method and skills, and another optional topic or research project. The programme ensures a competent working knowledge of core legal principles. It also develops core legal skills such as problem solving, critical analysis and contextualising the law. Modules such as a research project ensure that you also develop skills such as legal research, analysis and construction of arguments.

Law degree or GDL?

If you are thinking you might want to become a lawyer, you might be wondering whether to do a law degree, or another degree followed by the GDL. While technically neither may soon be necessary for the solicitors' profession at least, as mentioned earlier, realistically some level of academic legal training is likely to remain all but essential for any legal career. But which is better? It isn't possible to supply a definitive answer to that question, but we'll do our best to help you make the decision that is right for you.

I WISH I'D KNOWN . . .

'I was unaware there was an option to take the GDL. I was conflicted when choosing what degree I wanted to do and if I would have known that I can do another degree and do the GDL I most definitely would have.'

Lul Sheikh-Salah, BPP University, LLB, Year 3

The law degree and GDL are quite different qualifications. The most important differences are the intensity and variety of the programmes. A law degree spreads the foundation subjects over two or three years and offers a range of optional modules covering a wide variety of specialist subjects, skills and experiences. The law degree can spend more time on each subject and offer more subjects. It provides a broader legal education than the GDL and longer in which to develop legal skills and a legal way of thinking. There is also more opportunity to undertake extra-curricular activities.

INSIDER KNOWLEDGE

'I could have done a GDL as I had a BSc in Mathematics, but I chose to do a full law degree to have a solid foundation in law. I love and enjoy law, from logic, to finding solutions, and most of all when you complete a transaction and have a happy client! It is very rewarding.'

Shahrzad Atai Ahari, Head of Middle East Desk, Child & Child

The GDL in contrast is an intense period of legal study. It doesn't allow much time to reflect on the law and legal skills and it can be difficult to squeeze in extra-curricular activity. But it immerses you into the law, with the benefit of having already studied at degree level. If you are not sure whether law is for you at the time of choosing your degree programme, or if you are keen to study another subject but still think you might want to be a lawyer, the GDL gives you that opportunity. It may also be helpful if you know you want to specialise as a lawyer in a particular niche area: you may choose to study that subject (such as computer science, or finance) before moving on to law.

There are also practicalities to consider. While the GDL provides an additional qualification for only the cost of a single additional year studying, that is still one extra year's fees and living expenses on top of your undergraduate degree. Student loans may not be available. These factors may be a powerful incentive for many students who know they are interested in law to opt for a law degree from the start. However for those who feel the attraction to law only later, the GDL offers the opportunity to join the party.

Does the choice of law degree or GDL make a difference to your future employability? Not of itself. Both law graduates and non-law graduates with a GDL are eminently employable in the legal profession in England and Wales—depending of course on grades, skills, experience and attributes. Some students (particularly those with desirable specialist experience) may even find individual law firms willing to fund their GDL year. As for whether applicants are preferred according to what type of legal qualification they have, we are continually assured by employers and recruiters (and believe) that there is no preference given to applicants with either the LLB or the GDL. Recruiters recognise that both have their advantages and disadvantages, and view applications in the round.

If choosing between a law degree or a non-law degree plus GDL, there is one additional point to bear in mind. Not all legal professional bodies outside England and Wales treat the GDL as having 'academic equivalence' to a law degree for the purposes of legal qualification in those jurisdictions. If qualification outside England and Wales is your eventual goal then check the position before making your final decision.

STUDYING LAW IN THE UK AS AN INTERNATIONAL STUDENT

Significant numbers of international students choose to study law in the UK, and are made very welcome. Some join for a full degree programme, others for just a period of study. The student body is diverse and includes students from just about every country in the world, taking the full range of law programmes.

The idea of moving to a new country may be both exciting and daunting, but can open up new opportunities in your career and life plans. As an international student you can apply to study any law programme, as long as you meet the core requirements. You will need to meet the necessary academic entry tariff: your preferred universities will advise you on the equivalent in your home country.

Where English is your second language, you will also need to achieve the required score in an English language test. Most universities have international offices that will help you with the various application processes, including visa and housing applications. We'll consider particular issues that international students might face when studying law in the UK at relevant points throughout this book.

As well as the option of studying a full course in the UK, there are also opportunities to study law in the UK for shorter periods through various programmes. Universities often link with 'partner' institutions in a variety of different countries, or may offer summer school programmes. These can give you an interesting perspective on another country's law and legal system. They also provide the opportunity to explore another country and culture, both for its own sake and to aid your future employability.

For some students, studying in the UK may be a less costly way of learning the law than studying at home. Your home legal profession may recognise a UK law degree as a qualifying degree, but most will still require you to take some competency exams in your home country. If you want to study in the UK and return home to practise law, make sure you understand the process you will need to follow.

SUMMARY—HELP YOURSELF . . .

- **Consider your options**
  - Think about what studying law entails, where your interests and skills lie, and what career you might choose.
  - Investigate the programmes on offer—don't assume you have to do a 'straight' LLB or full-time LLB.

- **Do your research**
  - Research the different courses available at different institutions, and how they are organised and taught; find one that seems right for you.
  - Research the universities you are interested in; visit as many on your shortlist as you sensibly can.
  - Check that you have the necessary qualifications to apply to the institutions and programmes that you are interested in.

- **Be prepared**
  - Ask questions to help you make an informed decision.
  - Be an active participant at open days.
  - Watch Professor Graham Virgo on 'Why study a law degree?' at: https://www.youtube.com/watch?v=tvgu918yFcM for a helpful consideration of what a law degree is all about.

3

PREPARING FOR SUCCESS

*'I will not pretend I wasn't petrified. I was.
But mixed in with the awful fear was a
glorious feeling of excitement. Most of the really
exciting things we do in our lives scare us to death.
They wouldn't be exciting if they didn't.'*

ROALD DAHL,
Danny, the Champion of the World

INTRODUCTION

If you are reading this book then you presumably want to be a successful law student. Or possibly someone close to you wants you to be a successful law student and has forced this book on you. Either way, success requires preparation: doing and thinking. That is what this chapter is all about.

The first part of this chapter explores what 'a successful law student' might actually be: it is hard to prepare to be one, without knowing what it is. We'll then explore the attributes that will help you to earn that title, and finish by giving you some suggestions of things you can do right now to help you on your way.

WHAT IS A 'SUCCESSFUL LAW STUDENT'?

It isn't easy to *define* a 'successful law student'. But that doesn't mean it isn't possible to *be* a successful law student; only that there is no single way of fitting that description. We've taught a huge number of successful law students in our time, but they all looked different, spoke differently, had different experiences, even studied different things. They all achieved different things too, whether in terms of grades or careers. So how can we say they were all 'successful'? That rather depends on what 'success' is.

Contemplating success

Oxford dictionaries online (https://www.oxforddictionaries.com) defines success as 'the accomplishment of an aim or purpose'. What is your aim or purpose in becoming a law student?

At its most basic, your aim or purpose is probably to complete your legal studies, whether graduating with a law or combined degree, or completing some other period of legal study and continuing your studies elsewhere. You may also be thinking longer-term. If so, your view of success may be to secure a job, or hopefully, a satisfying career, whether in the law or elsewhere. This book is designed to help you achieve those basic goals. But we'd also encourage you to think more widely. Success is not just about graduating and getting a job, although of course these are important.

To us, a successful law student:

- Completes his/her legal studies within a period reflecting the opportunities and challenges faced during that time;
- Achieves a grade reflecting his/her ability and potential;
- Is able to pursue a job or activity that s/he finds satisfying;
- Enjoys, or at least appreciates, studying and learning;
- Develops useful skills and the desire to develop further;
- Engages meaningfully within a diverse community;
- Is resilient and able to learn from experiences;
- Is largely satisfied and contented with his or her life.

Success in the broad sense of being 'a successful law student' is thus not just about clearly measurable results. It is not just about getting a 'good' degree and a 'good' job. In any event, most of those more fluid notions of success, even if not easily measurable, will actually help you to achieve the degree result and career of your dreams. 'Success' is a complicated thing.

Success—an absolute concept?

You'll have noticed that our list carefully avoided aims along the lines of: 'come top in the class', 'get a first class degree', 'complete degree within three/four years' or 'get a job with a City law firm'. That is because, while success is about accomplishing an aim or purpose, it can be very easy to become distracted by 'absolute' perceptions of success—the top mark, the highly paid job, coming first in the mooting competition and so on.

But these are outside measures of success, often based on what we think other people perceive as success. They can mean we feel a 'failure' if we do not achieve them. They can impose pressures that can be hugely destructive of well-being.

Measuring success in absolute terms also has the potential to devalue the different experiences and challenges that you will have. It could easily exclude someone who absolutely has the capacity to be a successful law student. Remember that true success can only be measured against whether or not you have accomplished your *own* aim or purpose. Furthermore, it is important to think about how you frame your aim or purpose, to ensure that it is actually within your control.

Dr Steve Peters, in his excellent book *The Chimp Paradox* (2012), explains how our rational 'Human' part of our brain is frequently highjacked by the powerful, but irrational, 'Chimp' part of our brain. Here's what he has to say about measuring success:

> 'There are always different ways to measure success. For example, if you want to take an exam course, there are two ways with which success can be measured. Of course you want to pass the exam, however, you could approach it from different angles.
>
> The first measure of success is passing the exam, which is more likely to be the Chimp's definition of success, to which the Human may agree.
>
> The second way might be completing the course, or even just trying, which is more likely to be the Human's definition of success. This is because logic says that if I have done my best I can hold my head up and deal with the consequences.

If you choose the Human's definition, then as long as you try, you cannot fail to be successful. Of course, it would also be great to pass the exam! However, if it doesn't work out, it doesn't imply anything more than you tried your best (and you can't do more than this) and therefore you can celebrate your successful effort.

Your Chimp will still insist this is a failure. Think carefully, you have a choice here. If you always wish to measure success in life by what level you attain, then you must accept the emotional consequences when you do not reach this level. If you measure success in life by effort and doing your best, then it is always in your hands to succeed and to be proud of yourself.

Sadly, we sometimes see students who are feeling very low because they have come to view themselves as 'failures'. Often these are students who have actually achieved objectively good marks, who have a lovely circle of friends, supportive family and good prospects for a satisfying career. But they insist on measuring themselves against absolute and punishing levels of attainment, and so, no matter how hard they have worked, they simply cannot appreciate their achievements.

It is true that these students are not really 'successful law students'. But this is not because they haven't reached a particular level of attainment. It is because they cannot see and appreciate what they have achieved and use this as a stepping stone for the next stage in their lives. Of course it is entirely normal to feel disappointed, even dejected, from time to time. But by framing your aims realistically you can keep success within your reach and bounce back. Your own well-being is also an essential ingredient of a successful life.

Let's be clear: we would not discourage you from having ambitious goals. There is nothing wrong with aiming high. Particularly if the goal is where you genuinely want to be and not just where everyone else wants to be, or where you think others in your life want or expect you to be. But remember that being a successful law student is not about achieving particular levels of attainment. It is about doing your best in the circumstances you find yourself in. That is what being a successful law student is all about—reaching your potential—and we will try to help you to do that.

I WISH I'D KNOWN . . .

'I would have defined "success" as getting a first in everything, but now I would class "success" as doing the best you can in everything and feeling in yourself you have done your best, no matter of the outcome.'

Charlotte Brown, Bournemouth University, LLB Law, Year 3

Success as 'a law student'

There is another problem with trying to define a 'successful law student' in an absolute sense. That is there is no single notion of a 'law student'. A very positive thing about legal studies today is the enormous diversity within the student body, and the range of different courses on offer (see Chapter 2 for more on different law programmes). This means there is very little point in measuring your 'success' against that of anyone else, when everyone has different aims, purposes, abilities and experiences.

So we won't define success as completing a three/four-year undergraduate law degree, because you might be undertaking a joint or combined honours degree, or studying part-time, or taking a two-year programme, or a one-year postgraduate programme, or even a single-semester course as part of a degree programme from an international university. What is more, you'll still be a success if completing your course takes a little longer than anticipated because you need to extend or interrupt your studies because of some unforeseen personal or external event.

Similarly, success is not dependent on attending a particular institution or studying in a particular format—you can be a successful law student while studying anywhere in the country, or indeed by distance learning. Even if you only compared yourself to other students taking the same law programme at the same institution at the same time, your different life goals, abilities and experiences mean that your notion of 'success' must differ from everyone else's if it is to be meaningful and achievable.

So while we talk a lot about 'the successful law student', that term brings no single individual to mind. There is no such thing as a 'typical' law student, and no barrier in your way to being a successful law student. What matters is to understand and benefit from your own unique position, and aim to do all *you* need to do to put yourself in the best possible place to succeed in your own legal studies.

I WISH I'D KNOWN . . .

'To me "success" is when I know I achieved something from anything that could be little or big. After starting the degree, knowing that I can move into the next year means more than a success. Knowing that hard work has paid off is a confidence boost.'

Victoria Chan, Nottingham Trent University, LLB Distance Learning, Year 3

COMMON ATTRIBUTES OF SUCCESSFUL LAW STUDENTS

While there is no such thing as a 'typical' successful law student, in our experience successful law students often share particular features that make their success more likely (see Figure 3.1). Let's be clear, we are not talking here about innate legal ability or talent, whatever that might be. We are a bit suspicious of claims that someone is a 'natural' lawyer, or that you should not consider legal study unless you already possess high levels of confidence or are a highly persuasive communicator.

FIGURE 3.1: Common attributes of successful law students

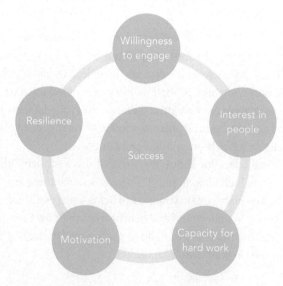

While some talents may make it more likely that you would enjoy working as a lawyer, our experience is that success as a law student is not dependent on particular 'natural' talents or abilities. It is important not to conflate 'being a law student' with 'being a lawyer'. Nor is it appropriate to focus entirely on the skills, abilities and interests you have now, rather than those you will develop over the course of your legal studies. What we are referring to here are approaches and attitudes that make success more likely. And even if you don't think you have them in abundance right now, they can be developed.

Willingness to engage

Key to success as a law student is a willingness to engage with learning and the whole experience of being a law student. It is about taking personal responsibility for getting the most out of the experience; going above and beyond the bare requirements in all you do.

It might be possible, although not easy, to gain a law degree by passively absorbing information that is provided to you. But you won't get much out of the experience and you certainly won't reach your full potential that way. It is really important that you don't just accept information, but think about it, challenge it and question it. That doesn't mean disagreeing with everything, but it does mean being thoughtful and critical (in a good way), looking for different points of view and approaches. Even the best judge, even the best academic, is not necessarily right, so keep your mind open and your brain engaged. We'll look more at approaches to learning later on, particularly in Chapters 8–10.

Successful law students tend to be active participants in their degree, not mere observers. Rather than just absorbing and noting down the contributions of teachers and classmates, they think and offer their own view. Even if they feel a bit unsure or nervous, they'll have a go at explaining a point. They attend talks and presentations that offer a different perspective or the potential for a different career option, join a club or society, and help out where they can.

Remember too that lecturers are more likely to go the extra mile for a student who is showing interest, as working with engaged students is far more rewarding. Active engagement is very much a virtuous circle.

Interest in people

Law both governs society and is moulded by society. Without an interest in other people it would be difficult to be a successful law student. It is that interest in others, in society, community and in the wider world, that stimulates and informs an interest in law.

Having the capacity to engage with other people is also important for effective teamwork. Almost all careers, whether legal or non-legal, will require teamwork in some form, and working with others is also important to your legal studies. You may find that teamwork is built into teaching and learning opportunities and assessments. Even if not, your studies will be far more rewarding and your learning more effective if you are able and willing to collaborate, share ideas, and support and learn from others. Successful law students tend to be engaged and supportive members of their learning community, and the community beyond.

Capacity for hard work

You obviously already have the capacity for hard work to have got this far. You won't be surprised to find that even more hard work is necessary to be a successful law student—worthwhile things tend to require hard work and dedication. The problem with hard work is that it is, well, hard. If it was easy, it wouldn't be *hard* work. All law students start their studies with every intention of working hard throughout, so why is it even worth mentioning this as an important attribute of a successful law student?

We recognise that, however good your intentions, it is not always easy to keep working hard. As a law student, you will, to a great extent, be left to your own devices. You'll be given guidance, support and suggestions, but ultimately you are responsible for your own work plan. You are highly unlikely to have weekly or even monthly deadlines during your studies, and you certainly won't have someone checking up on how much work you've done for each class and assignment.

INSIDER KNOWLEDGE

'As my managing partner used to say, if it was easy, everyone would be doing it. It isn't easy and you only achieve your objectives with hard work, determination and learning from your experiences as you go along.'

Roger Taylor, retired solicitor, now in business development, charity work and a practising Notary Public

Alongside this you may well have friends who are able to work very efficiently, or are on less immediately demanding courses. They may be very happy to tempt you away from your work. The most successful law students keep working hard throughout. That doesn't mean that you shouldn't relax and take a break from time to time—that is essential. But try not to get into the habit of 'clocking off' when you've only done the bare minimum of reading or preparation for a class, or coasting when you suspect you won't be asked to contribute. Although keeping up the habit of hard work is difficult, it is easier than getting back into the habit later, and much easier than having to cram for urgent assessments.

I WISH I'D KNOWN . . .

'Don't slack off. It's hard and demanding but, if you start slacking, then before you know it you're behind and burning the candle at both ends to catch up, which is absolutely exhausting.'

Sammee Hart, University of East London, LLB Law, Year 2

How to keep up your hard work? Taking personal responsibility for your own studies is essential. The next attribute contributes a lot too.

Motivation

Don't underestimate the importance of motivation for achieving your goals. When yet another essay is due, or yet another Monday morning lecture looms, it is so much harder to do what you know you *should* do if you have forgotten quite why you are bothering. It is important then to keep in mind why you are here.

Assuming you are just about to embark on your legal studies, you are probably feeling pretty well motivated at present, hopefully excited and enthusiastic. Try to capture that feeling; your aims, your goals, your motivations. Why do you want to be a successful law student? Think about your goals and keep them in mind. (We'll talk more about goals in a moment.)

Keeping motivated also makes it much easier to be enthusiastic about your studies, and fully engaged with them. Think about your favourite teachers from school, or your favourite colleagues at work and we'll guess many of them were enthusiastic. It is much easier to be inspired by something when the person you are with is enthusiastic.

Enthusiasm and motivation feed off each other, and can be infectious. So keep motivated by keeping your goals in mind, use that to keep your enthusiasm alive, and respond openly and positively to other people's aims, ambitions and excitement.

Resilience

It is not uncommon to become demotivated at times, particularly when facing a setback, such as a bad mark, or getting something wrong in class, or a problem or disaster in our personal life. There is nothing wrong with that; it is only human to have a negative response to those kinds of events. What matters is how we pick ourselves up after that— our resilience to such setbacks.

Successful law students, indeed successful people more generally, tend to be resilient. It isn't that they are particularly lucky or gifted, or are just maniacally positive. But when they face a setback, they deal with it in their own time, process disappointment, and then get back on with things. They 'bounce back'. They might be fortunate in having a particularly strong strand of resilience in their character. More commonly, they simply learn to be resilient—resilience can be developed, even if you feel you are not a naturally resilient character.

Throughout the book, we'll look at how to deal with some of the bad stuff that might come your way, as well as how to find and enjoy the good stuff. In the meantime the following tips can help to develop a more resilient attitude:

- Identify something positive in everything—the silver lining in every cloud.
- Challenge your own and others' negative thinking.
- If you have a bad experience, look for what it has taught you.
- Act kindly towards others, and accept kindness shown towards you.
- Unwind and manage your stress levels through relaxation and exercise.
- Keep a sense of humour, and don't be afraid to laugh at yourself sometimes.

INSIDER KNOWLEDGE

'A lawyer needs resilience, a team ethic and an interest in people. I see on a daily basis that individuals with these qualities achieve the best results.'

Chris Yates, Partner, Clifford Chance LLP

Other important attributes?

You may be wondering why we haven't included 'intelligence' or 'strong academic ability' in the list of important attributes of a successful law student. It is true that without intelligence—academic ability and common sense—you would find it very difficult to complete a law degree. But you have obviously got the basic intelligence you need to succeed in a law degree. If you hadn't, you wouldn't have got this far.

Remember too that success is about reaching your own potential, not about coming first. To be a success, all you have to do is the best you can. It is inevitable that there will be people in life who are 'cleverer' than you are, there always are. But your own success is not dependent upon what they achieve.

Another attribute that people seem to associate with legal study is 'being good at arguing', although you'll have noticed we haven't included it. It is not at all uncommon for teachers or parents to say things like, 'you'd make a great lawyer—you are always arguing'. That might lead you to suppose that if you don't enjoy arguing you shouldn't study law.

That's not the case. Thinking like a lawyer is not about arguing as such, but about exploring, investigating, proposing, testing, questioning, challenging and applying. Yes, you will learn to develop arguments and communicate persuasively, but that does not mean someone who dislikes 'arguing' should not study law. Of course some lawyers are very argumentative individuals, just as in any group of people. That does not mean that only argumentative people make good lawyers, and it certainly doesn't mean that only those who like to argue can be successful law students.

GETTING READY FOR SUCCESS

We've considered what 'success' means, and the attributes you can cultivate to make that success more likely. Now we'll look at practical steps you can take to help prepare for your successful legal study.

It is likely that you are reading this shortly before you head off to start your legal studies, and our suggestions are made with this in mind. But it is never too early to prepare for success. If you are reading this at an earlier stage, perhaps deciding whether or not to apply for a place on a law programme, then you can still follow up these suggestions. They might even help you to make up your mind about whether legal study is for you. Equally it is rarely too late to do a little preparation. Even if you are just about to go to your first lecture, or are already some way into your legal studies, there are still things you can do to enhance your chances of success.

SWOT: Strengths, Weaknesses, Opportunities and Threats

In business, projects often start with 'SWOT' analysis, shown in Figure 3.2. This can also be used at a personal level. You might want to keep SWOT in mind as you get ready for success.

FIGURE 3.2: SWOT analysis

Strengths	Weaknesses
• What strengths do you have that will help your studies?	• What weaknesses do you have that might make your studies harder?

Opportunities	Threats
• Are there opportunities you can take advantage of to improve your position?	• Can you foresee anything in particular that might cause you problems?

Thinking about your skills

To be as well prepared as you can be, it helps to spend some time understanding your current skills and experience. This enables you to:

- recognise where you have particular strengths or gaps in your skillset;
- make a confident start by reminding you of what you have already achieved;

- identify the most relevant opportunities available to you once your studies commence;
- develop your reflective skills.

Whatever your age and whatever your background, you will have developed a range of skills and accumulated a lifetime—your lifetime—of experiences. They probably won't be obviously 'legal' skills and experiences, but they will nonetheless help you on your way to being a successful law student.

Think back over the training, skills and experience you have already gained. This may be formal training, for example a computer skills course, an enterprise workshop or language training. It also includes training and experience in the workplace. Depending on whether you are approaching your studies direct from school or as a mature student, this could range from part-time work during your studies, work experience, or a lengthy spell as an employee or running your own business.

Just as importantly, your experience may come from your personal life. Again depending on your stage in life this could include anything from caring for a relative or helping at a local sports club, to volunteering for a local charity or acting as a local councillor or school governor.

Take some time to make a note of all the experiences you can call upon. This may be much longer than you might think at first. Now think about what skills each experience has brought or developed and write it down—just thinking is never enough. Table 3.1 shows an abbreviated example. Think widely about the types of skills your experience has developed, for example:

- Interpersonal skills;
- Resilience;
- Written communication;
- Oral communication;
- Social awareness;
- Commercial awareness;
- Leadership.

TABLE 3.1: Sample skills review

EVENT, ACTIVITY OR EXPERIENCE	SKILLS DEVELOPED
Working in Marks & Spencer	Working with others Dealing with difficult customers Managing money Awareness of business pressures
French GCSE and exchange visit	Basic French Confidence in communication Fitting in to a new situation
First aid course	Basic first aid Working with others
Babysitting/housesitting	Responsibility for others Dealing with unforeseen issues Knowing when to seek help Putting first aid skills into practice

By making your own list, you will see that you have a range of skills, many of which will be of use to you in your studies and beyond.

Now think about whether you could further develop existing skills, or where there are some gaps. Make some notes. Table 3.2 gives an abbreviated example. Use your reflection not just as a pointer for where you might usefully spend any pre-university time, but also as a reminder as you go through your studies to see what further opportunities you should consider taking up.

So, if you have some time before going to university, use some of that time to develop the skills where you think you are most in need. It need not cost anything. For example if you are already working part-time, or have taken on a job over the summer, or are fully occupied as a carer, then you are already gaining very valuable experience.

Make the most of any experience by really taking an interest in what you are doing. Think about how any business you are working in

TABLE 3.2: Sample skills reflection

SKILLS NEEDING FURTHER DEVELOPMENT	POSSIBLE ACTION	WHEN?
Languages—improve my French (and/or learn another language)	See if my university offers free/discounted language courses or language options Explore possibility of taking a working holiday abroad Keep in touch with my exchange visit family	Look at website now; ask tutor later Research on web Write email now
Leadership	Volunteer to support leaders in my youth group Join a club at uni and help with organisation	Speak to leader on Tuesday Explore options when arrive at uni
Oral communication	Offer to talk to my old school about my experiences at college/applying to university Try mooting at university and/or join the debating society Speak up a bit more in class	Email school on Monday Look at website now; ask tutor later Now and at uni

operates and what makes it a success, what skills the tasks you are undertaking are developing, how the personal relationships you are dealing with work and so on. If you have some time on your hands, then consider doing some additional voluntary/community work to benefit from the interpersonal skills and social awareness this will develop.

You may be lucky enough to have the opportunity for a long break before starting your law programme. We don't want to stop you enjoying yourself, so go ahead. But as well as relaxing, you could use this opportunity to explore more widely, seeing the challenges faced in other countries and communities, and improving language and communication skills. Grab any opportunities that come your way, and seek out opportunities you might not previously have contemplated.

Another easy but important way to enhance your skills and experience, in a way that will directly and positively impact on your legal studies, is to take an active interest in the world around you. Take a little time each day to deepen your awareness of and interest in society and in local, national and global challenges, by reading a respected newspaper or online news site. The celebrity gossip or sports pages are not enough! Talk to those around you about their own careers and experiences. You will also start to notice, once you are looking, just how much the law gets into everything—homes, families, money, business, jobs, global challenges and so on. That is possibly the most useful preparation for success any law student can have.

I WISH I'D KNOWN . . .

'Law is all around us. For example, look at the Court's decision about Brexit. Watch the news, read papers. Engage in debates and have an opinion.'

Frances Easton, University of Birmingham, Law, Year 2

Thinking about yourself

Most of us don't particularly enjoy reflecting on our strengths and weaknesses or our character more generally. But understanding a bit more about yourself can help to ensure you are ready to meet challenges as they arise. It also means that you have a better chance of organising your learning to best suit your abilities. We'll look further at learning preferences in Chapter 8.

Our discussion of motivation earlier highlighted the relevance of goals in identifying and maintaining that motivation. It is important that you take some time to identify what being 'a successful law student' means to you, and the goals that *you* want to achieve. You have probably already come across the notion of goal-setting in previous studies and work, so we won't go into much detail here, but it is useful to remember that goals work best when they are *SMART*:

- **S: Specific**

  What are you going to do (and why)?

  Be clear about what you want to achieve and how you are going to do it.

- **M: Measurable**

  What will show that you have achieved the goal?

  This may be a final outcome or a series of steps.

- **A: Achievable**

  Do you have what you need to achieve the goal; is the goal attainable?

  If you need to, break up a larger, more daunting, goal into smaller achievable steps.

- **R: Relevant**

  Is the goal consistent with your wider aims and ambitions?

  Check your goals are not inconsistent with one another or your longer-term aims.

- **T: Time-based**

  When will you complete the goal?

  You need a time-frame: this can be demanding but must be realistic.

Different formulations of SMART sometimes use slightly different terminology, but the essence remains much the same.

While it is important to have long-term ambitions, remember that goal-setting is about setting challenging but realistic, achievable goals. Not everyone can be Prime Minister (nor indeed Lord Chief Justice), but everyone can complete an assignment if they set their mind to it. Keep longer-term aims and ambitions in mind as these help to keep you motivated and enthused, but direct your energies to the completion of your more immediate SMART goals.

For goal-setting to be effective, it is really important that you revisit your goals as you progress, and that you feed in your growing knowledge and experience to develop your goals as you go along. At an early stage in your legal studies your goals may necessarily be a little indistinct, so add to and adjust them as your experience increases and your circumstances change.

We've already discussed reflecting on any strengths and weaknesses in your existing skills, knowledge and experience. Don't forget too to think about strengths and weaknesses of your personality and approach to life, so you are better prepared for your legal studies. So, for example, if you know you have a tendency to procrastinate, explore how you might cope with this. (And have a look at https://waitbutwhy.com on procrastination—if nothing else it gives you an excuse not to get on with what you should be doing! https://waitbutwhy.com/2013/11/how-to-beat-procrastination.html). Or perhaps you recognise that you can be impatient or intolerant of other's opinions. If so, keep exposing yourself to different ideas and points of view before you start your course.

All sorts of things might impact on your ability to succeed:

- How self-confident are you?
- Do you get easily distracted?
- Are you competitive? Does this motivate you or cause you to lose focus?
- Do you find it easy to listen to other viewpoints?
- How resilient are you?

There's no need to be super-critical. Just be honest with yourself so you can be alert to things that might trip you up on your road to success and take steps now to meet those challenges more effectively.

Thinking about the law, and more

Law does not exist in a vacuum, but exists to regulate, protect, support and benefit those to whom it applies. Learning the law is therefore not just about learning what the law is, but also considering and questioning how it applies. The more you engage with the world about you, the better placed you'll be to think about the law in context, and to make a confident and

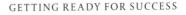

committed start to your studies. Likewise, by taking a wider interest in the law and the legal system, you will be better able to understand how things fit together and so more readily understand the law you will be learning.

Work experience

If you have the time and the opportunity, then additional work experience prior to university can obviously be beneficial. But don't worry if you can't get any formal legal work placements, in solicitors' firms or barristers' chambers for example, as they are difficult to obtain, particularly prior to starting at university.

Think more broadly, and take up any opportunities that come your way. Perhaps you could get some experience in a business or the voluntary sector. You might even be able to spend a short period of time in a local company or charity's legal or human resources department to get some more law-focused experience. Or explore the possibilities of work experience in the court service or with a law enforcement agency, or with your local council or the civil service. All will give you valuable experience of work and law in action. Take advantage of any paid work, voluntary work or extended holidays you are taking, to enhance your commercial and social awareness and develop your skills.

The courts and legal system

You can develop your legal awareness outside the confines of work experience. For example, why not visit one of your local courts or tribunals? You can do a search online at https://courttribunalfinder.service.gov.uk/search/postcode?aol=All to find different courts that are local to you. For the courts in Scotland, see https://www.scotcourts.gov.uk/.

You'll probably be given the chance to undertake a court visit at the start of your law programme anyway, but the pre-university period is a great opportunity to see different kinds of court and tribunal and so get a sense of what is going on in practice. It is particularly valuable as you probably won't find time to go more than once after your course has begun. Extra visits will also allow you to make comparisons between your pre-study and post-study perceptions of the court system and how the law is administered. As not all courts are open access, check online and call before visiting if you want to be able to sit in on a hearing.

If you get the chance to visit a court, it is also often worth taking a walk around the area. Legal businesses often congregate in certain areas, particularly around the courts—it can be interesting to stroll around the 'legal quarter', particularly in larger cities, to get a feel for the legal profession at work.

If you are in or visiting London a visit to the UK Supreme Court is highly recommended. The UK Supreme Court is open to the public and offers guided or self-guided tours around the highest court in the land: https://www.supremecourt.uk/visiting/index.html. You may get the chance to watch part of a case being heard. You can also visit the magnificent Royal Courts of Justice where the Court of Appeal and High Court sit. Tours are also available, although more expensive than at the Supreme Court: https://www.justice.gov.uk/courts/rcj-rolls-building/rcj/tours. While in London, try to find time to take a walk around the Temple area (near Temple tube station), or the Gray's Inn/Lincoln's Inn area (near Chancery Lane tube station) to soak up the legal, and sometimes still almost Dickensian, atmosphere.

If you would like to read more about the court and legal system prior to starting your studies then there are lots of books available. However most of these are quite substantial textbooks. As you will probably be recommended a particular book covering this topic to purchase as part of your law programme, it is not generally advisable to buy an expensive book now in case it is not the one your university wants you to follow. If you do want to get a bit of a head start on the basics at zero/low cost, try:

- The Supreme Court website: https://www.supremecourt.uk/about/the-supreme-court.html

- The Supreme Court: the highest court in the land (documentary): https://www.youtube.com/watch?v=PZtYENfNa7k

- Gary Slapper, *How the Law Works*, 4th edn, 2016.

To keep up-to-date with general legal news the best advice is to read a quality newspaper. *The Times* is particularly popular with lawyers, but all the broadsheets are good for legal news and views. You could also check out the following from time to time:

- Ministry of Justice: https://www.gov.uk/government/organisations/ministry-of-justice

- *The Lawyer* (including 'Lawyer2B'): http://www.thelawyer.com/
- All about Law: http://allaboutlaw.co.uk/law-news.

Law . . . and more

As enthusiastic, committed and hard-working individuals, prospective law students are often very keen to do some reading before starting their legal studies, and to start buying or borrowing textbooks.

We don't want to dampen your enthusiasm, but getting started on textbooks on particular areas of the law tends not to be the best way to do this. For one thing, we don't believe that reading a textbook on, say, Contract Law or Criminal Law, would be the most productive way of spending your summer before a September course start. There is a limit to the value you can get out of such an exercise before you are immersed in your legal studies. You'd certainly end up putting in a lot more effort than the benefit you'd gain. Furthermore, as every programme and every institution has different arrangements and approaches, you could inadvertently be wasting your time by studying a subject that you won't be covering for a year or two, or by reading about topics that you don't need to know about. We recommend leaving your substantive legal reading until you are given specific recommendations from your lecturers or tutors.

So we don't suggest you use your time to learn substantive law. There'll be plenty of time for that very shortly. Instead take the opportunity to read and think about the law more generally and stretch your mind. You can do this without reading textbooks, and can also take the opportunity to read and watch some fun stuff too. What we and your lecturers want is for you to start your course buzzing with ideas and enthusiasm. So don't just read and watch passively—think about the issues that are raised as you read or watch and formulate your own views. Start to get a sense of the enormous influence law has on society, business, the community and relationships at all levels. Think about how—in your opinion—that influence should operate.

Following are some recommendations for pre-course reading/watching/listening. None of this is 'essential' material, we have provided these suggestions for a blend of the informative, interesting, thought-provoking and fun. Pick and choose what you fancy, and keep that enthusiasm for the studies you are about to start. The list is in alphabetical order, not order of importance/preference. And bear in mind that while the US legal system is disproportionately represented, particularly in the film section, you aren't watching to learn about the legal system, but thinking about the issues raised.

Books:

- Catherine Barnard, Janet O'Sullivan and Graham Virgo, *What about Law?: Studying Law at University* (Hart Publishing, Oxford, 2011)
- Tom Bingham, *The Rule of Law* (2010) (Penguin, London, 2011)
- Gerry Conlon, *Proved Innocent/In the Name of the Father* (1990) (Penguin, London, 1991)
- Alfred Thompson Denning, *The Discipline of Law* (1979) (Oxford University Press, Oxford, 2005)
- Charles Dickens, *Bleak House* (1853) (Wordsworth Classics, Hertfordshire, 1993)
- John Grisham, *The Pelican Brief* (1993) (Arrow, London, 2010) (and many, many more . . .)
- Allan Hutchinson, *Is Eating People Wrong? Great legal cases and how they shaped the world* (Cambridge University Press, Cambridge, 2010)
- Harper Lee, *To Kill a Mockingbird* (1960) (Arrow, London, 2010)
- Michael Mansfield, *Memoirs of a Radical Lawyer* (2009) (Bloomsbury, London, 2010)
- Gary Slapper, *Weird Cases* (Wildy, Simmonds & Hill, London, 2009) (see also *More Weird Cases*, 2011 and *Further Weird Cases*, 2014).

Films:

- A Man for all Seasons (1966, dr. Fred Zinnemann)
- Amistad (1997, dr. Steven Spielberg)
- Erin Brockovich (2000, dr. Steven Soderbergh)
- Judgment at Nuremberg (1961, dr. Stanley Kramer)
- Legally Blonde (2001, dr. Robert Luketic)

- My Cousin Vinny (1992, dr. Jonathan Lynn)
- Philadelphia (1993, dr. Jonathan Demme)
- The Verdict (1982, dr. Sidney Lumet)
- Twelve Angry Men (1957, dr. Sidney Lumet)
- Witness for the Prosecution (1957, dr. Billy Wilder).

A note on required pre-course reading

Most universities now direct their new students to some recommended reading to undertake before starting your course. These suggestions can be very helpful, whether covering substantive legal content or legal skills, because they should be closely tailored to the particular course you are about to start.

Of course you should do as advised and read anything you are directed to read. Some of these may even overlap with some of our earlier suggestions, or at least with our more high-brow recommendations.

But a slight note of warning. Our experience is that some, although by no means all, of the reading recommended by law schools can feel a bit overwhelming at first. If you do find that is the case, *please* don't let this put you off. We promise that legal study is much more interesting and accessible than some commonly recommended early reading might suggest. If you find a recommended book too difficult, or struggle to see its relevance at the moment, don't despair and think you are not cut out to be a law student. Instead, put the book aside and come back to it once you start your course—you'll be surprised at how quickly you can then get into it.

SUMMARY—HELP YOURSELF . . .

- **Think about what success means to you**
  - Think about your own aims and goals: be ambitious but realistic.
  - Make sure you are aiming for things that *you* want and can achieve.

- **Reflect on your own position**
  - Think constructively about your own skills, experience and knowledge and your own strengths and weaknesses.

- Identify and take steps to fill in gaps and further develop existing skills.

- Explore sources of advice and strategies to play to your own strengths and weaknesses.

- **Be involved**

  - Take an active interest in the world around you and develop your social and commercial awareness.

  - Look for the influence of the law in everything you see or hear about.

  - Consider and question the approach taken to different challenges, whether local, national or global.

  - Seek out and take up opportunities to enhance your legal and wider awareness.

4

STARTING OUT AT LAW SCHOOL

'The distance is nothing when one has a motive'

JANE AUSTEN,
Pride and Prejudice

INTRODUCTION

Starting your legal studies is an exciting time. But you might also feel a bit apprehensive. You are about to commence a new and challenging programme of study, join a new institution, approach new ways of working, face new expectations and meet new people.

Whether you are moving away from home for the first time, changing degree courses or changing your career, some nerves and concerns are completely natural. Things may seem even more daunting if you are about to study law after a long break from education or are coming to study in another country. But whatever your situation, the better prepared you are, the better start you'll be able to make on your legal journey.

This chapter will look at both the transition to university, and your introduction to the law school itself. We will explore some of the different challenges you may face and help you meet those challenges. We'll also explain a bit more about the law school and your early days to help you to settle in as quickly as possible.

STARTING OUT AT UNIVERSITY

Transition to university

The move to university is often described as 'transition', defined by Oxford Dictionaries online (https//www.oxforddictionaries.com) as 'the process or a period of changing from one state or condition to another: *students in transition from one programme to another*'. Starting university study often represents much more than a stage in the educational process. It can be an important step in becoming an independent adult or a new chapter in your life through changing careers or aspirations.

Significant changes are exciting and, of course, bring challenges. As a successful law student, it pays to think ahead and be prepared for some of these likely challenges. This can make your own transition as smooth as possible.

Meeting the challenges

Universities and law schools all offer new students a great deal of support in different forms. After all, successful degree study begins with effective transition and everyone wants to ensure you have the tools to be a successful law student.

Nonetheless this transition period can be challenging for all students. Change may be welcome, but can nonetheless make you apprehensive. You might even start to doubt whether you have made the right decision. Remember that nearly everyone feels at least a little nervous, however confident those you meet might appear to be. As well as accepting your very natural nerves, try to enjoy the excitement that you and every other student will be feeling. Everyone is keen to make friends, to work together and to share the university experience. All the challenges you may meet—illustrated in Figure 4.1—can be overcome.

Academic challenges

Self-directed learning

A significant challenge when starting your legal studies can be adapting to self-directed learning, or independent study. You will be

FIGURE 4.1: Challenges for the successful law student

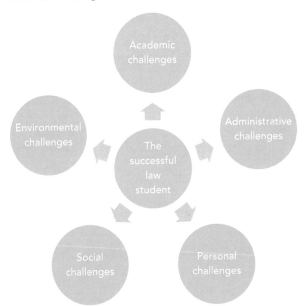

expected to undertake research and reading in preparation for learning activities such as lectures and tutorials, with only limited guidance. You will often have to make your own decisions about what to read and when.

I WISH I'D KNOWN . . .

'I wish I'd known how much independent study is expected. It can be destabilising to have only two or three contact hours a day (be it lectures or tutorials). Yet the amount of expected independent work is considerable, notably the recommended and further reading.'

Gabrielle Bargas, University College London, LLB Law with French Law, Year 2

This can be a significant change from previous study habits, but you will gradually develop your skills, and will be given more guidance in the early days. Learning to plan your time effectively can be a great help.

Consider managing your weekly and daily tasks using a study planner. Some basic tips for managing your time appear in Figure 4.2.

FIGURE 4.2: Managing your time

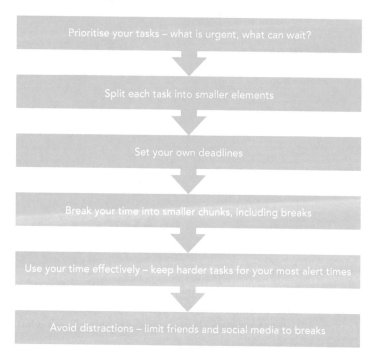

New teaching methods

Another big change is likely to be the size and style of classes. Lectures are usually an important form of class instruction. They are large—often very large—group classes. Learning alongside 100–500 other students can seem intimidating, particularly in the first week when you may not recognise any one else in the room. But say hello to the person next to you, and don't worry—you will settle in to the lecture routine very quickly.

Tutorials and seminars are smaller group sessions containing around eight to twenty students, and give you the chance to get to know other students a little better. Chapter 9 has lots of tips on how to get the best out of your law classes.

Workload

You may be concerned that as a law student you will have an overwhelming workload. Law can be a demanding subject but law schools do not want to overload anyone. In fact, some students may find that they actually have time on their hands in the first week or two, although the work always arrives before long.

Of course, the workload is often demanding, particularly when you begin and it is all rather strange and new. Plan your time carefully (see Figure 4.2) and seek advice from tutors if you find you are struggling. Before long you should find your workload little different to that of other students, or at least those who are as keen on being successful as you are.

The grading system

Starting at law school usually means a completely new grading system. At university, marks are usually awarded as a percentage mark, which in turn converts to an overall classification:

- 70–100 per cent: First class, or 'a first'
- 60–69 per cent: Upper second class, or 2.1 (said 'two-one')
- 50–59 per cent: Lower second class, or 2.2 (said 'two-two')
- 40–49 per cent: Third class, or 'a third'
- 0–39 per cent: Fail.

You may have been used to consistently receiving marks above 80 per cent (or 8/10) at school or college. But in law schools in the UK marks above 70 per cent are not very common, and even though higher range marks are becoming more widely used for deserving work, marks above 80 per cent remain rare. So bear this in mind and don't be dejected if your marks seem much lower than you have been accustomed to.

A new subject

Most law students have never studied law before, and so the first few weeks can feel a little overwhelming. It takes a while to get to grips with an entirely new subject, but you will get there. Generations of law students have worked through that initial unfamiliarity to success, and you can too.

Students who have studied law for A-level will have had some exposure to the study of the legal system and certain core subjects in law (for example, contract law or criminal law). This can give the advantage of some familiarity in the early weeks but the benefit doesn't last very long. Some students do feel that their transition was made easier from having studied A-level law, while others do not feel that it made much, if any, difference.

Whether you have studied A-level law or not; all students are considered to be new to the study of law, and the same level of work is expected from all students. All law schools have compulsory courses for law students to introduce them to legal skills and systems, and the study of each subject starts from the very beginning. And the A-level curriculum does not explore in depth the legal substance, legal decision making, and critical, evaluative skills that are developed in the degree programme.

As we saw in Chapter 2, A-level law won't therefore be a *disadvantage* unless you find yourself not concentrating or working hard in the first few weeks because you, wrongly, think you know it all already. But neither does it offer any significant benefit to legal study at university. You will successfully find your way into the subject either way.

Administrative challenges

The institution

Universities are enormous institutions. They cover a large geographical area, cater for huge numbers of students and employees, provide a wide variety of services and function very differently from schools and colleges. No wonder it can seem confusing.

Remember that much of the university's activities will be behind the scenes and have little impact on you directly. Most of your contact will be within the much smaller law school itself. You will become familiar with the people and bodies you deal with regularly. And if you need help finding your way around the system, just ask for it, whether from staff or fellow students.

Keeping up to date

In most universities email is the primary method of communication and you are expected to check your email messages regularly, at least once a day.

Build this in to your social media routine and be sure to sync your phone, tablet or other devices to your university email provider. Most university websites will have guidance on how to do this or IT services will provide drop-in sessions during the first few weeks of term. If your university or law school uses other methods of communication, get access established as soon as you can.

Also check your timetable regularly. Most universities have electronic timetables. These can be synced to calendars on phones, tablets and laptops and should automatically update if there are any changes.

If you print or copy your timetable into a study planner, check regularly to make sure there are no sudden room or time changes for scheduled teaching activity. It is worth checking your timetable for the day first thing in the morning to confirm your schedule. And if you make an appointment to see a tutor or administrator, don't forget to add this to your main calendar or timetable.

Taking care of administration

It can be worrying if something important goes wrong on the administrative front. This might be an issue with the payment of student finance, being registered for incorrect courses or even clashes within your timetable. But there is no need to panic—you will not be the first or last student to experience any of these problems.

Contact your law school's administrative office as soon as possible. They will be able to signpost you to the relevant person to deal with the problem. Get problems sorted as soon as they become apparent.

I WISH I'D KNOWN . . .

'I wish I'd known about all of the admin! From registering with the university, signing up for the library, registering with a GP—it is actually much more work than it seems at first glance. I wish I'd been more prepared and had a checklist of things "to do", rather than realising too late I had to do more administrative errands, when I don't have time.'

Rebecca Agliolo, University of Cambridge, Law, Year 4

Personal challenges

Moving away

Moving to a new place is often a powerful positive motivator in choosing your university. But it can still be a significant personal challenge to move away from your friends or family and leave behind established support networks. Don't worry if you feel a bit homesick—it is natural but soon passes. Usually in a very short period of time you will develop new friends and support networks—housemates, course mates, fellow members of clubs and societies.

Balancing commitments

All students have to balance the demands of legal study with other commitments. Students with young children, students on sports scholarships and the many students who have to support their studies by working part-time will all have to juggle to keep numerous balls in the air. Even if you just want to maintain outside interests, you will have to make choices and organise your time carefully.

When you have outside commitments it can be tough to see other students without the same pressures. At times, you may feel overwhelmed by a hectic schedule. You will need to be determined and flexible, adapting your routine where necessary. Reflect on the benefits of taking on work and other activities to keep positive—we'll look further at this in Chapter 18. But speak to your personal tutor if your commitments begin to impact significantly on your studies or well-being.

Another challenge is balancing work and the social aspect of universities. However you define your social life—whether book groups and coffee shops, or pub-crawls and rugby, or indeed a combination of all those things and more—the opportunity to engage fully in a variety of activities with like-minded people is an important part of the university experience.

There is a balance to be struck. Occasionally, students lose focus on either studying or their social life for a while. But nearly all students find a way of securing a sensible balance. The relative importance of work and play will naturally ebb and flow as the year progresses. While the successful law student has to work hard, it remains important to enjoy your time in university and build a good work/life balance. It can help to think of your degree programme as a job. Your daytime and maybe some of your evening will be consumed by your university study and teaching time. But the rest of your evenings and weekends should be free for social activities and down-time.

Some extra-curricular activities you undertake may also feel like work. We'll look at some of these in Chapters 17–18. They provide valuable opportunities for you to engage more deeply with the law, and to get to know people. But that doesn't mean you can or should do everything. Take stock if you feel things getting out of control. If you feel yourself falling behind, think about how you are dividing your time between your commitments. The successful law student needs to reflect and adapt, and keep an eye on their immediate goals.

Social challenges

Making new friends

It is common to worry at least a bit about making friends when you arrive at university and of course you may feel rather alone at first. But at university it is almost impossible not to make friends. You will meet people on your programme and beyond, and meet people with similar interests through clubs and societies.

You may also find a friendship group within your accommodation. If you are moving into university accommodation and want a head start on making friends, try bringing cake and a few extra mugs on arrival day—few people will resist an offer to share tea and cake after (or during) unpacking.

You will also meet friends by just attending social events and welcome meetings. Get out and about, even if you are feeling shy. Don't worry if it appears at these events that everyone knows someone else already. They have almost certainly only just met and will be very happy to add a new friend to their collection. Be prepared to ask (and answer) what seem to be the three most important questions of the new student: 'Where are you from?' ... 'What course are you studying?' ... 'Where are you living?' ....

Remember to be open-minded about the people you meet. University is a wonderfully diverse place and you might find the most loyal and kind-hearted of friends lurking behind the most fearsome faces or intimidating accents.

I WISH I'D KNOWN . . .

'I wish I'd introduced myself to more people and just been more forward in meeting friends. Now I'm in third year I know or would at least recognise everyone in my year and I would say my best friends and those I often work with aren't the people I met in the first week or so. It's so important to not just stick with the first friendly group of people, introduce yourself to as many people as possible. Some people will have come with friends from high school but make sure you don't just use them as a safety blanket. The people you meet at university will not just be friends now but also colleagues and contacts further down the line in your career.'

Alexandra Townsley, University of Nottingham, LLB Law and American Law, Year 3

A new culture

University culture can sometimes be a bit of a surprise. All institutions have their own traditions. Many societies and sport teams have their own rules and customs. These may seem confusing, particularly if you are also experiencing a new national culture as well. Nonetheless, you will generally learn to embrace these traditions and enjoy the way they often work to bring together a group of individuals.

Other than those institutional traditions that are an essential part of university practice, don't be afraid to say no if you are uncomfortable with a particular tradition or expectation. And always speak to representatives from your student union, guild or association if you feel that a university society is not operating in an inclusive way.

Environmental challenges

The campus or university area

A university campus, precinct or other area is usually huge compared with a college or school. The thought of navigating from your accommodation to your department or from the student union building to the library can seem like a daunting prospect. Even finding your way around some university buildings can at first seem impossible!

However confusing it seems at first, you will find your way around soon enough. Many universities will give you a map when you arrive or in your welcome pack. If you don't receive one, find one on the university website. Keep it with you! And don't be too proud to ask for directions—there is no shame in not knowing your way around. You may even find that the person you ask is heading to the same class.

I WISH I'D KNOWN . . .

'Where all the different lecture halls were for the different modules! I spent long periods running around campus like a headless chicken trying to find these historically named buildings that all looked the same. It felt like groundhog day for the first year. Take the time in the first couple of days to get a map of campus, and locate your relevant lecture halls. Document on your map and make sure you keep your map in a safe place for future reference and not leave it on the desk on Day 1 of lectures, so that all that orienteering is not in vain.'

Andrea Garvey, Swansea University, LLB Law Single Honours, Year 2

Obtaining essentials

Most university campuses have convenience stores where you can pick up essential items. But eventually you will need to find the local shopping centre for food, stationery, books and clothes. Most universities will provide a basic city map, or use a map app on your phone. Take the time to explore your new city. It will be your home for several years so look out for hidden gems and interesting places to visit.

Doctors and other public services

If you are in university accommodation, you should be able to get information there on anything you need. Your university's student advice service will also help on issues such as this. A further source of guidance is the student welfare officer in your university student union, guild or association. There are plenty of people happy to help you find what you need—just ask. It is important to register for things like medical services as soon as you can if you have moved away from home.

Finances

It is a rare student who has no money concerns at all. Make sure you have explored all the funding opportunities, such as student loans, available to you and your obligations to the provider. These opportunities will differ according to your home nation and circumstances. Keep your personal information, such as changes of address and phone number, up to date with funders.

Many students take on part-time work to support their studies, and we look at this further in Chapter 18. Remember too that many universities have access and hardship funds, so if you are getting into financial difficulties, speak immediately to your student union/association or university student support centre.

Other challenges

We can't hope to have covered every challenge you may face when coming to university. Equally we may have mentioned things that will simply never be an issue for you. The experience of starting a law degree will vary according to numerous personal factors. Just as there is no such thing as a typical law student, there is no such thing as a typical student experience. You will face different challenges depending on your own characteristics, qualities and experience. However, as particular groups of students may have distinct challenges, or may find that challenges present themselves in slightly different ways, we will look at this next.

Stepping into the unknown: school and college leavers

Leaving school or college to go to university should be an amazing time in your life. You get to specialise in a subject you are interested in, begin on your career path and meet new people. You may have more freedom, enjoy different experiences, have fun, and will learn skills to prepare you for the rest of your life.

We can't predict exactly what your undergraduate experience will be, nor all the challenges that may arise in transition. But the biggest challenge for school/college leavers is often overcoming the fear of the unknown—the understandable apprehension at leaving home, and starting a new and demanding way of studying.

Getting ready

However nervous you feel, within a few weeks we guarantee that you will feel very much at home. Help yourself by seeking out and engaging with the information you need. Your university will send you a great deal of information before you even leave home and you will be given even more when you arrive. Ask questions.

And don't be disheartened if the academic leap initially seems too high. Any big change takes time to get used to, and you can't expect to find it easy nor to instantly obtain the marks you were used to. Don't be disheartened if subjects are initially confusing or studying is initially difficult. Do your best to keep up-to-date with all your reading and tasks, prioritising the most important, and remember to *think*. No one is going to force you to work, nor to stretch yourself. You are obviously intelligent, able and thoughtful or you would not be embarking on a law degree. That means you have the ability to adjust your learning habits to work independently and think more critically, and to succeed.

I WISH I'D KNOWN . . .

'Organisation is key. As students at school we do not realise how much we are spoon fed. Going to university, the biggest change was the level of freedom you had and therefore, the amount of organisation and self-discipline you needed to be able to meet deadlines.'

Zoe Lindsey, Postgraduate student, University of Nottingham

Taking control

A particular challenge if you are living away from home for the first time is the management of your own affairs. It is not unusual to feel overwhelmed by the pressures of balancing work and social life, administrative tasks and extra-curricular activities, household chores and other commitments.

Help yourself by thinking in advance of the things you will need to do for yourself, from washing clothes to buying essentials, and from cooking and cleaning to paying bills. Get some basic skills in these areas: being able to cook more than just beans on toast is very helpful when you've got lots of other things to think about. You'll find that new tasks quickly become familiar chores, and you will find it easier to manage your time.

Budgeting is also an important part of being a student and may be a new challenge. Any financial assistance you have through loans, grants, bursaries, scholarships or family assistance will need to last throughout the term. Consider whether you need a part-time job to fund your studies or 'extras' such as books and travel, and explore what is available (see further Chapter 18). Take advantage of student discounts in many retailers, restaurants, bars and outlets.

Another concern may be the thought of living in halls of residence or shared housing. The experience of living with people from different countries, backgrounds and places can be very rewarding but isn't always easy. Despite the challenges it is actually very rare to have such difficult housemates that a student feels they need to move. Advisors in your student union/association will be happy to help with accommodation difficulties.

Welcome back: the postgraduate law student

As a postgraduate entrant to a law programme such as a Graduate Diploma in Law or accelerated law degree, you will have a good understanding of the critical rigour of degree study and workload, and the challenges posed by transition. However, beginning a graduate law programme also presents its own challenges, particularly as these programmes are often very intensive from the start.

Settling in

Settling in can sometimes be an issue for returning graduates. If you are joining a new institution you will have a new system to understand and new expectations to meet. You may be leaving a friendship group or support network. But having gone through this process before, you are well equipped to handle any issues you may face.

It is natural to feel great affinity for your first university and tempting initially to compare everything unfavourably against the institution you have left. This negativity is often down to lack of familiarity. Just as when you were an undergraduate, take time to explore the university and the area. Attend induction sessions so that you quickly become familiar with new systems, procedures, services and support networks. Don't assume it will—or should—all work in the same way as your previous institution or programme.

And don't just rely on old friends—take every opportunity to make friends and contacts through welcome sessions, clubs and societies. You may have a separate common room for postgraduate students which will allow you to socialise easily. And make sure you get involved with extra-curricular activities in your law school, both to gain valuable experience, and to integrate fully into your learning community.

Learning from experience

As a postgraduate student you have the opportunity to begin with a clean slate and review previous habits, practices and experience. Take the opportunity to learn lessons from your previous studies. Focus on your past practice, reflect and look forward. Ask yourself the following questions, and write down your answers to force yourself to think deeply and honestly:

- What worked well during my last programme of study?
- Why did it work well?
- Could it be improved?
- If so, what can I do to do this even better?
- What didn't work so well during my last programme of study?
- Why didn't it work?
- How can I improve it?

Now choose four things that you are going to do differently this time. They could be big or small, but make sure they are realistic and achievable. Put a reminder on your phone for the end of each term and check off whether you've done them.

A truthful reflective process is fundamental to improving personal performance. Hopefully, in this quick exercise you can isolate strengths and weaknesses in your previous performance and create an action plan for your coming course. Consider talking to your personal tutor about any problems you foresee.

Having completed a previous degree, you bring a level of expertise and unique perspective to your legal studies. Don't be afraid to draw upon your experience and use your knowledge to enrich the legal curriculum. But keep sight of your goals and remember that the aim of a legal programme is to learn the substance and practice of law. Your expertise can enrich but cannot replace your legal learning.

Balancing the scales: the mature student

As a mature student you have valuable skills and experience to offer. Just taking the step into legal study at university shows great commitment and self-motivation. As a mature student you may have no previous experience in higher education but are likely to have a great deal of real-world experience. You may also have a greater number of outside commitments and responsibilities than many undergraduates.

Fitting it all in

It can be difficult to organise home and family responsibilities and still fit in the amount of work needed to complete your legal studies. While if you are moving from regular structured employment to a freer university structure this can also be challenging. But draw upon your experiences and expertise to help you cope.

If, as is likely, you have been in employment or had equivalent commitments, you are already an expert time manager. Use these skills to enable you to manage your studies. Treating study as a day at work can be a good starting point. Or you may prefer to attend only during timetabled contact hours and return home, fitting studies around other responsibilities. Where possible try to set aside clear time for your studies to separate the distinct areas of your life and make most effective use of your time.

But there is no magic solution. Try a number of strategies in your first few weeks to see which works best for your situation. And although life has a habit of upsetting the most organised routine, university staff will be understanding and as flexible as they can be. Most universities also have mature student societies or support groups who are good for moral and practical support.

Keeping an open mind

Draw upon your range of experiences to provide new perspectives on your legal work, and be willing to share those perspectives with your classmates. Be open to others. It can be tempting to keep the company only of existing friends and fellow mature students, but don't ignore the younger undergraduates who will make up the rest of your cohort.

Mature students sometimes report feeling a bit isolated. Socialising outside class may take the form of late-night sessions you are unable to join because of family commitments. Discussions might centre on interests that you do not share. Or you might feel intimidated by being greatly outnumbered by younger students in a class, and at first it can seem as if younger students are choosing not to engage with you.

Take the trouble to talk to your colleagues, to start conversations, and suggest alternatives for socialising. Remember that younger undergraduates are almost certainly not deliberately excluding you, and in fact may well feel rather intimidated by your greater experience and need you to make the first move of friendship. Try to recall how you felt at the age of 18, 19 or 20. You may recall that all that exterior confidence and banter often masks a great deal of uncertainty and you all have much more in common than at first might appear to be the case.

A new jurisdiction: the international student

As an international student you will face issues very similar to those faced by the other student groups we have examined here but with the added challenge of being in a new country and/or studying in a second language. If it all seems a bit overwhelming, keep in mind the reasons why you took up this opportunity.

Taking advantage

Studying away from home provides a unique opportunity to explore another country and meet people from a variety of diverse cultures. You can also immerse yourself fully in a second language. Treat it as the adventure it is. For students from different continents, the UK can also act as an excellent base for exploring Europe. While it is important that you focus on your studies, take advantage of the wonderful opportunity you have been given to explore and appreciate another part of the world.

Such is the diversity of the student body that you are likely to find plenty of fellow students from your home nation, and possibly a student society. Make good use of these contacts and support systems. But don't be tempted to spend all your spare time with other students from your home country. It is natural to want to spend time relaxing with people who share your language and culture, but if you do so exclusively, you are missing an essential opportunity to improve your language skills and understand more about your host country. You will also miss the opportunity to make good friends from across the globe. Make the effort to speak to your fellow students on your course, wherever they are from, and be an active member of your study groups.

I WISH I'D KNOWN . . .

'As an international student, you may be overwhelmed by the amount of British students at the university, especially in Law. Do not feel insecure about your linguistics and stick to a group of friends from your country only. Try to make as many friends as possible because you are here to emerge yourself in the English culture.'

Quynh Anh Thi Le, University of Warwick, LLB with study abroad, Year 2

Language and culture

A key issue as an international student can be a language barrier between your first language and your adopted 'study' language. All international students who wish to study in another language will have completed an accredited language test as part of the application, but unless you are truly bilingual it is unlikely this means that you fully understand the language—particularly with the complexities of legal language.

There may be times where you feel like you are struggling. Don't panic or try to hide your difficulties. Instead take the time to reassess your language skills now you are in the UK. All universities offer excellent support for international students, and will offer support to students who are struggling with their learning. Learning support centres will offer courses on adapting to learning in another language.

Learning support can also help you to understand the British academic system. This can be initially confusing. Your student handbook and other information provided for international students in your law school may also include information on the British academic tradition. This includes the importance of critical thinking and evidence-based opinion, and ways to avoid academic problems like plagiarism. Being aware of different academic cultures and expectations from the start can help to prevent later difficulties. Don't assume that everything will be the same as at home; you may well have to develop new ways of working and thinking.

Always keep in mind any conditions of your stay. There may be strict attendance requirements as a condition of a student visa, so make sure you are fully aware of the rules that apply to you and stick to them.

Seeking help through transition

Whatever your background, when starting out it can sometimes be difficult even to acknowledge that you need support. But successful study of law at university depends on taking responsibility for yourself and that includes asking questions and seeking help when you need it.

If you need advice or guidance, use the various support structures that your university has in place. Speak to your personal tutor, or a university student support advisor, or your student union/guild. There is no such thing as a stupid question and we guarantee that your questions will have been asked before. Make use of specialist support systems where appropriate, for example, the international student office, student societies, the postgraduate office or accessibility support. And ask other students for advice if you are unsure of something: they'll probably be pleased to have the excuse to ask you questions too.

GETTING TO GRIPS WITH THE LAW SCHOOL

To get the best from your legal studies, it is essential that you become familiar with the law school and course structures that you will work within for the next few years. You can't expect to know everything within the first day or two. Focus on understanding the basic arrangements, what is expected of you during the first few weeks, and perhaps most importantly, where to find out more information when you need it.

Finding out

Induction sessions within your law school, usually held during Welcome Week (discussed a little later), will give you key information about your course and how to complete your studies successfully. You will find out things such as which modules are compulsory and which are optional, how much each year and each module counts towards your final degree classification, and the basic teaching structure for your initial modules.

I WISH I'D KNOWN . . .

'Knowing the grade structure is very important as you can work out the amount of time you need to spend on independently studying/revising.'

Quynh Anh Thi Le, University of Warwick, LLB with study abroad, Year 2

The amount of guidance you receive at the beginning of your course will vary, but all schools will have a student manual or programme handbook related to your degree. This will probably be provided to you in hard copy or electronically during this first week, or you will be told where to find it online. It will have all the important information you need for successfully completing your degree, including answers to many administrative questions and guidance on various other aspects of your course. If you are not given or directed to a specific handbook for your programme, there will be a general one for your wider faculty/college or the university.

Check out any online resources that you are directed to. If you have specific questions, search for the relevant information on your university website. Do your best to find the information yourself but if you can't find it then ask someone. Law staff do their best to tell you what you need to know but can't always second guess what is important or unclear to you.

If you are studying a combined programme or a flexible degree, you will need to check the particular requirements and information for these combination subjects too. These different degrees may have different requirements and rules for passing. They may also have differing assessment methods and be delivered differently. You must ensure that you attend any induction sessions relevant to both/all your combination subjects so you understand all aspects of your course.

Knowing what is expected

During the introductory week, you will usually be given some guidance on the amount of contact time you will receive. You should receive your timetable for your first term. You will also be given some guidelines on how much independent study you will need to do.

The majority of law schools deliver about ten to twelve hours of lectures and small group teaching each week. There is quite a bit of variety though, from perhaps six to eight hours in some universities to fifteen or more in others—much depends on methods of teaching. You will also be given opportunities for optional contact such as drop-ins and additional workshops. It is worth finding out this information early on so each week you can plan your time accordingly.

Alongside this formal contact time, you will also be expected to complete a considerable number of hours of independent study each week. Again, individual law schools will give you differing guidelines. You should expect to work in total the equivalent of a full working week each week, taking into account both individual study and timetabled classes. Once you have attended lectures and other teaching activities, the rest of your day should normally be spent undertaking reading and preparing for teaching activities.

Remember that it is your responsibility to monitor how much independent study that you do. Make sure to time manage yourself properly. If you feel yourself falling behind, perhaps reassess with honesty how much work you are doing each week and adjust your schedule accordingly.

GETTING TO KNOW YOUR LEARNING COMMUNITY

Law schools are often very large, with as many as 500 new undergraduate students each year, and many postgraduate students too. The law school is likely to be part of a broader faculty or college within the university, with even more students. Across the university there will be many thousands of students, and a vast number of academic and support staff.

Meeting your colleagues

As we've discussed earlier in this chapter, many students find making contact with fellow students quite difficult in such huge institutions and will be nervous initially. What matters is that you take up opportunities to meet your fellow students when you can, whether socially or in class.

Don't be intimidated if your new colleagues have studied law before and you haven't, or if they already have a degree or work experience. Instead, use this as a way to make conversation and even get their advice. Your fellow law students will be the people you spend the most time with at university, so get to know them and enjoy the experience of meeting people from all walks of life, with different backgrounds, interests, experiences and stories to tell.

It can be tempting to socialise only with those students you find yourself sharing accommodation with, or those with particular interests. But having some friends and contacts on the same degree programme as yourself is a valuable support through your course. View your classmates as colleagues and collaborators, not competitors.

I WISH I'D KNOWN . . .

'I would say that you should not worry about feeling a bit lost or stressed in the first week, as almost everybody feels that way!'

Fiona Lin, University of Cambridge, Law, Year 3

Meeting the law staff

You will also have plenty of opportunities to meet many of the teaching staff on your programme. You could look at the staff profiles on your law school's webpages beforehand to get a sense of who's who in your school. This will be easy in a small law school, less so in law schools with numerous staff members. Don't worry, you won't be expected to remember them all. Just become familiar with some of the faces that you will see regularly.

Most members of the law staff are happy for students to address them by their first name. But to avoid any possibility of offence, it is usually safer to greet staff members initially using their title, for example Ms Smith, Dr Ahmed, or Professor Zhang. The same is true if you are contacting them for the first time by email. Most will ask you to call them by their first name thereafter, but some prefer to be referred to by their title. Whatever you call them, it is good to talk to the law staff.

Some students can initially feel intimidated by the thought of talking to law staff, particularly professors. But remember that your lecturers are people—and most would not be in their jobs if they didn't like talking to students. Members of the law staff, whatever their title, can be a really valuable source of advice, hints, and tips for studying law. After all, they were in your position once and have seen numerous students pass through different institutions.

You will also meet various administrators during your first week in university. These are not teaching staff, but are vital points of contact for you as a student. These administrators or support managers will often be your first point of call for a number of queries. They will also be ready to support you and answer any questions you have throughout your degree.

Who's who in the law school?

You'll meet various people over the course of your legal studies, and while names and titles can vary from institution to institution, the basic concepts are usually pretty similar. Some of the key people you'll meet or hear about in the first few weeks are likely to include:

- Head of School/Department
  - Your law school will be led by a senior member of the law staff, often a professor. You'll probably meet them in the first week, as they will usually give a welcome address. You'll also probably meet the 'Director of Education' or 'Director of Teaching and Learning'— this will be the member of law staff with overall responsibility for student education in the law school.

- Lecturer, Teaching Fellow, Reader, Professor
  - Members of the law staff have different titles, with different levels of seniority and responsibility and varying roles. Titles vary between institutions with many additional permutations, including Principal Lecturer, Senior Teaching Fellow, Associate Professor etc. You'll be taught by many members of the law staff. Some will probably give introductory talks in the first week. One of them will also act as your personal tutor. Individual members of staff with particular administrative responsibilities may have titles such as 'Director of Employability'; 'Exams Officer', 'Mooting Co-ordinator' and so on.

- **Personal tutor**
  - This member of the law staff acts as your main contact point and has responsibility for your general welfare and progress. We look more at this role and relationship later on in this chapter. Your personal tutor will also be able to direct you to further sources of help such as the university counselling service or accessibility support.

- **School (or departmental) manager/administrator**
  - This person has responsibility for the general running of the law school. They will usually lead a team of people, often called the Law Office or Undergraduate/Postgraduate Office, who deal with administrative matters. Members of this team are usually very helpful and happy to answer any queries you've got about the course. If they can't give you an answer they will direct you to the person you need to speak to.

- **Student mentor/buddy**
  - Many law schools have schemes whereby other law students act as mentors or buddies to a group of new law students. You may be allocated a mentor/buddy automatically, or you may be able to request one. They can provide very useful support and guidance, particularly in your first few weeks. You may also come across student guides who help to show new students around and explain what you need to do.

- **The student union, student guild or student association**
  - This is run by students for students and provides a wide range of services and support. A representative of the student union will normally give a talk during the first week of your time at university, and many of the events that are laid on, and clubs that are run, will be through the student union.

- **The law society**
  - The student law society will be run by law students and offer many activities and events over the year. Joining the law society is a good way to make friends and contacts both in and outside the university, for developing your skills and expanding your career

opportunities. Usually you will be able to join the society during welcome week (see later in this chapter).

- **Law librarian/library representative**

  - The law librarian or law specialist on the library team will help students find and use legal resources. They can be a key support in your study so make good use of their expertise and guidance. We'll look more at legal resources and the law library in Chapter 7.

- **Careers and employability advisor/careers service representative**

  - The careers advisor with responsibility for law in your university careers/employability service can be a very useful contact through your studies. Some law schools even have their own dedicated career advisor. We'll consider the careers service further in Chapter 19.

- **Student well-being advisors/counsellors**

  - Most universities have student support workers or counsellors, sometimes even embedded within the law school itself. If you are feeling stressed, depressed, anxious or just need someone to talk to, make contact sooner rather than later. Your personal tutor or any other member of staff will be happy to point you in the right direction.

Networking

You will develop an important skill during these first few weeks. This is the ability to network. Networking is an important part of employability—building the skills that will get you the career you want.

The idea of networking may well be familiar to you: networking is the ability to create and expand your network of contacts in a professional and/or social field. Simply put, it is meeting people who can provide you with information or advice on your chosen field, be it law, business or anything else. Of course, digital networking is an important part of being a professional in the internet age, but being able to converse with people from all walks of life and make conversation face-to-face with strangers remains really important. Engaging with course colleagues, teaching staff and administrative staff is a great way to practise your networking skills, gain confidence and learn to think and act professionally in a safe and soon-to-be familiar environment.

I WISH I'D KNOWN . . .

'Join societies, clubs and do lots of extra curricular. Develop a relationship with those that will help guide you, such as personal tutors, careers advisers, members of staff. They are a real help. Also make the most out of the university experience: step out of your comfort zone, take advantage of every opportunity that comes your way. Don't see everyone as a competitor, because you will not make friends and just rivals. Finally, be yourself.'

Isabel Anderson, Aberystwyth University, LLB Law, Year 3

Personal tutors

During your first week in your new law school, or shortly afterwards, you will meet your personal tutor. Most, if not all, law schools now have a personal tutoring system. This is an important part of your academic and personal experience. The personal tutor system may vary from law school to law school, but in most cases every single student on every programme will have a named tutor. It is this tutor's role to provide the student with guidance, support and advice throughout their time in university.

You will usually be allocated your personal tutor immediately on arrival. Very soon after, you are likely to have a meeting with the personal tutor to welcome you to the university and explain their role. This initial meeting may be one-to-one, or may be a group meeting together with that staff member's other personal tutees. Subsequent meetings are usually one-to-one. But some law schools run introductory skills sessions through the personal tutors and for these you are likely to be in a group.

The personal tutor role has a number of facets, and the precise combination will differ between institutions. Most commonly the personal tutor:

- acts as an academic mentor during your time at university;
- provides advice and guidance as required on academic matters and skills development;
- helps you to address issues that impact on your studies;
- signposts relevant university support services where needed, from study and research skills to counselling or careers;
- liaises with other academic and administrative colleagues where necessary.

Your personal tutor may also help you complete any PDP (professional development planning) that you do as part of your programme. Take advantage of any opportunities that your personal tutor or school offer you to aid your professional development. If you are given tasks to think about developing skills, dedicate sufficient time to completing them properly as they will help you on the road to success.

It is common practice for students to meet with their personal tutor once or twice a term. This means you can update your personal tutor on your progress and plans and ask any questions that you wish to clarify.

You should also see your personal tutor outside any scheduled meetings—usually you can just email to make an appointment—if you have problems impacting upon your studies. Many students face difficulties during their degree and it is better to get help promptly, than to suffer in silence and alone. Your personal tutor is not a counsellor of course but will be able to help you by explaining to you what support is available and what help they or the school can give you. Other than in exceptional circumstances, anything you say to, or personal information you share with, a personal tutor is always treated in confidence.

INSIDER KNOWLEDGE

'Remember that your Personal Tutor is there to advise if you encounter any problems between meetings. He or she is a good first port of call whatever the nature of the problem: if you are uncertain where to go to get specialist advice, or just want a chat about how things are going or are concerned about some feedback you have received on coursework, for example.'

Dr Laura Bennett, Associate Professor of Law, Director of UG Programmes, University of Reading

Your personal tutors will also be the main person to write you references for future employment. That might not seem very important right now, but it will be. So let your personal tutor know how you are getting on in your studies, your involvement with extra-curricular activities and wider interests. That enables your personal tutor to give you tailored advice and support, and ensures a meaningful reference when needed. There is only so much a tutor can say from looking at a student record.

MAKING USE OF WELCOME WEEK

What is 'Welcome Week'?

Before your law programme starts in earnest, your university will provide a Welcome Week or Induction Week. This may be more familiar to you by its more common name of Freshers' Week.

These weeks are designed to help you settle in and enjoy the beginning of your university experience. You will be given plenty of information. And there will be numerous events organised to help you meet new people, find your way around, have fun and get used to studying and living at university.

It would be impossible to list all the types of events offered during Welcome Week as these are so varied. Everything from tea and toast drop-ins to pie and mash afternoons, or from archery taster lessons to Zumba sessions and from wine tasting to live music club nights. Don't feel you have to attend absolutely everything. Make informed choices to get the most out of this important week or two.

A common misconception about Welcome Week is that it is all about going out to bars, parties and clubs. This can be true if you want it to be, but it needn't be; there will be very many other activities you can do. And it is not all about social activities.

I WISH I'D KNOWN . . .

'Don't feel under pressure to go to every type of event straight away. Choose a couple to try out each week; you can make every semester a new experience if you so wish.'

Alice Munnelly, King's College London, Law with European Legal Studies, Year 3

Induction programmes

Welcome Week is about introducing you to both the university and the law school. So the university will provide a number of orientation sessions and induction meetings. These might cover the library, IT services, health and safety (especially if you live in halls of residence), sustainability, and even picking up your university ID card.

Your law school will also provide an induction programme. This usually involves a series of introductory lectures, meetings and events. These are really important to introduce you to your course, law school and colleagues, and welcome you to your new academic home. Sessions might include a welcome from a senior member of staff, initial lessons in problem solving, an introduction to the law library or a welcome party with lecturers and fellow students.

Activities and opportunities vary between law schools, but it is from these specific law school sessions that you are likely to gain the most directed information you need for studying law and the procedures for learning within your school.

You may also be introduced to the student law society during this induction programme. As mentioned earlier, nearly all law schools will have a student law society offering a wide range of social and career events over the year. Welcome Week provides a good opportunity to understand what the society does and see what they offer in the way of extra-curricular activities. They will offer lots of legally related activities and events that will be really valuable in developing your skills for your future employment. They should also provide loads of valuable information, advice, hints and tips for studying law.

With everything that goes on in Welcome Week, it may be tempting to miss classes or sessions timetabled by your university or school. Don't do it! These sessions are important to starting your journey as a successful law student. The last thing you want to do is start your law programme without essential information, or having to catch up on missed sessions.

I WISH I'D KNOWN . . .

'Don't miss the first lectures and workshops, it is very important to meet your lecturers and the group that you will be in.'

Lita Aguimoy Jones, Staffordshire University, LLB Law, Year 2

SUMMARY—HELP YOURSELF . . .

- **Be prepared for challenges and new experiences**
  - Reflect on particular challenges you may face.
  - Approach the early days with an open, enthusiastic and questioning mind.

- Be inclusive: support other students in the same position, and be aware of pressures on other student groups.
- Don't be afraid to ask questions; remember you are not alone.
- **Find out about your course and the institution**
  - Identify the key people and your own personal tutor.
  - Find out what you'll be learning, and when and where.
  - Don't overwhelm yourself with information. Make sure you know the basics—where you should be and when—and where to find out anything else.

- **Don't expect to be an instant expert**
  - Both the subject and the nature of study will be new; be prepared to take some time to adjust.
  - New grading systems can be initially disheartening; take the time to find out how the system works and set yourself realistic goals at the start.

- **Take all opportunities to meet people**
  - Attend welcome talks and don't miss any induction events specific to your law school, or any other departments with which you'll be studying.
  - Explore the clubs, societies and activities offered through the student union, guild or association.
  - Talk to student guides or mentors about their experience, and don't be afraid to talk to staff members.
  - Go to some social events as well as formal talks.

- **Make full use of your personal tutor**
  - Understand the role of the personal tutor and the supportive but professional relationship it represents.
  - Attend all personal tutorial meetings and keep your personal tutor informed of your progress, successes and challenges.

PART 2
SUCCESSFUL LEGAL STUDY

5

STUDYING LAW: ACQUIRING LEGAL KNOWLEDGE

*'I'm hungry for knowledge. The whole thing is to
learn every day, to get brighter and brighter.
That's what this world is about. You look at someone
like Gandhi, and he glowed. Martin Luther King glowed.
Muhammad Ali glows. I think that's from
being bright all the time, and trying to be brighter.'*

JAY-Z
quoted in 'Men's Health', 5 October 2010

INTRODUCTION

Legal knowledge is fundamental to being a successful law student and for undertaking any legal work. It is also key to understanding society around us, and our relationships with other individuals and public and private organisations. One of the main objectives of the law degree, alongside the development of essential legal skills, is to acquire legal knowledge. Even if you don't want to be a lawyer, knowledge of a range of legal subjects provides an enriching and eye-opening perspective on the world.

Law programmes all therefore require you to study a variety of different legal subjects over the course of your degree. And almost all law programmes will make certain key areas of law compulsory. In other words you are likely to *have* to study some legal subjects as part of your degree.

These compulsory subjects are usually those making up the 'foundations of legal knowledge', and are crucial to attaining a qualifying law degree. We discussed the qualifying law degree (or 'QLD') more generally in Chapter 2. Although the legal professions have proposed changes to the QLD, the current foundation subjects are likely to continue to play a major role in legal education for the foreseeable future at the very least. These proposed changes to the law degree and the progression route into the solicitor's profession are discussed further in Chapter 20.

In this chapter, we will explain what subjects make up the foundations of legal knowledge. We will outline in simple terms what these foundation subjects commonly include. We will consider how these subjects relate to real life, and also encourage you to think more deeply about the role of law in society and develop social and commercial awareness.

UNDERSTANDING THE FOUNDATIONS OF LEGAL KNOWLEDGE

Foundations: breadth and depth

The subjects that make up the foundations of legal knowledge (the FLKs) together show the breadth and variety of law, provide the foundations you need for expanding your legal knowledge into new legal areas and are a base for thinking more deeply and critically about law and justice. It is essential to understand the importance of developing this foundational legal knowledge.

As we'll discuss later, law is a pervasive subject that affects all of society. Law is not just in a book. It underpins everything we do and every part of society. From the moment you get up in the morning to going to bed at night, and from birth to death, law affects your life in innumerable ways. There are legal implications and consequences in just about all we do. Think about your own experiences, good and bad—from shopping to divorce, from being a victim of crime to renting a house—all will have involved law. Keep looking for practical examples of law in action before and during your studies. Watch the news and think about how the law influences the stories told, or how the stories told will impact on the law—you might be quite surprised at just how relevant the law is to everything.

Thinking about law in its wider context will also help you to appreciate the importance of concepts such as commercial and social awareness and engaging with current affairs. We'll look more at this later in this chapter.

The importance of the foundation subjects

As we considered in Chapter 2, most law programmes include a number of core compulsory modules. These typically include the subjects that make up the foundations of legal knowledge, the FLKs.

The FLKs are the core subjects currently prescribed by the legal professions in England and Wales as necessary for a degree to be a qualifying law degree (QLD). As we explained in Chapter 2, attaining a QLD means that you will have completed the academic stage of legal training if you want to go on to become a lawyer. (But remember that there are other requirements to become a professional lawyer, this is just one stage.)

The FLKs are therefore the subjects that the legal professions think are essential for all potential lawyers to know about. However while the legal professions decide on which subjects make up the 'foundations of legal knowledge', the precise content of each of those subjects is down to each individual institution. So the particular topics you focus on within each subject may be slightly different from a friend at a different law school, even though you are ostensibly studying the same subjects.

The FLKs are not just important for those who want, or might want, to become a lawyer. They also provide a deep and broad understanding of the legal framework that shapes and is shaped by our society.

Perhaps unsurprisingly then, even if you are not studying for a QLD, these foundation subjects are often taught as modules on non-qualifying law degrees. These include programmes such as a BSc in Law, or combined degrees with law as a major/minor combination. So even if not studying for a qualifying law degree, you are likely to engage at least to a certain extent with the foundations of legal knowledge. They will enable you to gain a good grounding in the law. A further advantage is that if you subsequently decide you want to convert your non-qualifying/

combination degree to a qualifying course by undertaking, for example, the Graduate Diploma in Law, you may be entitled to some exemptions. Ask your programme leader about this.

The FLKs can still be important even if you have absolutely no plans to move on to further legal study or legal practice. They are often good subjects to study alongside other non-legal modules. For example, modules in Politics can be complemented by FLK subjects such as Constitutional and Administrative Law and European Union Law. Or business modules may be well supported by FLKs like Contract Law and Tort Law.

INSIDER KNOWLEDGE

'The core modules of a law degree are not only the cornerstone for a career in legal practice but, by studying these, it helps hone an analytical mind, which is useful to a number of professions.'

Lali Wiratunga, National Manager Davidson Institute at
Westpac Banking Corporation, Australia

When are the FLK subjects studied?

In a standard three-year law programme, the FLK subjects tend to be taught predominantly in the first and second years of the programme. Obviously quite what is taught when depends on the particular institution and programme.

Subjects taught in the first year of a law programme usually do not count towards your final degree result. And second-year subjects often have less weighting than third-year subjects when it comes to calculating your degree result. (Check your own law school and institution's rules to find out how your degree is calculated.) But don't think that means the FLKs or any other subjects taught early on don't matter!

As a successful law student, of course you will aim to excel in all your studies. And even if passing is all that matters from the perspective of simply obtaining a QLD, you should still aim high. Fully understanding each one of the FLKs will support your learning in other legal subjects. And your marks in all subjects, whatever the year of study, will be looked at by future employers, whether applying for a job or work experience. The better you do in the FLKs, the better your chances of impressing employers.

What are the foundation subjects?

Figure 5.1 shows the current FLK subjects for England and Wales. We've used the names most commonly used in law schools for their modules. But individual subjects are sometimes referred to by different names at different universities, while Scotland uses different terms for some subjects (such as 'Delict' instead of 'Tort'). Note also that although the FLKs are usually each taught as individual subjects, sometimes they may be combined in different ways.

Most law programmes also include a compulsory introductory course. This is commonly entitled something like 'Introduction to Law' or 'Legal Foundations'. The content of these courses can vary, but they are fundamental to understanding the law, its institutions and processes, and its relationship to the FLKs.

FIGURE 5.1: The foundations of legal knowledge

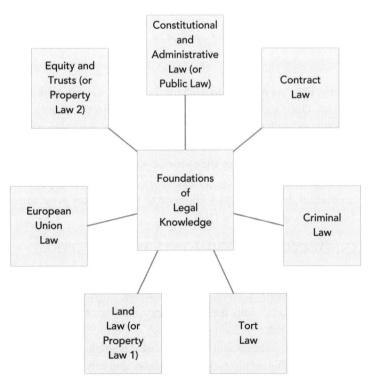

As well as the FLKs, over the course of your law degree you will study a range of other legal subjects. Some may be compulsory, depending on your institution and programme. Otherwise you will be free to choose your other subjects from a list that varies between institutions, programmes and year of study. We've already looked at some of the very varied subjects you might get to choose from in Chapter 2. And your experience of the FLKs can help you to decide your options, by looking for subjects that are similar to or different from those you have already studied.

INSIDER KNOWLEDGE

'Don't be tempted to concentrate on your favourite modules at the expense of those you like less. You will inevitably also find students who have already completed these modules will express their views to you about these modules, saying that "x module is boring" or "y module is really hard". Ignore them! Part of the skill of being a lawyer involves forming an opinion based on the evidence in front of you, so keep an open mind when starting these modules and decide for yourself what you think of them when you are studying them and not before. It is very possible that you might like modules that others do not!'

Dr Laura Bennett, Associate Professor of Law, Director of UG Programmes, University of Reading

Whilst the FLKs are essential to studying for a QLD, all your modules are important. Optional modules may not be 'core subjects' but are equally important to your law degree. They may even count more towards your final degree result than some FLKs if studied later in the degree and so weighted more heavily. They may provide you with a future specialism or a deep and abiding interest. So all areas of legal knowledge you study are important, but the FLKs are common to nearly all law programmes and currently essential to the QLD.

EXPLORING THE FOUNDATION SUBJECTS

Introduction to Law courses

As we mentioned earlier, nearly all institutions will provide a law introduction module. (Occasionally the introductory material is instead covered within other compulsory modules.) Although not technically a FLK subject, we've included it here because of its importance. These courses will have different names at different institutions. The names tend to be indicative of the particular content and characteristics of the course, for example, Introduction to Law; Legal Foundations; Learning the Law; Legal Skills and Systems.

The introductory course will usually introduce you to the English Legal System. This will include its vital concepts, structures and mechanisms—the basic understanding you will need to enable you to study law successfully. This might include things such as:

- Different legal sources, including the difference between primary and secondary sources of law;
- The doctrine of precedent, which is key to when and how one legal case is followed in later decisions;
- How a bill before Parliament becomes an Act (and so statutory law);
- How judges interpret statutes, a concept called statutory interpretation;
- The structure of the courts;
- The relevance of European and international law and courts.

We consider many of these points a bit further in Chapter 7 in particular.

You will often be encouraged to consider the wider social and cultural influences of, and on, law. Many introductory modules start by simply asking the question 'what is law?'. We did much the same in Chapter 2! There is no 'correct' or simple answer to the question, but it is always an interesting place to start your legal adventure.

If you studied A-level Law, some of the initial material covered in an introductory module may be familiar to you. But your studies will now ask you to think more critically about these concepts. You will need to evaluate your own opinions on the law and the legal system.

A number of vital legal skills that are needed for completion of the degree may also be introduced in this early module. These may include:

- Reading cases and other legal materials;
- Effective legal research;
- Thinking critically;
- Legal analysis;
- Constructing arguments;

- Problem solving;
- Legal drafting;
- Referencing sources.

These are valuable sessions that will give you a toolkit of fundamental skills to support your legal learning. You will probably need to revisit them to refresh your skills as you go through the programme.

If your programme does not offer an introductory course, or does not cover both the legal system and legal skills in it, do not worry. If this is the case, your programme will be designed so that you acquire the relevant knowledge and skills through other modules that you will study. For example you may focus on problem solving in Contract Law, or the foundations of the legal system in Public Law. You will find that the whole law degree is based around both developing skills and building knowledge.

The introductory course is not strictly one of the FLK subjects, although it may cover matters such as legal systems and procedures that are being given increasing weight by the legal professions. In any event the introductory module is an important aspect of your legal education and personal development.

Constitutional and Administrative Law (Public Law)

Constitutional and Administrative Law usually examines the central theories and concepts of the British constitution, and their application and practice. It is usually taught as a single module, but is sometimes separated into 'Constitutional Law' and 'Administrative Law'.

Constitutional law is an interesting and fluid subject, not least due to the unwritten nature of our constitution. You will find it particularly interesting if you have any interest in politics, government, or social affairs. You will look at the development of the Parliamentary system and the relationship between the Crown and individuals. This will include interrogating concepts such as:

- Separation of Powers: keeping the legislature (Parliament), the executive (Prime Minister and the Cabinet) and the judiciary (the courts) separate;

- Parliamentary Sovereignty: the idea that Parliament is the supreme legal authority in the UK.

You may have already noticed that these two concepts do not necessarily fit well together. This is just one of the things that make the study of constitutional law so thought-provoking. You will also look at the relationship between our governmental institutions and supranational bodies. Supranational organisations are those that cross national boundaries, such as the European Union. You may also examine the relationship between our governmental institutions and society. It may well include consideration of human rights.

This subject tends to be a lively, interesting and very contemporary area of law. It is obviously very relevant to society, exploring the power balance between individuals and the state. Numerous contemporary legal issues emerge from this subject including the ongoing human rights debate, and the negotiations towards 'Brexit' since the triggering of Article 50.

Administrative law is the part of the subject that examines the procedure of public bodies and their decision making. The law seeks to ensure that public bodies undertake their duties and use their powers fairly and reasonably. It is the relationship between individuals and these organisations of power, specifically the state, that makes this an exciting subject to study.

So, for example, constitutional and administrative law may examine the compatibility of government legislation with human rights. One recent high profile issue is the right of prisoners in the UK to vote. Currently, prisoners are unable to vote in elections, but the European Court of Human Rights has said that this prohibition is in contravention of the Human Rights Act and the European Convention of Human Rights. Other fascinating topics this subject may cover include examining how, if it all, the law is supreme and applicable to all people, and how our 'unwritten' constitution has developed through history.

I WISH I'D KNOWN . . .

'I found public law and land law rather challenging. The best advice I can give is to ask help from your lecturers. Go to them to get clarification on the things you do not understand or affirmation on the things that you do understand.'

Panashe Musabayana, Keele University, LLB Law with Criminology, Year 2

Contract Law

Whereas constitutional and administrative law examines the relationship between individuals and the state, contract law largely concerns the relationships between individuals.

A contract is a concept that you will almost certainly be familiar with. The word contract conjures up numerous images. Long, wordy documents being signed in boardrooms. Smiling football players or singers putting pen to paper in front of a room full of photographers. Or just getting a new phone. However, contracts are everywhere.

Contracts are pretty much any agreement that can be deemed legally enforceable. Often formality is not essential. The study of contract law explores how agreements and promises become enforceable. It examines how we interpret the terms of such agreements to understand each party's responsibilities. Contract law also outlines the consequences if people don't fulfil these promises.

Contract law underpins many of our daily interactions and social engagements, even if we don't usually think of them in that way. Have you ever thought about the legal implications of going to the shop and purchasing a carton of orange juice or a new coat? Probably not. But as a consumer, you are a party to a contract. Even buying the bus ticket to get to the shop involved making a contract.

So what questions might arise in contract law? Here's a few for starters:

- When does the contract form?
- What are your obligations under the agreement?
- What are the seller's obligations?
- Should different sellers have different obligations?

Let's look further at the first question. At what point does a contract form? When we pick an item up off the shelf in the shop? When we take it to the till point? When we pay? What do you think?

Contract law tells us it is when the cashier agrees to accept our offer to buy the item at the till point. This is because when the item is on the shelf, it is not an offer to buy, instead it is inviting us to make an offer to the cashier, which they can accept or reject. This is because a shop is seen as a place of bargaining and bartering. This is one of the first legal principles you will learn in contract law—you will be acquiring legal knowledge. But your knowledge will go much deeper: you will be taught complexities and exceptions, and will even consider whether these legal principles reflect the true nature of shopping in the twenty-first century. Contract law explores these interactions and seeks to see what makes such agreements, promises and interactions enforceable in the eyes of the law, and whether the law is fit for purpose.

An always topical area of contract law is balancing the rights and protection of the consumer against the freedom to make agreements. This has been in the news again recently as the government tries to rebalance the rights of the consumer through the Consumer Rights Act 2015. The pervasive nature of contract law means that it is constantly evolving. What is more, contract law principles underpin many other important legal subjects that are common optional modules, such as Commercial Law and Employment Law.

Criminal Law

Criminal law is the subject most people immediately associate with law and the legal system. The study of criminal law includes examination and evaluation of various aspects of criminal behaviour, the categorisation of numerous criminal offences, punishments and defences.

These can include the elements of criminal behaviour, including *actus reus*—the guilty act, and *mens rea*—the guilty mind. It also studies various offences, often including murder, manslaughter, non-fatal offences, sexual offences, fraud, theft and other crimes against property. Criminal law also looks at the sentences that individuals receive for such crimes and any defences that defendants raise to such charges. As you can imagine, criminal law also has a wider social perspective, which includes the purpose of criminal law and punishment.

One interesting debate lies around the purpose of imprisonment. How should we balance matters such as rehabilitation against the punishment of wrongdoers? What is the purpose of the criminal legal system? You might want to reflect upon the purpose of criminal law as social protection or state control. The very public nature of criminal law and its popularity as a topic of discussion especially in the mainstream media means that we are constantly surrounded by stories of crime and punishment.

Tort Law

If you haven't studied any law before, the term 'tort' may be alien to you. But the type of situation tort law deals with will actually be very familiar. The word 'tort' has its origins in medieval French (the historical language of English law) meaning 'wrong' or 'injustice'.

So tort law deals with many of the wrongs suffered by an individual as a result of things done, or not done, by another person or organisation. This includes things such as personal injury, medical negligence and professional negligence. Your tort law studies may also consider the invasion of privacy and damaging an individual's character (defamation), or perhaps the liability of building owners, employers and manufacturers.

You will also consider the relevance of tort law to society. For example how far should an individual be protected from the negligence and incompetence of others? What wider consequences might this protection have? You have probably seen adverts from companies asking if you've had an accident and offering 'no-win, no-fee' assistance. These are all based on making a claim in tort. Are these organisations helping people right the wrongs that have been done to them? Or are they a dangerous development in the law leading to pointless or speculative lawsuits, and resulting in overly defensive behaviour? Tort law has to balance the protection of everyone—considering both those being harmed, and the risk of imposing liability too broadly. Where would you draw the line?

Land Law (or Property Law)

Land law, sometimes called property law, is the study of the law relating to rights in and over land, and the different systems of land ownership. Rights or interests in land can include the ownership of estates in land as well as things such as leases, licences, mortgages and adverse possession (often called squatting).

At first land law might seem a bit dull, or remote to your current experience. But we will all have some interest in land, whether renting a room or house, staying in a hostel, or buying or sharing a property. It is fundamentally important that we understand who has rights and obligations in relation to land, to avoid disputes and ensure clarity in ownership. If you have already owned or rented a property, you will know how complex the system can be. If not then it won't be long before you are engaging directly with land law as you find a place to live.

Land law plays a fundamental part in modern society and can be a highly contentious subject. People often have conflicting interests and intentions for the usage of land. This is often embodied in planning disputes, whether concerning two neighbours, or wider local and national issues. For example, wind farms in rural locations often divide public opinion. If someone owns the land, is it their right to do with it what they please, or should they consider the impact on others? What about the rights of someone to access another person's land to reach his own? Or how can the needs of 'squatters' be balanced against the interests of an absent landowner? Land law seeks to explore these issues and resolve these disputes.

I WISH I'D KNOWN . . .

'In land law—I wish someone had advised me to look at my family's property deeds for our house. I found it a challenging subject and when someone suggested I tried to make it a practical exercise, then the concepts started to fall into place. If you're struggling with this I would also suggest drawing plots of land and boundaries, depicting the question in a more practical creative setting that you can visualise.'

Alexandra Townsley, University of Nottingham, LLB Law and American Law, Year 3

European Union Law

European Union (EU) law examines the relationship between EU Member States through treaties, and looks at the enforcement of legislation, rules and decisions of institutions in the European Union. This can include legislation from the European Parliament, the Council of Europe and the European Court of Justice.

When studying EU law, the emphasis is often on the way in which EU law is enforced and an examination of substantive legal areas. These include the free movement of persons, which is the right of EU citizens to move unhindered throughout the Union. Another substantive area is the free movement of goods, which is the right to sell and distribute goods unhindered through the Union. Finally, competition law is an interesting topic in EU law that examines how the

EU institutions have tried to maintain competitive markets for goods and services within the Union.

EU law is an influential and interesting subject but is also highly contentious. Even if you do not live in the UK, you will probably be aware that the Prime Minister triggered Article 50 of the Lisbon Treaty on 29 March 2017. Since then there have been ongoing negotiations around the relationship that will exist between the UK and the EU. In studying EU law, you will examine the profound effect that this withdrawal may have on the legal system and society in the UK.

Even after 'Brexit' it is likely that EU law will continue to have a significant influence on UK law, and will remain an important component of law programmes in this country.

Trusts and Equity

Trusts and Equity (or just 'trusts law') is unlikely to be a subject familiar to you. However, you may well already have had some engagement with this area of law. You may have had to consider someone's will, or just seen wills being read on television. You might live in a house that is jointly owned. You might have a pension—if not you will almost certainly start one some day. The law of trusts impacts on all this—wills, jointly owned property, pensions—as well as much more.

Trusts are fundamentally relationships where someone holds property, of any kind, for the benefit of someone else. They include family arrangements—big and small—but also commercial arrangements such as investment funds, or banks holding money for clients or property development. The law of trusts also concerns the administration of charitable funds.

Trusts law has huge relevance to commercial law, often influencing who gets what when a company fails or a person becomes bankrupt. It is also the basis for many of the obligations on directors of companies and other commercial positions. While you won't study every type of trust, you will find that an understanding of trust principles is a valuable underpinning of many other subjects.

The term Equity may seem a little surprising—you might think that all law should be about 'equity'. But trusts are based in the law of Equity, which is a fundamental part of the English legal system. 'Equity' as a system of law originated in the need for early judges to modify the operation of legal rules applied in cases to lessen their severity or prevent an unfair result. Judges don't have quite such flexibility today, but Equity does retain a rather different approach to many other areas of law. This makes it a fascinating subject to study. It also gives a great opportunity to explore the development of the law and consider the balance of fairness, justice and certainty.

I WISH I'D KNOWN . . .

'Land Law and Equity and Trusts has been particularly challenging for me as they are quite similar in terms of content and terminology. Reading the recommended reading, keeping a glossary of the key terms and their definition, as well as reading the cases was particularly helpful in understanding certain notions or principles.'

Lul Sheikh-Salah, BPP University, LLB Law, Year 3

Are legal subjects all distinct?

Law programmes have to organise the material they teach in a coherent fashion. That usually means identifying particular legal subjects and placing each into its own module. And so the subjects we've been considering, the FLKs, are usually taught as separate and largely distinct modules. The same is true of the many optional subjects you will come across. But it is worth bearing in mind that there are strong relationships and some considerable crossover between many of legal subjects, including the FLKs.

For example, contract law and tort law share the same root in the law of obligations. Judges have drawn together various component parts of these subjects and adapted doctrines from one to benefit the other. Land law and the law of trusts share some doctrines due to their common focus on rights and interests in property. EU law and constitutional law are also closely linked. And Equity has influenced other areas of law as well as being fundamental to the law of trusts.

You will come to realise that all legal subjects have elements of overlap. You will notice elements of law you have considered in the FLKs appearing in further optional subjects too. Crossovers, whether of principles, policies or problems, can be very helpful when learning a new subject, and can be valuable in encouraging you to deepen your critical thought.

IS LAW EVERYWHERE? THE PERVASIVE NATURE OF LAW

We've already touched on the pervasive nature of law. What did we mean by this, and why does it matter?

By pervasive, we mean that law is everywhere. It underpins most of what we do in society. The FLKs help us to appreciate this as they cover often very different but arguably equally important strands of the law, all with real practical relevance. Whether going to the movies or voting in an election, taking a holiday or giving money to a charity—all are governed by law and relate to the foundations of legal knowledge.

As you progress through your legal studies, you will see how the foundation subjects and further subjects interconnect. You will learn how the law has a real impact on what lies outside the textbook. As we've said before, an awareness of and interest in how law relates to the real world is a very real advantage to the successful law student.

I WISH I'D KNOWN . . .

'After reading law, I now appreciate how pervasive law is in society. Law is everywhere—when you board the bus or enter a classroom; when you buy a sandwich or cross the road; when you bump into someone or receive too much change. I find it very exciting to know that what I learn can be so applicable to everyday life.'

Godwin Tan, University College London, LLB Law, Year 3

Making connections

Essentially, law is everywhere, not just in the crime and politics stories that we see in the media. Most contemporary issues have an implication for the law or an underlying legal dimension. Most contemporary current affairs can be viewed as a contemporary legal issue. Much of the daily news has ramifications for the law or has a legal issue at its heart.

Law both influences and is influenced by contemporary affairs. Real life can prompt legal challenge and legal change. This means that law is always changing and adapting to changes in society: one example is the recent changes in marriage. But the law can also encourage social, political or cultural change—it is a two-way relationship, as Figure 5.2 demonstrates.

FIGURE 5.2: The two-way relationship

All this reflection upon the pervasive nature of law could simply be described as making connections. Studying law is all about making connections. For example, connections between:

- The various subjects you are or will be studying;
- The law and the people it serves;
- Law and contemporary events and issues;
- Different concepts or ideas in your legal studies.

Keep looking for these and other connections. They will assist in your critical thinking. The ease with which you can identify legal issues comes at least in part from your ability to think critically.

All of your lecturers will tell you the importance of critical thinking. We agree, and we'll look more at critical thinking and writing in Chapter 10. For the moment just keep in mind that the ability to question, analyse and evaluate everything is a vital skill for being a lawyer. This means that you should question everything, analyse every 'fact' and evaluate every opinion.

Exploration and challenge

You can make use of the pervasive nature of the law to develop not just your broader and deeper understanding of law and society, but also your critical skills.

For example, when reading a news story, be prepared to disagree with it. Just because somebody wrote it, doesn't mean it is right, or even true. Evaluate the accuracy of the report. Look at where the source came from: is it a reputable news provider, or a 'click bait' article on social media? Think about the author: are they a respected journalist or expert in the subject; can you find any information about them? Think about the sources that the article cites, if any: are you able to find this evidence; is it from reputable sources? Take it further: what is the 'agenda' of the newspaper or website or the political ideology of the source; is it independent; does the author or publisher have any particular motivation? All these questions can help you to evaluate the accuracy of sources. This is an essential skill that we'll look at again in Chapter 7.

Having evaluated the source, think about the implications of the news article on various different areas of your life, and on the law. What does it mean for you? What does it mean for others? Are there conflicting interests? How could they be resolved?

Much of what you will do as a law student, and in employment, will include analysing and evaluating arguments and opinions of others. You will have to think critically about weaknesses and strengths in their argument. You will also need always to consider how these will impact you, your employer or a person you are representing.

So acquiring legal knowledge isn't just about learning 'the law'. It is really important to be up-to-date with contemporary issues, whether they are general interest or more obviously legal. We have already spoken in Chapter 3 about the importance of engaging with current affairs by reading a newspaper and engaging with broadcast news services.

What is more, the growth of social media has put news media at our fingertips in very different formats. Twitter, for example, has become a major broadcaster of news and, with a little bit of research, can be a really useful resource for legal news and issues. Remember though to be as critical, analytical and evaluative with this as you would be with other resources. Remember that you can't always believe everything you read online. Get used to relying on, and citing, only trustworthy sources, and treat all publicly available material with some caution.

COMMERCIAL AWARENESS

A final point related to putting law in its pervasive context is the concept of commercial awareness. Commercial awareness is something that you may not encounter in your legal studies until you begin to think about applying for work experience in various spheres.

Commercial awareness is a fundamental part of applying for professional jobs in many spheres, including the legal profession. But it is not something that matters only to those wanting to be lawyers, or indeed relevant only to future employment. It is also important more generally to a broader understanding of law, responsibility and society.

At one level commercial awareness is simply an awareness of the 'industry' you are becoming part of so you understand how it operates and your role within it. For example, there have been numerous recent cuts to legal aid. This will have affected the income of some solicitors and barristers in local firms and may affect an individual's access to legal services. This is relevant to the legal system and legal employment of course, but also relevant to your studies, as pressures such as these may impact on the development or administration of the law.

Commercial awareness also encompasses a wider appreciation of business and commerce, and the responsibilities of individuals within this world. This means reading widely and understanding how general and subject-specific current affairs relate to your chosen field. Any employer will want to know you have an interest in recent developments and can evaluate how information impacts on a particular area.

For example, a law firm may monitor changes in local and regional property prices to forecast changes to the firm's workload in the coming financial period. How might a national 1.2 per cent property increase announced by the Treasury affect their operations in the region? This was a question posed to a student at a recent interview for a legal position. (The same student was also asked to assess how 'Leave' votes in the then forthcoming Scottish referendum and EU referendum would affect the firm's merger with a Scottish law firm!)

Don't be too daunted by questions like these. But as a law student, particularly if you wish to pursue a legal career, you will be expected to take an interest in and understand key changes and current issues that affect the legal profession. These might be financial pressures, issues that could affect individual clients or issues affecting the administration of justice.

You should also take an interest in different businesses, structures and professional areas within and interacting with your chosen field. Using law as an example again, this might be demonstrating an understanding of different legal business structures, or how particular industries, or large companies, deal with lawyers. It could include considering things as diverse as how a law firm or business can market itself more effectively to new clients or, as already mentioned, how changes in the prices of property can affect your practice or your client's business.

Again, don't be daunted. No one expects a brand-new law student, or even an established law student—however successful—to have extensive and deep commercial awareness of all possible relevant matters. But employers do expect you to have taken an interest in these things. And commercial awareness is useful more generally in understanding, applying and critiquing the law. By exploring areas of interest and keeping up-to-date with legal and wider issues throughout your studies, remembering the pervasive nature of law, you will be in the best possible position to demonstrate a level of commercial awareness should you need to. And to benefit from this in your studies and beyond.

I WISH I'D KNOWN . . .

'Law is a social institution that underlies every aspect of our life. A good idea would be to talk to lawyers (maybe you know people working in the field who are friends of your parents or something; or once you get to university, apply to formal open days and insight weeks) and try to get work experience early on. Seeing law in practice will help you appreciate its significance in society.'

Monica Chen, University College London, LLB Law, Year 2

SUMMARY—HELP YOURSELF . . .

- **Acquire broad and deep legal knowledge**
  - Understand why most law schools teach the 'foundations of legal knowledge' as core/compulsory subjects, and what they commonly cover.
  - Study hard in the foundation subjects to provide a strong base for further learning, regardless of whether the subject marks count towards your final degree result.
  - Recognise that optional, or 'non-core', subjects are just as important to your degree as the foundation subjects.

- **Understand what acquiring legal knowledge requires**
  - Remember that acquiring legal knowledge is not just about memorising information.
  - Always think critically about what you learn—develop a life-long questioning habit.
  - Aim to put your learning into wider context.
  - Look for connections between the foundation subjects, and between the foundation subjects and other subjects.

- **Deepen your knowledge and understanding of the wider world**
  - Seek to relate everyday matters to the law, to gain a better understanding of how the law applies in practice.
  - Engage with the world and society around you, considering the relevance of current issues to the law, and your views on them.
  - Keep up-to-date with legal issues—not just changes to the law in subjects you are studying, but matters relating to the administration of justice or pressures on legal practice.
  - Take an interest in the wider commercial world, and in particular how it relates to the law and legal practice.

6

STUDYING LAW: DEVELOPING (LEGAL) SKILLS

'In my youth', said his father, 'I took to the law,
And argued each case with my wife.
And the muscular strength that it gave to my jaw,
Has lasted the rest of my life.'

LEWIS CARROLL, 'YOU ARE OLD FATHER WILLIAM',
Alice's Adventures in Wonderland

INTRODUCTION

Studying law is not just about learning what the law is. It is also about developing a range of skills that are essential for legal study, legal practice and for a wide range of professions and fields of employment. Employers like law graduates or students who have studied elements of law during their studies. This is not least because of their ability to think critically, their proven skills in problem solving, and other important skills for employability that the law degree helps to develop.

This chapter will explore the general skills for employment that you will develop while studying law. It will also focus on some of the more specific 'legal' skills you will acquire. Arguably not all law schools emphasise sufficiently that the law degree teaches skills as well as knowledge. But even where your lecturers do not explicitly identify learning activities as 'skill learning,' often that is what you are doing. The skills you will use and develop while studying law incorporate a whole range of transferable skills for future employment, whether legal or not.

SKILLS AND STUDYING LAW

We have already explained (in Chapter 2) that you will probably study a range of compulsory modules that usually include the foundations of legal knowledge, plus a number of optional modules specialising in particular areas. Embedded within your programme and the various modules you study will be opportunities to develop various skills.

These will make you a confident and successful law student. They will also make you more employable, whatever career you pursue.

When and where will I learn skills?

Some law schools clearly highlight opportunities for skills development within their programmes. These will take a variety of forms and may be embedded within the whole programme. This is particularly true where a law school's curriculum is based for example on problem-based learning. But skills development is also part of law programmes and law modules even when not explicitly flagged as such.

Many law programmes will have specific modules that enable you to develop certain general and subject-specific skills. For example, modules entitled Legal Writing, Legal Research, Legal Skills or some variation of these. These skills development courses naturally have a legal focus because you are studying for a law degree. But they help you develop valuable skills for use in any form of employment, ie they are 'transferable' skills.

For example, just because you have done a specific course in legal writing, doesn't mean these skills are only of use in law. The ability to construct well-supported and analytical argument, present your work professionally and to cite references properly (we will discuss referencing and other connected matters in Chapter 11), will be valuable for countless different careers.

I WISH I'D KNOWN . . .

'How law prepared me for completing job applications. When I completed my first vacation scheme application, I really struggled. I thought I couldn't answer any of the questions and had nothing to add to the law firm. However, my personal tutor made me make a list of all the things I had done so far on my degree and encouraged me to map any relevant skills onto these things. Suddenly, it dawned on me. I had done loads of things that I had never associated with skills. I just thought it was about learning my legal subjects. It's not. It's so much more than that!'

Anonymous, Plymouth University, LLB with CCJS, Year 3

Some skills learning that you will undertake during your degree will be less obvious and sometimes you will gain and develop skills without even realising it. One of the biggest challenges for many law students is identifying what skills they have developed just through studying their law modules. You will obviously become knowledgeable in the intricacies of the law, but you also develop a range of general and subject-specific skills for working. It is easy to overlook this—don't!

Making use of skills

Skills you learn during your law studies are obviously essential to doing well in your degree, and being a successful law student. But the value of these skills is not confined to your degree.

When it comes to making applications—whether for legal and non-legal jobs—employers will often ask for you to draw on your experiences to explain why you would be valuable to their organisation. You will also be asked to provide evidence of the experience you have. For example, job application questions might include:

- Please give details of when you have been part of a team. What was your common goal? What part did you play in particular? How well did the team work together and why?

- Please give details of when you have had to handle some form of conflict or disagreement. What was the situation? What did you do? What was the outcome?

- Please give details of an idea you've had, and how you have told others about it. How did you get them to take it on board?

- Please give an example of when you have had a difficult problem to deal with. How did you approach it? What was the outcome? What did you learn from this?

Questions such are these are designed for you to highlight skills you have, and demonstrate your wider experience. You will need to explain skills you possess, such as teamworking or problem solving, *and* situate them in specific examples. These examples may come from studying on your degree, or part-time or full-time employment, or in extra-curricular activities.

By the end of your degree, you should be able to demonstrate evidence of various skills. For example there will be numerous occasions on your degree where you will work as part of a team. This may be working on a group project, as part of team for a mooting competition, or even playing for the law society football team. When it comes to problem solving, studying law is full of it. You will be able to evidence your legal problem solving, and extra-curricular activities may provide yet further evidence. Teamworking and problem solving are fairly obvious examples to select in explaining the skills met during your legal studies. The number of skills you acquire and develop is far greater.

Skill development and reflection

As Figure 6.1 shows, the skills you will develop during your law programme come in various forms. And of course many will overlap to some extent.

FIGURE 6.1: Different types of skills

All these skills that you acquire, develop or refine during your study of law are skills for employability. They are all skills that will benefit you in the future world of work and very many of them are transferable.

Before we look at the skills themselves, there is something important to remember. In order to maximise the value of your skill development, you need to *reflect* on the skills you are using and developing in your day-to-day study of the law. We started the process of reflection in Chapter 3, and this needs to continue as you move through your legal studies.

This requires an element of record keeping. This gives you the opportunity to reflect, and to see the bigger picture of your skills development. Don't limit your recording and reflection to specific skills-based modules, or distinct training courses. Jot down everything that uses or develops a skill, whether those are general or specific skills, or more general attributes. You could record your experiences and development in a number of ways:

- **Learning journals**
  - A weekly, or even daily, learning journal can be an excellent tool for keeping track of your intellectual and skill-based achievements. Even by the end of your first year, you will have a repository of information that you can draw upon to help you populate a CV or complete application forms.
  - Many institutions offer their students an online resource for keeping track of your skills and experience (often linked more broadly to personal development) so do use this if you have one.

- **Online blogs**
  - An online blog can be a good way to reflect on your study. Many lawyers and professionals keep blogs and they can be good networking tools, if they are professional. Or keep your blog hidden from the public if you want it to be for personal use only.

- A 'running' CV
  - If you don't already have one, a really good exercise is to design a CV (sometimes called a résumé). There will be careers services on campus that can help you do this, and we look further at CVs in Chapter 19.
  - Once you have a basic CV in place, use it as a 'running' document that you can update regularly.

- A 'living' personal statement
  - Many job applications ask you to attach a supporting statement or personal statement to your application. These must be tailored to the job you're applying to, and we'll look at this too in Chapter 19. But it can be a good exercise to write and frequently update a personal statement. It provides a valuable opportunity for reflection, and you can tailor what you have to any jobs that you apply for in the future.

- Video blogs
  - Much like blogging, you can reflect on your learning through private, or less commonly, public video blogs (vlogs).
  - The ability to reflect orally is a valuable skill and something most employees do regularly as part of their professional development.
  - To do this you could create a private YouTube channel and record yourself on your laptop, tablet or phone. This develops a library of reflection on skills and learning which you can use whenever you need it.

All of these can be a valuable way of reflecting on the skills you use, develop and learn on your programme. It will also ensure that you remember everything you do. However you choose to do it, reflection on and recording of your skills development will give you confidence in your progress. It will help you to see where you have skill gaps and will make job applications a whole lot easier.

GENERAL SKILLS

General skills are true transferable skills. This means that they are applicable in most, if not all, spheres of employment. You will be able to draw upon specific examples, with evidence, to support your applications for jobs and work placements. Employers, both legal and non-legal, need you to show what skills you have and provide evidence of how you can be an asset to their organisation.

I WISH I'D KNOWN . . .

'I wish I'd known that being a law student gives you a lot of transferrable skills—including how to present your law degree in that best possible light to non-legal employers.'

Fiona Lin, University of Cambridge, Law, Year 3

We will now discuss some of the important skills that you should develop during your legal study. It should help you to reflect on the skills you currently possess. And it should give you some guidance as to the skills you will be developing as you study law at university. The skills that follow are not intended to be an exhaustive list—there are bound to be even more. Keep reflecting on what skills you engage with for every activity you pursue.

Collaboration/teamwork (online and real-time)

Most law programmes will incorporate elements of group work or team-based collaboration. This may be in the form of a group project or having to research and deliver a group presentation. Some people relish the opportunity to work with others; others can find group work challenging. Either way, it can be a rewarding experience. Even if there is no formal teamwork embedded in your programme, you can develop collaborative skills through informal arrangements such as study groups.

Reflect on the way in which you work with others, and how you accommodate other people's ways of working. Evidence the ways in which you have collaborated as part of a team and developed your ability to work with others.

Some law programmes will provide you with an online platform for collaboration with fellow students, either generally or for specific projects. This can provide you with experience in using online environments for working. If you are not provided with a specific university platform you may be able to adapt more general social media platforms for this purpose.

Problem solving

Problem solving is a skill that is often particularly associated with the study of law. The practical study of law and its applications is all based around problem solving. Being an effective problem solver is a really valuable transferable skill. Law graduates are often attractive to employers for this very reason.

You will have numerous sessions with tutors on effective problem solving. This may be explicit or implicit, so keep reflecting on what you are doing and identify your skill development. While you will specifically develop skills around solving legal problems and applying the law, you will also be able to demonstrate generic problem solving skills through the usual challenges of studying for a degree, for example:

- Finding specific sources for research;
- Working out how to access course materials;
- Dealing with a difficult group member.

You will have to evaluate the situation, isolate the individual problems, consider the numerous ways you could solve each issue and apply the most appropriate way of solving it. This process is essential to success as a law student and is a particularly valuable transferable skill. Many applications for future employment will ask you to demonstrate evidence of where you have approached and resolved problems.

Researching (hardcopy and digital) and referencing

The ability to research effectively is important for any future employment. By the end of your law degree you will be adept at researching. You will be able to explain to potential employers how you are able to effectively research using hardcopy library resources and using digital databases. You will also be able to show certain specific legal knowledge in this area, alongside more general research skills. (And see further Chapter 8 on reading and research.)

You will also develop valuable skills in evaluating sources, referencing, and citing and using material appropriately. Even if you do not pursue a legal career, being able to identify the sources of your information and using an appropriate system for doing this is important in many spheres of employment. We will discuss referencing further in relation to your legal studies in Chapter 11.

Writing

By the end of your degree, you will have completed numerous assignments and made pages-upon-pages of notes. You will be a very proficient writer.

But it isn't just about doing lots of writing. You will need to convey your ideas and concepts effectively, and this means developing the ability to write:

- Concisely;
- Precisely;
- Persuasively; and
- Professionally.

The law degree develops the ability to do all these as they are key to most of your assignments.

Decision making

Your law studies will encourage you to make careful, considered decisions, drawing upon your knowledge and experience to ensure you make the best decision you can. You will do this across the whole of your degree study.

This will be explicitly legal through the substance of your work, making decisions about what legal source is most relevant, what route to recommend in a problem and so on. But will also relate to your wider learning experience. Everyday decisions such as whether you continue working on an assignment or move onto doing core reading in advance of your next lecture can be difficult, and engage your decision-making skills. You will learn to make the best decision you can at the time you make it.

Time management

Being a successful law student entails a lot of work. You will have to ensure that you manage your time efficiently. You will need to undertake preparatory work and essential reading for lectures and small group sessions, prepare and write assignments, attend all your scheduled classes, and make use of other contact time—as well as the everyday stuff like eating, sleeping and socialising.

This is all manageable, but only if you manage your time. Time management can be a good skill to discuss in interviews, and it is something that everyone relates to. If you undertake extra-curricular activities alongside your successful legal study you will have even more evidence to demonstrate effective time management.

Organising meetings

Effective organisation and administration is an important skill and you will have numerous opportunities to schedule meetings. This could be as part of completing group work, arranging to study with friends, meeting lecturers or personal tutors, or more formally, as part of a society. The ability to organise meetings, scheduling them and ensuring they are effective, is important to any future employment.

Project management

While this may seem a less obvious skill, increasingly employers are looking for individuals who have the ability to manage projects, lead teams and work under their own initiative to achieve specified goals. This is obviously closely linked to time management, but also connects together a number of different skills and abilities. Managing a group project or a large individual project (such as a dissertation, legal research project or a practical portfolio) allows you to develop specific project management skills that you can use to evidence how you have efficiently and effectively managed such a project.

Note making, minute taking and record keeping

You will take copious notes during your degree study, whether during lectures and tutorials or when undertaking research, and will revisit and refine your notes as you progress through a module. We will explore note making in more depth in Chapters 8 and 9 as it is such an important skill for the successful law student. You will also have to keep minutes from various meetings you will have, from dissertation supervisions to club meetings.

Notes will need to be filed and organised so you can find them and use them when you need them again. You will also organise your research materials, case notes, academic readings and other resources to easily find them again. This is record keeping. The ability to take effective notes, expand and modify, and organise them is a very valuable skill for all employment, and can demonstrate more generally your ability to organise yourself.

Oral, written and digital communication

Skills in different forms of communication will be developed as you undertake different parts of your degree. The ability to deliver a presentation, ask insightful questions and answer questions posed by a lecturer will all display your ability to communicate orally. Your assignments, emails, lecture notes and research summaries will all develop your ability to communicate in written form.

The ability to use forums and engage with online discussions on your institution's digital learning environment, and email contact with your tutors and other university staff will help you develop your digital communication skills. Remember that your university email is like a work email address. You should always send professional emails to staff and other students: respectful, to the point and using clear, effective language. It is good training quite apart from being good practice.

If you develop communication skills in a particular form or forum, remember to make a note of it as part of your reflection and record keeping. But even your standard day-to-day interactions as you complete your legal studies will develop your ability to communicate.

Reflective practice

Through your legal studies you will regularly reflect upon your performance and achievements. Some law modules now include specific activities or assignments that involve reflection on elements of your learning—take advantage of these if they come your way. Even if this is not offered, you will need to reflect if you are to benefit from feedback from tutors or feedback on assignments. And, as we've touched on before, it is important to reflect more generally on your learning, your skills and your goals.

The ability to reflect is a valuable skill that enables you to learn and develop effectively. It is not easy, and requires practice. Unsurprisingly it is much valued by employers.

SUBJECT-SPECIFIC SKILLS

Subject-specific skills are the employability skills that are relevant to specific types of employment or academic subjects. So, within a law degree, they will be specific legal skills. That is not to say they aren't transferable. Many subject-specific skills relate to the general skills already outlined, such as researching, or may also be subject-specific to other disciplines. For example, negotiation and client interviewing are essential to many different spheres of employment, not just law.

Advocacy

Advocacy is a skill particularly associated with law. The lawyer at the bar of the court, addressing the judge and a packed courtroom, is an image that often comes to mind when we consider legal practice. Advocacy is the art of putting forward a particular case, of persuasion. In legal practice it is usually associated with persuasive oral communication. Advocacy develops many skills, including oral communication, argument building and the ability to formulate responses quickly.

INSIDER KNOWLEDGE

'Advocacy, written or spoken, is the art of persuasion and a potential employer will view your application form from that perspective; if you cannot be persuasive on your own account you are unlikely to be able to be persuasive on behalf of a client.'

Anna Vigars QC, Barrister, Guildhall Chambers

As a law student you may develop your advocacy skills in specific advocacy modules, or within advocacy exercises in other modules. But another very important way of developing skills of advocacy is through mooting. Mooting is an activity, usually competitive, where two teams of students undertake a mock court hearing, presenting legal points to a 'judge', who is usually a lecturer or local lawyer. The moot judge gives a decision on the point of law being discussed, but also evaluates the skills of the individual mooters. Mooting is an important extra-curricular activity for law students, although rarely compulsory. It is explained and discussed in more detail in Chapter 17.

Negotiation

Negotiation skills are essential for working in the legal sector and many other areas of employment. In law, less than 10 per cent of disputes go to a full hearing in court or a tribunal. A vast majority of disputes are settled at some point in the pre-trial process—and this usually involves negotiation.

Negotiation means getting what you want, or at least something you are prepared to settle for, from someone else through agreement rather than outside direction. It usually necessitates a back-and-forth discussion, aiming to find some common ground and reach an agreement.

Negotiation skills are usually taught through specific negotiation modules, or through extra-curricular negotiation training or competitions. Negotiation competitions usually involve two teams negotiating over a set of issues to try to reach a compromise, and are considered in more depth in Chapter 17. Occasionally individual modules may incorporate negotiation exercises as part of the learning process. Negotiation skills can also be developed in less formal ways, such as through group work.

Negotiation develops numerous interconnected skills, not just the ability to negotiate as such. These skills include decision making, active listening, oral communication, rapport building, problem solving and others.

Client interviewing

Client interviewing is a legal skill that is now quite commonly offered in law schools. In legal work, you will need to be able to engage with people from various backgrounds with various legal problems. It also develops your skills in fact-finding, specific questioning, interpersonal skills including empathy and compassion, and a professional approach.

Client interviewing is sometimes taught through the curriculum, either as a distinct module, or within other law or legal skills modules. More commonly, client interviewing is made available as an optional extra-curricular activity. There are also client interviewing competitions, as for mooting or negotiation. See Chapter 17 for more on client interviewing.

Letter writing

The ability to write clear, coherent and appropriately worded legal and non-legal letters is very important. Many law schools are now teaching letter writing as part of their courses, often within general legal skills or legal writing modules. You may also develop letter-writing skills as part of extra-curricular activities such as law clinic or other 'pro bono' work you do (see Chapter 18 for more on these).

The skill includes the ability to write formal, professional letters to potential employers and other individuals and organisations, as well as legal letters to clients or other lawyers. The ability to write an articulate and professional letter is important and is occasionally overlooked. If you aren't given skills training in letter writing and find you need practice, perhaps when preparing to apply for a job, ask your personal tutor or careers advisor for guidance.

Legal drafting

Some law courses also embed opportunities in the curriculum for drafting legal documents. These may be court forms, claim forms, specific legal documents or even research memos. While this is not currently commonplace in university legal education—it tends to be dealt with in depth during subsequent professional legal training—it is becoming far more common. Some students also do this as part of their volunteering in law clinics and in other pro bono projects.

Legal research

Practically all degree programmes allow you to develop research skills. But law degree programmes tend to put significant emphasis on research, and give you a specific set of skills for finding and utilising legal materials.

Legal research skills may include locating cases and statutes in the library and on one of the legal databases (such as Westlaw and Lexis-Nexis), finding and engaging with scholarly legal opinion or even trying to expand your research into other fields to place your research in context. We'll look more at legal resources and research in Chapters 7 and 8. Much of any work within the law is based around researching, synthesising the material you find and presenting your research. The law degree trains you to do this from the very beginning of the programme until you put your pen down at the end of your last exam.

Developing subject-specific skills

We don't pretend that this is a full list of the specific legal skills you will develop, nor that you will necessarily come across all listed legal skills as distinct parts of your formal learning. Law schools differ in what they offer, both within and outside the curriculum. There will be variation in the extent to which you encounter subject-specific skills and the ways in which you develop them.

As some of the skills will be developed as part of extra-curricular provision, it is really important that you get involved. Opportunities may be offered by your university, law school, outside providers or through your student law society. Take up all the experiences you can that develop your skills and help to make you a successful law student. We'll look further at this in Chapters 17 and 18.

COLLECTIVE UNDERSTANDINGS AND ATTITUDES

As well as legal knowledge and legal skills, legal studies can also help you to think about your role in society, and the role of law and the legal professional. So, while collective understandings and attitudes may seem a rather vague concept, it is actually quite straightforward. It means the acquisition and development of understandings and attitudes that are beneficial to the collective existence of society. Many collective attitudes and understandings that are transmitted by legal study are valuable for professional practice and to wider society.

INSIDER KNOWLEDGE

'The attributes of a lawyer vary between the different pockets of the legal profession, but what is always worth keeping in mind, in my view, are developing your research, analysis and communication skills, as well as having an ethical awareness.'

Natasha Bellinger, Barrister, Magdalen Chambers

These can include broad but fundamental concepts such as justice. What does 'justice' mean? Is it retribution or vengeance for a victim or someone who has had their rights infringed? Is it rehabilitation of an offender or a change to practice to ensure no one is hurt again? Is it balancing rights and interests, or ensuring there is a clear winner? Is it being certain, so everyone knows exactly what the law is, or being flexible to ensure the fairest result can be obtained in every case? Does the law deliver justice?

This can also include thinking about concepts such as access to justice. Should everyone have access to justice? Does everyone have the right to access justice, in relation to every legal issue they might face? Does everyone have the right to fair hearings and legal processes? Access to justice is particularly topical due to recent cuts to legal aid and changes to court fees.

Collective understandings and attitudes may also include concepts around professional behaviour. This may be quite law focused—what code of ethics should guide a legal professional, and why. Or more general: being honest, fair and free of prejudice. This can include examining concepts such as neutral partisanship. This is when a lawyer or other professional takes an unbiased view on a client's morals when representing them. This can be associated with the notions of 'innocent until proven guilty' and the right to representation, but is much broader in its scope.

Finally, collective understandings and attitudes may also include wider considerations of socio-political and economic issues and how these affect the law and any other sector of employment. These are really important for employment in the legal and non-legal sector and they are closely linked to the discussion in Chapter 5 on law as a pervasive subject.

SUMMARY—HELP YOURSELF . . .

- **Understand the different types of skills that your legal studies develop**
  - Remember that acquiring legal knowledge is only one part of studying law at university.
  - Recognise that both general skills and subject-specific skills are relevant to employability, both within and outside the law.

- Be aware of the collective understandings and attitudes you will develop, and their importance to successful work and wider society.

- **Seek out opportunities for skills development**
  - Take advantage of any skills-based modules you are offered, whether by your law school or other departments.
  - Engage fully in learning activities in modules that give you the opportunity to try out new skills or develop existing skills; don't view them as extraneous to your learning of the law.
  - Keep an eye out for extra-curricular activities that develop your legal and wider skills.

- **Make full use of your skills development**
  - Keep a record in some form of your skill development, don't wait until the end of your programme.
  - Remember to include all relevant experiences—not just those that have been labelled as skills-based or training exercises.
  - Reflect on your development, identify any skills gaps, and seek to remedy them.

7

LEGAL MATERIALS AND RESOURCES

*'A mind needs books as a sword needs
a whetstone, if it is to keep its edge.'*

GEORGE R. R. MARTIN,
A Game of Thrones: A Song of Ice and Fire: Book One

INTRODUCTION

When you begin studying law at university, you will be greeted with a
plethora of new and unfamiliar sources that you will need to discover
and explore. Part of the learning journey is navigating your way to the
right resources and using them to guide you to greater understanding.

Finding relevant and appropriate legal resources can be one of the
biggest challenges you may face when arriving at university. It can
be initially difficult but is an important challenge for a successful
law student.

This chapter aims to help you start that journey. We will be considering the various resources available to you in the modern university—both traditional library resources and additional digital
resources. And we'll consider resources in the wider context of the
changing nature of legal study, the increasing use of technology and
the accessibility of sources.

While much of this chapter is relevant to all law students, at times we
refer to the legal system and sources of England and Wales. There are

differences between the law and legal systems of England and Wales, Scotland, and Northern Ireland, and this should be kept in mind if you are studying in those jurisdictions.

APPROACHING LEGAL RESOURCES

Preconceptions and realities

While you may have certain preconceptions about the study of law, the reality is possibly very different. You might imagine yourself spending many hours in an oak-panelled library, poring over dusty leather-bound books and debating intricate points of law with your colleagues (think the library in Legally Blonde!). This may well be part of your studies, but law has evolved.

Law schools and universities have embraced technology to aid your quest for knowledge. While most law schools still have a dedicated law library or extensive library collections for law, many legal sources are also now available online or in digital form. It is becoming ever more common to see law students huddled around a tablet or laptop reading legal cases or discussing an Act of Parliament projected onto a digital screen. That's not to say that books are no longer an integral part of legal education, but students now have more options than ever for engaging with this ever-evolving subject.

The scale of the challenge

The sheer quantity of different legal sources available may be intimidating. Many of these sources may be unfamiliar and initially difficult to comprehend. This will be true for students who have studied law previously at A-level as well as those who are completely new to the subject. This is because degree level students are expected to engage in depth with primary sources alongside a wider appreciation of the critical thought found in secondary sources. Therefore, all law students have to develop their skills, regardless of their previous experience.

You'll also need to develop your skills in using technology in this area. The way students interact with legal and teaching resources has changed in recent years due to advances in everyday technology.

Many universities use eLearning tools (computer-based tools that facilitate learning) to engage students and host learning materials. These 'virtual learning environments' can be a really valuable resource for the successful law student and can effectively supplement your core learning.

WHAT ARE LEGAL RESOURCES?

While this might seem an obvious question, it is important to understand from the outset what legal resources are and why they are important. 'Legal resources' is a deliberately broad term, including the:

- Sources of law that establish and define legal principles;
- Accompanying commentary that helps us understand and evaluate those principles;
- Tools we use to access legal material.

So legal resources include the primary sources of law (such as cases and legislation) and secondary sources of law or sources of legal commentary (such as textbooks and academic works). We'll explain these further in a bit. They also include documents such as papers from Parliament and government reports, which help us to understand the law and its application in our society.

But 'legal resources' also encompass the way in which these sources are presented to you. That might include case law collections and databases, legal dictionaries, journal collections and various other resources.

The internet age has seen many legal resources digitised. This has led to greater breadth of available sources, added functionality and enhanced potential for their use in education. These resources will become your best friends, and possibly, at times, your worst enemies. But they are the essential pillars that will support your legal education. Within these sources, you will find the answers to (nearly) all your legal questions and will learn the language and spirit of the law. Figure 7.1 summarises some of the sources of law and the resources through which you'll find them.

FIGURE 7.1: Sources of law and where you'll find them

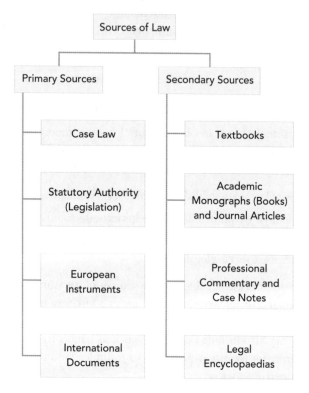

PRIMARY SOURCES OF LAW: THE LAW ITSELF

The primary sources of law are the sources you should become most familiar with during your time at law school. They contain the law itself and you will be expected to read them extensively, engage with them effectively and construct argument or opinion around their content. These primary sources are the bones of your legal study, an essential part of your legal education.

The law of England and Wales (like the USA, Canada, Australia and India to name but a few) is a common law system. It differs markedly from civil law systems (for example, most of Europe and South America) that are based on long, written 'codes' covering the law. Common law is sometimes referred to as 'judge-made' law or decision-based law. It is formed from many individual judgments by judges in different courts. The judgments from the higher courts bind the lower courts—this is called precedent or '*stare decisis*'. The system of precedent is easy to understand as a concept but more complex in operation; you'll study this early on in your legal studies.

England and Wales are also governed by Acts of Parliament (called statutes) that work alongside judgments of the court. Judges also interpret these statutes, through a process called statutory interpretation, in order to give life to the stated will of Parliament. Again, you'll study the principles of statutory interpretation early on in your legal studies.

Alongside these sources of law, there are also international sources of law that have direct or indirect influence on the law of England and Wales. These include European legislation, in the form of treaties, Regulations and Directives. Decisions of the Court of Justice of the European Union and the European Court of Human Rights also have an influence upon our courts. Finally, international documents such as international treaties and conventions can influence governmental behaviour and domestic legislation.

Case law

Domestic case law

The main source of law you will engage with in your studies is domestic law, which is the law of the superior courts of England and Wales. It is found in the reported judgments of the higher courts. While not every case is reported, cases that relate to a significant legal point will be. The judgments you will read will usually come from:

- The High Court
  - Consisting of three divisions: the Queen's Bench Division, Family Division and Chancery Division, which deal with different areas of law;

- The Court of Appeal
  - Consisting of two divisions: the Criminal Division or the Civil Division;

- The Supreme Court
  - Formerly called the Appellate Committee of the House of Lords, or in short 'the House of Lords'.

These judgments are the basis of our common law system. You may also come across judgments from the Privy Council, which hears appeals from some Commonwealth countries. These decisions can be important but are not strictly 'binding' on domestic courts, ie they do not create a direct precedent that must be followed.

I WISH I'D KNOWN . . .

'I wish I had known how much easier I would have understood an area of the law just by looking at the cases.'

Charlotte Brown, Bournemouth University, LLB Law, Year 3

European judgments

The judgments of the Court of Justice of the European Union and its related tribunals all have some effect over our domestic courts. Another important—but quite distinct—court is the European Court of Human Rights. Contrary to popular belief, our courts are not subservient to this court, but instead look to this supranational court for guidance on human rights matters.

Judgments from European courts will be a specific source of law for you when studying European Union Law. They can also be a valuable source for analysis alongside domestic judgments in lots of other areas of law, particularly where European cases have been consulted, followed or rejected.

International case law

There are numerous international courts and tribunals that issue judgments which can guide or affect domestic courts and law makers. These are too vast to explore in detail here, but should you take modules such as International Human Rights, International Public Law or International Criminal Law as options during your programme, you will be instructed on using this source of law. Also bear them in mind when considering domestic law; especially regarding issues that concern our actions as individuals and as a country overseas.

Statutory authority (legislation)

The second principal source of our law is statutory authority. This is generally considered to be the supreme form of law. This is because of

Parliamentary sovereignty—once legislation is in force the courts must interpret and apply it.

Primary legislation

Statutory authority consists firstly of Acts of Parliament, or primary legislation. This means that a Bill has passed through the House of Commons and House of Lords, been debated and discussed, before being given royal assent. The detailed process may be covered within your legal studies. Acts of Parliament are definitive documents setting out the law in a particular area.

Secondary legislation

Statutory authority can also come from secondary, or delegated, legislation. This is new law or changes to the law that don't require a full Act of Parliament to be passed. Delegated legislation is passed by bodies empowered to do so by an Act of Parliament. A good example is the Welsh Assembly, which was given delegated powers to make law under the Government of Wales Act 2006. An example of delegated legislation is statutory instruments, which may be issued from government departments to update or modify the law in certain areas.

European instruments

Our membership of the European Union gives rise to numerous outside influences on the law of England and Wales. Treaties of the European Union place certain legal obligations on member states and afford wide-ranging rights to European citizens. Legislative acts, such as Regulations and Directives, from the European Parliament guide domestic policymaking. When these provisions are combined with European case law (mentioned earlier), they have a substantial influence on the law of England and Wales. We have also seen that the jurisdiction of the European Court of Human Rights impacts on parts of our law.

International documents

Various international treaties and their accompanying organisations have an influence on a diverse range of governmental policies and our law. For example, you will have heard of the Geneva Convention. This is actually a number of treaties that agreed the treatment of military personnel, civilians and prisoners of war. These treaties dictate government policy and outline the charges for war crimes should they be contravened. This is just one example of an international document that has a bearing on our domestic law. There are numerous international documents, relating to various subjects, which will form a distinct primary source in your legal education.

SECONDARY SOURCES OF LAW: COMMENTARIES ON THE LAW

If primary sources are the bones of the law, the secondary sources provide some flesh. The secondary sources of the law are generally commentaries on the law which help you understand the primary sources. Academics, judges, politicians, legal practitioners and others create these sources, and they can provide a well-informed, contextualised approach to learning the law.

These sources will help you understand the law. But they also develop your critical opinion of the law and help you observe how legal principles work in practice. These secondary sources may also provide background to the enactment of legislation, the development of particular legal principles and their operation in society.

Textbooks

This term will undoubtedly be familiar to you. Generally, textbooks are instructional works based around specific areas of law. These books often draw together many primary sources of law and other types of secondary commentary to create guides to a particular subject.

In law, textbooks are valuable resources for learning the law and considering the law in its wider context. They will be part of your core reading, but you will need to build upon them by using primary materials and other secondary sources, such as academic monographs and journal articles.

Your module leader will usually recommend a particular textbook or textbooks for you to use on that module. But if you find you can't engage with a recommended textbook easily and effectively, be discerning. Go to the library to look at alternative textbooks to see if one better suits your style and needs, or flick through the offerings of your university bookshop to see if one there appeals.

I WISH I'D KNOWN . . .

'Law textbooks are a life saver when it comes to breaking down obtuse statutes and legislation. They usually come with an index indicating the precise page(s) in which the author discusses the specific section in the legislation.'

Godwin Tan, University College London, LLB Law, Year 3

Academic monographs and journal articles

Academic monographs (individual books on specific areas of the law rather than textbooks) and academic journal articles (essays, reports or papers published in legal journals) are vital secondary sources that a successful law student must engage with. Law schools expect their students to read widely and critically, and this requires engagement with academic opinion.

These monographs and journals can, and will, develop your critical opinions on the law. They will also inform your understanding of the strengths and weaknesses of key debates within an area of the law. These articles may also inspire you to make connections between law and other subjects that you wouldn't otherwise think about.

As we've seen in Chapter 5, law is a pervasive subject and academic journals reflect this. Reading widely and deeply allows you to see the intersection of law with almost every sphere of society, and you learn to formulate your own scholarly informed opinions. It is also worth noting that modern judges often inform their decision making by drawing upon academic scholarship.

Professional commentaries and case notes

The growth of the internet has led to a proliferation of material written by and for the legal professions, particularly solicitors and barristers. Such material has always existed in the form of professional publications, but the internet has opened publication opportunities to all legal practitioners. Most law firms and barristers' chambers host articles on their webpages. These usually focus on commentary on recent cases (often those in which the writer has been professionally involved) or changes to the law.

Professional commentary can help you to consider the effectiveness of the law in practice and its impact on society. These sources can broaden your understanding of the law away from the classroom, moving it from the theoretical to the practical. Professional case notes can also aid your own case reading, and are generally good examples of distilling legal argument. These case notes will almost inevitably have a practical application, so bear this in mind when reading.

Remember that law firm (or equivalent) commentaries should be regarded as a supplement to rather than a substitute for reading about the law in primary materials, textbooks and academic monographs and journals. It is also essential that you verify all the sources that you find online. Ensure that they come from a legitimate law firm or chambers and that the author is legally qualified (you should be able to search for the author and find their online portfolio). Consider also whether the article genuinely adds anything to the legal picture before making direct use of it.

Legal encyclopaedias

Legal encyclopaedias are useful reference books to establish definitions of legal words, principles and concepts. They can also act as an excellent point of departure for researching specific legal areas. Most legal encyclopaedias will give a brief explanation of the specific point you are investigating, but go on to give numerous references to case law, statute and academic research. You can use this to guide your initial research for essays and projects. A legal dictionary can also be a useful first step if you are unsure of the meaning of a particular word, phrase or concept.

ACCESSING LEGAL INFORMATION

Students new to legal study often have concerns about locating legal resources. It can be daunting to look at a reading list and not know where to start. And the thought of going beyond the reading list might initially seem ridiculously ambitious. However, the successful law student will read widely. They will go beyond the textbooks and often beyond the reading list to add rigour and breadth of argument to their assignments.

All students can develop the skills necessary to locate appropriate legal information. But you will need to take up opportunities, and practice your newfound skills. Many law schools will have induction sessions to help you locate important information, often run by the law library. Others will set a library exercise early in your studies to ensure you practice finding resources in the library and online. Figure 7.2 gives a flavour of the different resources you might use.

FIGURE 7.2: Library resources you may use

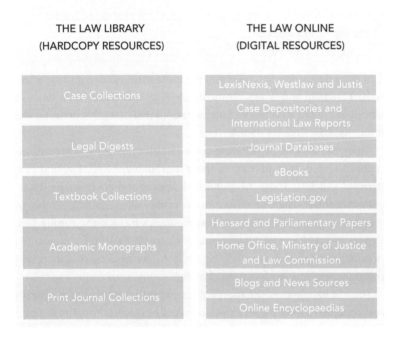

THE LAW LIBRARY
(HARDCOPY RESOURCES)

THE LAW ONLINE
(DIGITAL RESOURCES)

Case Collections

LexisNexis, Westlaw and Justis

Case Depositories and
International Law Reports

Legal Digests

Journal Databases

eBooks

Textbook Collections

Legislation.gov

Hansard and Parliamentary Papers

Academic Monographs

Home Office, Ministry of Justice
and Law Commission

Blogs and News Sources

Print Journal Collections

Online Encyclopaedias

The law library (hardcopy resources)

Case collections

The case collections are the hardcopy collection of the law reports that you will be expected to read throughout your law degree. They will be reference only, ie not for taking out of the library. While many students still use these reports regularly, it is becoming more common for students to access law reports using online resources.

All universities will have numerous collections of law reports. The main collection is the 'Law Reports', the official reports published by the

Incorporated Council of Law Reporting for England and Wales (ICLR). These include selected cases from the following courts:

- The High Court
  - Queen's Bench (QB) or King's Bench (KB);
  - Chancery (Ch);
  - Family (Fam), formerly Probate (P).
- Court of Appeal, Supreme Court (formerly the House of Lords) and the Privy Council;
  - Appeal Cases (AC).

The official reports are considered the most authoritative report collection in England and Wales. However, the ICLR also publishes a series of weekly law reports (WLR) that include additional cases that do not make it into the Law Reports themselves.

There are also many different commercially published series of law reports. The most important of these is arguably the All England Law Reports (All ER). These are published weekly and cover many different areas of law. There are also a great number of specialist law reports, focusing on particular areas of law. Examples include the Family Law Reports (Fam LR) and British Company Cases (BCC). While your institution may not subscribe to all of the available law report series, there will certainly be plenty for you to work with.

You will have noticed the abbreviations in brackets by each of the law reports outlined above. These abbreviations will be used to cite individual case reports, to enable you to identify and locate the relevant law report.

Legal digests

There are many hardcopy legal digests. These are brief, abridged versions of law reports. An example is 'Current Law', which is a popular monthly round-up of legal developments including case law, statute and other sources of law. The content is arranged by legal subject, and can be a speedy way of ensuring that you are up-to-date in a particular area of the law. Your law library is likely to subscribe to at least one legal digest.

Don't forget too that legal encyclopaedias cover the whole range of legal topics and provide valuable references to case reports and other sources. This can be a good place to start if you have a tricky essay or project question, or to begin your research trail. The most famous legal encyclopaedia is 'Halsbury's Laws of England'.

Textbook collections and academic monographs

Your library should have at least a few copies of the core textbooks that your lecturers recommend for the various legal subjects you will study. The library is likely to include other textbooks, and you can use these to broaden your knowledge of the subject, and help you to understand difficult topics. Remember to check the date of publication though, as sometimes quite out-of-date textbooks remain on library shelves.

I WISH I'D KNOWN . . .

'Sometimes you don't need to buy all the textbooks and the law library can be a great resource. If you don't understand a topic in the core materials or from the judgment then sometimes it can be a good idea to research the case in another textbook and clarify your understanding. To hear it in alternative words can sometimes help.'

Alexandra Townsley, University of Nottingham, LLB Law and American Law, Year 3

The law library will also include many academic monographs (books) on different topics. These provide more in-depth analysis of specific areas of law and can aid your research and arguments.

Print journal collections

You can also find academic journal articles in your law collection. Quite what is available will depend on the library. Many journals are now on-line, but most universities still have hardcopy versions of important journals. Academic scholarship is vast, and journals cover subjects as varied as Law and Literature to Commercial Law. Wander along the shelves that contain the hardcopy journals and see if any subjects catch your eye. Take a look and have a browse. You may find your future specialism.

The law online (digital resources)

LexisNexis, Westlaw, and Justis

LexisNexis and Westlaw are the primary legal databases, and are widely used by students, academics and the legal profession. They provide a full search function of many law reports, legislation, academic and professional journals as well as legal compendiums and practice manuals. You will probably find these to be the most useful of all the online resources available for your legal study and they will often be your first port of call for research. Later in this chapter, we'll discuss the various training options available for LexisNexis and Westlaw.

INSIDER KNOWLEDGE

'Online legal databases such as WestLaw and LexisNexis are fundamental. They save vast amounts of time when it comes to legal research, which will have to be undertaken. The best advice with regard to both of these tools is learn how to use them fully at the start of your course. Most universities will run workshops to assist you with this; so take advantage. If you progress to further study or work in the legal sector you will be expected to have a good working knowledge of these tools.'

Jamie Hill, Barrister

Justis is another case law archive that includes English and Welsh, Irish and Scottish decisions. However, its companion, JustCite, is what makes Justis a really valuable tool for the successful law student. JustCite is an online research platform that, alongside the case report itself, provides a summary of the current state of the law to help you locate the best authority in a given area of the law. If your university offers JustCite, it is well worth familiarising yourself with it early on in your studies.

Case depositories, eg BAILII and InfoCuria

Numerous case depositories are available online, which are freely available. BAILII is the British and Irish Legal Information Institute, which hosts a free database of legal material, including decisions from England and Wales, Ireland, Scotland, the European Court of Justice and the European Court of Human Rights. While these are unlikely to hold *all* the relevant reports you will need, they do hold a vast amount. InfoCuria is the database for all judgments of the European Court of Justice and its related tribunals.

International law reports

The Justis database (mentioned earlier) also holds a digital record of the decisions of international courts and arbitration panels. This may be useful if you elect to study subjects such as international law or international criminal law during your degree.

Journal Databases eg HeinOnline, Web of Science, JSTOR and Google Scholar

The best place to find academic scholarship and journal articles is by using your university's digital library search facilities (guidance will be on offer at the library or on the library's website). Very often university libraries have a single catalogue search that searches both their hardcopy and digital collections. Always start here.

You can take your search further by exploring other journal databases. While LexisNexis and Westlaw (see earlier) are useful for searching for legal articles, they don't contain everything. Other databases can have a different spread of subscriptions for legally related material. For example, HeinOnline is a database providing access to a different range of legal scholarship; JSTOR is a shared digital library that holds copies of academic journals, books and some primary sources; Web of Science generally holds scientific papers, but may be useful if you're studying optional modules such as Medical Law and Ethics.

Google Scholar can be a valuable search tool. Do note though that we are talking about Google Scholar, not just 'Google'—'googling' instead of proper legal research is not the way to be a successful law student. Google Scholar works best if you are connected to your university's network, as it can link directly to databases that your university subscribes to. It also provides access to many free articles which can enrich your research.

When using databases, precision is crucial. Type key search terms into the databases and use relevant search connectors. Search connectors are words that help to narrow search results. Some examples are AND, OR and AND NOT. You should also put key terms in quotation marks. For example, if you were looking for journal articles relating to the doctrine of consideration in contract law, just searching for 'consideration' would return too many, non-specific results. However, if you searched for 'consideration' AND 'contract law', it would narrow the results significantly.

Most universities will offer courses on using journal databases through their libraries. It is really worth taking these courses to make your research process more efficient and effective. The earlier you take these courses, the more benefit you will get from them. But don't be too embarrassed to do them later if you missed out, or to retake a training course later on to refresh your library and research skills if you need to.

I WISH I'D KNOWN . . .

'I would say to have a play around with [a database] first to familiarise yourself with it before attempting to find something specific as you then will be able to find what you are looking for in the future much more easily.'

Charlotte Brown, Bournemouth University, LLB Law, Year 3

Subscription to eBooks

Some institutions now have subscriptions to various eBook collections and individual digital texts. These are great for reading, noting and note making as they allow you to copy, highlight, annotate and manipulate text to supplement your course notes. These eBooks can often be read on tablets and smartphones as well as computers, so provide flexibility in your research and where and when to study.

Some students find it difficult to use eBooks when studying. If you need to switch between pages when considering a topic or completing an assignment, it can be harder to do with an eBook. But even if you prefer hardcopy materials don't dismiss all eBooks. They can be a useful additional resource. This is particularly so if there are a lot of students wanting to read the same book in the library, which can be common around assessment time. If you like reading on tablets or on computer, then enjoy the flexibility of eBooks as an additional resource in your research arsenal.

Legislation.gov.uk

Legislation.gov.uk is the central government depository for currently enacted legislation. Through this portal you will be able to access most enacted legislation and important explanatory notes to help you understand these documents.

One of the most useful functions of this source is the ability to 'track' legislation and subsequent changes made by Parliament. As you may be aware, new Acts of Parliament may change elements of earlier Acts. Legislation.gov.uk allows you to see these changes and link between the relevant legislative provisions. This can be helpful when looking at how particular statutory principles have developed.

Hansard and Parliamentary papers

Hansard is the official report of the debates that take place in Parliament and can be an interesting insight into the progress of particular laws. Hansard is edited to avoid repetition and correct mistakes but provides an accurate record of Parliamentary proceedings. It also features written statements and written answers to questions and includes votes cast by MPs.

Parliamentary papers is a catch-all term to describe the output of Parliamentary business, including the findings of Royal Commissions and Select Committees, Parliamentary Inquiries, drafts of Bills and statutory instruments, and papers that have been presented to Parliament by outside bodies. These can be especially useful when studying subjects such as Constitutional and Administrative Law and for expanding your research around particular legislative principles.

Hansard is available online and Parliamentary papers can be accessed via the same portal. Historical Hansard reports and historical Parliamentary papers may also be available via your university's library portal or in hardcopy.

Home Office, Ministry of Justice and Law Commission papers

As we've seen, alongside the courts, Parliament is the major law-making body in England and Wales. Changes to the statutory law are often proposed by governmental bodies. The Home Office, the Ministry of Justice (MoJ) and the Law Commission all explore current legal and social issues and make recommendations to Parliament, other government departments and government committees.

The recommendations of these bodies often guide policy drafting and the creation of primary legislation. Their reports can therefore be valuable in understanding the reasons for legal changes and the influence that political procedure has on law making. These papers are available online via the relevant government organisation's website.

Blogs and professional online publications

In the digital age, many academic researchers and professional lawyers blog about changes to the law that interest them. The rapidly changing and evolving nature of the common law in England and Wales means blogs are an excellent way for individuals to comment upon the law in real time, rather than waiting a year or so to publish a paper or essay in a book or journal.

Blogs can be a valuable insight into the opinions of an academic or professional expert and they can support your preparation for tutorials and assignments. However, all internet sources need to be treated with caution. Check the author. Ask yourself questions such as: are they an academic or professional lawyer, or otherwise concerned in the study or practice of the law? Are they an expert on the topic? Look at the organisation purporting to publish the blog. Appropriate questions might be: is it a law firm, barristers' chambers or law school? Is it from some other organisation active to the law? Does the organisation have a particular aim or political stance that I should be alert to?

As well as blogs, law firms and barristers' chambers often expect their individual lawyers to publish articles on changes in the law within their practice area, on firms' or chambers' websites. These can provide interesting insights into the law and practice and can add an element of legal practice to your academic research.

News sources

News sources can be useful non-legal resources that allow you to put the law that you're learning into context. Law affects most aspects of society. Keeping abreast of news stories broadens your understanding of the social, political and cultural climate in the UK, and helps to demonstrate social awareness to employers. As we mentioned in Chapter 5, it is worth getting into the habit of reading the news daily and thinking about how the biggest news stories of the day relate to the law. However, much like other online sources mentioned here, only use reputable sources and read critically. Remember to take account of the political stance of many media outlets.

Online encyclopaedias

Online encyclopaedias have now largely overtaken hardcopy versions, and can be useful for defining terms, and starting research. But make sure you use verified content from respected sources. Try to avoid peer-contribution sites such as Wikipedia. While Wikipedia's reviewing and verification system has become more sophisticated, there is always a substantial risk that the information is incorrect. Even if correct, an entry may relate to the situation in another country and so be irrelevant. and this may not be immediately obvious.

THE VIRTUAL LEARNING ENVIRONMENT (VLE)

Most, if not all, universities now host a Virtual Learning Environment, or VLE, for their students. These go by various names depending on the institution. One of the most common VLEs is 'Blackboard'. For many new students, VLEs are completely new resources.

What is the VLE?

VLEs are generally web-based platforms that you log into. The VLE will usually be organised with separate pages for your programme (eg LLB Law) and your individual subjects/modules.

There is a lot of variety between institutions, but programme pages will generally include all the important information related to your course. This might include programme and student handbooks, course-work manuals, deadline dates, careers and employability information, web links to relevant information etc. Check out these materials at the beginning of your course and ensure that you understand how your course works. Come back to these resources and consult them throughout your degree as and when you need them.

It is the subject or module pages that are more likely to be integral to your legal education. These are the pages you will become most familiar with. These pages will be used by your lecturers to display course materials, such as lecture handouts, copies of slides/power points, workbooks, tutorial questions, reading lists and much more.

Media content is also becoming more prominent in legal education, and many lecturers now use video and audio podcasts to support their teaching, which will often also be embedded within the VLE. Resources may be arranged by subject matter, or as a weekly guide to materials that you will use.

Importantly, the VLE is not merely a repository for course materials; it can be used as an interactive learning tool. Most VLEs allow lecturers to create various online activities to assist and support your learning. These might include:

- **Multiple-choice and short answer quizzes**
  - Test your knowledge and get instant feedback on your understanding of specific subjects.

- **Discussion forums**
  - Debate and explore contemporary legal issues and decisions, and/ or ask questions for your colleagues and lecturers to respond to.

- **Wikis**
  - Contribute, with your peers, to a collective legal resource.

These are just some examples of more common eLearning activities made available through a VLE. As technology develops, lecturers are creating more and more interesting ways of supporting students.

Finally, the VLE is increasingly being used for digital 'eSubmission' and 'eMarking' of assignments. This means that students may be able to submit essays, reports and assignments via the VLE. In some universities these may then be marked online by the lecturer and returned to the student with feedback in electronic form. If this is used at your law school you'll be given specific guidance about how to use the system. It makes sense to become familiar with how these systems work well in advance of any critical submission dates.

I WISH I'D KNOWN . . .

'How vital [the VLE] is to the study of the course. Lecture handouts will be posted on there, lecturecasts (i.e. lecture recordings) as well, suggested readings, articles, important deadlines for essays ... It is important to keep up to date and log in regularly on the system to avoid missing important information. There is nothing worse than coming to a lecture with the wrong lecture handout because the lecturer posted an updated handout the night before and you were not aware of this change!'

Gabrielle Bargas, University College London, LLB Law with French Law, Year 2

How do I use the VLE?

At first glance, a VLE may appear daunting. Get stuck in—log on and have a look around. This will give you a feel for how it is arranged and what is available.

Many universities will offer some instruction in using the VLE. But continued engagement with the VLE is your responsibility. To gain anything from the resource you will need to be an active participant and make use of the resources that the lecturer puts up.

Ideally you should really check the relevant VLE subject pages every day (or at least in advance of any teaching session) and the programme page every week. This will keep you up-to-date with relevant information and will ensure you can prepare fully for your classes and assignments.

When it comes to using the interactive learning tools and exercises, you'll only get out what you put in. The VLE can be an innovative and sophisticated method for learning and support, but you will only reap the benefits if you use it actively. Degree study is time-consuming, but it is worth finding the time to use VLE hosted resources to support and enhance your learning.

Online collaboration

Teamworking is becoming an important part of legal education because of its relevance to twenty-first century employment. Many jobs, including those with a legal focus, now involve teams collaborating online, researching and writing collectively. Some law schools have embedded this in their curriculum to varying extents, and the VLE often acts as a platform for this collaboration.

Online collaboration usually involves being placed into groups, and working together on a project or task. This might include creating a group presentation, a report or reflective journal. You will often be able to communicate through message boards or a chat function, edit and share documents, display research findings and contribute to the collective efforts of the group. These online projects develop important employability skills. And working in a collaborative online environment can be really enjoyable. Even if it isn't your favourite way of working, it is still a valuable experience.

GETTING HELP AND ASSISTANCE

We're hoping that by this point in the chapter, you are feeling excited by the challenges ahead, rather than slightly concerned at the variety of resources you may need to find and use. Either response would be understandable! Remember that everyone at your university wants you to succeed. There are numerous places to get help and assistance with all your legal research and resource needs. We can't predict all of the support you will receive at your chosen institution, but Figure 7.3 indicates some important common sources.

FIGURE 7.3: Common sources of support

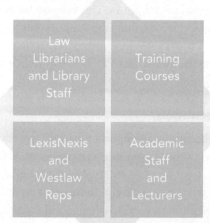

Law Librarians and Library Staff

Training Courses

LexisNexis and Westlaw Reps

Academic Staff and Lecturers

Librarians and library staff

A good first port of call for issues with resources is often the library itself. Most university libraries offer training courses or library tours, usually in the first few weeks of term. These are an excellent way of learning how to navigate the law and other collections, and the learning spaces available to you. Do go on a library tour if it is offered, even if you plan to do most of your research online—familiarity with the library is a huge advantage, particularly when you start to work on longer research projects in the latter years of your degree.

Some law schools will have a dedicated law library (either on its own premises or otherwise separated from the main university library) that will be run by designated law librarians. They are the gatekeepers of legal knowledge. They may not be able to tell you directly the answer you desire—they are not supposed to do your work for you! But they can guide you towards the best resources for finding your answer or identify the source you need.

INSIDER KNOWLEDGE

'The law librarian is your friend! You will spend lots of time in the library so get to know the law librarian!'

Karina Rooney, Progress Tutor, Queen Elizabeth Sixth Form College

In other universities, the law collections will be part of the central library but may still have their own specific law staff. Very often, these will be called subject librarians and they are the specialists in their subjects. That's not to say that the subject librarian for law will necessarily be a trained lawyer, instead (and much more usefully) they will be an expert in the collections and resources available for the study of law.

Librarians will also be able to arrange access to sources that are not in your own university library by borrowing it from another. This is called an inter-library loan and can be very useful when conducting longer research projects, such as dissertations. Law librarians and subject librarians will also be happy to hear feedback from you on their collections. This may include requests for further copies of books or journals and ideas to improve the collection. Many law schools and libraries have designated funds for just such purposes and need you to provide this information so the funds can be used to best effect.

You will also find the general library staff very helpful. They are specialists in navigating the library and using its classification system efficiently. They can also help if you have an issue with the overall environment of the library—whether it's fixing the photocopier or the noise levels! Much like everything else at university, the library is full of people who are willing to help you. If you have a question, can't find something you're looking for or have an issue with the learning space, ask.

I WISH I'D KNOWN . . .

- -

'Be willing to consult your university websites or to ask librarians for help! There are almost always more resources available than you thought, that are really helpful.'

Fiona Lin, University of Cambridge, Law, Year 3

LexisNexis and Westlaw representatives

It is common in modern law schools for second and/or third year students to act as representatives for LexisNexis or Westlaw. Their role, in return for a small bursary, is to assist and support other students. They may also offer workshops and training sessions, whether on their own or with LexisNexis or Westlaw professionals.

These representatives are usually based within your own law school, and are very approachable. They can provide prompt support and hands-on guidance with any queries or issues that you may have. You may even be tempted to become the next LexisNexis or Westlaw representative later in your studies.

Training sessions and online tutorials

Many law schools offer training in specific legal databases, which may lead to certificates of competence that can enhance your legal CV. Sometimes training like this will be arranged in the first few weeks of your course. If so, take advantage of this. If your law school or law library does not offer the training directly, you can still complete it online. For example, Westlaw and LexisNexis both offer free online training courses with certificates on completion.

If you require further assistance or need to know how to do something quite specific, there are numerous online tutorials available. If you can't find what you need, your librarian should be able to point you in the right direction. And don't underestimate the usefulness of online resources, such as YouTube or Vimeo. These include student-made walkthrough tutorials and video guides. When used with caution (we can't vouch for everything on YouTube or Vimeo . . .), these can be useful resources for the successful law student.

Academic staff

There may be times during your studies when you feel lost or confused about the resources you need. That is very common, particularly at the start of the course and around assessment times, when accessing (and understanding) legal resources can just seem all too much. There will be times when you cannot find a particular resource or may feel like you are drowning in material, or you may feel entirely under-skilled for the task at hand. Nearly every student feels like this at some stage, although some are very good at hiding it.

Don't be afraid to ask your friends, lecturers, subject tutors or personal tutor for help. If you encounter a problem, and can't easily find the answer yourself, ask someone for assistance. Every member of staff wants you to succeed and will help you as much as they can. They might not give you a direct answer, but they'll help you to find out for yourself.

Remember there is no such thing as a silly question. A reluctance to ask for help is often one of a student's most significant shortcomings, but one that is easily remedied. The sooner you ask for clarification and guidance the better learning experience you will have. Staff can help you find the resources they recommend, guide you to additional resources and help you develop the skills needed for using these resources in your learning.

University training courses, eLearning and IT services

To state the obvious, universities are centres of learning and you are here to learn. Make the most of this, in every way possible.

Many universities have specific study centres offering their students training in a variety of skills. What is on offer will vary from institution to institution, but might include:

- Using library resources;
- Effective note making;
- Avoiding plagiarism;
- Research tips;
- Essay writing;
- Time management.

These courses (whether person-to-person or online) can be very helpful and may introduce you to new ideas for studying and skills for learning.

Student learning services may also offer subject-specific training courses, courses to develop specific skills related to the study of law. These might include:

- Reading cases effectively;
- Writing legal essays;
- Using legal databases.

Your university will probably have webpages for its study skills or learning centre, or a learning portal hosted on the VLE. If not then check your emails, as they may alert you to upcoming events. If you need specific guidance, ask your personal tutor or academic mentor, as they'll be able to guide you in the right direction.

OTHER STUDY TOOLS

There are countless examples of software and apps that can assist in the study of law and support your learning. They include tools for:

- Note making;
- Recording research material and creating bibliographies;
- Mind-mapping.

Tools such as these can make your learning, research and revision more effective and increase your productivity. Efficient working is an important skill—both for successful study and for employability. Experiment with relevant study tools, to find what works best for your learning style and needs.

Note-making tools

There are various note-making tools in the software/app market that allow you to create expansive digital scrapbooks and bring all your notes together.

However you create your class notes—whether electronically or on paper—you will need to bring together information from different sources. The most successful students tend to take notes written in lectures and small group sessions, add to them from core reading and elaborate on them through reading additional legal resources. We'll look further at note making in Chapters 8 and 9.

Software such as Evernote, Microsoft's OneNote, Apple's Pages and Super Notes are sophisticated note-making tools that allow you, for example, to type in your lecture notes, supplement these with slides from the lecture, and then add in anything from excerpts from cases, eBooks or articles, summaries of academic or professional opinion and visual aids such as mind-maps or flow diagrams. You can even drop in media files, such as voice memos or video notes. Most also enable you to back up your notes onto cloud-based file saving.

Mind-mapping tools

Many law students find that they learn best when they convert their legal knowledge into different forms. For example, lots of students like to visualise legal concepts and demonstrate the relationships between them.

Mind-maps are an excellent way to do this and can act as brilliant revision aids. While many students make these by hand and often find this process valuable in itself, there are numerous free programs that can allow this process to be done digitally. Software such as XMind, MindMaple, MindMup and SimpleMind+ are all easy to use on your computer, tablet or phone.

Bibliographic software

As you begin researching for projects, essays, and dissertations, you will quickly realise you are collecting a large amount of material from different sources. You may worry about referencing properly and avoiding inadvertent plagiarism if you can't keep track of it all.

Programs such as Endnote and Refworks can help you organise your research and aid referencing. They act as an evolving library for your references, which you enter manually or by exporting them from online resources. These can then be imported directly into your word processing program. These tools can save you time and ensure that the referencing in your written work is accurate. Most universities include bibliographic software as part of their suite of available IT programs and can also provide training on how best to use them.

SOME USEFUL LINKS

- **BAILII:** http://www.bailii.org/

  BAILII is a free, searchable database of primary legal materials (specifically cases) that you will find useful in your day-to-day studies

- **Google Scholar:** https://scholar.google.co.uk/

  Google Scholar is a useful first port of call for finding scholarly literature and secondary sources

- **Hansard:** https://hansard.parliament.uk/

  Hansard is the record of UK Parliamentary business, which can help you understand the background to legislative changes. The online database is searchable

- **HeinOnline:** http://home.heinonline.org/

  HeinOnline is a large, fully searchable database of legal and historical materials. It is US focused but also contains many historical legal journals to provide context

- **Home Office:** https://www.gov.uk/government/organisations/home-office

  Being aware of government publications and pronouncements can help you understand the political context of legal changes

- **InfoCuria:** http://curia.europa.eu/juris/recherche.jsf?cid=224772

  This is the searchable database of judgments from the European Court of Justice

- **JSTOR:** https://www.jstor.org/

  JSTOR is one of the biggest searchable databases of academic books and articles

- **Justis:** https://www.justis.com/

  Justis is an international case law and legislation database

- **Law Commission:** http://www.lawcom.gov.uk/

  The Law Commission is an independent body that reviews and

recommends changes to the law of England and Wales. Their website has links to current projects and previous reports and recommendations

- **Legislation.gov.uk:** http://www.legislation.gov.uk/

  This database publishes all UK legislation, including repeals and amendments. It is an excellent source for the most up-to-date legislation

- **LexisNexis:** https://www.lexisnexis.com/uk/legal/

  LexisNexis is one of the most famous legal databases, containing case reports, legislation, journal articles, practice manuals and much more

- **Ministry of Justice:** https://www.gov.uk/government/organisations/ministry-of-justice

  Useful for contextual information about the administration of justice in England and Wales

- **Westlaw:** http://legalresearch.westlaw.co.uk/

  Westlaw is another particularly important legal database, hosting a wide range of legal materials from case reports, journal articles, legislation and more

SUMMARY—HELP YOURSELF . . .

- **Explore the important legal sources**
  - Familiarise yourself with the primary sources of law—the law itself. Be prepared to read and engage with these sources.
  - Use secondary sources. These are generally commentaries on the law that assist in understanding the primary sources, and help to provide an informed, contextualised approach to learning the law.

- **Check out primary and secondary sources**
  - Practice finding sources both in hardcopy in the law library, and in digital form.

- Familiarise yourself with a range of resources, including case collections, legal digests, legal encyclopaedia, textbooks, monographs and journals.

- Explore electronic legal databases, such as LexisNexis, Westlaw, Justis, BAILII, JSTOR and Google Scholar.

- Check out websites such as Legislation.gov.uk, and websites for bodies such as the Home Office, Ministry of Justice and Law Commission.

- Critically evaluate your source: whether it is an academic or professional blog, professional online publication, news source or online encyclopaedia.

- **Locate help and support**

  - Explore the various support services available and be prepared to use them when you need them.

  - Utilise sources of guidance including library staff, legal database representatives, training sessions (in person and online) and academic staff.

  - Make friends with the VLE—the more you use and engage with the resources available, the more benefit you will get.

PART 3
SUCCESSFUL LEARNING
Making the most of teaching
and learning in law

8

LEARNING IN LAW—READING, RESEARCH AND MORE

*'You must never feel badly about making mistakes,' explained Reason
quietly, 'as long as you take the trouble to learn from them.
For you often learn more by being wrong for the right reasons
than you do by being right for the wrong reasons.'
'But there's so much to learn,' he said, with a thoughtful frown.
'Yes, that's true,' admitted Rhyme; 'but it's not just learning things
that's important. It's learning what to do with what you learn and
learning why you learn things at all that matters.'*

NORTON JUSTER,
The Phantom Tollbooth

INTRODUCTION

A good part of your legal education will take place in classrooms and lecture theatres—you will be *taught* a lot of law. But successful learning in law also relies to a great extent on individual, autonomous study: reading, research, thinking and reflecting. Learning law is about much more than what and how you are taught.

Of course it is not really possible to separate 'teaching' and 'learning' in practice. Individual study, whatever form it takes, informs and supports your law classes and vice versa, and teaching has no purpose if it is not about your learning. For convenience though we will focus on learning generally and particularly reading and research in this chapter, and then look at getting the best out of particular law classes in more depth in the next chapter, Chapter 9.

So in this chapter we'll look at your crucial role in the learning process, and how you may be able to enhance your learning in law by understanding your learning strengths and working with them. And we'll spend some time looking at effective reading, research, note making and reflection—how to make best use of your time and the material available.

YOUR ROLE IN THE LEARNING PROCESS

Studying law at university may be your first experience of a different way of teaching and learning, with new styles, approaches, terminology and expectations. The learning process is made up of different elements, some more directed, some more self-guided. All require your full engagement.

Learning opportunities

The classes you have in law (see further Chapter 9) provide the backbone of your legal learning, as well as the springboard for exploring further and more deeply on an individual level. Formal teaching sessions thus guide, support and deepen your individual reading and research.

You could learn the law entirely on your own, from books and other resources, but this is *much* more of a challenge. Many law students discover this the hard way if they allow other distractions to keep them away from classes for too long! Lectures, tutorials, seminars and other classes provide the essential framework and direction you need to be successful in law, as well as providing opportunities to engage more deeply in complex or topical issues, ask and respond to questions, test your understanding and skills, and receive feedback.

Equally you could probably just about manage to learn the law only through your law classes, doing the bare minimum to get by. But you are unlikely to be satisfied with the outcome.

So it is your law classes combined with your individual study that enables you to be a successful law student. Figure 8.1 shows how important it is to engage with the whole range of learning opportunities, because they are all connected.

FIGURE 8.1: Different elements of the learning process

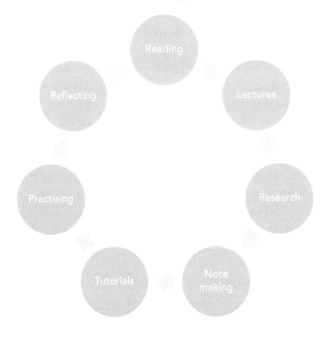

INSIDER KNOWLEDGE

'Attend them all, contribute actively to seminars, carry out independent study to augment the content of the lectures, and spend plenty of time understanding and digesting the information gained. Don't leave it all to the last few revision weeks! I did not follow that advice, and consequently gained only a third class degree.'

David Willingham, Retired, formerly Head of Risk Financing at Save the Children

Individual study

As we've already touched on, individual study plays an important role in supporting, developing and enhancing the learning you do in class. You will engage in individual study in preparation for a class, and pursue further research and reading after classes.

That study may be under high levels of guidance, for example when you are given very specific things to read and tasks to do in preparation for a class. Or it may be more lightly guided, for example when you have to select appropriate material from a wider reading list, or find and read the relevant pages in a textbook and then start your research from there. Different lecturers, tutors and modules will give you different levels of guidance, but you can expect a little more guidance in the early stages of learning the law, and less in the later stages as your legal skills develop.

Some students fall into the habit of only studying for specific events such as tutorials or assessments, and only studying material they are directly referred to. This means they do not get the benefit of, and develop the skills of, self-directed study. By engaging with different texts, seeking out different articles and following through an academic debate or reform proposal you can stretch your understanding and develop your skills of research, criticism and analysis. A successful law student doesn't do *only* what s/he is told expressly to do.

PPAR for the course

When studying law at university you will have much less contact time with teaching staff than you might be used to from school or college. As we've seen, individual study is essential. But it is also important that you maximise the value of the time you do get with your lecturers and tutors. That requires taking a focused and active approach to your learning. We call this being 'PPAR for the course', illustrated in Figure 8.2.

FIGURE 8.2: PPAR for the course

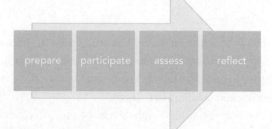

prepare   participate   assess   reflect

All these elements are important when approaching learning opportunities if you are to get the most from them. You need to:

- Prepare properly;
- Participate appropriately;
- Assess your skills and understanding, as well as the law, on an ongoing basis; and
- Reflect on what, and how, you've learned.

You will see aspects of these reappearing when we consider particular classes in Chapter 9. Your role in all elements of teaching and learning is therefore critical. It will be up to you to decide quite what work to do, and when to do it, and whether you want to push yourself further to seek out additional material or further intellectual challenge. You may need to keep your immediate and longer-term goals in mind (see Chapter 3) to remain focused and motivated.

I WISH I'D KNOWN . . .

'It's a big change from the learning style at school. No more spoon-feeding, it's over to you.'

Madeleine Burrell, University of Oxford, Law with German Law, Year 3

With effort and application, you will develop the independent study skills you need to succeed in learning the law as your degree programme progresses. And even some skills that you undoubtedly already possess—like reading—need to be honed if you are to use your study time effectively. You may find it a little easier to develop your skills if you first reflect a little on your own preferences for learning.

YOUR LEARNING PREFERENCES

Individuals learn in different ways. You probably already have a good sense of things that have or haven't worked for you in the past.

There are a number of ways you can assess, categorise or reflect on your learning styles or preferences. Of course, the notion that everybody has a particular learning style is not without controversy. But even if you are not convinced, or don't feel any of these styles resonate with you, considering the way you think and learn can still be helpful in finding more effective ways of learning for you. At the very least, consideration of learning styles can encourage you to try out new learning and study techniques that you could find helpful.

Exploring your learning preferences

You may be asked to undertake a number of exercises when you start university to help you identify your learning type or style. Even if you think you already know your own personal learning preferences it is worth engaging with these exercises—you might be surprised. If you are not directed to any particular exercises, you can find plenty of further information on learning styles, including some questionnaires, online.

One of the best-known ways of understanding how you learn is VARK, developed by Neil Fleming. It helps you identify what type of learner you are by working through an inventory that shows your strengths in particular learning styles. VARK stands for: V=Visual, A=Auditory, R=Read/Write, and K=Kinaesthetic, which can be summarised briefly as follows:

- Visual (V)
  - Learners with a visual preference engage best with material that is presented using visuals like mind-maps, diagrams, arrows or graphs. They like things that could be presented as words, represented *visually*.

- Auditory (A)
  - Auditory learners learn best through methods which convey information through the medium of *sound*. They generally have a preference for information that is 'heard or spoken' and often learn best from lectures, group discussion, speaking, or similar, including talking out loud/talking to yourself.

- Read/Write (R)
  - Those individuals with a preference for read/write preference prefer information to be displayed as *words*. Text-based materials and text-based learning processes are preferred—reading and writing in all its forms, including manuals, reports, PowerPoint and lists.

- Kinaesthetic (K)
  - Kinaesthetic learners learn best through *experience*, preferring their learning to be connected to reality. In law, this might include

role-play; such as mooting, negotiations and client interviewing, or problem solving. It can also include demonstrations, simulations, case studies and applications.

You can visit Fleming's website (http://www.vark-learn.com) for further information.

The idea is that by better understanding your learning style, you can better tailor your study techniques to suit your preferences. Many students also find the Honey and Mumford Learning Styles helpful in deciding how to approach their legal studies, and to encourage them to try out new techniques and practice other ways of working.

Honey and Mumford (1982) identified four distinct styles that people use when learning, but concluded that most people only use one or two of these styles. The four styles are:

- Activists;
- Pragmatists;
- Reflectors; and
- Theorists.

A summary of these styles can be found in Table 8.1.

TABLE 8.1: Learning styles and associated attributes

LEARNING STYLE	ASSOCIATED ATTRIBUTES	TYPICAL ACTIVITIES
Activist	Learn by doing. An open-minded approach to learning, involving themselves fully in new experiences	Brain-storming Problem solving Group discussion Role-play
Pragmatist	Need to be able to see how to put learning into practice in the outside world. Experiment, trying out new ideas, theories and techniques.	Case studies Problem solving Discussion Thinking about applying learning

(*Continued*)

(*Continued*)

Reflector	Observe and think about what happened. Stand back and view from different perspectives. Take time to work towards conclusion	Observation Feedback from others Interviews and paired discussion
Theorist	Learn by understanding the theory behind the actions, using models, concepts and facts. Draw new information into a systematic and logical theory.	Applying theories Stories and quotes Statistics Background information

Further information on Honey and Mumford's learning styles can be found at: http://www2.le.ac.uk/departments/gradschool/training/eresources/teaching/theories/honey-mumford.

Like the VARK questionnaire, the Honey and Mumford Learning Styles Questionnaire (available online) can suggest effective learning activities and study techniques for you. This may help you to develop the important skills you need more easily by working with your strengths, and put you on your way to being a successful law student.

READING IN LAW

As a law student, you will spend a lot of time finding and reading legal material (we looked at sources of law and legal materials in more depth in Chapter 7). Your research and reading will broaden and deepen your understanding, support and develop your classroom learning, help you prepare for assignments and develop valuable transferable skills. So the successful law student needs to know how to find what they need and what to do with it once they've got it. We'll look at research skills in a bit, after exploring the critical skill of reading.

Learning to read

Do you really need to learn to read? Of course, the simple answer is no. You must be able to read well to have got this far in your education. But you do need to ensure that you can read *effectively* for the tasks that you now face as a law student.

Reading for information

Reading for *information* is a key skill. And focusing on information that is relevant and pertinent to a particular problem or task at hand is essential to being a successful law student. Needless to say, you can't read everything about a chosen subject. You need to be selective, and avoid reading things that are irrelevant to your area of study or task as this will waste time you could spend more constructively. So it is worth learning to read again, in the sense of developing skills to make you an efficient and effective reader.

It is important to recognise the difference between reading for study and reading for pleasure. The fact you have chosen to study law means that you are, presumably, interested in law. But enjoying your subject, and being interested in what you are reading, is not the same as reading for pleasure—the aims and approaches differ.

What is more, most law students will at some point encounter a subject that doesn't engage them as much as others, or that they don't enjoy, and so reading 'for pleasure' may seem very distant. Reading material effectively and efficiently, even when it does not immediately engage you, is an important skill in studying law, but also for future work. Whether you are enjoying your reading on a particular day or not, it is important that you learn to read relevant material effectively and efficiently.

So reading for learning is very different from reading for pleasure. A successful law student develops a set of skills that take this into account. When reading for pleasure, most of us will put down and pick up books after chapters, we might scan read, we let our imagination fly, and we may not think too hard about the contents of the book. And, we will read the whole book! That is the only way to get the whole story. This is because reading for pleasure is usually reading to be entertained, whether through fiction or non-fiction.

But reading in law school is task-based: you need to learn key information, engage with and understand new concepts and arguments, and identify the importance of what you are reading to the task at hand, whether a specific assessment, or acquiring more general or deeper knowledge of a subject.

In order to do this, it may be necessary to read a number of chapters at once to see the development of an argument or concept, or to pick out a particular chapter (or just part of a chapter) for deep consideration. It will be necessary to question and evaluate what you read, and think about the evidence presented to support an author's argument.

You will need to think carefully and critically about the information you are reading in order to allow this to inform your own understanding of the subject and to allow you to reconsider or adjust your own opinions.

I WISH I'D KNOWN . . .

'Legal texts are daunting in the first few weeks of first year but you quickly become acclimatised. However, you must put in the effort to understand.'

Monica Chen, University College London, LLB Law, Year 2

Learning the law rarely requires you to read a whole textbook or journal—it might not even be necessary to read a complete report or article. To use your time effectively, you may only read an introduction or abstract, or scan a few sections, in order to identify whether the material is relevant. And even relevant books or articles may only have a chapter or two, or a few sections that are directly relevant to your task. You will need to tailor your reading accordingly.

Selecting and combining material

If you have a textbook that accompanies a course, you will be directed to read chapters as you progress. You will supplement this with chapters from other books or individual articles from journals, and primary material.

Imagine you were studying a module on human rights law. You would probably use a general textbook on human rights and read individual chapters to complement the material in lectures, although you won't read them all at once, and you might not read them in order. When you supplement the textbook, you will not be reading a whole journal or other book on a particular topic. You will read articles relevant to the specific topic and a number of chapters from different authors where they interrogate a similar subject matter. This wider reading gives you broader and deeper perspectives on the issues, and enables you to become a well-informed, critical thinker.

I WISH I'D KNOWN . . .

'I was given a reading list in my first year as with every other year, and it was quite straightforward. However, I found that I was going to the library to find books that were not on the reading list as they were more straightforward, not full of waffle and cut to the chase.'

Isabel Anderson, Aberystwyth University, LLB Law, Year 3

So, reading as a law student both transfers knowledge and information, and processes it to create understanding and the ability to assess and apply that knowledge. Reading widely enriches your learning. But while a few lucky individuals are blessed with exceptional memories and can remember all they read, most of us need to make notes on our reading to assist in this process. This is where the process of assimilation largely takes place. This process is illustrated in Figure 8.3.

FIGURE 8.3: Assimilating information

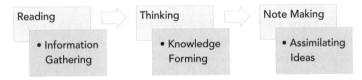

Reading
- Information Gathering

Thinking
- Knowledge Forming

Note Making
- Assimilating Ideas

The importance of note making in the learning process will be considered further a bit later. First it is necessary to make sure you can locate appropriate and relevant material effectively.

SUCCESSFUL RESEARCHING

You will need to read and engage with a sufficiently wide range of sources to get a broad and balanced outlook on your particular subjects. In order to do this, you will need to use as many resources as possible.

Make sure you use both primary and secondary sources in your research, using the materials that are most appropriate to the specific task at hand. So, if you were preparing an essay for contract law for example, you would use the primary sources of cases and statutes (and possibly reform proposals and reports), and the secondary sources of academic books and academic journal articles. But if you were doing an assignment for a law, literature and film course, it might well be necessary to use films, books or television series as primary sources, with academic books, newspapers and academic journal articles as secondary sources.

You need to select the right kinds of materials for the task, using different sources to inform your own knowledge and argument. This is true whether you are preparing assignments or undertaking wider reading related to the courses you are studying. Be sure to read widely. Read beyond your textbook(s) and casebook(s) by reading a mix of primary and secondary sources, to enrich your learning.

INSIDER KNOWLEDGE

'There is so much now available on the pressing of a key board ... use everything that is suitable and available but don't rule out discussions with your fellow students, a lot is to be learnt that way also.'

Jonathan Brew, Senior Partner, Harrison Clark Rickerbys

So far, we have emphasised the need to research and read widely. But reading in depth, albeit selectively, is also extremely important to the successful law student. Having researched widely, you need to explore particularly relevant material in depth. So, for example, once you have found a particularly pertinent case, don't just read a summary, read all the judgments carefully and compare and critique the different approaches. Or, if you have found a couple of academic articles on the same point, read them carefully to find competing arguments or policy concerns.

Making a start

Research trails

A good place to start any research is your reading list for the course. Most, if not all, courses will give you a recommended reading list at the outset, or in relation to individual topics as they are covered. These provide a starting point for research and will help you to find further works that may be relevant. This is because most material in your reading lists will cite other sources, which you can move on to explore yourself. This is sometimes called 'referencing mining'.

As well as helping to you find further relevant sources, referencing mining helps you to understand how a particular writer developed their ideas. This will critically inform your arguments and understanding of the subject.

The research trail you develop by using sources in this way will guide you through the subject in relation to both primary and secondary sources. For example, with case law it is valuable to look at other cases the judge cites to examine how they reached their decision. This can include cases that they have followed, those that they have decided not to follow and those that they use to give them guidance. By looking at the thought process of judges, you get a real sense of how the law has developed in a particular area.

Similarly with academic books and articles, the author will have drawn together numerous primary and secondary sources to provide an evidence base for their analysis, and by engaging with these directly you can better evaluate and critique their conclusions. These secondary sources also tend to provide a particularly rich and varied set of references for mining. Get stuck in!

Law library

The law library (and library catalogue) also helps you find resources for research—for both assignments and to supplement your lecture and tutorial reading. Start with your university online library catalogue, using key search terms relevant to the topic to find books and articles. If you need advice on using the library catalogue—even if you've already had library training, but have forgotten it—speak to your law librarian.

Using key words is a good place to start. We saw in Chapter 7 how important it is when searching databases to be as precise as possible in order to return focused results. And despite the importance of electronic catalogues and e-resources, it is also worth walking around the library, exploring what books and other materials are on the shelves. This gives you a sense of what sources the library holds in particular areas, and may help you to see further links that you might not notice simply by searching online using key words. Flick through a few books, have a look at the contents pages and think about whether the book might be of use itself, or whether it suggests further areas for exploration.

The internet

The internet is obviously a valuable resource for your research. However, as we discussed in Chapter 7, you *must* exercise care over the relevance, value and reliability of your sources. Remember that specific search engines that search for academic articles such as Google Scholar (https://scholar.google.co.uk) are much more useful than a general search engine. And don't forget that you still need to evaluate the sources that even specialist search engines locate.

INSIDER KNOWLEDGE

'Your time is precious. Don't use your time reading poor quality, freely available web resources when developing your understanding. Use only quality resources, which you can access through services like Westlaw. This applies to law reports (cases) as well as academic commentary.'

Dr Richard Bowyer, Senior Lecturer, University of Exeter

Even general search engines can have a role to play sometimes—they may throw up interesting debates and less conventional resources. But your search terms will need to be precise and it is particularly important to treat every source with caution. The same rules apply here as they do for the validity of resources that we discussed in Chapter 7.

Identifying relevant material

It can be a big challenge to narrow your field of research sufficiently to make your research efforts as efficient as possible, while not prematurely excluding material and topics that could prove to be valuable. Similarly, ensuring you consider sufficient relevant material, but having the confidence not to use things that are irrelevant or only peripherally relevant, can be a difficult balance. Reading abstracts (the short summaries at the beginning of articles), introductions and conclusions can guide you on their relevance to your research.

I WISH I'D KNOWN . . .

'That you should be highly strategic in your reading—skimming is often as valuable as agonising over and highlighting every single useful phrase.'

Fiona Lin, University of Cambridge, Law, Year 3

Sometimes though there is no substitute for reading a whole article, or chapter, in order to evaluate its usefulness. Think really carefully about each source you read, and don't be afraid to put it to one side if it is not relevant or is of questionable value—even if you've read it all and made notes. It is better to be selective with your materials, than to try to force irrelevant material into your essays and notes. Using everything may indicate to the reader that you have not really understood the topic, or may confuse you when you come back to your notes later.

The ability to distinguish between relevant and irrelevant material is a very important skill. It is one that you will develop with practice, and as you grow more familiar with law and legal materials, but is something that you need to think about from the start of your legal studies. You are likely to get more guided support on reading in your early days. This doesn't exempt you from the need to consider relevance. Instead use these opportunities to help you spot why material is relevant, so you can develop your own skills for the future.

Beyond your university library

On occasion, you may need to access material from other libraries and/or visit other libraries. Don't be afraid to ask your own library for support when locating specific resources. If your university law library does not have access to a book or a journal article that you believe would be helpful to your studies then speak to your law librarian. They may be able to order you a copy, or arrange an inter-library loan. This is more likely to be possible in relation to specific research projects than for general reading.

You may also be able to benefit from materials held by other libraries if you are prepared to travel, or if you spend your vacations away from your home university. Consider making use of your local library or a university library in your home town, if you are studying during vacations. Most universities will permit students from other institutions to access research materials and may provide you with associate or temporary membership of their library.

TOP TIPS FOR SUCCESSFUL RESEARCHING

- **Plan your time**
  - Particularly if you have a deadline, ensure you plan your research process carefully, to give yourself enough time to undertake enough research and explore a range of sources. Build research time into your work schedule, and 'project manage' your assignments so you know where you are and what more you need to do.

- **Start simple**
  - Start your research by reading the appropriate section of a simple textbook or introduction to the subject, and/or your lecture notes to

get a firm grounding and essential background knowledge. Move on in stages—after the introductory reading, read the core text and key cases before moving on to further cases, academic texts and journal articles.

- Focus

  - Focus your research on the sources that are most relevant to your work. Read introductions and/or abstracts, or a couple of pages of the work in question, to select the best material from a wide initial range. This takes time and can be frustrating, but will be worth it in the end.

- Choose a variety of sources

  - Explore a variety of sources to ensure you understand a topic fully, and to give you the breadth of argument and context needed to be a successful law student.

- Organise your material from the start

  - Keep track of your sources, maintaining good notes on your reading, organised in a way that you can use effectively. Sort your material in a way that is useful to your particular task—perhaps by source type, topic or chronology—so you can locate and use the information later. Make sure you record full references as you go along in case you need to find a source again later, or need to refer to it in an assignment.

- Be ruthless—throw things away

  - Don't be afraid to disregard irrelevant research or reading. Just because you've read something doesn't mean you should necessarily include it in your notes or in your assignments. If it doesn't fit, chuck it! It will make your notes more focused and your assignments well considered.

- Develop your own ideas

  - When you're researching, you will have thoughts and ideas. Write them down, think about them and develop them. They will help you in evaluating your research material and forming arguments and will add depth and sophistication to assignments. The independent thought that will help you to achieve the best marks will only be developed if you get used to exploring and recording your own ideas—supported where possible of course with evidence.

NOTE TAKING OR NOTE MAKING?

Everyone can take notes, but *making* a clear, concise and coherent set of learning materials is the challenge. This is a key skill to set you on the path to being a successful law student, and is of value in any future employment. Not all law students recognise the importance of effective note making—which means they may not get the most out of law classes, professional opportunities and experiences (such as mooting, negotiation, client interviewing, work experience or internships), or their reading and research.

Effective note making

Notes shouldn't simply be a repetition or summary of material. They should form a record of knowledge, and your own thoughts, ideas and opinions of this. Your notes should allow you to map your learning, and then help you to understand it.

The process of note making allows you to explore different ideas and critically analyse them using prior learning, other ideas and your own opinions. This will be immensely useful when revising for exams and researching for assessments.

Note making may seem like a really easy skill that should pose no problems. After all, it's just writing stuff down. Well not entirely. It is a skill to be developed. It is quite usual to make longer notes at the beginning of your studies as you learn effective techniques. Don't worry if you find this is the case, but do guard against trying to write down every word that you hear or against copying out (or printing, or highlighting) every sentence that you read.

To make effective notes, you need to focus on the key points that are relevant to your learning. For example, if you were making notes of a particular article, you would want to pull out the central argument, with a brief summary of any significant supporting evidence or examples. More extensive notes would also record important connected lines of argument, rebuttals of well-known counter-arguments and any suggestions for changes to the law. This should trigger your own thoughts and enable you to link to other material. By being selective with the notes that you take, you move beyond the passive activity of note taking and begin the active learning process of note making.

Developing note-making skills

To test and develop your note-taking and note-making ability, try this short exercise. Select a short YouTube video (about 10 minutes) that deals with a particular topic—a TED talk for example, or a short documentary, and try taking notes on the subject.

First, just take notes as you would normally take notes, right until the end of the video. Once you've finished, look back at your notes—are the key messages of the video clear, or not? Now watch the video back and reflect again on what you have written. Some questions to think about:

• Did you find it easy or hard to make notes? Did your notes clearly identify key points of the video?

• How much did you write? Do you think it is too much or too little? Why?

• Did you struggle to keep up with the speaker? Why might this be the case?

• Are you writing down whole sentences that the speakers are saying? Would it be more valuable to have just noted key points or phrases?

• When you do this exercise again what will you do differently?

You can do a similar exercise to test your note making when reading, by picking a short article from a magazine or newspaper. Again, make notes on what you are reading, and then review them, re-reading the article and then reflecting on the experience.

Now think carefully about how you can make more efficient notes. Once you have thought about how you can improve your practice, then try the exercise again. Keep practising. It is also worth experimenting whether you make better notes when writing by hand or when typing on your computer. You might assume that notes made on the computer would always be better, but often typed notes tend to be more detailed, but less effective. Note making by hand can be a more active learning experience, although computers do allow you to move text around more easily later on. See what works best for you.

Combining sources

The really valuable part of note *making* comes after the more basic and initial note taking. So after taking notes while reading a particular book, or article, or from a lecture, you need to review those notes and put them into a meaningful order, begin to add in further notes from reading and your own ideas, and add your own personal flourishes to them.

So your initial notes are just a skeleton for development of your learning. By combining notes from textbook reading, lecture notes, tutorial guidance points and notes from further articles and reports you can build up a valuable—and focused—library of information.

When making notes on your reading—whether it is a textbook, an academic book, a journal article, a case report, a statute or any other resource—be precise. Your notes should not be big chunks of text copied from your sources, but should be summaries of key points, and collections of ideas from the reading (carefully referenced of course).

Only include direct quotes that are particularly pertinent (and again, reference them carefully)—it is usually more valuable to your learning to be able to formulate points in your own words as this means you've had to think about what you are writing. If you are making notes to use in assignments, then you must be careful that your notes make clear where material has come from so you can reference properly. (See Chapter 11 for more on referencing.) Using different colours or codes can be helpful if you are bringing various sources together in your notes, so there is never any doubt as to where material came from, and which ideas and explanations are your own.

You can even take this further and divide your notes by source type and cross-reference across them all. For example, some students will have a set of notes with lecture and tutorial material, a set for case reading, a set for textbook reading and a set for further research (including journal articles). Many students find it useful to compartmentalise their work in this way, and it effectively creates a homemade 'text and materials' book that can help you as a reference tool for revision. However, some students find it frustrating to jump between note sets and prefer to have all their material in one place.

Finding your style

It should be clear that there is no single right or wrong way to arrange your notes—whether you like using full sentences, bullet points, highlighters, ink colours, diagrams or pictures, it is all up to you. Try a variety of techniques to see which works best for you, taking your learning preferences into account.

If you are a traditional learner, making handwritten notes, highlighting specific passages of reading, re-reading, rewriting and redrafting your notes will usually work best. You could write out your notes on flashcards and re-read these, or create workbooks of all the material. You may also find it helpful to use a notebook to jot down ideas and build them into your notes as you redraft.

If you are an auditory and verbal learner, you are likely to learn best by listening and developing ideas through talking them through with others. This may seem strange when it comes to note making, but remember that notes can be in any form. You may find it useful to record lectures or tutorials (with the lecturer's consent) and listen to them back later. You may also find it helpful to make podcasts of your own notes, readings and ideas. Use your phone, tablet or laptop to create your own multimedia resources. You may also find it helpful to form a study group to talk work through with other students, and read to each other. Using voice recognition software to dictate notes to your computer may also help you to think about information more carefully.

If you learn best through seeing and visualising concepts—a visual learner—traditional learning methods such as underlining and highlighting text and writing in different colours to code your text will help your note making. You may also find mind-maps and flow diagrams helpful, as well as illustrating your notes and using symbols for concepts. Try sketching or copying photographs into your notes to act as memory aids. Or record videos of yourself reading through your notes, presenting them and watching them back later.

As a kinaesthetic/tactile learner you can learn through experiences, by touching and doing. You could try making your notes on flashcards, then spend time laying these out in particular orders. This process of moving knowledge around will help you to engage with it. You may also find that holding different objects or tokens when reading through particular notes will help you learn the material better, as you will associate the feel of that object to the subject matter. It has been suggested that techniques such as chewing different flavour chewing gum for different subjects can help tactile learners to learn or even squeezing a stress ball.

Even if you are not convinced by the notion of personal learning styles, or have not identified yourself as having a distinct learning style, try experimenting with some of the ideas above to see what works best for you.

REFLECTION IN READING AND RESEARCH

Reflection—really thinking about what you have just done and how you can do it better—is important when it comes to note making and learning in general. During this process of reflection you will draw together the different strands of research, consolidate your learning and create new ideas and opinions—and you will begin to understand how you can study most effectively. The ability to reflect upon the work you have done and how you have done it keeps you developing as a law student.

Reflection on your reading and research enables you to assimilate the knowledge that you have gained at every stage:

- Read back through your notes regularly and think carefully about their contents;
- Make sure your notes are readable and you understand them;
- Consider where more work or research/reading is needed, and identify whether you need to ask questions;
- Reflect on what you have learned and the different approaches and views you have explored;
- Use this to develop your own ideas and arguments about the subjects you are studying.

Finally, keep reflecting on the effectiveness of your research and reading:

- Are you able to find the material you need?
- Are you reading enough, and reading efficiently?
- Are you reading the right things, and in a sensible order?
- Are you making effective notes?
- Do you need to revisit research skills tutorials or re-do library exercises?

Explore your university or law school's study skills advice guides, and speak to advisors or your tutor if you need further support. Reading and research are essential to your success as a law student, so keep working on them. And of course reflection is important more generally to learning, as we'll see in relation to your law classes in the next chapter.

SUMMARY—HELP YOURSELF . . .

- **Remember the most important person in learning and teaching is you**
  - For successful learning—prepare, participate, assess, reflect.
  - Engage with any work set *and* the topic more generally—don't get in the habit of just doing the bare minimum.
  - Remember the importance of individual study and engagement.
- **Identify your own learning style and preferences**
  - Play to your strengths when developing your skills.
  - Don't assume you already know how you learn—look at things afresh as you start your legal studies.
- **Read efficiently and effectively**
  - Reading in law school in generally task-based. Think about why you are reading particular material.
  - Be selective in your reading: you don't always need to read a whole book or journal to get the relevant information.
  - Take time to understand what you are reading and develop your own ideas.
- **Research successfully**
  - Explore a variety of sources but focus on the most relevant
  - Use reading lists or textbooks as starting points then 'mine' for further resources.
  - Make use of the resources available to you: law library, library catalogues, internet, etc, but only use trusted and reliable sources.
  - Plan your time effectively to ensure that you have sufficient time for research and organise your material from the start.
- **Make useful notes**
  - Focus on key points that are relevant to your learning, not just everything you read or hear.
  - Reference any quotes or notes you make properly.
  - Experiment with note-making techniques to find what works for you.

9

TEACHING IN LAW—SEMINARS, LECTURES AND MORE

*'Personally, I am always ready
to learn, although I do not always
like being taught.'*

WINSTON CHURCHILL

INTRODUCTION

Every law programme will make use of a range of different teaching opportunities, with differing aims and approaches—all designed to help you learn. As we've seen in Chapter 8, during your legal studies you will engage in a great deal of individual study, but your law classes nonetheless play a very important role in your success. This chapter will look at the different classes you may come across during your legal studies, particularly lectures, tutorials and seminars, and how to get the best out of them.

Although many law schools take quite a traditional approach to teaching and learning, you may come across different approaches, such as problem-based learning, peer learning or clinical legal education. These may be found within individual modules or across the whole curriculum, and embedded in the teaching structure or just used to enhance a more traditional approach. We'll look at some of these forms of teaching and learning towards the end of this chapter.

To maximise the benefit of your law classes, whatever the type of class, or the style of teaching, you will need to keep in mind the importance of being an active and engaged participant in learning. The PPAR principles—prepare, participate, assess, reflect—that we looked at in Chapter 8 should guide your approach to all your learning.

UNDERSTANDING TEACHING IN LAW

Most of your law classes will fit one of three main types: lecture, tutorial, and seminar, although the names used for different classes differ between institutions. Even within these standard class structures, the types of teaching and learning can vary considerably. Sometimes classes may be quite traditional and teacher-led, others will be much more interactive and innovative, and may incorporate new teaching ideas and technologies.

Classes and contact hours

In most law schools the majority of subjects, particularly the compulsory modules, will be taught through both large group and small group teaching sessions. These are commonly timetabled weekly (lectures) and fortnightly (tutorials and seminars). Some subjects, particularly smaller optional modules, may be taught only through seminars, while research-based modules such as a dissertation or project (discussed in Chapter 14) will invariably have fewer timetabled sessions.

Classes will usually be timetabled across the full week, although Wednesday afternoons are often kept clear to allow for sports fixtures and the like. Occasionally small group classes will be arranged directly by the tutor rather than centrally timetabled.

Your timetabled class time is sometimes referred to as contact hours— as they involve teaching 'contact' with a member of teaching staff. For many students the number of contact hours provided is a significant factor to be taken into account in deciding on the merits of a particular law school or institution. It is a popular question to ask about at open days (see Chapter 2).

Of course, the amount of guidance and support you receive from lecturers and tutors is very important, and contact hours are a partial reflection of this. But the quality of contact and the availability of other guidance and resources are also important—as of course is the amount of time and effort you are prepared to put into your own learning.

Law schools vary in the total number of contact hours, the regularity and quality of that contact, the styles of teaching and how far individual or peer-supported study is favoured over traditional contact time. All these factors will influence how many hours of classes you have each week. Around ten to twelve hours per week of timetabled classes is fairly typical for a student on a full-time law degree programme, but there is a lot of variation between institutions, and from year to year depending on the subject options you choose.

Who does the teaching?

Classes, particularly lectures, will usually be led by a member of the law staff, ranging from senior professors to brand-new lecturers. You are more likely to see professors leading optional modules, or small sections of compulsory modules, based on their research area, than taking small group classes, but much depends both on the institution and the individuals. You might find your lecturer has years of experience in the subject—they may even have written the textbook—or s/he could be quite new to the subject. Don't assume one is necessarily better than the other!

Ideally you will experience lecturers from lots of different backgrounds, and with different styles and approaches—there is no single 'right' way of teaching, and you may find your own preferences differ from those of your friends. You may also be offered guest lectures from local practitioners or past graduates (alumni) from your law school. These can really add depth to your legal learning—as well as expanding your wider legal, social and commercial awareness.

Small group sessions may be taught by postgraduate students or part-time tutors as well as by full-time law staff. Postgraduate teaching assistants, often referred to as PGTAs or GTAs, are students who are teaching alongside studying for a doctorate (PhD) or other higher level degree. Part-time tutors will usually be doing a small amount of teaching alongside other jobs (usually they are solicitors or barristers).

Sometimes you won't even be aware that your tutor is a GTA or part-time tutor rather than a full member of the law staff because it rarely makes a difference in practice. GTAs are often particularly good tutors because they were recently undergraduates themselves, and can give lots of hints and tips to help you become a successful law student. Part-time tutors can often provide interesting practical perspectives on issues to enhance your understanding.

GETTING THE MOST OUT OF ALL YOUR CLASSES

The type of class and the style of teaching you face will differ according to your institution, and from module to module. But the same basic principles underpin your success—prepare, participate, assess, reflect. While the preparation you do and the way you participate will be different for every class, what matters is that you engage fully.

INSIDER KNOWLEDGE

'The most important thing to do is ask questions. Although finding the confidence to do so may be difficult, it is the most effective way of clarifying uncertainty and something I personally have always liked as it shows the student is engaging with the course.'

Richard Costidell, PhD Student and Assistant Teacher, University of Bristol

Adaptability

It is also very important to be adaptable. You will inevitably prefer some types of teaching and learning, and some lecturers/tutors. But don't simply reject other classes or teachers, or assume that they are of less or little value to you. Every teaching method and every teacher has something different to offer.

All lecturers and tutors—senior or junior, full-time or part-time—are individuals, with different teaching styles and approaches. So if tutor A tells you to prepare a question in a particular way, do so—don't simply continue working in the same way that you did last term with tutor B. If lecturer C expects you to read the relevant chapter of the textbook before the lecture, do so, even if lecturer D doesn't expect any pre-lecture preparation. Work with each lecturer and tutor to get the best from his or her particular approach and benefit from new skills and perspectives. Even if you don't particularly like one person's teaching style, this won't be a major issue, as you will be taught by lots of other people too.

It is also worth reflecting on why you prefer certain methods of learning. Is it because it plays to your strengths? If so, that is great, but that might mean it is not helping you to address any weaknesses or develop new skills. Other methods of teaching might benefit you more overall by developing your capacity to learn, even if they are harder for you to engage with at the start.

Or might it be that you find the method unchallenging, and so can relax and enjoy yourself? Enjoying learning is important but learning is not always comfortable. We all need to be challenged sometimes, to be pushed out of our comfort zone. So whatever you face, and however it makes you feel, get stuck in regardless—it is often not the most comfortable teaching and learning that leads to ultimate success.

Attendance

As a law student you are given a great deal of responsibility over your own learning. So, to some extent attendance at classes is a matter for you. But as we saw in Chapter 8, your classes make up an important element of your learning and you should take all the opportunities provided to you, even if at the time you'd rather be somewhere else. Engaged students are typically far more successful that disengaged students. If you need a more pragmatic reason for attending, remember that you are probably paying for your education, so you might as well get your money's worth!

I WISH I'D KNOWN . . .

'I wish I had known that the lectures give you a lot more information than just what is on the slides, therefore you would miss out on crucial information if you just studied from home.'

Charlotte Brown, Bournemouth University, LLB Law, Year 3

You may also find that you attract unwanted attention if your attendance record isn't good. Students who do not attend class are statistically more likely to do badly in their final assessments or to drop out of the programme, which are outcomes no one wants. So, attendance is usually monitored for small group classes and you can expect your law school or university support centre to be in contact if you do not attend. (Your law school and/or university will set out their own rules for attendance, registration, absences etc. Make sure you find out about them from your student or programme handbook.)

For overseas students, non-attendance can affect the validity of your student visa so the consequences can be particularly serious. But even for UK students, persistent non-attendance will cause you problems with your institution and may affect any later reference you need for work or further study.

Where attendance is not monitored, as is usually the case for large group sessions (lectures), you will not normally suffer any immediate consequences from staying away. The consequences for your learning are another matter. There are serious downsides to not attending classes and it is up to you to weigh up the benefits of attendance against more immediately attractive options.

INSIDER KNOWLEDGE

'Turn up—Attendance is the key ... even at 9 am on a miserable Monday.'

Jane Alice Murray, Legal Assistant, Local Authority

Of course there may be legitimate reasons why you can't attend—caring responsibilities, work pressures and more. Illness or unexpected disasters do happen. So occasional absences might well be unavoidable, and as long as you haven't missed too much, you will be able to catch up. Access any available material, work through it properly, and see if a friend is willing to share his or her notes with you.

If you miss a small group class or other monitored session then contact the tutor or law school, as advised by your own institution, as soon as possible to explain your absence. But if you find yourself missing classes frequently, or on a regular basis, you need to speak to your personal tutor as a matter of urgency to explore what can be done to help you stay on track.

If you know in advance you won't be able to attend a small group class, for example because you have an interview, then it is usually worth contacting your tutor beforehand. They may be prepared to let you attend an alternative tutorial group class for that week, so you don't miss out.

Don't just go along to an alternative class without checking with the tutor first—it isn't polite and there may not be space to accommodate extra students without notice. Where you can't attend a timetabled class on a regular basis because of another commitment then speak to your law school administrator. It is possible you may be permitted to change to a different class (if available), but only if you have a very good reason, such as caring responsibilities.

Law class 'etiquette'

Every class is a valuable learning opportunity, and one of the most important ways in which you will interact with fellow students and lecturers. But if you feel a bit unsure of what is expected of you when attending classes, we've included a few tips below. As you'll see, consideration for others and engagement in the learning process are all that is required—that way everyone is able to get the most from the class:

- **Coming and going**
  - Always aim to be punctual, and ready before the class starts. Otherwise you may miss the focus of the class, disrupt planned learning activities and disturb other students.
  - If you are late then join the class quietly and sit in the first available seat. In small group classes the tutor will appreciate an apology. If you have to leave unexpectedly, for example if you feel ill, then do so as unobtrusively as possible.
  - In small group classes, if you know in advance that you will be late or will have to leave early then let the tutor know.
  - Resist the temptation to start packing up before the lecturer/tutor finishes: it is distracting and you may find that you miss an important point or instruction. If a class is running over time you might need to alert the tutor politely to this. But don't set an alarm for the end of class—that won't go down well!
- **During the class**
  - Be prepared, with electronic devices charged or plugged in and pens and paper ready, so you don't have to hunt around for things during class.

- Remember you are still visible and audible, even in the largest classes. Don't chat to friends unless you have been asked to discuss a particular issue.

- Turn phone and email alerts off or to silent and don't use electronic devices for anything other than work during classes. If you decide you don't want to engage in a class, it is better not to attend than disturb others by not listening.

- If you want to record a class then you *must* get the permission of the tutor beforehand.

- Be a good member of the group. Join in, and allow other students to join in too. Help out by taking on a point if your classmate is struggling but don't interrupt if someone else is trying to answer.

- Be respectful of other students' right to express their opinions. And of course, you are free, indeed encouraged, to express politely your own contrary views.

- Try not to take offence at things others say—offence is rarely intended. If there is a problem then let the lecturer/tutor know at the time or after class so it can be addressed appropriately.

- Speaking to lecturers/tutors

  - Respect your colleagues and your lecturer/tutor, but don't feel intimidated or nervous and ask if you don't understand something.

  - Use opportunities given in class to ask questions: if you've got a question you can be sure that others have too.

  - While lecturers/tutors are usually happy to speak to you before or after class, time is often very limited so keep it brief and use office hours for longer discussions.

LECTURES

Understanding the format

Lectures are the main form of large group teaching in law. They enable lecturers to engage with large numbers of students at the same time. Even if you've yet to start your studies, you've probably got a good idea of what a lecture is, whether from previous studies or viewing lectures online. For example, the very popular TED talks (http://www.ted.com), are simply short, engaging, one-off lectures.

A lecture in law school can encompass any large group teaching session, usually led by a single lecturer. Depending on the size of the law school and the particular module studied, the group could range from ten to 500 students, although both extremes are unusual. As universities have expanded and law has become ever more popular, it is common to find classes of between 200 and 400 students for lectures in compulsory modules on undergraduate programmes.

Usually lectures last an hour. Typically this means fifty minutes in practice as time has to be allowed for students and lecturers to get between classes. It is also quite common in law to have a double lecture slot so the lecture will last two hours, often with a short break.

Depending on your institution and size of the class, lectures may be in a variety of teaching rooms. For a relatively small class such as a specialist optional subject, the lecture is likely to be in a standard teaching room, with seating at flat tables or work stations. But for larger classes, particularly compulsory subjects, lectures will take place in large lecture theatres. These can range from impressive ancient wood-panelled auditoria, where the back seats may be vertigo-inducing, to modern hi-tech spaces with comfy movable seats and power sockets.

Although lectures tend to look much the same, the format can vary. While commonly the lecturer will just talk to the audience, usually using PowerPoint or other visual aids, other lecturers will be more interactive, inviting questions and comment, requiring you to discuss issues with your classmates or giving you tasks to undertake. You may be encouraged to offer your view out loud, or some lecturers may make use of learning technology that enables the class to answer questions via phone, tablet or laptop. So don't expect every lecture to be just listening and taking notes, although there will be a lot of this.

What is a lecture *for*?

Law lectures traditionally focus on delivery and exposition of the law. A lecturer will often aim to provide a summary or framework for all the issues you are expected to be aware of as a base for your further reading and research. Other lecturers may look to provide in-depth analysis of a few particular areas of interest and difficulty with the gaps to be filled by your further reading and research.

Both aim to aid your understanding of the law and to interest you in the particular subject, by different routes. Lecturers may use a combination of both approaches. Modern lectures also often seek to develop your legal skills and understanding by engaging you more directly in tasks within the lecture space. A particular way of doing this is through 'flipped lectures' which we'll discuss later.

Lectures are often popular with students as a method of learning law, and this isn't *just* because they commonly involve less hard work than a seminar or tutorial! For example lectures can be valuable in providing an overview of a topic, and an introduction to more complex ideas. They enable a lecturer to explain and illustrate concepts in different ways. They provide the opportunity to introduce new developments in the law, and for you to ask questions.

Despite the popularity of lectures, it has been said that 'a lecture is the means by which the contents of the notebook of the professor are transferred through the instrument of the pen to the notebook of the student without passing through the mind of either'. This definition, sometimes attributed to Mark Twain, highlights a potential problem with lectures. Is it true that no one in a lecture room is engaging their brain at all—is there really no learning going on?

Well there is some truth in the statement, but it is based on the traditional view of a lecture as involving passive delivery and passive receipt of information. That is increasingly not the case in law teaching, which often utilises interactive teaching techniques and aims to inspire as well as inform. The 'definition' is helpful though because it reminds us that if a lecture is to go beyond simple transmission of information, it is essential that there is full engagement by both the lecturer and the student.

You can't do much about the approach of your lecturer—some are naturally more engaging than others. But while the lecturer is important, s/he is not the only person who influences the value of the lecture. It is the extent to which *you* personally engage with each lecture that is critical to maximising its learning potential.

Getting the most out of law lectures

Preparation

The better prepared you are for a lecture, the more you will get out of it. Preparation enables you to pick up more quickly on points made by the lecturer, see the broader picture and identify things that might be more complex or where you have questions. It puts you in a much better position to think as you listen and engage with the lecture at a deeper level, rather than simply creating notes on a new topic.

Occasionally a lecturer may not want you to prepare in advance, for example if they want to explore an issue of policy or critical theory with you from an entirely fresh perspective, but usually preparation will enhance your experience of a lecture.

Figure 9.1 shows some simple ways you can prepare for a lecture.

FIGURE 9.1: Basic lecture preparation

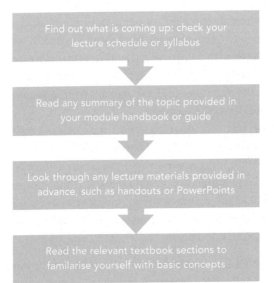

Find out what is coming up: check your lecture schedule or syllabus

Read any summary of the topic provided in your module handbook or guide

Look through any lecture materials provided in advance, such as handouts or PowerPoints

Read the relevant textbook sections to familiarise yourself with basic concepts

There is no need to try to understand everything—the lecture is going to help you to put all this in context and highlight the important elements. You are simply alerting yourself to the main issues and material. This will put you at an advantage over other students who are hearing about everything for the first time, as you will be in a better position to understand what the lecturer is saying and think about the concepts. All this helps to ensure the lecture is much more than just the transmission of knowledge.

For some lectures you will be given specific work to do in advance. This is usually some basic reading, such as a particular case, statutory provision or journal article. Less commonly you may be told to undertake a task such as preparing a summary of an article, or writing a mini-essay. This is much more likely if your lecturer takes an interactive approach.

Engaging with the lecture

To benefit from a lecture it is important to engage with what is going on. That means giving the lecture your full attention, not just turning up and hoping knowledge and understanding will magically transfer from the lecturer's head to your own.

Of course, it is easy to get distracted in a lecture. It is not like a smaller classroom where the prospect of being noticed or asked a question is usually enough to keep everyone pretty well focused. If you know you are easily distracted then turn off any notifications on your phone, tablet or laptop and keep off the internet. If you really struggle to avoid these temptations then consider only taking handwritten notes and keeping any electronic devices in your bag.

Quite apart from obvious distractions, it isn't always easy to maintain a good level of attention for a full fifty minutes, or longer. There is plenty of evidence indicating attention spans typically fall away after about fifteen to twenty minutes or so. Of course it is much easier to stay attentive if your lecturer is entertaining, and/or you have tasks and discussion within the lecture, but that won't always be the case. To help you to maintain your attention during the whole lecture, try:

- Actively listening to the lecturer—concentrate on the points being made, rather than letting it wash over you;
- Thinking about whether the approach is the same as in your pre-lecture reading, and whether difficult points have been clarified;
- Looking up regularly—don't spend the whole time looking down at your screen or notepad;

- Engaging with the lecturer as an individual—smile, nod, or look confused, as appropriate! This also helps the lecturer to gauge whether s/he is pitching the material appropriately, making it more likely that you can stay engaged;
- Asking questions if something is unclear;
- Making notes of key points rather than trying to write down everything;
- Creating diagrams of points as they are raised;
- Underlining important points;
- Coffee . . .

If you do find you have tuned out for a bit, don't give up listening. Just bring your attention back to the lecture and do your best from this point. Don't try to catch up by asking your friend or you'll both miss the next bit. Your friend might be able to help by pointing out where you've got to in a lecture handout though.

Note making in lectures

Taking notes during a lecture helps to keep you focused, and provides a record of points that you will need to recall later. We looked at note making in general terms in Chapter 8. The need to pick out important points rather than trying to record everything is particularly important in lectures—there is little thinking going on if you are just writing everything down, leading to much less valuable notes. And don't bother recording lectures to transcribe later on—a transcription of a lecture is not nearly as useful as individually created notes, and takes a lot of time to do.

I WISH I'D KNOWN . . .

'You do not have to transcribe your lecturer's words. Focus on the key points: what does a certain case stand for? What are academics saying about the said case? What are the contentious issues in this topic?'

Godwin Tan, University College London, LLB Law, Year 3

How you make your notes is up to you. The majority of law students now bring a laptop or tablet into lectures and make notes on screen.

Many students find this enables them to write down more than is possible by hand, and it can be helpful for organising your material. You can type your notes onto a fresh document, or add notes to lecture handouts that you've been given in electronic form, or use the 'Notes' page under PowerPoint slides to link your notes with specific parts of a lecture. Think about how best to make use of the material you've been given, and how you will find your own notes easiest to access later on.

Plenty of law students continue to make notes in the traditional way on paper—either using fresh paper or annotating printed material or slides. This can be easier to work with in cramped lecture halls, and there is some evidence that information is easier to recall when it has been written down by hand. It is also usually easier to highlight links and add in points when writing than when typing, or to present information diagrammatically, which provides more flexibility to your note making. Note making by hand tends to mean that although you may write less than when typing, what you write is more pertinent as you have to focus more clearly on the key issues. It is worth trying both ways of taking notes and seeing what works best for you.

When making effective lecture notes keep the following things in mind:

- Use whatever technique works best for you (laptop or pencil, linear or diagrammatic etc); try everything;
- Focus on recording key points and concepts;
- List points or create a diagram to show how things connect;
- Link together the law and the relevant authorities;
- Note any important cases, texts or articles that are mentioned that you might want to look up later;
- Make a quick note to yourself if you need to fill in more information later;
- Make sure your notes are labelled or stored sensibly so you can find them later and linked to the relevant lecture material;
- Review your notes after the lecture, making sure you can understand them.

Reviewing and reflecting

Make sure you build in time to review the lecture. You should do this as soon as you can after the lecture has finished, while things are fresh in your mind. That doesn't mean spending time rewriting your notes neatly. What matters is not producing beautiful or verbatim notes, but creating useful material, and reflecting on what was covered and what you need to do now:

- Revisit the lecture material and your notes, bringing them together into a single document if necessary;
- Read back through your notes ensuring you have understood the key points from the lecture;
- Summarise the main theme or key issues. This provides a reminder for revision purposes, and a useful check that you have grasped the essence of the lecture;
- Create an ongoing diagram of how the different lecture topics interconnect. Add to this each week to build up a full picture of the subject;
- Follow up connected reading. Read your textbook chapter carefully and explore relevant statutory material, key cases and pertinent articles, and add notes on these to your lecture notes directly or by cross-referencing;
- Follow up any areas of difficulty. If you don't understand a point, read about it in a different textbook, discuss it with friends or see your tutor.

Creating a dialogue

To get the best from a law lecture it can help to think of it as a dialogue, not a monologue. That might seem strange when the lecturer is the only one speaking, but ultimately a lecture is a learning process, and that involves more than one person.

So join the conversation—be prepared, think things through, listen actively, join in discussion, ask questions, reflect and engage. Remember that the value of a lecture doesn't come just from that single hour in the classroom—it comes from the work you do before and after the lecture too.

Lecture recording

Increasing numbers of law schools now record lectures, sometimes known as 'lecture capture'. This is usually organised centrally, although sometimes individual lecturers will record their lectures and make them available. Even where lecture capture is available, it is unusual for all lectures to be recorded—it is more common for compulsory modules.

The availability of lecture recordings can make it particularly tempting not to bother going to lectures. Why go to the effort of going to the lecture theatre, particularly for lectures early in the morning or late in the evening, or if you've got a long commute or an essay deadline to meet, when you can watch it later in your own time?

Lecture recording is undoubtedly a useful facility for some purposes:

- For catching up if you were too ill to attend a lecture;
- To pick up a point you didn't quite catch when it was made in the lecture, or when you can't quite understand your notes;
- If English isn't your first language and you need to take a bit more time to understand what the lecturer is saying;
- For revision as a refresher on certain topics.

But lecture recordings are a poor substitute for attendance for a number of reasons. Having a recording of a lecture is not the same thing as watching the lecture. Even with the best of intentions, once you have downloaded the recording, you may not get round to listening/watching. This gets increasingly likely the more lectures you have lined up to watch, so by relying on recordings you may miss out on learning opportunities. What's more, it is much harder to maintain concentration when watching a recording than when watching in person.

Connected to this, lecture recordings are passive—you do not have the opportunity to engage with the lecturer or ask questions. And while lecture recordings may be a reasonable (if imperfect) substitute for a classic lecture, they do not work well with the more imaginative class work that now often takes place.

Quite apart from teaching and learning, lectures also have an important social function in bringing you together with your classmates and lecturers—it is much easier to become isolated if you do not regularly attend lectures. So do make full use of recorded lectures if you have them as an additional support and revision resource, but we strongly recommend you don't use them as a regular substitute for lecture attendance.

INSIDER KNOWLEDGE

'I would advise all students to attend all lectures and seminars. Crucial documentation or information could be missed which could relate to topics covered in exams or assignments. That information that is missed may make a difference of 1% but could be the difference between getting a 2:1 or First Class Honours. Think about how much you are paying for your course and the amount of hours you spend with your lecturers. When you work out the value of each lecture or seminar, you will not want to miss anything.'

Gavin Teasdale, Solicitor, PGS Law LLP

'Flipped' lectures

Traditionally a lecture is seen as the starting point in the learning cycle for a topic, with deeper learning taking place thereafter. With 'flipped' lectures you will instead be given work to do *before* each session, with deeper learning taking place in the lecture itself. In the lecture you may work through problems using the reading you've done in advance, or undertake further tasks and discuss issues. The lecturer may move around the class, engaging directly with individuals and groups. Often use is made of learning technologies so that all students can participate easily, even in large groups.

You'll only get value from a flipped lecture if you both prepare fully and participate actively. So they aren't always popular because they are harder work than a conventional lecture. You might even feel you haven't been 'taught' properly because it is easy to associate learning with receipt of information. But you learn as much, and probably more, by discussing issues, testing your knowledge and practising applying what you know, than when you are simply absorbing information. Whatever form your lecture takes, go with the flow and work with the lecturer to get the best out of all your classes.

TUTORIALS

Tutorial or seminar?

In this section we are using the term 'tutorial' to refer to standard small group teaching sessions and 'tutor' to refer to the person leading the class. These classes are almost invariably offered alongside and supported by lectures. There is quite a lot of variety in what these classes are called—some law schools call these seminars, others tutorials, while others use names like workshop or supervision.

Traditionally *tutorials* were one-to-one classes between student and tutor for which the student would write an essay to be read, discussed and explored. In contrast *seminars* were larger group classes of up to about fifteen students, with more general discussion of series of pre-set questions. Over the years, these two concepts have become merged and the traditional one-to-one (or two-to-one) small tutorial has become much less common, other than in universities such as Oxford and Cambridge where the old tutorial system remains integral to law teaching.

Understanding the format

Tutorials aim to deepen your understanding of a topic, explore the issues and further debates, and enable you to practise using and applying your knowledge. Tutorial classes vary in size, length and approach, depending on the institution, module and tutor. Groups may range from four to twenty-five students, but most commonly involve about eight to twelve students. They usually last for an hour (actually fifty minutes), but may be longer.

You will usually be with the same students for all your tutorials for a particular module. Less commonly you may find yourself in the same group for all your modules in a particular year. This has the benefit that you really get to know your colleagues and may be more comfortable talking in front of people you know well. It is obviously less positive if you don't get on with someone in your group.

Tutorials are usually held in central teaching rooms, either in the law building or elsewhere in the university. Rooms are often set up with the chairs and tables in a horseshoe shape, to encourage class discussion. Or you might find tutorials held more informally in the tutor's office.

A tutorial will usually be designed around a particular topic within the subject, often recently covered in lectures. You will be given work in advance. This usually requires you either to undertake specific reading or select appropriate reading material from a wider reading list, and then prepare answers to set questions which often mirror the type of questions you might expect to find in the final exam. See Chapter 12 for how to approach different styles of law question.

In a standard tutorial you won't normally be expected to prepare full written answers for the questions. Instead you will be required to work through the issues arising in the questions, discuss the topic and respond to additional questions posed by the tutor or arising through discussion. You may be expected to answer individually, or discuss issues in small groups and share your conclusions. You won't necessarily work through the questions you have been set in order, and some may be covered in more depth than others.

You may also have discussion on the topic more generally and explore other connected issues not directly covered in the questions. Your tutor will often guide you on how to answer questions of the type you've been set, as well as on the law and context more generally.

Quite what you do, and how you do it, will depend on the tutor's own preferences and style. Rather than standard questions, tutors may set a variety of tasks to engage you in the topic and develop your skills, from reading and discussing an essay you've written, to evaluating other people's work, presenting on an issue to other students or working through a selection of material to advise an imaginary client (problem-based learning, discussed later in this chapter).

Getting the most out of law tutorials

Preparation

It is essential that you prepare fully for tutorials. Tutorials are not like most lectures, where you can get something out of the experience even if you have not prepared. Tutorials are designed to be interactive, with tutor and students working together to draw out and develop understanding, and apply knowledge and understanding to a range of issues and problems.

That means you'll need to answer questions, think about issues you might not have thought about explicitly before, work through new scenarios, contribute to discussions with your tutor and classmates, and support and justify your views. You can only do that if you have prepared.

That does not mean just reading through your lecture notes before the class. Preparation for a tutorial should take you several hours—ideally the equivalent of about one working day per tutorial—of serious work. And while reading is important it is not sufficient. Even more important is thinking about the issues and reflecting on the state of your knowledge and understanding. Preparing for a tutorial encompasses a number of steps, illustrated in Figure 9.2.

FIGURE 9.2: Effective tutorial preparation

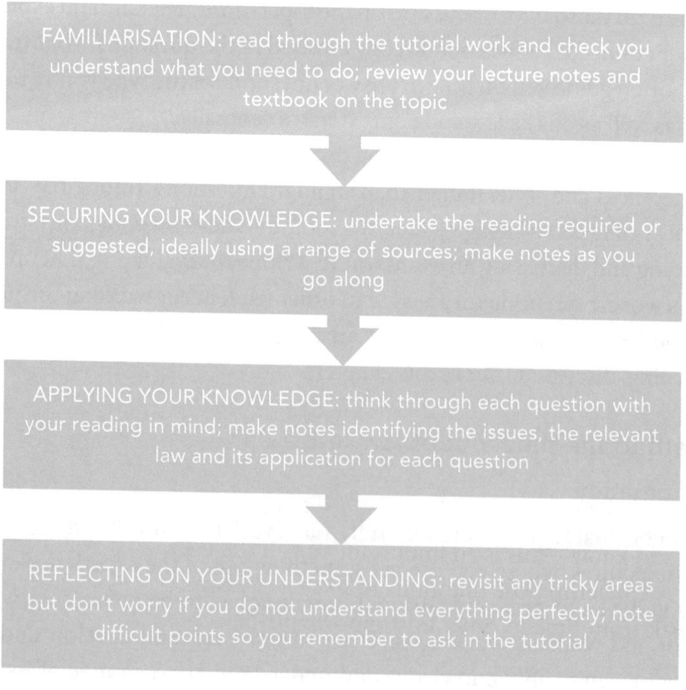

FAMILIARISATION: read through the tutorial work and check you understand what you need to do; review your lecture notes and textbook on the topic

SECURING YOUR KNOWLEDGE: undertake the reading required or suggested, ideally using a range of sources; make notes as you go along

APPLYING YOUR KNOWLEDGE: think through each question with your reading in mind; make notes identifying the issues, the relevant law and its application for each question

REFLECTING ON YOUR UNDERSTANDING: revisit any tricky areas but don't worry if you do not understand everything perfectly; note difficult points so you remember to ask in the tutorial

Preparation is key to learning successfully in tutorials. If you do not prepare you cannot participate, and if you cannot participate, your learning opportunities will be significantly curtailed. A lack of preparation also impacts on your fellow students, who miss out on learning opportunities from interaction with you.

I WISH I'D KNOWN . . .

'There really is no point in attending a seminar/tutorial if you haven't prepared for it. You will also sit there the entire time praying that the tutor won't pick on you. So make sure you do your preparation!'

Emily Barrett, University of Bristol, Law with Study in Continental Europe, Year 4

Tutors do not expect you to be expert in every topic. The tutorial is a learning environment, where you are free to make mistakes and ask questions. But tutors do expect you to make an effort. In the university environment turning up to a tutorial unprepared is simply unacceptable and some tutors will either ask students who have not prepared the set work to leave the class, or will notify the student's personal tutor.

Engaging with the tutorial

Getting the most out of a tutorial is not just about preparation. Even a well-prepared student will not get much benefit from a tutorial if they sit passively. It can be tempting, particularly if you lack confidence, to treat a tutorial like another lecture, just writing down things the tutor or other students say. But this really isn't the function of a tutorial, and is not the way to get the most out of it. Joining in is essential.

Sometimes you will have little choice about participation because the tutor will ask you questions directly, and you need to be willing to answer. Even if you are not sure of the answer, try to work it through from what you do know—this is an important part of the learning process. Other tutors prefer to pose questions to the group, but expect all students to speak from time to time. It is important that you do. Not only does it enable you to test your own knowledge and understanding and receive feedback, but it also develops important skills of communication.

INSIDER KNOWLEDGE

'There is a simple correlation between those students who participate in discussions and complete the tutorial prep—read the cases, prepare draft answers to tutorial questions, or even just highlight the legislation—and those who do better in the final exam. It gives you the opportunity to ask questions of your own, clarify interpretations of the law and generally take a weight off your shoulders.'

Edward Burtonshaw-Gunn, PhD student and Land Law Tutor, University of Bristol

Of course, some students are more shy than others, and can find it really difficult to speak up. This is true of students from all nationalities, but it can feel particularly strange for those who have come from very different educational traditions. However nervous you feel, or however alien it seems, it is important that you engage with the learning—don't let nerves stand in the way of your success.

Try answering a basic question first, to get used to speaking up. Or even start by asking questions if there is something you need help understanding. Gradually you will find it easier to contribute more fully, and join in discussion and express your own views. This is an essential part of developing your understanding of a topic, and learning to question, challenge and analyse—all things that enable you to reach the higher marks in law. As a side benefit, a tutor will be more willing to write a reference for you later on if you have participated effectively in class; not only are they more likely to remember you, they will be able to say positive things about your approach to learning.

It is increasingly common for students to bring their laptops or tablets into tutorials. This is generally fine but can create a barrier to engagement. Open laptops effectively create a wall between students and tutor. Suddenly it feels easier to hide, and more nerve-racking to breach the wall by speaking. What is more, having your laptop can make it feel that you should be trying to type whatever the tutor says, and some students seem to think this is the right thing to do. It isn't, so don't fall into this habit. The tutorial is a testing ground—you need to be thinking, talking, listening and practising—and you can't do that if you are typing.

If you really find it easier to access your notes on screen, then you probably do need your laptop, but just use it for that purpose. If you are

using the laptop for anything else, then get rid of it for tutorials. Bring in notes in paper form, look up as well as down, and really engage with what is going on. Don't worry at all if you find you don't make many notes, the learning in tutorials is about much more than note taking.

Reviewing and reflecting

Tutorials are, or should be, quite an intense learning experience. You need to find time to review and reflect on them. Just as with lectures, try to do this not long after the class, while things are fresh in your mind:

- Revisit the tutorial questions, making sure you have identified all the issues arising and relevant law;
- Try again. If the tutorial showed that you'd taken a wrong approach, work through the question again;
- Clarify any difficult points by re reading your textbook or trying a different book;
- Catch up with any reading you didn't do but now realise is important;
- Follow up connected reading and read any additional material your tutor recommended;
- Make notes on the key points from the tutorial, and from further reading.

A really good exercise after tutorials is to attempt to write an exam-style answer to one or more of the questions you covered. You will have good awareness of the topic, and now have the benefit of the guidance and further analysis from the tutorial. Activities such as this enable you both to cement your learning on a topic to get the most out of the tutorial, and to practise relevant skills.

Many students claim they don't have time for such an exercise. Of course you are busy, and have new classes to prepare for. But it needn't take long: just allow yourself the time you'd have in an exam, commonly forty-five to sixty minutes per question. If you don't feel revisiting a tutorial question provides you with enough challenge then look through past exam papers for your subject, or a textbook or Questions & Answers book, to find a question on the tutorial topic, and do this instead. The practice alone is worthwhile, but ideally then evaluate your own work, checking whether you've covered all the points and explained the law and its relevance clearly. Your tutor may well be willing to have a quick look over your work too, during the time set aside to see students, if you want reassurance.

SEMINARS

Understanding the format

As we've seen, in some institutions, 'seminar' is the term given to standard small group teaching sessions that are supported by lectures—what we've called tutorials and discussed under that heading. And some institutions may use the term seminar just to indicate that teaching groups are a little bigger than a standard tutorial—perhaps fifteen to twenty students—although the essence of the class is still much the same.

However, the term 'seminar' is also used for classes designed to replace both lectures and tutorials. This is particularly common in modules involving smaller numbers of students. These kinds of classes are often longer than either a tutorial or a lecture (two or even three hours) and will usually be held weekly or fortnightly. They may be small groups of under ten students or as large as fifty students, but twenty to thirty students is typical. You will almost invariably be given reading to do before the class, and will be expected to prepare work that will be discussed in, or will inform, the class.

The flexibility of a longer class with a relatively small group means that seminar work can vary a lot between modules, and even from week to week. It may involve, at least in part, a lecturer instructing the class, but typically involves much more student discussion than a lecture, and often more wide-ranging debates than a tutorial. Seminars also often require students to present to the group on particular aspects of a topic, either individually or in small groups. Other students (those not presenting in a particular week) will be expected to respond formally or ask questions, to enable further analysis of the issues.

Seminar classes are often held in more flexible workspaces, sometimes with students sitting round small tables, to facilitate group work. However, depending on available rooms and the size of your class, you might also find yourself in small lecture theatres or larger standard teaching rooms.

Getting the most out of seminars

Preparation and engagement

To get the most out of seminars you need to prepare well and engage fully—just as for lectures and tutorials. Both these things are perhaps particularly important for seminars. From a practical perspective, the size of a seminar group makes it difficult to hide, as you might be able to do in a lecture. And the nature of a seminar is such that simply absorbing information passively isn't really possible. If you don't both prepare and engage, it is likely you'll find the class of limited value.

I WISH I'D KNOWN . . .

'At first I had no idea how to tackle a seminar so I did not attend any of them. Don't do this. Just ask for help, as staff are more than willing to help. They understand that the university experience at first may seem a little daunting and everything is new. They are more than happy to help.'

Isabel Anderson, Aberystwyth University, LLB Law, Year 3

Preparation requires you to undertake all the work you are given—reading, questions, other tasks. As for tutorials, secure, apply and reflect on your knowledge and understanding. If you are going to be presenting then it is essential that you are fully prepared so you learn from the experience. You will also benefit from the further discussion and analysis that a good presentation will trigger. While presenting might be a bit daunting at first, you should view it as a great opportunity to engage really deeply with an element of the course and develop additional skills.

Even if you are not presenting in a particular seminar, preparation is still really important. That is because you need a good base of knowledge and understanding prior to the seminar if you are to be able to understand the discussion, respond to the presentations of others and develop your ability to analyse and apply the law. If you are not prepared then at best you will leave the seminar having picked up a basic level of knowledge, but at worst you won't have understood anything because everyone else will be discussing matters at a higher level.

Seminars are often longer classes, so it is important to keep focused and engaged throughout the class. Preparation helps here too as it makes it possible to listen actively—make notes, think of questions, compare approaches and so on. If nothing else, remember that you may be called on to respond to another student's viewpoint or presentation, so stay alert.

Time management

Time management when preparing for seminars can be an issue because activities tend to be more diverse, and your role may change from class to class. It is important therefore to check your timetable and syllabus, and see what is expected of you from week to week.

In some ways, it is not very different from tutorials, in that you need to allow for plenty of time to prepare for every class. But with seminars you may not have the support of lectures, so may need more time to ensure you have the basic points clear in your mind before moving on to more complex issues.

You will also need to build in more time if you are presenting, as this inevitably takes more time, or should do, if you do it well. Where you are working in groups, you will have to allow time for group meetings, and will need to liaise with your colleagues to timetable those well in advance.

DIFFERENT TEACHING METHODS

There are lots of different ways of teaching law. The full range of teaching methods can be, and often are, incorporated within classes bearing the traditional names of lecture, tutorial and seminar. But sometimes certain approaches to law teaching are made central to a particular module or law school. This section looks at some particular approaches you might come across instead of or alongside more traditional law teaching.

I WISH I'D KNOWN . . .

'You will encounter different teaching methods—some might be more suited to you than others, but nonetheless even if you are not enjoying a particular teaching style, you should persevere for at least a while.'

Fiona Lin, University of Cambridge, Law, Year 3

Team-based or peer learning

Law students are often quite independent in their outlook and learning approaches. But the ability to work in groups is an important one for any future career, developing wider skills beyond university and legal practice. And working together has the potential to enhance your learning.

Much learning at university has a component of peer learning—for example through discussion or completion of a specific task in a small group within a class. However, team-based learning (TBL) is further embedded within the curriculum, with cooperation and engagement with other students central to the learning process.

TBL thus envisages students working together outside the classroom as well as inside. There are typically fewer lectures, but more small group sessions both with and without staff input. Students work together to research and present topics and answer questions, learning from each other and stimulating further discussion and learning.

With TBL the tutor's role is more to guide discussion and assist in identifying problems, rather than to 'teach'. This can be unsettling if you are more accustomed to listening to a figure of authority than working with your peers, and requires trust in both your colleagues and the tutor. Student perceptions of TBL can vary markedly, and much may depend on your experience in a particular learning group. There is no doubt that working with others, and being interdependent in your learning, can be both rewarding and, at times, difficult. Much of the advice in Chapter 12 on group assessment applies also to TBL.

I WISH I'D KNOWN . . .

'I wish I had known how difficult it was to motivate everyone and get people to pull their weight as that can be a huge burden, however, if you have a good group you will love working in a group as you will learn so much more than you think you will.'

Charlotte Brown, Bournemouth University, LLB Law, Year 3

Problem-based learning

Problem-based learning (PBL) approaches the study of law through simulated legal problems. At one level, this happens in traditional tutorials where many questions are typically problem-based, but PBL embeds this further into the learning process.

With PBL, materials for study will typically mirror documentation that might be seen in practice, such as letters, forms or witness statements, as well as more conventional law reading lists. This way you learn to identify the issue(s) from 'real' material, see how issues connect, and you can see how your reading relates to real legal problems. A particular set of facts may be added to as the course progresses, with new material and more issues being added to incorporate new topics, or entirely new simulated disputes may be brought in.

PBL is flexible. You may find it within lectures, tutorials or seminars, or encompassing the whole teaching cycle. Most typically in law it is used within tutorials/seminars, with more traditional lectures providing the knowledge framework underpinning the PBL.

Although PBL does not necessarily require working in groups, in practice law PBL is almost invariably based on teamwork—sometimes with an outside legal professional as a mentor—because this echoes the reality of much legal practice and other work, and develops wider skills. As such PBL typically shares many of the benefits and potential drawbacks of team-based learning, and the two concepts are not always clearly distinguished from one another.

Clinical legal education

Clinical legal education (CLE) is more commonly a distinct module within a law programme, rather than encompassing the whole legal curriculum. With CLE you learn, at least in part, by actually 'doing' law, not just discussing and writing about it. The learning will be based around a law clinic or other legal advice centre, or supervised case work with another organisation. Law clinics and advice centres tend to offer basic legal help, advice and support to individuals who might otherwise not be able to access legal advice. You will therefore be interacting with real people with real problems. Alternatively, CLE may be supported by simulated examples rather than real clients, or with a combination of both.

CLE is quite different from traditional law teaching methods, but just as, if not more, demanding. It actively engages you in the learning process, and with the wider community. It focuses more on legal skills, activities and values, including the complexities and ethics of legal practice, than on subject-specific learning. However you will also have to undertake legal research when dealing with particular problems, often in areas of law with which you are not very familiar. You will also have to engage with a wide range of materials when considering wider issues and preparing for assessment. There is often a strong reflective element to CLE work, as well as the challenge of dealing with clients directly, so it is far from an easy option.

If you are not offered a module based on CLE as part of your law programme, or do not select it as an option, you may still have the opportunity to work with a law clinic or other advisory centre as an additional voluntary activity. Activities of this nature—often referred to as 'pro bono work'—are considered further in Chapter 18.

Socratic teaching in law

A way of teaching often associated with law is the Socratic method. You may be familiar with this, particularly if you have watched films about law schools in the USA, where it is an established approach to law teaching.

Socratic teaching is highly participatory, with the lecturer posing series of challenging questions to individual students in the class. There is no chance of sitting passively simply hoping to absorb information in a Socratic class. Students are 'put on the spot', so they are forced to develop their thinking and apply their knowledge. The rigorous process enables the student, and the class as a whole, to work through issues, develop and deepen their understanding and recognise the complexities of an issue.

However some students undoubtedly find it intimidating. Socrates said: 'The only true wisdom is knowing you know nothing'—but realising this in front of all your classmates can be unsettling!

In fact in UK law schools, Socratic teaching is not very common. In many large group sessions you will not be asked any questions at all, while in others questions will be posed simply as things to think about. Even in more interactive sessions, it is very rare for lecturers to require individual students to answer. While smaller group sessions tend to be more Socratic in approach, they remain typically collegiate and supportive. Law classes should and will be challenging and stimulating, but not intimidating.

SUMMARY—HELP YOURSELF . . .

- **Supplement what you've learned in classes**
  - Individual study and engagement are critical to successful learning.
  - Don't limit your learning to specific tasks or timetabled events.

- **Always prepare well for classes to get the best out of them**
  - Check your course information for guidance on how you'll be taught and speak to current students to ensure you are well prepared.
  - Recognise that different classes engage you in different ways and will require different levels of preparation.
  - Don't underestimate the time you should be spending on preparation.

- **Make the most of what you have**
  - Attend and participate in all your classes.
  - Be open and adaptable to new ways of working and don't expect every class to be the same.
  - Don't rely on lecture recordings as a substitute for attendance, and catch up on any missed work.
  - Develop your note making skills and practise different techniques to find what works best for you.
  - Think actively about issues and problems and try to work things out—don't use 'I don't know' as an instinctive response.
  - Be considerate of others' views and needs.
  - Reflect on what you've learned to get full value from each class.

10

THINKING LIKE A LAWYER: CRITICAL THINKING AND LEGAL ANALYSIS

'It is not so very important for a person to learn facts.
For that he does not really need a college. He can learn
them from books. The value of an education in a ... college
is not the learning of many facts, but the training of the mind
to think something that cannot be learned from textbooks.'

ALBERT EINSTEIN

INTRODUCTION

You may be familiar with the phrase 'thinking like a lawyer'—it may have come up at a law school open day or when looking at degree choices. If not, you will almost certainly hear it during your first term of law school. Thinking like a lawyer is—to a great extent—about thinking critically and analytically.

As well as teaching you what the law is, a core part of legal education at university is developing the ability to assess, question, reason and evaluate. The successful law student must analyse, critique and criticise.

Learning the law is not just about remembering principles, cases and statutes. It is about applying these things to specific problems and considering the consequences. It is about questioning and evaluating legal principles, balancing different viewpoints and approaches, and recognising complexities and uncertainties. It is about thinking beyond individual cases to consider the suitability of law in the world around us, both generally and within specific contexts. Law is not just the study of law, but also its relationship to society, other institutions and jurisdictions, culture and art, business and economics, and many other parts of our daily life.

As we discussed in Chapter 5, law is pervasive and the successful law student needs to be able to place the law in context, analyse its effects on different parts of society, apply these rules to different problems and reflect upon the suitability of both individual laws and the law as an institution. This ability to think critically and undertake broad and deep legal analysis is important to becoming a lawyer, but is also valuable for any other career.

In this chapter, we explore the importance of critical thinking to the law degree and beyond, and look at how you can bring analysis and criticism into your work. With this in mind, this chapter will explore techniques for problem solving and for essay writing, and the importance of constructing arguments balancing 'content' and 'thought.'

CRITICAL THINKING

What is critical thought?

Critical thinking is defined as the 'objective analysis and evaluation of an issue in order to form a judgement' (http://www.oxforddictionaries. com). This applies to the study of any subject, but it is particularly important in law. It can apply to the theoretical study of the law and in its application to problems. Critical thought may not always end in a concrete answer, but by raising more questions and identifying further points to consider, it enables you to work your way towards finding a solution or developing a reasoned and nuanced conclusion.

Critical thought is vitally important to the study of law and assessing the impact of laws on society. A key part of critical thinking is thinking as an individual and having your own thoughts and opinions, and developing your own views and arguments. Rather than gut feelings, prejudices or pre-conceptions, this is about reaching considered views based on exploring the evidence, facts, theories, the opinions of others, principles and alternative options. Or at the very least being able to justify your initial gut feeling!

Opinions and argument

You will need to recognise the difference between opinions and argument. An opinion is your own subjective and personal view on something, whereas an argument is a logical idea that you support with evidence.

Now, an argument may grow out of an opinion and your opinion may very well change after being exposed to differing arguments. The two are inherently interlinked. But you must be able to understand the difference between someone presenting an argument and someone presenting an opinion. Opinions are valid, but evidenced and reasoned arguments are what we need to develop as lawyers. We are asked to develop arguments around chosen topics, explore all potential perspectives and develop our own logical conclusions. This can stop us from sitting on the fence, and allows us to inform our opinions with evidence.

You will already have views and opinions on lots of things, and a successful law student develops the confidence to formulate views and opinions on the law and its impact. So critical thinking in law is not about presenting and explaining the views of others, although you should take these into account, but about developing your own reasoned thoughts.

Developing critical skills

Think about a recent news story, or an opinion piece you've recently read or watched. Did you agree with what happened, or the opinions given? Entirely? What facts or evidence would need to change to make you agree or disagree with the actions taken or opinion given? What consequences, negative or positive, might flow from what has happened, or if the writer's opinions were followed? What would you do differently and why?

Questions like this provide a starting point for critical enquiry rather than simply accepting something at face value. It is this that leads to critical thought.

I WISH I'D KNOWN . . .

'I wish I'd known that my opinion actually matters! I thought studying law was all about learning rules, reading cases and using them to answer problems. But it is more than this. I learnt really quickly that I'd have to be able to think carefully about whether these rules were actually good or bad. One of my modules was all about how the law works in society, and I realised that I held some strong opinions that often went against what the law says.'

Anonymous, University of Plymouth, LLB with Business, Year 2

However, critical thinking is not just looking for argument for argument's sake or questioning things at random. There has to be a point to it. In university, critical thinking is about getting as close to the truth as possible. This includes challenging preconceived notions and your own ideas about subjects.

Being a critical thinker

Critical thinkers don't just accept things, but question why this is the case and look for evidence to support these arguments before entertaining them as true (or close to the truth).

I WISH I'D KNOWN . . .

'It is perfectly fine to disagree with leading academics on certain issues as long as you are able to justify your standpoint.'

Godwin Tan, University College London, LLB Law, Year 3

Critical thinkers don't just describe the law, but explain why this is, or may not be, the case, and evaluate their own and others' arguments.

As we saw when looking at developing critical thought, critical thinkers use probing questions to interrogate the facts. These can be simple questions like what, how and why, and these can lead to more difficult questions: what consequences might there be if it was a different way? Why should it remain the same or change? Why is this important? However simplistic this might seem, it is this ability to question that will make you a successful law student. Some points to think about are shown in Figure 10.1.

To be a good critical thinker:

- Position yourself in an argument
  - You will need to examine a number of sides to different arguments, whether in essays or problem questions. But avoid sitting on the fence: it is not about just 'on the one hand . . . but on the other hand . . .', you need to take a view.
  - It is important to recognise different possibilities, but then put forward the best argument based on your material and evidence and position yourself within it, reaching a conclusion based on the evidence.

FIGURE 10.1: Critical questioning

WHAT?	• What should the law be on this matter? • What consequences are there for different people? • What would happen if the law was different?
HOW?	• How did we get to this position? • How has the law changed, if at all? • How could we do it differently?
WHY?	• Why does this law matter? • Why has the law changed? • Why should we consider changing the law?

- Imagine getting an essay or tutorial question such as 'Human Rights are being abused by criminals and wrongdoers'. Clearly you need to think about what this statement is saying, and what evidence there is for this, and indeed why it is saying it (the context). So you might want to consider the deportation of terrorists to places that condone torture or the recent prisoners' campaign for voting rights. You will need to explore the varied and numerous sources relating to this. However, you will also need to consider why this might *not* be a good thing and support this with evidence. Importantly you need to make an objective assessment based on the evidence, and position yourself in this argument. This may or may not be in agreement with the statement; you might even argue the statement doesn't go far enough, goes too far or is based on a false premise or misconception—keep thinking and questioning.

- **Develop your own argument**
  - As you explore critical questions and the evidence that will help you answer these questions, you will start to formulate your own views, which may or may not be the same as those you started with. You may also begin to develop arguments that you have not read—your own arguments. Use them!

- Developing your own arguments based on the evidence you are using, or extending or challenging the arguments of others, is key to being a good critical thinker and a successful law student.

- **Balance content and thought**

  - You need to show you know and understand the law, but as a critical thinker, don't just dwell on the details. Describing the law, or the facts of a problem is not enough, you need to balance this with thought, analysis and evaluation.

  - That doesn't mean you should disregard the basics. Some students can be so keen to show their critical thought that they forget to explain the law. Balance the evidence with your own argument and thoughts.

Considering the wider picture

As a critical thinker in law you will learn always to question the law, its suitability and applicability to the facts of any problem before you and how well it serves the people for whom it has been formulated. What are its aims and does it meet them? Don't just accept that the law is what it is—the successful law student questions the law presented to them and thinks about its value and appropriateness.

INSIDER KNOWLEDGE

'Law covers all areas of modern life; you become an expert in random and niche areas of society. I expected to learn law and I learned so much more about modern day life.'

Damien Seddon, Paralegal, Woodfines

A decision in a case can have positive and negative impacts on the individuals in the case, but also on the wider law and on business and society. Similarly legislation can be both beneficial and detrimental—and different people may experience it in different ways.

Imagine if a court held that tobacco manufacturers were responsible for ill health from smoking; or that the government banned the sale of all tobacco products. This might be a good idea for public health, and many people might benefit. But there would also be a great number of people negatively affected. Does the potential damage to people's health justify infringing their freedom? What about the economic impact of those decisions, on business, employees, the health service, insurers and so on?

Thinking like a lawyer involves considering the wider picture, as well as whether what is done is legally possible—and this is so whether considering 'little' questions such as interpretation of contractual terms or 'big' questions such as the death penalty or a Bill of (Human) Rights. As a law student, learning points of law and engaging with judgments and legislation is only a part of your study; engaging with larger, more pervasive issues is also really important. So think critically, question the law and challenge preconceptions.

So far, we've been focusing on the big issues—what should the law be, why and how? These are the things that we tend to think of in terms of 'critical thought'. But there are other important questions about the law, often based around which points of law are related to the facts we are considering, whether the law is clear in this area, or how the specific point of law will apply to the facts in front of us. This aspect of critical thinking is often called legal analysis and we will discuss this next.

LEGAL ANALYSIS

What is 'analysis' in law?

During your legal studies you will often hear reference to analysis (or legal analysis). This can be a difficult concept to define though. The practising lawyer may see analysis as the process of understanding the facts of a specific situation, appraising the law that is relevant to those facts, and applying it appropriately whilst being mindful of the outcomes.

The academic lawyer may view analysis more as the appraisal of various conflicting legal principles and their effects on society, or the theoretical examination of the law and its relationship to other theories and concepts. To some it will be a combination of both, or even more besides. Many law students struggle to understand what analysis is, even though it is included on many marking criteria in law schools and is undoubtedly a fundamental part of legal study.

Questioning and evaluation

Analysis has at its core the ability to question, evaluate and come to a conclusion on the information you are exploring. Careful consideration of the material you are investigating begins this process of analysis.

Analysis requires you to study strengths and weaknesses, assess good and bad. In law, this may be the strength or weakness of a legal principle, specifically with how it relates to the problem you are trying to explore, which will impact on the outcome. Exploring whether a legal principle is good or bad for the individuals or groups it serves may support or justify your conclusions and enrich your argument. You can see clearly here the link between analysis and critical thought.

It is important to understand that in this context we are not talking about good law in the legal sense. You may hear the phrase 'good law' a lot during your studies, and this generally means a legal principle that remains supported by the leading authorities (ie the court decisions or statutory principles) on the particular issue. But in this context, we are looking at how the law works for society and the people it serves. So 'good law' is not necessarily *good* law; it might be bad for society, or sections of society. For example it is 'good law' that abortion is available, within set limits, but some people may see that as very bad due to their personal, religious or ethical beliefs, or, conversely, bad because of the restrictions currently imposed on that right.

Analysis is all about taking your learning from description to something more. As Einstein said in the quote that opened this chapter, anybody can learn facts, but it is the ability to think critically and analyse all you learn that is important. Legal analysis involves a multitude of things, including:

- Identifying the legal issue behind a problem or set of facts;
- Understanding what law governs that particular legal issue and where the law is, or might be ambiguous, unclear or uncertain;

- Applying the law to the facts, recognising the (often subtle) differences between the current facts and how the law has been applied previously;
- Reasoning logically to find a solution where the law is unclear;
- Exploring different legal arguments and evaluating their likelihood of success;
- Considering the wider consequences of the application of the law from multiple perspectives, including its impact on individuals and wider society, and the strengths and weaknesses of the law as it stands.

It is this application and analysis of your legal knowledge and the ability to recognise subtle differences and consider alternative arguments and possible consequences that will demonstrate you can think like a lawyer. Analysis and application, coupled with critical thinking about the law in a wider sense, makes you a successful law student and problem solver.

INSIDER KNOWLEDGE

'I imagined that law was about knowing the answers to legal questions. In fact, I found that there are rarely black and white answers, and that it's usually a case of 'on the one hand … but on the other hand' (that's why so many cases get to court—different lawyers have different answers, and only the court can give a final answer).'

David Willingham, Retired, formerly Head of Risk Financing at Save the Children

Analysis and criticism

We are sometimes asked, usually by students reading feedback on their essays, whether there a difference between analysis and criticism. Well, yes, but you probably don't need to worry too much about it! Better to think about what you need to be doing, rather than be concerned about how to describe it. And if you are thinking critically, you'll be doing a bit of both.

A colleague explains the difference in the following way: analysis is packing things into boxes; criticism is taking them back out again (with thanks and acknowledgements to Dr Aurel Sari). That is rather a clever explanation. Of course it is incomplete as a definition, but it helpfully highlights that analysis requires you to identify things and see how they fit together, while criticism is more about challenging conceptions and questioning previously accepted notions (and possibly finding some new boxes). It is hard to criticise effectively and convincingly without prior analysis. Ultimately, though, if you are thinking about the issues, the law and the wider context, you don't really need to worry about whether what you are doing is technically analysis, critique or criticism.

INCORPORATING ANALYSIS AND CRITICAL THINKING INTO YOUR WORK

Analysis and problem solving

Legal analysis is often related to problem solving. It is obviously linked to *applying* the law, and the term 'application' is sometimes favoured by markers when dealing specifically with problem-based questions, but it is still about analysis of the facts and law. Much of what you do during your law degree will be based around problem solving, and it is this skill that sets law graduates apart from many others. Employers like graduates who can problem solve in a logical and critical way.

In this section we will look at a four-step approach to problem solving that can help you break down individual issues, interrogate the law, then apply it and develop a conclusion. You'll meet this approach again in Chapter 12 when we look at assessment skills.

You may have already heard the term IRAC, or ILAC. This is a step-by-step process for examining issues in problem questions, and it can also encourage you to analyse the law more generally and effectively. Some law lecturers may ask you to address problem questions (either generally or in certain subjects) in slightly different ways, but, if not, IRAC is a good place to start when developing your skills in legal analysis.

You may be able to follow these steps for a whole problem, but this is not usually very effective. It is usually much better to break the problem down into individual issues and deal with them in turn, so applying IRAC for each issue.

FIGURE 10.2: Understanding IRAC

Figure 10.2 shows the basic steps of IRAC, which we also explain in more detail:

- **I—Issue**
  - The first step in your legal analysis revolves around accurately identifying the legal issue(s). So you need to state what the question of law is, and where there is more than one issue, break these down into individual questions to address.

  - Most problem questions in law school will have more than one legal issue, so identify and deal with these separately. Similarly if you are advising different people or looking at the potential liability of different individuals, you should usually deal with them separately—there is more advice on answering problem questions generally in Chapter 12.

  - It is important to remember that identifying the legal issue is not the same thing as restating the facts of the problem, which is a common mistake. You need to explain what issue of law the facts give rise to.

- **R—Rule (sometimes expressed as L—Law)**
  - The next step is to identify and explain the legal rules that relate to the issue you have just identified. You need to focus on the law that is applicable to the issue at hand, don't just recite all the law in a specific area. This shows that you really understand the law, and enables you to be precise in your application.

- An important part of being a successful law student is identifying which rules—whether statutory principles, judgments or treaty provisions—are relevant to the issue and which are not. You will need to explain what the point of law or principle is and the source for this rule, ie the authority. This is also where you should identify any conflicting decisions from different courts and use judgments as appropriate to expand upon any statutory principles.

- You should be clear as to what is the most authoritative decision on a subject, remembering binding and persuasive authority, and the position of the court issuing the judgment in the court hierarchy.

A—Application and Analysis

- This step is where you will develop the rules you outlined earlier and apply them to the facts at hand. You will need to analyse the decisions and principles you have identified and differentiate between conflicting decisions in order to apply the most accurate and effective of these to the facts you have been given. You will need to argue why a particular decision or principle applies to your case, or why it may not. You might need to distinguish cases, explaining why they shouldn't apply in this particular scenario.

- You should interrogate your own argument too, and assess both sides of the argument, as a lawyer would do, to come to the most likely and accurate conclusion based on the law and the facts in your problem.

- You may also wish to analyse and evaluate some of the wider issues in a particular area if relevant to the problem, bringing in some secondary scholarship to support your argument. Sometimes the law must be followed, but you can still argue that the law has been criticised, and put forward arguments as to why it could, and should, change.

C—Conclusion

- The final step is the conclusion on the issue at hand. You may argue that the facts in the problem and the state of the law mean that the likely outcome is fairly certain, or you may need to explain that conflicts between cases or uncertainties in the law leave the matter wide open. Even here though you should explain which outcome you think is most likely (or most justifiable) and why.

- However balanced you think the arguments are—and you may find they are quite evenly balanced—try to avoid conclusions that just say 'it is up to the judge to decide'.

- You might also need to make the point that additional facts are needed to be able to conclude clearly on the likely outcome, but explain what facts and their significance.

- It is crucial that you conclude on the issue you have been exploring, don't avoid it or get distracted. If you find you really can't reach any kind of conclusion on an issue then you need to revisit the first three steps.

When it comes to developing these skills, practice is all important. You may have specific sessions on problem solving and legal analysis built into your degree programme, but practising problem solving by answering tutorial questions is also really valuable. This allows you to practise your legal analysis regularly within the context of individual subjects, and get feedback from your tutors. It is also worthwhile to explore some past exam paper questions, and develop your methodology for legal analysis.

Analysis, critical thought and essay questions

Obviously, you will apply your skills of legal analysis and critical thought in essay questions and discussion type questions too. However, IRAC does not work as well for these types of questions and some students find another system more helpful. That is CEEO. We'll touch on CEEO again in Chapter 12 on assessment.

CEEO encourages you to evaluate specific positions more directly and allows more scope for you to develop your own opinion based on the evaluation you have undertaken. Some students like to use this to structure their whole essay, while some use it for specific arguments within an essay. It can be helpful as a starting point for structuring your whole essay or discussion, but do remember to think about all these points

FIGURE 10.3: Understanding CEEO

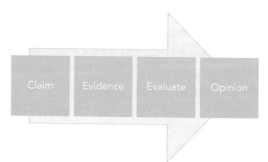

within individual sections of your essay too. Figure 10.3 shows the basic steps of CEEO, which we also explain in turn:

- C—Claim

    - This is the first step in approaching an essay question. What is the claim being made by the statement or question and what are the claims that can be made in support or against the question being asked?

    - Most essay questions present you with a presupposition which you will be asked to explore. The example we gave earlier was 'Human Rights are being abused by criminals and wrongdoers'. It is your job to discuss this.

    - Remember that although the question may present what looks like a single claim, it will incorporate a number of different elements, all of which need to be considered. The claims you consider should be both those that support and those that counter this argument. For this question example just given, you might wish to start by outlining that this is a view held by a number of people, and then develop your counter-claims that you will explore. The claim should be the opening point of your argument, the idea that you will interrogate.

- E—Evidence

    - You must present evidence to support your claim or a specific claim in your essay. This may be cases, legislation, commentary

234

from secondary sources such as books and journal articles, or any other reliable sources that you can use to develop your argument.

- This evidence should help you explain your claim, support the proposition put forward and allow you to state clearly how you have come to this assertion.

- E—Evaluate
  - The next step is to evaluate. This is where you will interrogate the claim you have made and the evidence presented to support this. You may use sources that contradict your original claim and you may develop a number of counter-arguments to your claim. These may not be as persuasive as your original argument, or they may be far stronger.
  - It is during this evaluation step that you will undertake a careful and considered analysis of your arguments and evidence. This will lead you onto making an objective judgement in the final step, the opinion.

- O—Opinion
  - Opinion here does not necessarily mean your own personal opinion, it may simply be a reasoned conclusion on the strength of a claim following your evaluation. It can give you the opportunity to present your own argument but most important is to present an objective, well-informed and considered opinion on the question you have been asked.
  - This should be the result of your analysis and evaluation, and be based on the evidence you have presented. This opinion should normally be expressed in the third person, for example, 'It can be argued here that . . .' rather than 'I wish to argue . . .'.
  - These concluding remarks are key to showing that you can follow through to a logical conclusion based on the evidence you have presented.

As you read through these points, you can probably see how this could provide a structure for your whole essay or discussion, or how you could follow these points for individual arguments within an essay. Much may depend on the particular question and the various points you need to address, and also what works best for you.

Like the analysis needed for problem solving, the only way to develop this skill is to practise. You may already have experience of writing essays through previous study, but focus now on developing that balance between description and analysis, content and thought. It is common to find this difficult when you start out.

Remember that you are not just telling the reader what the law is, or just offering two clear alternative points of view; consider why the law is what it is; how it got there, what it is aiming to do and where it should go next. Don't be afraid to disagree with the status quo and keep thinking critically.

CRITICAL THINKING AND ANALYSIS FOR THE FUTURE

Your future career

Lawyers need to be critical in order to solve problems and construct arguments. Being able to see different solutions to a problem is clearly very valuable when instructing a client.

It is essential to be able to develop rational and logical arguments based on thoughtful considerations of different viewpoints, and to be able to examine evidence and come to a logical and objective conclusion. Generally, critical thinkers also develop an excellent ability to strategise. By being able to see multiple viewpoints and considering numerous potential outcomes, critical thinkers are able to make the correct, or at least the best possible, decision.

Critical thinking and the ability to analyse complex ideas is valuable for any future employment, not just legal careers. In most jobs you will need to question things, think critically and solve problems on a daily basis. Many employers particularly like law graduates for their questioning minds, and their ability to examine evidence objectively and present logical conclusions. They also like the way in which law students can problem solve—spotting issues, evaluating options and finding solutions. Remember this when you are applying for positions!

Social awareness

While being a critical thinker is important for law students, lawyers and employment, it is also important more generally. We think you can even describe being a critical thinker as being an important life skill.

Particularly in the emerging age of 'fake news', social media headlines and 'click bait', it is important to be able to consider the validity of sources, think critically about the subject and evaluate evidence independently. You don't have to view everything negatively, but be able to ask thoughtful questions about the source and its supporting evidence.

You will develop all these skills as you progress through your programme, so do as much as you can to develop them as you go. Don't be afraid to question everything. Look at the strengths and weaknesses of different arguments, and be sure to think about the big questions as well as the technical points of law. That way, by the end of your law degree you will be an expert problem solver and a critical thinker, with excellent skills of analysis.

SUMMARY—HELP YOURSELF . . .

- **Be a critical thinker**
  - Don't just describe the law, be sure to question it, using What, Why and How.
  - Position yourself within the arguments you are exploring and where possible, develop your own arguments.
  - Balance content and thought throughout your legal studies.
  - Try to reach objective conclusions based on the evidence you have presented.
  - Be sure to think more broadly too by looking at how the law affects or can affect society.

- **Develop your skills of legal analysis**
  - Study strengths and weaknesses, assess good and bad. Keep questioning and evaluating, and push yourself to reach a conclusion.

- Remember that to analyse in law you will need to identify issues and the relevant law, apply the law to a situation, reason logically to reach a solution, explore different legal arguments and consider wider consequences.

- For techniques to encourage analysis, try IRAC when problem solving, and CEEO for essay writing.

- **Take these skills forward**
  - Reflect upon your skills of problem solving, critical thought and legal analysis and think about their use in future employment and more broadly.

  - Use examples from your studies to enrich your CV and job applications.

PART 4
SUCCESSFUL ASSESSMENT
Making the most of assignments,
assessments and feedback

11

COMPLETING ASSIGNMENTS: CORE SKILLS FOR ASSESSMENT

'. . . we exceeded expectations just by turning up for the exams.'

GEORGE WEASLEY,
in 'Harry Potter and the Order of the Phoenix' by J.K. Rowling

INTRODUCTION

Assessments are important. But lecturers can sometimes get a bit frustrated if they feel they are only ever being asked about assessments, or how to get a particular mark. That is because a legal education isn't all about assessment. Learning and education are important in their own right and should not just be viewed as a means to an end. Lecturers do genuinely believe this, we promise: there is undoubtedly benefit and pleasure in learning and stretching yourself intellectually, regardless of how that learning experience is going to be measured.

Nonetheless, we think it would be rather unrealistic to tell you not to focus on assessments. After all, even if you agree that learning is beneficial in its own right, your aim is to achieve a law degree or other legal qualification. Particularly when you are putting a lot of time, effort and money into your education, it is understandable that you will focus to a great extent on achieving the best possible return from that investment in terms of the visible end result.

In this chapter we will consider some general points and core skills for success in your law assessments. By success, of course we mean achieving the best you can at the time you take that assessment. Because the topic of assessment is so important, it stretches over several chapters—in the next chapter we will look at specific skills and tips for particular types of assessment. You will probably find it most helpful to read this chapter first for an overview of assessment and core skills, and then turn to other chapters for guidance on preparing for specific types of assessment as and when you face them. Advice on coping when assessments don't go well can be found in Chapter 15.

LAW ASSESSMENTS

Formative or summative?

During your legal studies you will undertake both *formative* and *summative* assessments. What is the difference, and does it matter? Figure 11.1 explains the key differences.

FIGURE 11.1: Formative or summative assessment?

Formative assessment	Summative assessment
• Any piece of work that contributes to your learning • Usually refers to a formally set piece of work where you get feedback and, usually, a mark, but the mark does not count towards your final grade in a module or course • Examples: non-assessed essay; mock exam	• A piece of work where the mark you get will count towards your final mark for the module and/or course • Examples: exam; assessed essay • For assessments other than exams, sometimes referred to as 'assessed work' or 'coursework'

You might see the term 'assignment' used instead of or alongside 'assessment'. This term most commonly refers to formative assessments, but it could refer to summative assessment, or to any piece of set work whether formative or summative, so make sure you check how it is being used if you come across it in your course.

From formative to summative, and on again

A simple way of considering the relationship between formative and summative assessment is pictured in Figure 11.2. This shows that even though the marks for formative assessments are not used in the calculation of the final grade, formative work feeds into the skills and/or learning needed for summative assessment, where the marks do count toward the final grade.

FIGURE 11.2: Formative and summative assessment

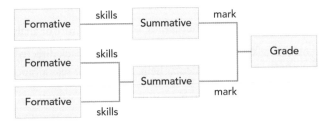

From a teaching and learning perspective, it is undoubtedly *formative* assessment that is the most important part of your education. That might seem surprising, and we understand if from your perspective it feels as if only summative assessment really matters. Of course that would be right in terms of the calculation of your final grade. But it would be too easy to follow this through to a conclusion that formative assessment doesn't matter and so not to bother engaging with a formative exercise when there are other things going on—it seems far too much effort for something that 'doesn't count'.

In our view that would be a big mistake. The more formative exercises you undertake, the more opportunities you get to test your understanding, develop your skills and receive feedback—and therefore enhance your performance in summative assessments, whatever form those take. Remember that formative assessments are designed by the people who know your course requirements the best—the very same people who will be setting and marking your summative assessment(s). It is therefore essential that you take formative assessment seriously, and don't just focus on assignments where the marks 'count'.

To make best use of formative assessment:

- **Take up all the opportunities you get**
  - It is better to have a go even if you are short of time and get some feedback, than miss out entirely. Make sure you use all formative opportunities, whether that means writing an essay for submission or preparing fully for seminars and tutorials.

- **Reflect on other formative work**
  - This may be formal set work that you have already completed such as essays or presentations, or informal work such as tutorial discussion.

- **Focus on particular areas of weakness, such as structure or analysis**
  - If you can, ask your marker specifically for feedback directed to an area where you need particular help, guidance or reassurance.

- **Practise skills you will need for a summative assessment**
  - Depending on the nature of your summative assessment(s) and your own learning needs, this could include analysis and critical thinking, referencing, essay structure, or writing coherently at speed, for example.

What is more, as Figure 11.3 shows, summative assessments throughout your studies also have formative value for future assessments. Keep

FIGURE 11.3: Building on assessments

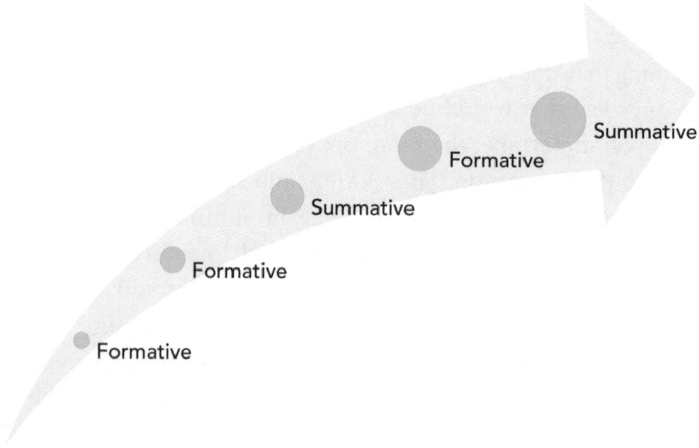

building on what you learn at each stage in your studies and don't just forget about an assessment when it is complete. A big part of this is through making use of feedback, which we consider in Chapter 13.

So it *does* matter whether your assessment is formative or summative. Only marks for the latter will count towards your final mark. And formative assessments will commonly be optional and have less stringent submission or presentation requirements than a summative assessment. But this does not mean that only summative assessments matter, and the guidance we give you on approaching law assessments applies to all your assessments—whether summative or formative. The successful law student approaches every assessment as if it counts. It does.

How many assessments will I have?

Most law schools will assess each module separately: you will have distinct assessments for each subject you study. Quite how many assessments you have will depend on various things, including the number of modules you study, the learning and teaching arrangements, the type of assessment and the credit value of modules.

You will have plenty of formative *opportunities* in every module, but not all will necessarily be obviously formative *assessments*. Formative opportunities include things like tutorial work, peer-discussion or working through an online sample essay. As far as formative assessment is concerned, most modules will offer you at least one opportunity to submit a formal essay or equivalent piece of work for individual feedback. You may have more.

Summative assessment for each module may be a single assessment, such as an exam or project; or two or more assessments, such as an essay plus an exam, or a presentation plus a reflective report. Less commonly your programme may use 'synoptic' assessment. This means that more than one module will be combined for the purpose of assessment. This can help you to make connections between subjects and may reduce the number of separate assessments you do.

However many assessment points you have, and whether assessment in your law school is separate for each subject or combined/synoptic, don't forget that formative and summative work in one module will still aid your learning in other modules.

THINKING ABOUT ASSESSMENT

Reflecting on your assessment experience

Whatever your current position and educational background, you will have had lots of experience of assignments and assessments. This may be very recent—you may be feeling distinctly over-assessed by this point, if you have recently completed school or college. Or it may be back in what feels like the distant past.

Your experiences of assessment will of course influence how you feel about upcoming law assessments. If you've always done well in assessments and haven't found assessment to be a particularly stressful experience, you might be feeling quite confident. That's great, although don't be over-confident as you do need to develop further and different skills for law assessments. On the other hand, if you've had negative experiences, whether recently or in the past, you might be feeling pretty apprehensive, and it is important that you don't allow this to impact too much on your legal studies.

Think briefly about your past experience of assessment to check if there are any areas where you know you should be prepared for potential problems. These could be as diverse as getting overly anxious before or in exams, or procrastinating when faced with an essay, or not working effectively within time limits.

Aim to address any issues that have troubled you in the past well before any assessment is due—whether by seeking advice, taking up training or counselling opportunities, or practising particular skills. It is much harder to acknowledge issues calmly, let along take up opportunities to deal with them, when assessments are actually bearing down on you. Don't dwell too much on past difficulties though. The same problems will not necessarily recur—we all change in our attitudes and approaches, and law assessments will be very different from other assessments you have taken—but of course it pays to be prepared.

INSIDER KNOWLEDGE

'Know your own personality. . . . If you have done all you can to prepare in good time this should help.'

Hazel Stones, Retired secretary/PA

Timed and non-timed assessments

We will look in more detail at particular assessments in the next chapter, but a more general and important difference between assessments is whether they are timed or not. You will have a set time in which to complete any assessment, but the time you are given could range from one hour for a short exam, to two weeks for an essay or eight months to complete a dissertation.

By 'timed' assessment we mean the kind of assessment where you have only a short period of time in which to complete the work—usually an examination. 'Non-timed' assessments are those when you are given a longer period of time to complete them, such as an assessed essay where you might be given several weeks from the time when the essay title is released to when you have to submit your work. There are of course also assessments that include elements of both, such as an advocacy or negotiation exercise, where you are given the information in advance to prepare, but have to turn up and deliver at and within a set time.

Although you will need to take different approaches to timed and non-timed assessments, in truth the key skills you need for both overlap to a great extent, and the advice in this chapter generally applies to both. However for timed assessments, while your preparation in terms of studying and revision goes on in advance, everything else has to be compacted—so planning your answer has to be done at speed, and you will need to reflect and self-edit as you go along. These things take some skill, and there is really no substitute for practising timed assessments to develop these skills. If you are on a course where all (or nearly all) your marks will come from examinations then this is particularly important.

Non-timed assessments offer different challenges—foremost amongst them the difficulties of managing your time when you have lots of other commitments to balance, and the potential to unsettle yourself by discussing with friends how much they have done. But they also offer you the chance to reflect on and develop your work over a longer period which can be very beneficial. The level and type of stress you may feel will also differ between timed and non-timed assessments, and you will know best how you react in such situations. It is worth exposing yourself to similar experiences as much as you can so that you can learn to manage this.

PREPARING FOR ASSESSMENT

You might view some of the points we are going to make in this section as rather obvious. They are—or at least should be. But our experience shows that they are points that too many students forget when preparing an assessment—probably because they are rushing, or because they think they already know what to do.

Know what is required

Before starting work on any assessment you need to make sure that you know *exactly* what is required. That means reading all the information you have been given, including the assessment rubric. The 'rubric' is the set of instructions that apply to the assessment, including things such as when the assessment is due, how long it should be, any formatting requirements etc. It is essential to read the rubric carefully and in full. That is true even if most of the information appears to be the standard assessment information that you've seen on other assessments.

If you don't read it carefully you may make a serious error or make an incorrect assumption about when or how you need to submit your work. Often late submissions for summative work attract serious penalties. If something has happened that is going to make it difficult or impossible for you to meet a submission deadline for summative work, or if you have particular educational needs that need to be taken into account when preparing or submitting work, then you need to speak to the relevant person in your law school as soon as possible. Check your own programme or law school guide for what you need to do.

Similarly, it is surprisingly common for students to answer the wrong number of questions in an exam because they did not read the instructions carefully, leading to a significantly lower mark than they would otherwise have obtained. So read through the rubric carefully, whether in an exam or coursework, and ensure you know what you need to do. And when preparing coursework, read the rubric carefully again both during the preparation of the assessment and shortly before submission to make sure you haven't misremembered the instructions or accidentally mixed up the instructions for two different assessments.

So, before even thinking about the specific question/s you've been set, make sure you are clear about what you need to do and when you need to do it by. Check any general rules, for example in any student or course handbook, as well as the specific rules for the assessment. If there is a discrepancy that hasn't been explained, check with your tutor or module leader which you should follow. It is common for quite severe penalties to be applied for things such as writing over a word limit, or not following formatting requirements, or forgetting a required element such as a bibliography, so it is in your interests to get all this clear before you start.

I WISH I'D KNOWN . . .

'I wish I'd known how to stay within the allocated amount of words. Go over the word count then you will get penalised.'

Andrea Garvey, Swansea University, LLB Law Single Honours, Year 2

Another element of ensuring you know *exactly* what you need to do involves spending time considering the question(s) you've been set. How long you can do this for will depend on the assessment: not long in an exam! But whatever the assessment, it is an essential stage of initial preparation.

Don't assume you know what the question is about: read it through several times to ensure you don't head down the wrong path. If the assessment is coursework rather than an exam, then it can be a good idea once you think you've correctly identified the topic to do some quite basic preliminary reading just to check your first inclinations were correct.

Reflect on your skills

Initial preparation also involves making sure your skills are up to scratch more generally. Check back through any work you've already done, whether formative or summative, and spend some time addressing any areas of weakness.

One area of particular importance is communication skills. It is not at all uncommon for students to drop marks because of lack of clarity and precision in their writing. Communication is of course the gateway to success, because however strong your knowledge, understanding and other skills and abilities might be, they count for little if you can't communicate them effectively.

This is something you can work on long before any particular assessment. Practise your writing whenever you can—don't just take notes, also practise writing essays, case notes and mini-explanations. Self-evaluate your writing critically, and also seek feedback from friends and tutors.

If English is not your first language then writing clearly can be a particular challenge when writing for law assessments because precision is so important. Nearly all institutions will have language support units, while some offer courses or drop-in sessions specifically aimed at international law students. It is really important that you make use of these and any other opportunities you get if you might benefit at all from any improvement in your English skills. Don't assume that passing an English language test at an acceptable level will be entirely sufficient to equip you for academic and legal writing, and don't be embarrassed to ask for a bit of help. Similarly make sure you've practised skills such as referencing, so you don't lose marks for something you could have really easily worked on in advance.

Understanding assessment/marking criteria

For every assessment you undertake, you should be provided with, or have access to, assessment or marking criteria. These are the things against which your work will be judged, so are really important, but are surprisingly often overlooked by students.

Assessment criteria should tell you each criterion that is being assessed, and will usually focus on particular competences and skills (eg Understanding, Analysis, Numeracy, Presentation), rather than the content you should include. Each criterion should include some explanation or an indication of how each criterion might be demonstrated, or you should be told where to find more information on the criteria, so you know what is meant by the terminology used.

Assessment criteria should ideally also indicate what is expected of you in relation to each criterion for both achieving a particular grade (eg first, 2.1, 2.2 etc) and your level of study (eg Level 4 (first year), Level 6 (final year)), but not all assessment criteria provide this much detail. Even very basic criteria are still useful to indicate what factors your marker must consider in reaching an overall mark or grade for your work. If you don't know what factors a marker is taking into account, it is very difficult for you to know what things you need to do or improve to get a better mark.

I WISH I'D KNOWN . . .

'I wish I had known that you do not have to provide a ground-breaking original view in any written work. You should have some originality and criticism in your essays, but it does not have to be radical. For problem questions, criticism can be included but the focus is on accurate application of the law.'

Fiona Lin, University of Cambridge, Law, Year 3

There is inevitably some fluidity in the concepts appearing in assessment criteria, but the gist should be clear. You will become more familiar with the requirements as they apply to your legal studies as you progress, provided you engage with the criteria and your feedback. If you do have real difficulty in understanding what the criteria mean, and how they relate to each other, then ask for more guidance from your module leader, if it relates to a specific subject, or your personal tutor for more general help.

Bear in mind that the assessment/marking criteria that could apply to your work might include, in order of increasing specificity:

- University marking criteria
  - These are often called 'generic criteria'.
  - They tend to be quite general as they have to apply to the whole range of different degree programmes but should at least show you what your University expects of you in order to achieve particular degree classifications.

- Law marking criteria
  - These are criteria applying within a law school to law modules, and may be quite detailed, or fairly brief.
  - Law marking criteria are often more useful than university generic criteria as they can focus on things that are really relevant to law, although they can't be too specific as they have to cover all law assessments.

- Assessment-type marking criteria

  - Your institution or law school may use marking criteria that relate to a particular type of assessment, eg essay, problem question, poster, presentation.

  - These types of marking criteria often focus on specific skills relevant to the assessment in question, and may be provided for each of the whole range of different types of assessment or only where the assessment is of a less common type, such as advocacy or negotiation.

- Assessment-specific marking criteria

  - These are the most specific of marking criteria as they apply only to a particular assessment. They may provide guidance on the content of the assessment in very general terms as well as more general traits.

  - Often, if you are given assessment-specific marking criteria, these will be additional rather than stand-alone criteria, so you need to have regard to either university generic criteria, or Law marking criteria as well.

  - Another possibility is that instead of detailed assessment specific marking criteria you could simply be told of any additional criteria that apply to your assessment, or which of the generic criteria are considered particularly important or unimportant for your assessment.

If you do not know what assessment/marking criteria apply to your assessment, and still don't know after reading the assessment rubric and your course handbook or equivalent, then ask your tutor or module leader. It is essential that you know what your work will be marked against if you are to prepare effectively.

Keep the assessment criteria in mind when working but particularly when reading back or reviewing your work. By taking the time to self-evaluate your work in relation to the assessment criteria you have the chance to identify areas of strength and weakness even before submission. This allows you to modify your work and improve your chances of success accordingly.

GETTING STARTED: PLANNING AND PREPARATION

Preparation and planning are essential if you are to achieve your potential in every assessment. Just as you wouldn't consider taking a driving test without lots of practice (well, we sincerely hope you wouldn't!), so you should never consider taking a law assessment without lots of preparation.

It might be tempting to get straight down to writing but you will do much better if you spend time planning and preparing your work. It is the things you do in planning and preparing your work that make up most of the core skills you need to master to be successful in assessment.

How much time is there?

Obviously you can only prepare and plan if you have allowed yourself time to do so. Time management is therefore essential (we discussed time management more generally in Chapter 4). Quite how much time you've got and how it needs to be managed is of course dependent on the nature of the assessment. This may mean:

- Ensuring you think about an essay as soon as you get the assessment title;
- Setting aside days for research and writing plenty of time before a deadline;
- Not leaving revision until the week before an exam;
- Committing to five minutes at the start of an exam to write an answer plan.

Whatever the form of the assessment you are facing, you need to allow an appropriate amount of time for preparing and planning your work. If you have coursework to do, you need to factor in time for preliminary reading, thinking about the brief, researching points in depth, writing, reflecting, rewriting, editing and referencing. You'll appreciate that this really can't be done effectively in a very compacted period of time, so you need to start early and take things steadily.

Structure

The planning stage is also really important in helping you to produce an effectively structured piece of work. Structure is critical to a strong piece of work in law. A good structure clearly identifies the issues and leads the reader through them clearly and coherently in order to reach a logical and reasoned conclusion. Without a strong structure, even the cleverest thoughts can get lost. We'll explore this more in the next chapter when looking at essay writing and other similar assessments, but it is important to emphasise here that the planning of every assessment requires a great deal of thought about structure.

Thinking and visualisation

An essential early stage in your planning process is to think long and hard about the question you've been set or the brief you've been allocated. Read it several times to identify the nature of the assessment, the topic and issues, and identify any particular constraints such as the length, or the way in which information must be presented.

It can be helpful straightaway to start jotting down ideas and see how they connect. If you are really feeling at a loss you may need to do some preliminary reading on likely topics just to help you locate the relevant areas. Don't spend too long on this, you want to start connecting your thoughts directly to the assessment as soon as you can.

Most people find it really helpful to visualise the work in some way, so organise your jottings in a way that works for you—a 'spider diagram' for example, or a simple linear skeleton plan. Spider diagrams, often better known now as 'mind maps', are often the most helpful visualisation process as they allow you to connect issues and join in new points easily, and can be used for all sorts of different assessment formats.

There is no need to produce something beautiful, and only you need to understand it. In fact the messier it is the more willing you may be to modify it, or even scrap it and start again, and this is one of the most important parts of planning. Once you've got a good sense of the basic issues you can fill in more detail as your research and thinking progress, and then translate a messy diagram into a more workable plan.

Research

You need to undertake appropriate independent research for your assessments, and the expectations on you in this regard will increase as you continue your legal studies. In your first year, it might be expected that you will only move a short way from the safety of primary sources and the main textbooks, perhaps considering in addition to these only a couple of key academic articles or reform reports. But as your skills develop, your markers will hope and expect to see that you have consulted a larger amount and wider range of materials, and will be particularly pleased if you have managed to find interesting quality sources beyond any course reading list as this indicates your growing research ability. We've looked at reading and research in Chapter 8.

But it is essential too that you *engage* with your sources to some degree. This means not simply citing the material, but showing you have thought about it, perhaps by considering the merits of an argument, or assessing the practical consequences of a reform proposal. You might want to look back at the points we discussed in Chapter 10 on critical thinking and analysis.

Of course the type and level of research will differ according to the type of assessment you are preparing. What is important is that you demonstrate that you can locate pertinent sources, both primary and secondary, and are able to make use of them appropriately.

Preparing your work

Preparation continues after the planning stage, as you have to translate your plan into a finished piece. This means continuing to research the points you have identified as important, while also starting to write the essay, problem answer, or whatever other form of assessment you've been given. Even less traditional assessments such as presentations or posters will need you to prepare them and put your thoughts into writing in some form.

We would strongly recommend combining the research and writing stages, at least to some degree. It is inadvisable to start writing in earnest too early as you need to have formulated and reflected on your ideas a bit. If you start writing too early you may inadvertently limit your research and analysis. However if you wait until you've completed all your research before starting to write, you might not leave enough time for editing, and you might not spot new issues or complexities that often seem to appear only as you try to formulate an argument. You may also feel overwhelmed by information if you leave writing until you've read absolutely everything you've found.

Writing, rewriting and editing

Even the most accomplished legal writers would struggle to write a convincing and polished piece in one go. The writing process is not a one-off event, whatever the format of the assessment. (The exception is obviously an exam, where you do have to produce a finished piece pretty much in one attempt, which makes the brief planning stage particularly important.) A successful outcome in non-timed assessments is therefore highly dependent on rewriting.

It can be painful to revisit work that you have put a lot of effort into, but rewriting and ruthless editing is an essential skill to engage with. It is only by reworking your initial thoughts that you can really develop your ideas and express them as effectively as you can.

Don't be afraid to ditch a sentence, paragraph or even whole piece of work that isn't working, or change a structure or approach if your ideas have moved on. You can always move material to a separate document if you are concerned you might decide you want to use it later. Provided you've been managing your time effectively, there should be enough time for you to work through several development stages, each one of which should move you closer to a more polished final effort.

I WISH I'D KNOWN . . .

'Even if essays are assessed, do not waste too much time in making sure they are perfect—after all, there are many other components to your law degree, so you may sometimes need to limit your perfectionism.'

Fiona Lin, University of Cambridge, Law, Year 3

Referencing

It is essential that you reference your sources properly in law assessments. The level of referencing will depend on the type of assessment—the very basic details will be sufficient in an exam, while in coursework you would normally be expected to reference fully, following an accepted legal referencing format, and include a bibliography listing all the sources you have used.

You will need to include a reference whenever you use material or ideas that are not your own and go beyond common knowledge, for example:

- Making a statement of law;
- Using someone else's diagram, statistics or research findings;
- A quote or paraphrase;
- A summary of a view or statement;
- Adopting a writer's argument, opinion or ideas.

Referencing is essential to:

- Support your work by giving authority for your statements of law and comments;
- Show the range of your research;
- Ensure you acknowledge the work of others and avoid plagiarism (see later in this chapter);
- Allow a reader to locate and evaluate your sources, and confirm or question your statements.

Different law schools may follow different referencing systems, and you need to become familiar with your system as soon as you can. If you are not given a specific referencing system to use in assessed essays and similar assessments, a good one to use is OSCOLA. More information can be found online, with a handy reference guide at: https://www.law.ox.ac.uk/sites/files/oxlaw/oscola_4th_edn_hart_2012quickreferenceguide.pdf. You can read more about different referencing styles and see examples in law study guides such as Finch and Fafinski's *Legal Skills* (2017). Whatever the system you use, remember that your references must be:

- **Complete**
  - Provide all the necessary information—follow the referencing system.
  - Include the precise page number when you are referencing particular passages or comments.

- Acknowledge the source you have used (eg a textbook) as well as the original source (eg a case or article) if you have not used the primary source directly.

- Accurate
  - Check your references are correct and up-to-date, don't just cut and paste references from elsewhere.

  - Ensure references align with the correct text—it is easy to find they have moved around during subsequent formatting or when moving text.

- Consistent
  - Whichever referencing system your law school prefers, stick to it. Follow the same approach throughout your work.

While preparing your essay remember that you need to keep very good notes about your sources and the location of material you are using. While you might think you will remember where information came from, and be tempted to leave referencing to the last minute, it can be very difficult to locate references at a later stage. So keep your references up-to-date as you go—it saves time in the long run, and ensures you avoid all risk of inadvertent plagiarism.

HOW TO RAISE YOUR GRADE

Students often ask for tips on how they can improve their grades, particularly how to reach those elusive higher marks. Perhaps just as important, although not asked as often, is how to avoid making errors or taking an approach that can easily drop you a grade, or more. So, Figure 11.4 presents our top tips for you to consider when looking to develop your assessment skills more generally, with explanations following. You'll find more tips in relation to specific types of assessment in Chapter 12.

I WISH I'D KNOWN . . .

'I wish I had known the little tips that can get you from a 2:2 to a 2:1.'

Charlotte Brown, Bournemouth University, LLB Law, Year 3

FIGURE 11.4: Don't drop a grade

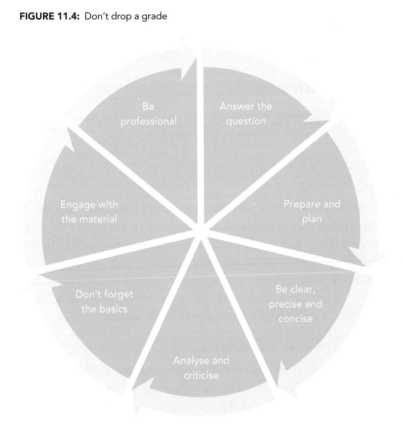

Answer the question

However much knowledge you have on a particular topic, you will not get a good grade unless you use that knowledge to answer the question. It is by answering the question that you demonstrate that you have understood the law and can analyse it and apply it appropriately, and this is what gives you access to the higher marks.

So make sure you direct your discussion to the question, picking it apart to identify the relevant issues. However much you wish the question was on something else, don't head off onto irrelevant matters, and don't try to rewrite or rephrase the question to make it suit your strengths. Markers are very alert to this!

Link your discussion explicitly to the question rather than discussing the law generally, and/or fulfil the brief as presented. Aim to reach clear conclusions, based on what you have been asked to do.

I WISH I'D KNOWN . . .

'The law is so important, make sure you get this right and then logically apply to the situations. The questions aren't there to trick you.'

Emily Barrett, University of Bristol, Law with Study in Continental Europe, Year 4

Prepare and plan

Follow our earlier advice and always spend time planning your work. However little time you have, planning your work will make a huge difference to the quality of your work, whatever the form of the assessment.

Prepare properly, making sure you follow the instructions for your assessment. If you write the wrong length of essay, or answer the wrong number of questions, your mark will be in serious jeopardy. In most institutions markers have *no* discretion in these matters.

Be clear, precise and concise

Inaccuracy, vagueness and 'waffle' are all easy ways to lose marks. It wastes time and also indicates to the marker that you are not sure about the law and/or its application. If you are not sure about a point, you don't make this any less obvious by discussing it in vague terms for a long time. Better make the point the best you can, and move on.

Work on your skills of communication, ensuring that you can express yourself clearly, and that you can make points accurately but concisely. Don't be tempted to try to write 'like a lawyer', using unduly complex or flowery language, particularly if you have any doubt at all about the meaning of the words you use. Remember that the best lawyers are masters of precision, not walking thesauruses.

INSIDER KNOWLEDGE

'Do not use up words in your word count by saying anything that does not directly answer the question.'

Gavin Teasdale, Solicitor, PGS Law LLP

Analyse and criticise

Particularly as you progress through your legal studies, markers of your assignments will want to see more depth of analysis and criticism in your writing. Remember not just to set out the relevant law, but also to make justified and reasoned evaluations of the law and its significance. Consider and challenge the law, question views and approaches, apply the law to issues and problems, explore practical consequences or theoretical conundrums, and engage with the primary and secondary material. Chapter 10 considers the important skills of analysis and critical thinking in more depth.

Don't forget the basics

There can be a risk that in aiming for higher-level analysis and engagement with academic writings, the basics can be forgotten. Remember that you need to provide enough explanation of the law, with relevant authorities, to convince the marker that you know and have understood the relevant law. Don't be tempted to skip this on the basis that the marker already knows the law—of course s/he does, but you need to show that you do too. The depth you include will depend on the question, but try to avoid just skating over a point unless it is really only peripheral to the question.

Engage with the material

Markers love to see that a student has a good grasp of relevant legal sources, and can not only use this in appropriate places to support their explanation of the law, but can also *engage* with the material. This means actually thinking about the material you are referring to, and considering whether you agree or disagree (and why), or assessing whether it takes a conventional or novel approach, or conflicts with other authorities or approaches, and whether this is a good thing or not.

Engaging with the material also means—*don't copy*. Obviously you should not be copying anyone else's work and presenting it as your own—this is plagiarism, and important guidance on this is included in the next section. But we would also urge you not to waste important time in an exam or space in coursework simply regurgitating material in any great length. There is usually little to be gained in setting out a full section of a statute, or a long quote from a case or article. While you will need to quote some material directly, and it is important to do so, be sparing with how you do this.

Similarly, while referencing thoroughly will avoid plagiarism, simply copying other people's words and splicing them together will not get you a good mark. Markers want to see evidence of your own thoughts, not just advanced cut-and-paste skills.

Be professional

Even if no marks are allocated to presentation, put your marker in a happy mood by ensuring your work is well presented. If you are not given specific rules to follow then use a sensible font type and size and set out your work neatly, using appropriate sub-headings and paragraph breaks for example. If you are hand-writing, you need to make sure that your writing is legible. It doesn't have to be attractive, but the marker does need to be able to read it.

Professional presentation also means following standard legal conventions for legal terms and titles, and complete and accurate referencing, as appropriate for the form of assessment. Make sure you are confident about these basics.

ACADEMIC MISCONDUCT, PLAGIARISM AND POOR ACADEMIC PRACTICE

Does this really concern me?

We don't believe that anyone reading this book starts with the intent to do anything that might be classed as 'academic misconduct'. You want to do your best and achieve your potential by fair means. But stuff happens.

Some law students, although happily a very small proportion, do indeed engage in academic misconduct—and face enormous stress, embarrassment and awful academic and professional consequences when that misconduct is discovered. Other students will have the worry of an investigation due to poor academic practice. This often involves very high-level members of the law school and university, and can be very stressful, whether or not it results in a penalty or other unwanted consequences.

So how can you avoid academic misconduct and/or poor academic practice, whether being tempted to engage in this deliberately, or inadvertently straying into murky waters?

Avoiding academic misconduct and poor academic practice

Academic misconduct and poor academic practice can be either deliberate or inadvertent. It usually occurs for one of two reasons:

- Where a student doesn't fully understand what they should, or should not, be doing; or
- Where a student finds themselves tempted, often through a feeling of 'desperation' from lack of time or disappointment in results so far, to attempt to take a short-cut to a better result.

With this in mind, you can minimise any risk of engaging in academic misconduct or poor academic practice by:

- **Ensuring you understand what amounts to academic misconduct or poor academic practice**
  - Read all the relevant guidance provided by your own institution and law school.
  - Undertake your institution's training courses on good practice. Often these are online modules that you can do in your own time, and can repeat whenever you like.

- **Adopting good habits**
  - Take a fresh approach to the preparation and presentation of your work if you have adopted habits at school, college or at institutions elsewhere that conflict with the expectations now on you.
  - Practise good technique.
  - Listen to, and act on, feedback.
  - Ask or check when in any doubt.

- **Using time effectively**
  - Keep proper notes and prepare proper references.
  - Don't be tempted to make up for lost time by inappropriate means.

- **Respecting yourself and others**
  - Understand that success is only meaningful when obtained through your own honest best efforts.

Plagiarism

Plagiarism is probably the most common ground of academic misconduct, and often causes a great deal of worry for students. In short, plagiarism amounts to presenting ideas, or work more generally, as your own without acknowledging and/or referencing your source(s) properly. It can cover a great deal of different behaviour, so includes, but isn't limited to, the following:

- Direct copying of someone else's work, whether from a book, article, the internet, a friend or anywhere else;
- Claiming the ideas of someone else as your own;
- Incorporating sections of a text or texts with only simple links between them;
- Re-using work you have submitted for another assessment, whether at the same, or another institution;
- Submitting work written by someone else, whether you 'borrowed' it, were given it or bought it.

You can see that plagiarism may be deliberately dishonest behaviour, such as buying an essay from an online essay writer—something that institutions have got increasingly good at detecting and punishing. Or just possibly inadvertent poor referencing, maybe not realising that you have to acknowledge all your sources, including textbooks. Good study and referencing techniques, practising these throughout your course, and good time management will ensure you don't engage in plagiarism.

Collusion

Although less common than plagiarism, collusion can also be a problem for law students, and again, it is possible to breach the rules against collusion inadvertently. Collusion consists of presenting jointly prepared work as if it was your own, or working together when this isn't permitted for the assessment.

If the assessment is group work, then obviously there is no collusion in working together—this is an important element of the assessment. However if an assessment is an individual piece of work, and most law assessments are, then you should *not* plan and write your work with someone else.

That doesn't mean you can't get together with friends as study buddies for topic discussion and revision more generally. But once it gets to preparing an assessment, and definitely when it gets to planning, structuring or writing your assessment, you need to work alone. Ultimately you just need to remember that work you submit as your work must indeed be *your* work. Equally, don't let a friend use your work, even if you feel pressured to do so—you could end up in just as much trouble as them.

Other types of academic misconduct

Any behaviour that does not involve presenting your own work honestly, or involves you seeking to obtain an unfair advantage, can amount to academic misconduct. Cheating in exams, for example by communicating with other students, or taking unauthorised material or electronic equipment into the exam room, will obviously be included. So will things such as misstating the word count of your essay to make it appear that you have not exceeded a word limit, or falsifying results of an experiment, or misreporting survey data.

Poor academic practice

This term is usually used to refer to behaviour that does not meet the standards of accepted academic practice, but falls short of clear academic misconduct. So any lack of academic honesty, attempt to obtain an unfair advantage, failure to give full credit for other people's contributions, not following academic form and style as directed, etc, will be poor academic practice.

You can see it is very easy for poor academic practice to tip over the line into academic misconduct. This is particularly likely to be the case if you have been warned about poor academic practice in the past, perhaps through inadequate referencing, or making too much direct use of other people's work in your essays, and then do the same thing again.

But don't worry

While academic misconduct and poor academic practice are very important and can have serious consequences, there is no need for you to worry *too* much. By being aware of academic standards and requirements, taking every opportunity to develop your skills and accepting personal responsibility for your study and educational development, you can very easily avoid any danger in this area.

Perhaps keep this in mind. If you would have *no* concern in telling a tutor openly what you are doing, you probably have nothing at all to worry about. However if you would rather your tutor did not know, then perhaps it is time to question yourself more closely.

SUMMARY—HELP YOURSELF . . .

- **Take both formative and summative assessment seriously**
  - Remember that although only the marks of *summative* assessments count towards your final grade; *formative* assessments are critical in helping you towards success.
  - Take up all formative opportunities that you can.
  - Make use of both formative and summative assessments to develop your skills for further assessments.

- **Prepare fully for all assessments**
  - Know the rules that apply to each assessment, checking carefully, and stick to them.
  - Reflect on your strengths and weaknesses, and aim to address them well in advance of any summative assessment.
  - Identify the assessment criteria that apply to your work and take some time to understand what they mean.
  - Be aware of good academic conduct, and how to avoid poor academic practice and academic misconduct.
  - Practise your skills and good technique.

- **Manage your time effectively**
  - Map out all your assessments, both formative and summative, from the start.

- Think about the time you'll need for each individual assessment and other commitments.

- Don't let poor time-keeping lead to poor academic practice or academic misconduct.

- **Submit the best work you possibly can**

  - Plan your work carefully, continually checking you are fulfilling the assessment brief.

  - Answer the question set as directly as you can, and keep on point.

  - Display knowledge of the relevant law and use of relevant sources, but also your understanding and ability to analyse and apply the law.

  - Present your work professionally.

12

COMPLETING ASSIGNMENTS: ASSESSMENT SPECIFIC SKILLS

*'As for accomplishments, I just did what
I had to do as things came along.'*

ELEANOR ROOSEVELT

INTRODUCTION

To successfully complete specific assessments, you will need to know what is expected of you, and develop the skills to deal with it. Depending on where you are studying law and the optional subjects you choose, you may come across many different forms of assessment, or only a very narrow range.

Some law schools continue a very traditional approach of assessing only by final exam. Some, possibly the majority, use a simple combination of exams and other written assessed work such as essays or problem questions. However, other law schools utilise many different forms of assessments, with the aim of promoting and testing a wider mix of skills and abilities. These might range from traditional exams and essays to oral presentations, group projects, posters, blogs and reflective exercises.

Are you better off with a range of different assessments or only one or two forms of assessment? There's no simple answer. Having only one form of assessment means you have plenty of opportunity to practise the specific skills for that type of assessment. But it doesn't cater for individuals who don't thrive on that particular type of assessment, or whose skills are stronger in other areas. A range of different assessments will encourage you to develop your skills more broadly, and allows a wider range of different individuals to showcase their abilities. But variety means you have to engage with different assessment environments, and, of course, you are unlikely to perform equally strongly in every different type of assessment.

Whatever your law school's approach, what really matters is that you can succeed, ie do your best, in whatever assessment you face. This chapter looks at some of the different forms of assessment you may come across, and gives you tips on how you can approach them to enhance your chances of success. You should also have regard to the core skills and principles we looked at in relation to assessment in Chapter 11. Remember, too, that if you need reasonable adjustment for an assessment because of a disability or learning need, you should discuss this with your personal tutor or university support centre as soon as you can in advance of the assessment.

EXAMS

The most common form of assessment in law is the exam. Even those institutions that have adopted a wide range of assessments, usually still assess the majority of modules at least in part by exam. Over the years there has been lots of discussion about whether exams are actually the most appropriate form of assessment in the modern world, but as long as exams survive—and their demise is certainly a very long way off—a law student can expect to take a good number of them.

Because of the significance of exams to law students, and the importance of preparing for them effectively, this book has a separate chapter devoted to 'Exams and revision' (Chapter 15). It comes a bit later in the book because you will usually be thinking about exams after you've been thinking about other assessments—exams are more commonly taken at the end of the academic year, while other assessments can pop up at any time. Remember though that law exams usually combine essays and problem questions, and may include multiple choice questions, so much of the following discussion about different forms of assessment is applicable to exams too.

ESSAYS

You will be writing lots of essays as a law student—practice (or formative) essays, tutorial essays, summative coursework essays and essays in exams. A common form of law essay question is a statement, or quote, followed by a direction to consider a point in relation to that statement, or simply to 'discuss'. Essays could alternatively ask you a question in relation to a topic, along the lines of 'To what extent is it true to say . . . ', or 'How far do you agree that . . . '. Another possibility is asking you to consider and comment upon a particular area of recent or proposed law reform, or to identify and explore an area where law reform might be needed.

Essays are a hugely flexible tool in a lecturer's armoury. They can encompass a fairly broad topic, or a narrow but interesting point within a topic. They can raise an issue stretching over more than one topic, or combining several topics, or a wider theme or theory. You should be prepared for anything.

Although we'll discuss some common essay-writing approaches, in truth there is no single 'correct' way of answering a law essay question. That might be disappointing if you were hoping for a single one-size-fits-all approach you could learn to guarantee success in writing law essays. But, on the plus side, the flexibility of legal writing means that any number of students could answer an essay question successfully using different structures, approaches and even, to some extent, content. Just because your style or view is different to someone else's doesn't mean it is wrong.

However, that doesn't mean you can just write whatever you want—you do still have to produce a coherent response to the question set. Here we'll consider a number of points and techniques that should help you to answer essay questions successfully, and you should also refer back to Chapter 10 on critical thinking and legal analysis.

Essay-writing approaches

There are lots of established approaches to answering essay questions. One of the best known is PEA (or, less attractively, PEE) which is often introduced in school to encourage students to make and support arguments. Although there are different views on what the letters should stand for, the essence is: Point, Evidence, Assess (or Point, Evidence, Explain/Evaluate).

These principles can be applied to law essays: it is essential that you identify the point you want to make, that you support it with evidence (usually legal authority) and explain and assess each point. However there is no need to follow the approach rigidly: the principles are important, but the precise approach less so. Certainly approaching an essay by setting out all the points, then all the evidence and then all your explanation, would make for a very dull essay.

The risk with PEA is that adhering too closely to it may not promote deeper analysis, nor remind you to respond directly to the question. So keep PEA in mind when writing, but use it as your servant, not your master.

Another established approach to answering essay questions is CEEO, also known as CLEO. This is better suited to law essays than PEA, as it more directly encourages engagement with the issues (and so is more likely to help you access the higher marks). It stands for Claim, Evidence (or Law), Evaluate, Outcome (or Opinion). We looked at CEEO in Chapter 10 in relation to including critical thinking and legal analysis in your work: refer back for more guidance on constructing arguments and using CEEO.

You can see immediately that by keeping CEEO in mind, you are reminded to evaluate the law, and consider and conclude on what that would mean. It also helps you to separate issues, so you deal with each one in turn, aiding your structure and reducing the opportunities for confusion. Just as with PEA, though, use CEEO thoughtfully rather than mechanically. Don't be afraid to approach matters in a different order, or to make links between different issues where appropriate.

Consider the question

It can be tempting to read an essay question, identify the topic and then simply write about that topic. This can be a particular problem in an exam, when panic sets in and you are rushing to set down the information in your head, but the problem is more widespread than just exams. Discussing the topic might get you sufficient marks to pass the assessment, but you may well not manage much more than that.

FIGURE 12.1: Using your skills to answer the question

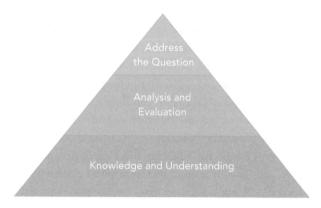

It is critical that your answer actually addresses the question, and doesn't just consider the topic more generally. This is because addressing the question itself shows the marker that you have not just learnt the law, but can use it effectively to consider a particular issue—making choices about what to use, what to leave out, and how to direct your material. Considering the question also encourages you to evaluate the law in the light of the statement, which is important to show that you can analyse and apply the law, and not simply recite it. Figure 12.1 shows how you must build on your knowledge and direct your analysis to address the question.

I WISH I'D KNOWN . . .

'Do not be afraid to have an argument. The law is created on judgments and students should not be scared to have an opinion and write about this in their assignments, providing it is respectful and uses the law as evidence.'

Zoe Lindsey, Postgraduate student, University of Nottingham

Structuring your essay

We saw in Chapter 11 that a strong structure is an important element of good work. While there are no specific rules for structuring an essay, there are a number of things to bear in mind.

Structural freedom

In some countries, and in some academic subjects, essays have to follow very strict structures, and will be marked down severely if they do not do so. That is not the case when studying law in the UK. You are therefore free to structure your essay however you wish, unless your lecturer tells you to follow a specific structure for a piece of work. (This would be unusual, but is not entirely unknown.)

If you had to learn a strict form of essay writing in previous study, it can be quite difficult to shake that off and start again. But it is important that you do so, and you should come to enjoy the freedom. You should start with no preconceptions about the number of sections or paragraphs, nor proportion of space to allocate to particular elements of the essay.

The basic structure

While you are free to structure your essay as you choose, a good essay will inevitably include an introduction, the main part of the essay (split into sections and/or paragraphs dealing with different points) and a conclusion.

Quite how much space you allocate to each part of your essay will depend on various factors: how much time or space you have, the topic and issues arising, and your own style and approach. You should however expect your introduction and conclusion to be significantly shorter than the main section of your essay.

Effective introductions tend to be relatively short, and grab the marker's attention. They will need to set the context, identify any important concepts, unless these are sufficiently complex to need a section of their own within the main part of your essay, and should ideally set out what your approach is going to be—both what you are going to consider and why you are going to consider it. It is this last element that clearly links your discussion to the question and reassures the marker that you are considering the question and not just the topic. If you can briefly set out your argument or indicate your conclusion then this can be very effective, but can be difficult to do in an exam where your ideas will develop as you write.

The main part of your essay should lead on neatly from your introduction, as the issues you have identified should make up paragraphs or sections of this part. Make sure you explain and assess each issue as you go through, drawing interim conclusions and linking between points, rather than drifting from point to point. It can be helpful to refer specifically to the question as you discuss issues, to show that you have identified the key themes from the question and are considering them.

If your main consideration has dealt with all the relevant issues, the conclusion should follow on fairly naturally—but there is a tricky balance to find. While you need to summarise the key arguments, you do not simply want to provide a summary of the essay. And while you want to show you have thought deeply about the issues and wider consequences, the conclusion is not the place for brand-new information. So aim to pull together key strands, linking issues and, most importantly, showing explicitly how your consideration addresses the question asked.

Using sub-headings

Most essays benefit from distinct sections with short and clear sub-headings. Sub-headings are really helpful in maintaining a clear structure, leading you and your reader through your discussion.

Sub-headings can be particularly useful if you tend to drift from point to point or merge points when writing. They force you to identify, consider, evaluate and conclude on each issue before moving on. Sub-headings shouldn't stop you from making links between issues, but mean you have to make clear transitions, which is a good thing. If a strict word limit tempts you to cut out sub-headings, think twice—the benefit of having a few extra words to play with will probably not outweigh the loss of clarity and structure.

Dig deeper

However, the essay question is phrased, it is essential that you engage with the question deeply. As a first step this means you need to pick apart the question, identifying the topic, key areas for discussion and particular points of complexity or controversy. If you don't do this, your essay will tend to be descriptive and topic-focused rather than question-focused.

To do really well in an essay, you need to consider and challenge the law and the point of view (explicit or implicit) in the essay title, as well as explaining the relevant law and basis for the statement. In other words, as well as answering the question, try to question the question. Consider the discussion on critical questioning in Chapter 10 to help you to engage more deeply with the question and produce a more thoughtful essay overall.

I WISH I'D KNOWN . . .

'That the lecturers require that we understand both sides of the topic and our own critical opinion.'

Lita Aguimoy Jones, Staffordshire University, LLB Law, Year 2

Case notes

Rather than a conventional essay, you could be asked to write a case note, although this is less common than it used to be as a form of assessment. A case note explains and explores a particular case—this will inevitably be a particularly important or interesting recent case on a topic. You can look in the good academic journals (not just practitioner blogs) for examples of case notes, but bear in mind that they will be longer than you are likely to be given for an assessment.

Just as with a standard essay, it is important to engage with the issues deeply, and not just explain what happened in the case. Use your introduction to explain the significance of the case, showing you have thought about the issues. Don't spend too much time reciting the case facts: the marker will want to see your skills in identifying the key facts and setting them out concisely and effectively. The most important parts of the case note in an assessment are your examination of the judgment(s), and your evaluation of their significance. As part of this you will need to consider how this case fits in with earlier cases and develops the law, and how it has been applied in any subsequent cases. Good case notes will also reflect on any wider policy and reform issues raised by the case directly or indirectly.

PROBLEM QUESTIONS

Other than essays, problem questions are the most popular format for assessment exercises, whether in exams or as coursework, as well as formative assessment of course. Problem questions normally involve a set of facts, sometimes quite lengthy and often involving several different characters and events, and ask you to advise a particular client or all the parties on their legal position. A problem question could simply ask you to 'discuss', but as that discussion will relate to the legal consequences of the events for the individuals involved, the approach is the same.

Students' views on problem questions differ sharply. Many students prefer problems to essays, as by simply working through the facts, it is usually fairly easy to identify at least the main issues, which can then be discussed in turn. It is probably less likely than in an essay that you will find yourself with absolutely nothing to say, or no idea how to structure an answer.

However, other students find problem questions more challenging than essays, perhaps finding it more difficult to locate the legal issues within a factual scenario than in an essay title, or finding the application of the law harder to discuss convincingly than analysis of the law more generally. Spotting and dealing with the more complex issues in problem questions can be difficult, as can allocating time appropriately to different points.

It certainly isn't possible to say that essays or problems are 'easier' or 'harder' than one another. And mark spreads tend to be remarkably similar for both types of question, whether in coursework or exams.

Problem question approaches

Just as with essay writing, there is no single 'right' way of approaching a problem question. However, just as CEEO can help you to remember what you need to do in an essay (and can be adapted for use in problem questions too), so IRAC can help you to focus on the right things in a problem question. We looked at IRAC when exploring how to bring critical thinking and legal analysis into your work in Chapter 10.

As we saw there, IRAC stands for Issue, Rule (or Relevant Law), Apply, Conclude. Or you may see it as ILAC, where 'L' stands for Law, or IPAC, where 'P' stands for Principle. The acronym reminds you that you need to identify the issue (the particular problem) clearly, explain the relevant law that applies to that issue, apply the law explicitly to the facts and reach a reasoned conclusion. It sounds simple, but it can be surprisingly difficult, particularly the application of the law to the facts. More guidance on problem solving and use of IRAC can be found in Chapter 10.

As with essay writing approaches like PEA and CEEO, remember that IRAC should be a tool and not your master. As long as you deal with the issues fully and apply the law coherently, the precise order in which you cover things isn't critical.

Remember more generally that although a problem question usually asks you to 'advise', you should not write your answer directly to an imaginary client, nor structure it as if it were a letter or legal opinion, unless you are expressly told to do so because you are developing particular skills.

Question focus

Just as with an essay, it is essential that you focus on the question itself. Particularly if you lack confidence in your understanding of the law, it is all too easy to identify the area of law and then simply set out all you know about it. Although you will get some credit for relevant knowledge, the marker will not be convinced that you understand the law and can apply it. So make sure you pick out the particular issues from the question—who are you advising, and what are they complaining about? Then think about how the law applies to those particular facts and advise. This is shown in Figure 12.2.

FIGURE 12.2: Using your skills to advise

I WISH I'D KNOWN . . .

'Make sure you know who you are advising and that you are doing this. If you need more information from the question don't be afraid to say that.'

Frances Easton, University of Birmingham, Law, Year 3

When considering the law it can be quite effective to identify the relevant broader principles and then narrow them down in stages to the specific points arising—this can also help you to identify where there are grey areas in the law, or where you would need more facts to advise conclusively. Don't ignore any facts—they will be there for a reason, even if that is to make you conclude that they are not relevant and why. Similarly, don't ignore any part of the instruction—if you are told to advise A *and* B, then do so, or be prepared to lose a lot of marks.

I WISH I'D KNOWN . . .

'Do not list cases simply by way of example. Delve into the case facts and holdings, and argue that the case is either similar for a certain reason or distinguishable for a certain reason. Be willing to wrestle with conventional understanding of certain cases.'

Godwin Tan, University College London, LLB Law, Year 3

Structure

Some subjects will give you quite clear guidance or instruction on how to structure a problem question for that subject: this is quite often the case for criminal law, although other subjects too may favour particular approaches. If you are told that you should structure a problem question in a particular way, then follow that direction. Otherwise, as with an essay, it is up to you. In a problem question an introduction is still valuable, but can usually be very short, just showing the marker that you have understood what you need to advise on and have identified the relevant area(s) of law.

You will almost certainly be advising either more than one person, or in relation to more than one complaint, or with more than one area of law applying, so use these as natural sections and headings for the main part of the essay. Remember to identify the issue and the relevant law and apply it expressly. You should be able to reach an interim conclusion on each point, so do so. Not only does this show the marker that you've understood and applied the law, but it keeps you focused so that you can lead on to appropriate further points and, ultimately, reach a final conclusion.

If you have done this, your final conclusion should be fairly straightforward. Make sure you do as directed and advise the individuals, or on the issues, as instructed. If you are unable to reach a final conclusion, look back through your work to see where you haven't managed to identify and apply the law.

Avoid cop-outs such as 'ultimately, it is up to the judge', or 'it will depend on the evidence'—reach a conclusion. If the facts are ambiguous or limited, you can make clear that your conclusion depends on your particular construction of the facts, or would differ if a specific additional fact came to light, and if the law is uncertain you could conclude 'on balance'—but be clear why you are unable to be more definite.

I WISH I'D KNOWN . . .

'I wish I'd known how much a structured answer counts. Providing a clear structure to frame the answer shows the examiner you understand the essence of the topic. Also, I wish I'd known how lucky you are when the topic is tricky: the messier the law, the better because it allows you to bring to light the complexities in the law and shine. Instead of just applying the law, you offer various solutions and discuss the value of each of them.'

Gabrielle Bargas, University College London, LLB Law with French Law, Year 2

Using secondary material

Views differ on whether secondary sources, particularly academic articles, should feature in problem questions. Although some lecturers indicate that they should not, the more common view is that it is perfectly acceptable, and can be very effective, to include such material. What matters is how you use that material.

You will almost certainly make less use of secondary material in a problem question than an essay question, because the focus in a problem question is so much more on identification of the issues and application of the law, than on broader, in-depth analysis of difficult legal issues. However difficult legal issues do arise in problem questions and where they do, they need analysis if the law is to be considered and applied effectively. Judges increasingly make reference to academic views when considering how to develop and apply the law, so it can hardly be the case that you shouldn't.

Accordingly, where there has been pertinent academic discussion, perhaps particularly if relating to the merits or otherwise of a case, or the likely future direction of authority, or law reform proposals, these can be highly relevant. So, always consider all relevant material, but make sure you keep your focus on the problem rather than producing an essay-like answer that more broadly evaluates the area of law.

MULTIPLE CHOICE TESTS

Although multiple choice questions (MCQs) rarely, if ever, make up the complete assessment for a module, they do sometimes appear as part of the assessment. They might be a separate test with a further assessment to complete, or one part of an exam.

Understanding law MCQs

You may well be familiar with MCQs from school or training courses, and the concept is very easy to understand. You will be given a question, and must choose the correct answer from a selection given (usually four or five possibilities). Although that sounds easy, it can be surprisingly difficult: even if you have revised very thoroughly, there is nothing like being given a choice of answers to make you doubt yourself. It is often advisable to try to work out the answer *before* looking at the possible answers, to reduce the chance of confusion.

Law MCQs can be particularly tricky. Not only will they be designed to offer a real test of your ability, they may include problems, with you having to choose the most likely outcome or appropriate advice, or consideration of complex or uncertain elements of the law, or require you to rank points in order. This means you need a really good understanding of the relevant law and can't just rely on good recall of information.

It is therefore important not to focus exclusively on 'knowledge' when studying for MCQs. Work on understanding the issues and the complexities in the law as well. Broad knowledge is of course very important for MCQs, and MCQs often trip up students who might try to 'question-spot' in other assessments. But knowledge alone is not sufficient to do well.

The good news with MCQs is that if you've worked hard and consistently, really high marks are often more achievable than in essays and exams. On the other hand, if your studies have been patchy, you may well find your mark is much lower than you might have achieved with good luck in a conventional exam.

Dealing with uncertainty

What to do if you don't know the answer to an MCQ? Well, if you find yourself having to choose between answers, as you undoubtedly will at least sometimes, then it is helpful to start by removing answers you are pretty sure aren't right. That process might be sufficient to highlight the likely correct answer, but even if not, your chances of success will be much higher if you have to choose from one out of two answers, than one out of four. Don't take too long over your decision though. You will usually not have much time per question for MCQs, so if you are really struggling with a question, leave it and come back to it if you have time at the end, rather than waste too much time. (If you can—some online MCQs will not allow this.)

Whether or not to make a guess on a question when you are really unsure of the answer must depend on how the test is marked. If marks are simply awarded for correct answers ('positive marking'), then you might as well guess—nothing lost, and you might get lucky. However a lot of MCQs use 'negative marking', so you will lose marks for incorrect answers, rather than simply not gaining marks for those answers. In that case you will have to think carefully about whether or not to make a guess, and probably shouldn't unless you are reasonably confident. Make sure you know how your MCQs will be marked before you start the test.

I WISH I'D KNOWN . . .

'Read the questions slowly. Under exam conditions our brain can play tricks on us and we see what we want to see; not what's actually written on the page. Take your time, read it carefully, then read it again. Once you decide the answer mark your selection and move on.'

Andrea Garvey, Swansea University, LLB Law Single Honours, Year 2

ADVOCACY, ORAL PRESENTATIONS AND VIDEO SUBMISSIONS

Oral presentations or video submissions can be a form of assessment in a wide variety of modules, and not just ones explicitly based on such skills, such as advocacy. Not only do these types of assessment develop and test different and important skills that are particularly relevant to wider employability, they also provide you with the opportunity to excel if you have stronger abilities in oral than in written communication. However, for a lot of students, oral presentations are particularly daunting—even quite confident students can feel very nervous when face-to-face with an examiner, 'judge' or video camera.

Whatever the format of an oral assessment, it is important to remember that it will be aiming to test a range of skills. On the one hand you will still be expected to display your legal knowledge, understanding, and skills of application, analysis and research—you won't do well if you don't know and can't explain and use the relevant law. However, you will also be assessed on the particular skills of communication and presentation, and you mustn't leave these to chance.

Preparation and planning

As discussed in Chapter 11, preparation and planning are the key to success in all assessments. This is just as true for oral assessments as for more traditional written assessments. As well as preparing in terms of researching and learning the relevant law, you will need to prepare and plan for the presentation itself.

Make sure you read the brief carefully, so that you know who your audience is supposed to be and can direct your material appropriately—both in terms of detail and approach. An advocacy exercise, seeking to persuade a 'judge' of your case, will be very different in focus to a presentation to a 'law firm' or 'business leader' on an uncertain point of law, for example, even if relating to the same subject. So focus on your own particular assessment, rather than just aiming more generally to 'give a presentation'.

INSIDER KNOWLEDGE

'Be bold, have a go, do your best. We all have to start somewhere and practice does improve one's skills. Learn off others so ensure you also participate as a spectator.'

Jonathan Brew, Senior Partner, Harrison Clark Rickerbys

Written material and visual aids

You must always check whether you are expected to produce accompanying visual aids and/or written material. This may be a required element, or an optional extra. Depending on your assessment you could be required to produce a written plan, a script or a summary, or might be allowed to use PowerPoints or equivalent or a handout to support your presentation.

If you are permitted to use visual aids, we strongly recommended that you do so, as it has the potential to add value to your presentation, as well as helping you to keep focused. Unless specifically directed to submit a script, your visual aid should be much more, and less, than simply what you are going to say. As you will know from the best lectures, visual aids should signpost the content and approach of your presentation, assist your understanding of a point and reflect on the point made—and ideally help you to engage your audience. Your visual aids must link effectively to and support your presentation, without drowning the viewer in information.

Video presentations

Video submissions have much in common with face-to-face oral presentations, and similarly need a focus on the brief and lots of preparation and planning. But video submissions tend to be less daunting because at least you have the opportunity to review, reflect and edit (or even start again), before submission.

A common mistake we see with video submissions is too much focus on the technology, at the expense of content and delivery. While slick presentation and clever effects can be great to catch the marker's eye and maintain interest, don't let these overwhelm your submission. Even in Hollywood the best special effects can't make up for lack of meaningful content.

Remember too that your submission is ultimately a presentation, so work on your presentation skills. Just because the marker isn't in the room doesn't mean you should ignore them. Make sure you connect with your viewer—avoid looking down at notes or fidgeting.

If you are unfamiliar with making videos, there is no need to be worried. Most institutions will offer training in these skills, and even if they don't, there are several simple and free apps that will enable you to put together a competent video very easily.

Timing

An important factor in all presentations, whether in person or on video, is timing. It takes real skill to use your time effectively—to balance what you want to cover and how you want to cover it, with the allocated time. Most oral assessments will stick very strictly to time limits. You may be cut short if you overrun, meaning you miss the opportunity to conclude, or you may be penalised, sometimes quite heavily.

When considering the timing of presentations, there are two common errors. The first is trying to squeeze too much content into the time available. This compromises the delivery of your material: you will have to talk very quickly, or may run out of time. It also affects how far the viewer can appreciate and understand your presentation. So stick to the essentials and do those well, focusing on the particular issue in question rather than spreading your net too widely. The second occurs when a student is careful to select an appropriate amount of content, but then rushes in the presentation—this leads to a presentation that is too short.

To avoid both these problems it is essential that you plan your presentation carefully, practise it and review it. Consider videoing yourself or asking a family member for comments—it can be painful, but it is definitely worth it. Practice also helps you better cope with nerves on the day and makes it less likely you will rely heavily on notes. Don't practise so much that your presentation becomes wooden, particularly if you need to respond to questions for example in an advocacy exercise, but you really don't want to be trying out a presentation for the first time in the assessment room.

I WISH I'D KNOWN . . .

'1. Fake it till you make it. Confidence or feeling confident is important! Don't worry about being a bad speaker. Tell yourself that you are the most amazing person in the world and you will be if you maintain that mindset. 2. Practise beforehand in front of friends or coaches! If you are self-conscious, do it in front of the mirror. 3. Find an experienced debater or public speaking expert to coach you.'

Monica Chen, University College London, LLB Law, Year 2

Skill development

Many university study guides and 'law skills' books provide advice on oral presentations that you may find helpful if you need further guidance on presentation technique. There are also many excellent sources of information relating to particular skills—for example Iain Morley QC's *The Devil's Advocate* (2015) is an entertaining read on advocacy and court skills. You can also work on your skills by taking part in extra-curricular activities such as mooting and debating (see Chapter 17), and even by taking a more active role in tutorials, or working in a group or society where you will have to present your ideas.

REFLECTIVE REPORTS

A key skill for success, whether as a law student or beyond, is reflection. It is only by reflecting on our experiences that we can truly learn and develop. Because of its importance, reflection is increasingly becoming a specific element in law assessments, and you may find yourself being assessed, at least in part, on the basis of a reflective report.

This could amount to a separate assessment or one part of a longer piece of writing, but as reflection cannot exist in isolation, it will be part of an experience or wider project of which other parts may or may not be assessed. This could be an event such as a presentation or negotiation, or a longer-term project involving group work, a law clinic or work experience, for example.

Why assess reflection?

Law students can sometimes be a bit thrown by the concept of a reflective report—after all, where is the law? It is important therefore to remember that reflection is a valuable skill that will assist you more generally in your studies as well as in future work, and is not merely 'fluffy stuff'. It ensures that you have engaged fully in an exercise, have gained from that experience and can demonstrate that. It also develops writing skills beyond those required for law essays and exams.

In essence, reflective writing involves considering an experience, not just to describe what it was and what happened, but to reflect on why things happened that way, what went well and badly, and how you would approach things differently, or what you have learnt from the experience. Reflective writing is not a simple matter of writing up an event or writing an account for a journal and can be very hard work because it involves your own thoughts and feelings, and deep consideration of the learning experience.

Developing reflective writing skills

If you are asked to write a reflective report you will almost certainly be given guidance on what your tutor expects in that report, so we don't want to be too prescriptive here. You should also pay careful attention to the applicable assessment/marking criteria. But there are some useful general tips on reflective writing to enhance your chances of success in this important skill:

- Remember this is about you and your experience. Consider what you did, why you did it, and your views before, during and after the event or experience. Unlike most law assessments you should expect to write in the first person ('I').

- Don't just describe events, engage with them. This is much easier if you've kept notes throughout the activity or experience on which you are reflecting.

- Be specific—give examples (evidence) to support the point you are making, rather than just generalised observations.

- Recognise your strengths and weaknesses—whether in preparing for the experience, or in carrying it out.

- Consider whether you could or should have done anything differently, and what effect that change might have had.

- Reflect on outcomes—positive or negative, immediate or longer-term. Will you change anything in the future as a result of the experience? Why?

- Introduce relevant academic literature where this has influenced your approach or response. This could be specific to the topic, or to the type of exercise you are reflecting on, or indeed more generally to the learning process and reflection.

Such is the importance of reflection to learning, that your own institution will probably provide guidance on reflection and writing reflective reports. Do check amongst any online study guides offered by your institution, as this should most closely reflect your tutor's approach. If you want more information, some helpful resources are included on the Learnhigher website: http://www.learnhigher.ac.uk/learning-at-university/critical-thinking-and-reflection.

OTHER FORMS OF ASSESSMENT

Instead of, or as well as, traditional one-off assessments such as exams and essays you may be asked to engage in ongoing forms of assessment such as contributing to blogs or wikis. Or rather than creating traditional written essays, you might be asked to communicate in a more visually exciting form, such as a poster or leaflet.

The core skills of assessment continue to apply, just as they do to more traditional assessments, but of course they may differ in importance, while other skills may become more important. Always consider why you have been given an assessment in a particular form—what skills are being tested; what do you need to demonstrate—so you know where to focus your efforts.

Blogs and wikis

Assessment through a blog or wiki contributions ensures that students who engage fully with a subject are likely to be more successful than those who only take a superficial interest. It is essential that you pay attention to the instructions with this kind of assessment because they tend to be ongoing and reward steady workers. If you don't check what you need to do from the start you may not have enough time left to complete all the tasks.

Trying to do it all at the last minute is unlikely to be sufficient: the marker will be looking for sustained interest, developing skills and even a reflective element. You may also be asked to respond to questions or discussion points raised by the tutor or other students and marked not just on the content of your responses, but on how you interact and communicate and your awareness of wider or deeper issues.

Posters

Posters are increasingly seen at academic conferences and legal workshops, and unsurprisingly have made inroads into legal assessment. A good poster combines appropriate content with visual impact, and the trick is getting that balance right. If you have a choice over the topic for your poster, then pick an interesting but relatively self-contained topic to ensure you can demonstrate depth of research and understanding, without overloading the poster with information.

As always, check the specific requirements for your particular assessment, but some tips for good law posters are:

- Posters are commonly produced in A2 size, so make sure yours works effectively at that size. If your assessment uses a smaller or larger size then modify your design and content accordingly.

- Your poster does not need to be read from a distance and if it can be, you have probably not dealt with issues in sufficient detail. But it should look sufficiently interesting for someone to want to cross the room to look more closely at it.

- Break your poster into sections covering different elements of your topic—structure is as important for a poster as for an essay.

- Ensure your poster conveys an overall message or theme—that it has some aim or purpose.

- Use at least some visual representations—pictures or diagrams work well, but even buzz-words can be effective—to catch the eye and break up text. Choose carefully to maximise the impact and value of every element of your poster.

- Use colour and different texts thoughtfully—they can be a very good way of adding interest and making your poster more attractive, but if overused can distract and confuse.

- Make sure you reference your research—plagiarism is still plagiarism, even on a poster.

Leaflets and guides

Just as with posters, leaflets require a careful balance of content and visual impact. Keep in mind your target audience—for example, have you been asked to write a guide to the courts for litigants-in-person, or review a new case or procedure for specialist lawyers? Your approach should be very different depending on the purpose of your leaflet or guide.

Assessments in this form will typically give you very little space in which to work—often a single sheet of A4, folded in half or thirds. You therefore have to consider very carefully what information can be included, and what will need to be omitted—and this is one of the important skills that will be considered by the marker. How you present your work should, of course, differ according to your audience—pictures or diagrams; information boxes or bullet points; type font, size and colour etc—but you should always aim to make the leaflet attractive and accessible to its audience.

GROUP WORK FOR ASSESSMENT

So far we have largely assumed that the assessment you are taking has been an individual assessment—that is you are expected to prepare and deliver the work alone. But some of the assessments we have covered, such as video submissions or posters, particularly lend themselves to group assessment, and group work may make up an element of many activities and assessments.

Assessment of group work

Although you will be working as a group, your final piece of assessed work may be submitted either individually or as a group. And the mark you receive may be the same for all students in the group, or may be an individual mark—this will depend on the nature of the assessed work, the assessment criteria and the allocation of marks.

Whichever form the mark takes, you will need to work successfully as part of a team. Even if no marks are specifically allocated to the group nature of the work, and they often are, there will be something about the task—perhaps its size or complexity or involvement of diverse skills and aptitudes—that means someone working alone would be unable to produce work as good as an effective group.

Allocating tasks

As part of group work you will need to discuss and analyse the overall assessment, and allocate tasks to ensure that no individual is overburdened, reviewing progress as you go along. It makes sense to play to the strengths or interests of individuals in the team, so initial discussion along those lines is very helpful. You might even decide to take a team personality test—there are plenty available free online. It can be a fun bonding exercise as well as helping you to link roles to individuals.

Appointing a group leader is pretty much essential to ensure there is someone with an overview of the work who can organise meetings and encourage activity. Remember though to choose your leader carefully; the most obvious candidate may not be the best. A good group leader needs to be able to engage all members of the group and delegate appropriately.

Managing group assessment

Not everyone finds group work easy—in fact we'd go so far as to say that most law students find it pretty challenging. It can be particularly so when you know that your mark rests, at least to some extent, on the efforts of others. However group work is an essential skill that all successful law students need to learn, that will benefit you throughout your studies and in your future career.

In our experience group work probably produces the most complaints and grumbles of any form of learning or assessment. This is because working together is not easy—there will always be perceptions that someone is not pulling their weight, or dominating the group, or is uncooperative or difficult. Sometimes these complaints have good foundation. After all we all know difficult, lazy or careless individuals, and sometimes personalities clash horribly. However, we must also remember that our views of others are influenced by our own experiences and expectations and may be unfair—is that person lazy, or do they just have commitments we are unaware of? Our own traits may also not always be viewed favourably by others.

Remember that everyone has something to contribute, even if it may take some effort to locate their particular skills. Successful group work means learning to work within a group dynamic, recognising that everyone has their own style and approach to work and learning, and working out how best to manage that.

To a great extent, working as part of a team means dealing with and managing difficult situations, so you should always start by trying to resolve problems within the team. However if the group has a significant problem—perhaps a member simply cannot be contacted, or the group splits into factions—or if difficulties descend into abuse or bullying then you should contact the person in charge of the module or assessment for advice. It is unusual, but sometimes problems do need the assistance of an outsider to reach a satisfactory resolution.

SUMMARY—HELP YOURSELF . . .

- **Be aware of the types of assessment on your course**
  - Find out what types of assessment you will take during your legal studies, and when they will be.
  - Practise those types of assessment—if you don't have the opportunity to practise in class, or with formal feedback, then practise on your own or with a friend.

- **Consider why a type of assessment has been chosen**
  - Different assessments test different skills or abilities, or test skills and abilities in different ways. By understanding why the assessment is in a particular form, you can better direct your work to your marker's expectations.
  - Take every opportunity you can to develop different skills and abilities.

- **Play to your strengths**
  - If you have particular skills or abilities, or particular weaknesses or dislikes, then consider how you will be assessed when selecting optional subjects.
  - Consider in advance how you can mitigate your weaknesses, and showcase your strengths; take up opportunities for practice, training and other support.

- **Engage with the new**
  - Approach all your law assessments with an open mind; they will all differ from your previous assessment experience in some way.

- Don't dismiss new forms of assessment out of hand; take the time to think about what is needed and why it is important.

- **Take personal responsibility**

  - Whatever the form of assessment, find out what you need to do and how you can enhance your chances of success.

  - Research relevant assessment skills, as well as the relevant law.

  - Practise the kind of assessment you will face.

  - Group assessment does not mean absolving yourself from personal responsibility. Engage fully with group work, act constructively and remember that everyone has the right to be treated with respect.

13

UNDERSTANDING AND USING FEEDBACK

*'Feedback is good for you—like exercise
and broccoli. It makes you stronger and
helps you grow.'*

DOUGLAS STONE AND SHEILA HEEN,
Thanks for the Feedback: The Science and Art of Receiving Feedback Well

INTRODUCTION

Feedback is an essential part of the learning process. It has a really significant role to play in your success, although its importance is often underestimated. Feedback enables you to learn from your experiences, to identify your strengths and weaknesses confidently so you can then work on your strengths and eradicate (or disguise!) your weaknesses. It ensures that you can build on your hard work and continually improve your performance to achieve your potential; it looks *back* in order to move on to the *future*. Management guru Ken Blanchard has said, 'Feedback is the breakfast of champions' and it is an essential component of the successful law student's diet.

The bad news is that feedback can only operate effectively if you are prepared to put a good deal of effort into obtaining, understanding and using it. The successful law student always engages fully with feedback, which means putting in that effort throughout your studies, as well as before, during and after every assessment.

Unfortunately, even those who recognise the importance of feedback don't always benefit fully from it. Admittedly this is sometimes because the quality of feedback is low, but just as often this is because of a lack of understanding about where to find feedback and how to use it effectively.

This chapter will look further at feedback—what it is and where you can get it—and about how you can make the most of the feedback that is available to you to enhance your chances of success. We will be concentrating on feedback within your legal studies, but remember that the general principles of finding and using feedback—taking opportunities, identifying strengths and weaknesses, building on experience and absorbing the advice and experience of others—have relevance to all aspects of your successful life and career.

UNDERSTANDING FEEDBACK

What is feedback?

Feedback comes in many forms but in essence is information or guidance on your work, whether that is an essay, exam, presentation or just contributions in a seminar. It is the process by which you understand how your present state of knowledge, understanding and performance relates to your goals.

Feedback includes any mark given for a piece of assessed work, but that is certainly not the most important part of feedback. What is essential about feedback to a successful law student is that it shows you how to improve. That doesn't mean that feedback will tell you explicitly what to do next time—a law degree is designed to create independent thinkers not producers of model answers—but it provides you with the tools you need to evaluate and improve your own performance.

Feedback and feedforward

Feedback you receive will normally relate to a specific exercise, assessment or activity. It is obviously immediately instructive in relation to that particular assessment. It gives you the mark (showing where you are in relation to established standards), explains why you got the mark that you did, identifies issues you missed and indicates where you got the law or its application right or wrong, for example. To that extent feed*back* is well named—it looks *back* at the assignment.

But feedback is much more important than that. Feedback also gives you guidance on how to improve your work in the future—not just showing you where your legal knowledge and understanding need work, but also enabling you to identify where your technique is good and where your skills need to be developed. This element of feedback is sometimes described as 'feed*forward*' to demonstrate how it operates (or should operate) to inform your future work. This element of feedback is not limited to a specific assignment, or even a specific module, but is relevant to other modules and future work as well. The difference between feedback and feedforward is illustrated in Figure 13.1.

FIGURE 13.1: Feedback and feedforward

FEED*BACK* ...
Tells you what you did right and wrong in the assignment

FEED*FORWARD* ...
Tells you how to do better in your next assignment

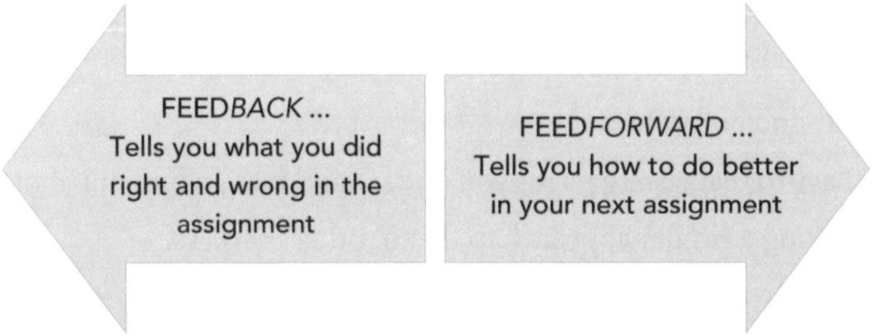

Is feedback necessary?

It should be obvious now why feedback is so important. If you don't know what you have done wrong, and what you have done well, it is very difficult to improve.

You might argue that just doing further assessments will lead to improvement. There is some truth in this—the more we practise the better we will get. But improvement is likely to be limited without expert guidance, and slight improvement is not what a successful law student is aiming for. And 'improvement' may not be so desirable if you are just getting more practised at something that was wrong in the first place! Constructive feedback enables you to see what you have done well, what you have done badly, and can give you indications of how you can improve in your next assessment.

Characteristics of good feedback

The *best* feedback you will get during your studies will be:

- **Specific and individual**
  - Detailed guidance, with examples of good and poor practice.
  - Related to the task and to specific elements of your own performance.

- **Constructive**
  - Highlighting good points as well as errors.
  - Identifying ways to improve.

- **Goal-orientated**
  - Related to your achievement of the relevant assessment criteria.
  - Identifying how your performance relates to recognised standards.

- **Clear and consistent**
  - Easy to read, using terms you understand (or can find out about).
  - Taking a similar approach to that of other markers.

- **Timely**
  - Given within a reasonable timescale.

Not all feedback will meet all these criteria, but hopefully much of your feedback will meet at least some of them. Of course the more opportunities for feedback you can take, the more likely it is that *overall* you will receive feedback that collectively meets all these criteria.

Feedback as a process, not an event

It is tempting to regard feedback as limited to the bit of paper (or possibly email or audio/video link, depending on your course and the technological inventiveness of your lecturers) that accompanies a returned assessment. As lecturers we don't help by calling this 'the feedback' and rarely referring to feedback outside this.

Because of this it is also tempting to regard feedback passively—as something that we, the lecturers, do to you, the students, so your role

FIGURE 13.2: Using feedback to improve performance—a virtuous circle

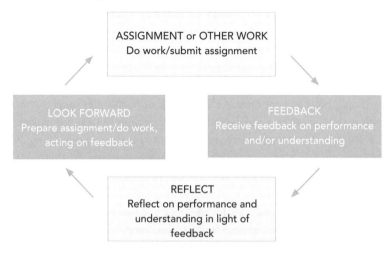

is just to sit back and receive the feedback. Both of these temptations should be resisted. As Figure 13.2 shows, feedback is an *active process* rather than a single event, and is relevant to all aspects of your work.

I WISH I'D KNOWN . . .

'Make sure you keep a record of your feedback and then read through it before you begin your next essay. You will only ever get better through feedback. This applies now in your law degree but also in later life during your career.'

Emily Barrett, University of Bristol, Law with Study in Continental Europe, Year 4

Passive receipt of feedback is just not enough to make a truly successful law student. It has to be used. And that means both finding opportunities for feedback, and making good use of the feedback you receive.

What feedback opportunities will I get?

If you think of feedback as just the formal written feedback you receive following assessments, you would be forgiven for thinking that you don't get much of it. In your legal studies at university you will probably only produce one or two pieces of work that are formally marked for each module each year—possibly even less. That may come as quite a shock if you have come directly from studies at school or college where you might have been producing an essay or attempting an exercise every week or so (or even more) that would have been marked and returned. You might even feel rather short-changed in terms of feedback.

But it is important to remember that feedback is much wider than formal written feedback, although of course this is very important. You will find that there are numerous feedback opportunities open to you, although they might not all be immediately obvious. As a successful law student you have to take active responsibility for your own learning by hunting out and using all possible feedback opportunities. Furthermore, you need to recognise these as feedback opportunities so that you know what to do with them.

If you simply wait passively for feedback to come to you then you will limit yourself to formal written feedback on compulsory work, and thus limit your chances of success. While you can get a lot from formal feedback as we'll demonstrate later, you can be even more successful if you recognise other opportunities for feedback, and take as many of them as you can possibly manage.

Sources of feedback

There are lots of different possible sources of feedback, for example:

- Individual feedback following an assignment, usually written;
- General feedback to the student group relating to an assignment, either oral or written;
- One-to-one discussion with tutor about an assignment, or performance more generally;
- Tutorials and seminars—practising questions and testing knowledge/ understanding with colleagues and tutor;
- Personal tutor or other advisor for general feedback;
- University skills/education/language departments or bookable sessions;
- Group study activities—receiving feedback from your friends, for example on exam practice questions;

- Quizzes—provided in the module or in textbooks or other resources;
- Self-evaluation—practising questions, critiquing and marking own work.

There are clearly ample opportunities for feedback. But only the first two in that list could be viewed as feedback that is simply 'provided'. And, of course, your tutor's time is limited. To make the most of feedback opportunities you are going to need to be proactive in getting them and making use of them.

Using feedback

To be of value, feedback opportunities have to be used. Even those feedback opportunities that don't appear to require your active involvement, like receiving a feedback form or listening to general feedback in a lecture, actually *do* require you to engage with the feedback if you are to benefit from it.

You will get little benefit from even very detailed and constructive feedback if you do not take the time to consider it carefully, re-assess your work in the light of the feedback, and attempt to put the advice into practice in the next piece of work you do. Remember the feedback cycle in Figure 13.2.

It is easy to put up barriers to feedback. Receiving feedback often challenges how we view ourselves and our abilities. Getting negative feedback, however constructive, can be hard to deal with, particularly if you've put a lot of effort into some work, or thought you'd done a really good job. Some people even find it difficult to receive positive feedback, and push it away.

It is important to remember that feedback relates to your work, not you, and to try not to be defensive or dismissive. Try to cultivate a 'growth mindset' that sees your characteristics and abilities as malleable rather than fixed. This will help you to see feedback as an opportunity for development rather than a reflection on you personally, and make it easier for you to engage with the feedback you receive.

INSIDER KNOWLEDGE

'Always take feedback positively. Do not see it as a negative. Hopefully, the feedback you receive from your tutors will be constructive. Think to yourself: what is my tutor telling me? Is there something I can do about this? Is this something that I need to remember for future assignments or exams? Do not just read the feedback and not act upon it. Nobody is perfect, we are constantly improving ourselves. So do not take feedback as an insult, but rather a way to improve and better yourself.'

Nina Ali, Administrator, Coventry University and People Manager, Jake Restaurants Ltd

MAKING USE OF FORMAL FEEDBACK

If you've completed an assignment, it makes sense to get full value from your effort. That is true whether the work is formative, ie non-assessed, or summative, where your mark counts towards your final module mark. You shouldn't regard your work as at an end when you hand in the assignment. What are you going to do now you've got your marked assignment and feedback sheet in front of you?

In all likelihood your first act will be to search for the mark, and what you do then may well depend on that mark. If the mark seems satisfactory you may well put the paper aside, possibly after a cursory look at the comments, as it seems to offer little of value. You did fine so you don't need any feedback, why waste your time? If the mark seems unsatisfactory then you might throw the paper aside in a fit of despondency, or else dismiss the marker as an idiot and the feedback therefore as clearly wrong. You won't be surprised to hear that while these reactions are completely understandable, they are not the way to get the most out of this feedback opportunity. Remember that 'growth' mindset?

I WISH I'D KNOWN . . .

'I wish I'd known that they are only giving you that feedback for your improvement.'

Charlotte Brown, Bournemouth University, LLB Law, Year 3

So what should you do? Ideally, we'd recommend that you don't even look at the mark before reading the feedback, but we know you wouldn't listen to us, and we almost certainly wouldn't follow our own advice if we were in your shoes. Being realistic, the first thing you will do is look at the mark. So—how is it? Okay? Disappointing? Excellent? Better than you'd hoped? Does it reflect the amount of effort you'd put into the piece? Whatever your feelings, take a deep breath before moving on. Take a short break if you need to—but you must come back soon.

Now you need to read the feedback—carefully. With any luck, your feedback will be clear, detailed, meaningful, specific to you and your work and provide you with examples of how you have met, or not met, the assessment criteria for the piece of work. If you are one of these lucky students then you need to reward the marker's time by taking time yourself to work through those comments.

Engaging with quality feedback

A useful first task on reading through the feedback is to try to separate those points that are specific to the question, such as points of law you might have missed or where you haven't applied the law correctly to a particular issue, from those points that are more general, for example not addressing the question directly or not communicating clearly. Make two lists. Of course some of these points may be connected, so the lists may overlap a bit. You should also check your essay itself to see if there are additional comments written on the essay that you can add to your lists. Table 13.1 gives an example:

Table 13.1: Identifying points of feedback

SPECIFIC FEEDBACK	GENERAL FEEDBACK
Missed out issue A	Imprecise in statements of law. (and lots of question marks in margins of essay itself)
Good analysis of point B	Insufficiently concise. Didn't use word limit effectively.
Application of *C v D* was not sound—misunderstood Lord X's analysis	Presentation generally good
Needed more detail on point E, including the views of Dr Y and Professor Z	Referencing did not follow consistent form
	Not enough detail on key cases and their application
	Needed more discussion of the academic arguments

Now you can look in more detail at the specific points. This is very important to aid your learning in the particular module as it will tell you where your understanding of the law or its application is sound, and where it is not, or where you needed more or less detail.

So check through your list, and re-read your essay to see whether you really understood the law. If there are problems, go back to your books and notes and revise the law. You should do that now, while it is still fresh in your memory. Of course, it may be that by looking back at your books you can see that you did understand the law but that you hadn't explained yourself clearly—if so then this is a general point to go on your second list.

Having checked the particular topic, now look at the more general points that you can use for feed-*forward*. Looking at your list, find the criticisms and re-read your essay with these criticisms in mind. Can you see why the marker has made these comments? It is unlikely that the marker is wrong, however much you might wish they were.

So you need to try to identify places where these criticisms apply and try to think about how you could have avoided them. Could you have approached things differently? Could you have explained things differently or discussed things in more depth perhaps? Think about how you could have dealt with the material differently.

Remember to use your list to identify the good points of your work as well—hopefully there will be a few! Positive feedback has great value too. Re-read your essay again to identify those good points. Did you realise you were doing these things well? Could you have extended this good practice to more of your essay? Think about how you could use these techniques or further improve on these skills in another essay.

We are not pretending that engaging with feedback is anything other than a time-consuming process, but good feedback requires your input in order to work, and the more work you put into it the more positive impact it will have. Successful law students never miss an opportunity to engage with quality individual feedback.

I WISH I'D KNOWN . . .

'I like to re-do any essays I haven't achieved a good mark in so I can apply the comments that my tutors have given me. This way it's still fresh in your mind and when it comes to revision you'll have a better grade of paper to use than the initial one you perhaps didn't perform so well on.'

Alexandra Townsley, University of Nottingham, LLB Law and American Law, Year 3

Engaging with poor or limited feedback

So far, we have assumed that the feedback you have received is high quality. What if the feedback you have received doesn't really meet those 'best practice' criteria?

The quality and quantity of feedback will vary—between universities and between, or even within, modules on the same course. While law schools constantly strive to improve the feedback provided, the reality is that numbers of students, work pressures and the limited time provided before work has to be returned mean that the feedback you receive may not be wholly satisfactory. Of course you can feel aggrieved, you could even complain in extreme cases, but a more constructive approach is to treat all feedback as valuable and see just what you can get out of it, however limited.

Let's take an extreme example of feedback that doesn't meet our good feedback criteria. This is the feedback on a Contract Law essay:

'A reasonable effort, but you completely missed the issue of implied terms.'

Not much to go on then, and certainly not detailed. But let's look again and break down the feedback a little more:

'A reasonable effort . . .'

This doesn't tell us much, but we can at least see that there was nothing seriously wrong with your technique or your coverage more generally—certainly nothing sufficiently awful to catch the marker's eye. Equally, though, there seems to be nothing that has particularly impressed the marker. The quality was clearly not high—otherwise it would say 'a good effort' or 'a very good effort', so it is not just the omission of a major issue that has impacted on your mark.

Let's see what else we can find out. Try going back to your marked essay—look for any comments or other marks on the paper. These are often ignored or just brushed aside but they can be surprisingly helpful.

For example, squiggly lines under passages or question marks in the margins will usually mean that the marker couldn't fully understand the point you were making. More than a couple of these gives you a strong indication that you need to be working on expressing yourself clearly and unambiguously. Are there lots of corrections to your English? Again, this tells you that you need to work on your communication.

If your marker is a 'ticker' then lots of ticks should indicate that you are making valid points. If there are only a few ticks then look again at the 'blank' passages and see if you are actually not saying much of value. Crosses will inevitably mean that you are making mistakes of the law or in its application so look carefully again at the law in this area. Omission marks (usually upside-down 'v' shapes) indicate that you have missed something out or the marker wants more detail on a point, so you either need to revise the law to discover what point you missed, or you need to be working on providing more depth in your discussion. If there are lots of searching questions in the margins, this suggests that you have not been developing your analysis sufficiently deeply, and were not adequately critiquing the law or its context.

And next:

'. . . you completely missed the issue of implied terms.'

At first sight this has benefit only as feed-*back*, but is still useful. It tells you that you need to remember to address the issue of implied terms in a question like this, and helps you to identify how particular issues might be connected in an essay or problem question. What's more. even a brief and apparently topic-specific comment such as this may offer us the opportunity for feed-*forward* if we look hard enough.

Think about whether you put enough effort into this particular essay—and whether that effort was appropriately focused. Did you read sufficiently around the most obvious topic(s) and think about the module content as a whole to see what else might be relevant? If you didn't, you will lack awareness of other issues and their inter-connectedness and that might be why you didn't think about implied terms. Did you just assume that you knew what the question was asking rather than thinking it through and questioning it more deeply? Did you double check all the facts in a problem or all the words in an essay to see why they might be included? Did you plan and structure your work so that you could ensure that all the issues were dealt with appropriately?

Or perhaps you had spotted the issue but then decided it wasn't relevant or that it wasn't important enough to include. If this is the case then you can work on techniques to improve your prospects even if you miss out on the big marks. For example if you have decided that an issue is only peripherally relevant and so not worthy of discussion, you could briefly indicate in your answer that you have thought about it, but have concluded that it is not relevant for a specified reason. That way, even though you might be wrong in your conclusion that it was not relevant, the marker can give you some credit for having recognised the existence of the issue.

You also need to think back through any previous essays you have done at university. Is this the first time your work has been criticised for missing a significant issue? If this comment is not the first like this then this tells you that you probably need to work on your problem/issue identification skills. Perhaps you could go through some past exam papers and make a list of primary, secondary and peripheral issues for each question—compare them with a friend, and/or see a tutor in their availability times to see if you are getting the hang of the process. You could also work through topics you have covered in your modules to make revision notes and diagrams that identify all issues and show their connections.

Even very limited feedback then can provide you with valuable insights into your performance and provide you with plenty of scope to work on your strengths and weaknesses. But you do have to make the effort to glean what you can from what you have been given, rather than dismissing it out of hand. Of course if the feedback you are receiving on a module is really unsatisfactory then do speak to your tutor or student representative about it.

Further feedback on assignments

There are other ways of maximising your feedback from an assignment. In many law schools, individual modules or lecturers may provide additional feedback opportunities, but it will be up to you whether you take advantage of these.

The most common source is general feedback on the assignment, either written or in a lecture or podcast. This general feedback will usually go through the topics/issues covered by the assignment, and may well also highlight common errors and/or good practice identified during marking. If you are lucky enough to have access to this general feedback then you should engage with it carefully. Use it to identify things that you did well or badly, and learn from others' mistakes as well as your own.

Other lecturers might provide a model answer, or bullet points of suggested content. While less helpful for feed-*forward*, this can ensure that you have fully understood the issues that arose in that particular question. Read it carefully, while the topic is still fresh in your mind, and make sure that you then compare and contrast it with your own effort.

You might also or alternatively be offered open door sessions or booked appointments with the marker, to allow you to discuss your feedback following the exercise. If you get such an opportunity, use it wisely. Make sure you have read through the feedback and re-read your work before attending, and try to identify any particular areas in which you are struggling to understand the feedback or where you want guidance on how to improve. Don't use the session to complain or get upset, although lecturers will always understand disappointment and frustration. Try to use it positively, looking to maximise the feedforward from the exercise.

INSIDER KNOWLEDGE

'Getting feedback from tutors is the best yet most underused resource in university. Tutors are the experts in their fields and having a one on one chat with them regarding your participation in class or an essay, even if you are satisfied with your performance, is excellent for self-improvement.'

Shubreet Kaur, Advocate, Punjab and Haryana High Court, India

Even if further opportunities such as those already outlined are not on offer, and they are far from universal, there are further steps you can take to maximise your feedback. You could for example sit down with a friend and critique each other's work—in a positive way of course! Sometimes students can be too protective or embarrassed to show their work to their peers—don't be. But don't simply compare how many cases you each cited; really read the work and try to evaluate it against the assessment criteria. Can you help each other understand the feedback given by the tutor, or can you provide further insight? Peer feedback is valuable whatever the level of performance of your friend; don't dismiss feedback just because it comes from someone apparently less able than yourself.

Other sources of guidance could be university study skills units or other skills sessions where non-subject experts may be able to give you feedback on essay technique for example. And don't dismiss the role of textbooks in providing feedback. Some textbooks, particularly revision books and 'Question and Answer' style books, can help to show you how to craft effective essays on particular topics—although be careful to use them to develop your own skills rather than simply as a source for 'model' answers.

So keep in mind that the written feedback you receive on an assessment is really just a starting point for a much longer conversation. It is up to you how much further you want to develop that.

INFORMAL FEEDBACK/FEEDBACK OUTSIDE ASSIGNMENTS

The feedback discussed earlier related to specific assignments. Feedback can also be obtained more generally on your performance, and in more informal ways. This can give you valuable guidance on whether you are reaching your potential.

Peer feedback

We've already touched on peer feedback earlier, in relation to getting additional feedback on particular assignments. Peer feedback can also be very helpful for feedback more generally, and you can use your friends in a variety of ways—remembering of course that you should be willing to give assistance to them in return.

Quite apart from peer feedback in formal group learning sessions, it can be useful to get together informally with a friend, or with a few friends to make a study group, to work through topics and problems together. The most successful peer feedback tends to be in relation to identified exercises, so rather than discuss a topic generally, set each other tasks and feedback on these.

Ideas for peer feedback/study group activities:

- **Hone your understanding**
  - Explain a previously agreed legal issue in a limited time or a limited number of words (you could do the same issue or different issues) and then ask each other questions, and offer feedback.

- **Boost your exam skills**
  - Write an answer to a past-exam question, either time limited or word limited, then swap and mark each other's work, with feedback.

- **Maximise your expertise**
  - Write a summary of a key academic article on a topic, or a pair of articles on the same topic, and swap and mark each other's work, with feedback.

- **Smart revision**
  - Prepare a revision plan, such as a skeleton list or a spider diagram, for a given topic, then swap and offer feedback on the issues covered and the connections identified.

Tutorials and seminars

It is easy to see tutorials and seminars as just 'class time'. But they offer excellent, regular opportunities for feedback—albeit they are not usually explicitly labelled as 'feedback'. Provided you prepare thoroughly for these classes, you will receive implicit or explicit feedback on your knowledge, understanding and ability to apply the law, as well as your ability to present your findings, by participating actively in class. This allows you to test your understanding and skills with colleagues and the tutor.

Make sure you answer questions thoughtfully, engage with discussion actively and ask questions where an issue remains unclear to you. If you have prepared thoroughly and participated to the best of your ability, most tutors will be only too happy to discuss matters with you further after the class should you need further feedback.

I WISH I'D KNOWN . . .

'Leave a good amount of time to prepare for your tutorials and really take the effort to do the further readings. Prepare a few questions before the tutorial that you'd really like to ask your tutor. No matter which module you are studying, you will definitely have questions along the way. Tutors are usually more responsive and thorough when you ask those questions in person, than when you try to email them during the revision period.'

Godwin Tan, University College London, LLB Law, Year 3

Lecturer/tutor availability

Many lecturers and tutors at university offer 'office hours', 'open door' or 'drop in' sessions, or bookable appointments, to see students on any matters. Most will be happy for you to use these sessions to go through practice work you have done to give you immediate feedback. Feedback may not be extensive, there will be other students waiting and time is limited, but it is immediate and personal and you will have the opportunity to clarify any issues there and then.

You can make the most of such opportunities by evaluating your own work before you attend, and making clear to the tutor if there are any particular areas you would like feedback on. You should also aim to work steadily through the year: you are less likely to be greeted warmly by a tutor if you bring five practice answers to the final busy open door session of the year, than if you attend with a single essay on five separate occasions. Little and often is usually best for you and the tutor.

I WISH I'D KNOWN . . .

'Do not be afraid to ask for feedback, as they are there to respond. Having said that, do keep in mind that if they are a bit slow in providing feedback it is because they are busy people.'

Fiona Lin, University of Cambridge, Law, Year 3

Personal tutor/student mentor

Your personal tutor, mentor, support staff or student mentor or buddy may be able to offer you general feedback on your performance. They are unlikely to have direct knowledge of all your particular modules but can be a valuable source of feedback on your general performance and skills development.

If you can, you should have regular contact with the individuals who make up your support network over the course of your studies. This ensures any feedback you need is individually relevant and pertinent to the stage you are at.

Additional activities

Always take advantage of any additional learning opportunities a module might provide you with. These can vary from quizzes and student forums to revision exercises, worked answers and so on. These tend to offer you the chance to receive feedback in a very flexible and informal way, enabling you to check on your understanding to date.

These activities will usually require you to undertake an exercise or participate to some degree in order to get full value from them, and it is easy to view such optional extras as something that will just take up your time. Put in the time now and benefit from the additional feedback.

Self-evaluation

Feedback is a process, and the most important person in that process is you. Self-evaluation is key to using feedback effectively and also provides you with additional valuable feedback, over and above that available from tutors and friends. Spend time becoming familiar with the assessment criteria, and practising your techniques to demonstrate that you are reaching your targets.

Learn to be self-critical. By this we mean you should approach your work in a critical light, evaluating it against the assessment criteria, comparing it with your earlier work and others' work, and trying to see it from an outsider's perspective, remembering that the marker cannot see what was in your mind when you wrote. Being self-critical does not mean that you have to tear yourself apart—this is about improvement, not self-flagellation.

Ways in which you can develop skills of self-evaluation:

- When reading a textbook or an article and making notes, make sure you read back through those notes and ask yourself whether they adequately explain the issues and highlight the complex points. Would your notes make sense to someone else? Try rewriting your basic notes as a briefing document for an imaginary law firm and evaluate its content and clarity.

- When you have finished an assignment, read it back through with a critical eye and with the assessment criteria in front of you. Try to identify places where you have met those criteria. Give yourself a mark, and reasons for that mark. When you get your work back, compare your comments with those of the marker.

- When preparing for a tutorial or seminar, always try to prepare full responses to any questions you are set and then read them through and evaluate them before the class. Identify any areas you feel you have not explained clearly or understood fully. Revisit the work after the class to see if your initial concerns were right and whether you could have approached the question more effectively.

- Practise past exam questions and read back through your answers. Pretend you are the marker, armed with ticks and crosses (and any other squiggles you fancy), and mark it critically—what could you have done better?

- Reflect on every learning opportunity. Consider what you learnt and what you could have done differently to have got more from the opportunity.

SUMMARY—HELP YOURSELF . . .

- **Locate and take all opportunities for feedback**
  - Look more widely than formal written feedback.
  - Participate actively in class and in any additional activities.
  - Use tutor time wisely—identify particular queries or concerns.
  - Use your friends (in a good way!)—make use of peer feedback.

- **Use your feedback for feed-*back* and feed-*forward***
  - Review your work in light of both specific and general comments.
  - Don't simply dismiss unfavourable or unexpected comments.
  - Identify strengths and weaknesses for you to deal with going forward.

- Re-read earlier feedback, whatever the module, before preparing your next assessment.

- **Learn to self-evaluate**
  - Become familiar with the relevant assessment criteria.
  - Mark and comment upon your own work before submission.
  - Undertake practice questions and other learning exercises and evaluate your answers.
  - If you have time, re-do assignments following feedback to put the advice into practice.
  - Aim to identify recurring strengths and weaknesses across modules.

14

DISSERTATIONS AND RESEARCH PROJECTS

*'It's none of their business that you
have to learn to write. Let them think
you were born that way.'*

ERNEST HEMINGWAY
quoted in 'With Hemingway: A Year in Key West and Cuba' by Arnold Samuelson

INTRODUCTION

A dissertation or research project is often an important part of your legal studies. It can be viewed as the culmination of three or four years of hard work because it is usually completed in the last year of your degree. A dissertation or research project allows you to demonstrate your skills as an autonomous learner and prove you can undertake a critical and research-focused piece of work. Students often find the dissertation one of the most difficult parts of their legal studies, but most relish the challenge. Most are rightly very proud of the final product.

In this chapter, we will explore the nature of legal research projects and dissertations. We will consider how to complete them successfully, taking a broadly chronological approach to the issues arising. While our approach may not follow precisely the guidelines set out by your law school, it can still provide markers to guide you through the process, from constructing and refining the project proposal, to writing and rewriting, all the way through to final submission. This chapter also discusses further the use of relevant resources, drawing upon our discussion of research in Chapter 8, and the important relationship with your dissertation or project supervisor.

WHAT IS A DISSERTATION OR RESEARCH PROJECT?

Essentially, a dissertation is a research project that undertakes an in-depth and fully researched examination of a research question agreed upon between you and your supervisor, and usually lasts a full academic year. Dissertations generally have a word limit of between 8,000 and 15,000 words, but the precise length will depend on your institution. Most commonly the word limit is either 10,000 or 12,000 words.

At first glance, this may seem a lot; especially if you are used to writing 2–3,000-word essays. But break it down and it seems much more manageable. A dissertation could be seen as a 1,000-word introduction, 4 x 2,000-word essays as individual chapters and a 1,000-word conclusion. Much more manageable! While the length of a dissertation may seem initially daunting, there is nothing to fear if you plan appropriately from the very beginning. This chapter will help you do that.

A research project is similar to a dissertation but is generally shorter in length. Like a dissertation, you will have to undertake a well-researched evaluation of a particular idea or legal concept, but generally this will be a narrower topic than the dissertation. A legal research project is usually between 4,000 and 6,000 words in length and may be completed over a term rather than the academic year. It requires you to be more succinct and focused in your choice of topic.

When students opt to do a research project rather than a dissertation, if they have a choice, it is often to get the experience of in-depth research, but maintaining flexibility in their studies to choose some other modules or courses. While a research project is shorter in length than a traditional dissertation, the basic principles of how to approach it are the same.

In the next section, we will explore the key points in your dissertation or project journey and provide you with guidance for each stage. As mentioned above, these can only be general markers to aid your journey as individual law schools may have differing requirements and provide different advice about completing the process. If you are given specific instructions for any particular elements of your dissertation or project, make sure you follow them.

THE JOURNEY

The process of preparing, researching, writing, editing and submitting a dissertation or research project may feel a bit daunting at the beginning of the process, once the initial excitement and sense of freedom has faded. The level of guidance you are provided with at the start can vary immensely: some schools will offer introductory lectures and skills sessions, while others won't; some will provide clear guidance for what needs to be done and by when, while others view the dissertation strictly as an exercise in independent research, writing and project management.

You may feel a little lost, if all your experience to date has been of very directed, teacher-led modules. However there are advantages and disadvantages to both guided support and much more hands-off approaches, and you will soon get to grips with what needs to be done.

Figure 14.1 shows key stages in your dissertation or research project. We'll consider these, and other points, in order to guide you on your journey.

FIGURE 14.1: The dissertation journey

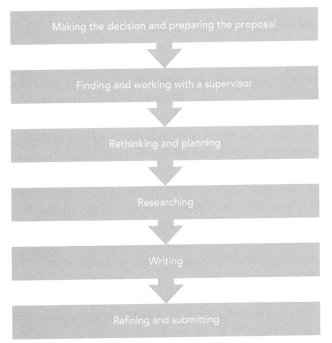

We'll deal with them in the order they are likely to arise so you can plan for all eventualities and upcoming tasks, although in practice they tend to overlap quite a bit. As you will have heard hundreds of times, failing to prepare is preparing to fail... or, as we prefer, always prepare for success!

MAKING THE DECISION

One of the first questions you face when you begin the journey towards completing a dissertation or research project is deciding whether or not you *want* to complete one. You may have no choice if it is a requirement of your degree programme. If that is the case it is worth reflecting on the benefits of such a project so you are fully committed to the journey and can get the most out of it. However, in many law schools the dissertation or research project is an optional module that you can elect to do, so you have to make the decision whether or not to go for it.

Why might you choose a dissertation or research project module if you have the choice? Depending on your own position you may identify various benefits, and some drawbacks.

One factor against doing a dissertation might be if there are other subjects you want to study—perhaps you feel you just don't have space for a research module once you've included all the subjects you are interested in and/or think would be valuable for your future career. This is understandable, but perhaps undervalues the benefits of a dissertation both generally and for its career-enhancing qualities. The dissertation is like no other module that you will study. It is a personal challenge and will develop your legal skills, such as critical thought, analytical ability and research to a higher level. Potential employers are often very interested in dissertations and similar projects because they recognise this. They also value the wider transferable skills a dissertation demonstrates such as time management, communication and organisation. It can also give you something to talk about at interview!

What else might put you off a dissertation? The length of the project can be off-putting to some students. But by breaking the project into chunks as we indicated earlier, this should not be a major concern. A bigger factor might be if you recognise that you are not particularly self-motivated or good at managing your time. A dissertation is a good way of developing these skills, but if you know that you will have great difficulty directing yourself and creating and sticking to self-imposed deadlines, then perhaps a dissertation or research project doesn't play to your strengths. That would be a shame though: the dissertation or research project is an excellent way to complement your subject-based legal studies.

The dissertation gives you a final project, a sense of personal achievement, and provides you with something you can show off, whether to family, friends or potential employers. If you are considering a dissertation or research project, and you should at least consider it, then read up on the requirements for the module and speak to the dissertation co-ordinator to get as much information as possible to make an informed decision. Perhaps chat through your options with your personal tutor.

If you think you'd like to do a dissertation or research project but are not sure about what topic you'd want to research, then think about the subjects you've been most interested in so far, or any topical issues you've seen discussed on the news. Speak to a member of staff with interests in the area to see if they can help you to formulate some ideas.

INSIDER KNOWLEDGE

'The sweet spot for a topic is a balance between what interests you, what is valuable to others and what may not already have been covered. To find this, start asking questions.'

Lali Wiratunga, National Manager Davidson Institute at
Westpac Banking Corporation, Australia

PREPARING THE PROPOSAL

The proposal form

Once you have decided you want to undertake a dissertation, you will often be asked to complete a proposal form. This will usually be submitted to your school before the summer break that leads into your final year.

Proposal forms will ask you for some information about your proposed project. Some will only require minimal information, such as the area of your proposed research. Others may expect more, such as a title, a brief summary of your proposed research, a research aim and some research questions, some key words related to your proposed research, and even a list of some important sources. Some tutors will accept or reject a potential supervisee based on this proposal.

Obviously, the more information needed at this point, the more you'll need to look into the topic beforehand, and you may need some informal help from a member of staff. Even if you only need to provide minimal information up front, thinking about these things in advance is still very useful. A good dissertation proposal is as precise as possible, but don't worry too much—law staff will be sympathetic when reading your proposal as they will understand this type of activity is new to you.

I WISH I'D KNOWN . . .

'Start first by looking, broadly, at textbooks and recent journals and cases to get a sense of where the current academic discourse is heading.'

Godwin Tan, University College London, LLB Law, Year 3

What should go in the proposal?

How much detail you include will depend upon the form you are given to complete. But here are some things to think about in relation to different parts of the proposal.

Title

Your title should focus on the proposed area of research as much as possible. It can be tempting to go with a broad title—but that can make it impossible to answer in 10–12,000 words. For example, we have seen titles such as 'The English "Law" of Privacy' or 'Are Lawyers Moral People?' While these are interesting questions/topics, they are too broad for a dissertation or research project—they would provide enough material for a PhD and then some. So keep your title focused to a fairly narrow area of study, and be prepared to modify the title in consultation with your supervisor as your research progresses.

Summary of proposed research

Within your summary, be sure to include three things:

* What you want to research;
* How you are going to do this; and
* Why it is important.

Outline the area you wish to explore and the specific area that you will interrogate in detail. You should also explain the sources that you will use to do this. This will probably include primary legal sources, such as case law, statutory provisions, historical documents or information you will collect yourself. You will also have to draw upon secondary sources, such as academic scholarship.

Finally, explain why your research is important: why is this area worth researching? This may be because the area of law is unclear or there's a problem that needs a solution; you may be arguing for reform to the law.

I WISH I'D KNOWN . . .

'Be smart—choose a topic that not only interests you, but is in fact intellectually manageable and relevant to your legal studies thus far. For instance, if you've studied contract law in your first year, you might choose to do something in that module but with a different spin (e.g. feminist perspectives on undue influence in contract law). If you are going to be studying conflict of laws in the same year, you might want to do a dissertation on something specific in the module, once again with a different spin. What you do in your dissertation would inevitably have some sort of relevance and may be applicable, even if indirectly, during the exam.'

Godwin Tan, University College London, LLB Law, Year 3

Research aim and questions

The research aim is essentially the desired outcome: what you want to discover, or the argument you want to make. The research questions are the questions that you will answer throughout your research in order to achieve your aim. Aim for about three or four simple questions.

Key words

These will just be a few key words related to your research. We would recommend the first one should be the broad area of the law the dissertation relates to, such as contract law or EU law, followed by some specific key words or phrases linked to your aim and research questions.

Important sources

This should reflect your preliminary research, and should contain examples of both primary and secondary sources. This provides evidence to the dissertation co-ordinator that you have already considered the subject area and have begun thinking critically about your research area.

After submitting your proposal

Once your proposal has been submitted, you should be told fairly soon whether you have been accepted on the dissertation/research module, assuming it is optional. However, you may not be allocated a supervisor until the following academic year. Don't just wait. Spend some of your summer undertaking some preliminary research and beginning to develop a plan. This will put you in a really good position for the coming academic year.

SELECTING OR BEING ALLOCATED A SUPERVISOR

If your law school allocates supervisors, you do not need to give much thought to this, although it might be sensible to read the law school's staff pages to check there is at least someone interested in your chosen topic. Submit your proposal, and see who you get—it can be a really good way of engaging with a member of staff who you haven't otherwise been taught by.

However, many law schools expect dissertation students to approach a potential supervisor before submitting their proposal. Generally, this will need to be done before the summer break that leads into your final year, or at the very beginning of your final year. A good place to start is approaching the person who normally lectures the subject on which your dissertation is based. For example, if you are planning to research unfair contract terms, approach your contract law lecturer or tutor to see if they can help, or can suggest someone else suitable.

If you plan to study a subject you haven't been taught, check your law school's website and look at the research and teaching interests of all staff in the school. You will be able to narrow down some potential supervisors to approach. If you are still struggling to find an appropriate supervisor, speak to your personal tutor or the dissertation co-ordinator and they will help you. Whether you have input into the choice of supervisor or are simply allocated someone suitable will depend purely on the protocols in your law school.

I WISH I'D KNOWN . . .

'Read widely, ask your tutor for suggestions on what to read as they are an expert in the field.'

Frances Easton, University of Birmingham, Law, Year 3

RETHINKING, PLANNING AND REFINING

Once you have chosen or have been allocated a supervisor, you will need to meet with them and discuss your proposal. This will probably take place within the first few weeks of your final year. The supervisor may contact you to arrange this meeting, but in many law schools it is left up to you to organise. This is the first clear indication that this is your project and your responsibility. Make a good first impression by being proactive, polite and flexible in organising the meeting.

Reviewing your proposal

The first challenge you will probably face will be to rethink aspects of your proposal and refine your research question in accordance with your supervisor's feedback. This may mean focusing your proposal further, redrafting your aims, and even refining your research questions. This can seem difficult and may be frustrating if you have carried out work previously. But your work will be so much better if you refine these key features early on. Keep your goal in mind. What are you trying to achieve and what is the best way to do it? Critique your own work, think hard and don't be afraid to throw some paper away.

Planning your time

Possibly the biggest challenge at this early stage though, is effectively planning your time. You have to be disciplined with the work you will undertake, especially with all the other modules you will be studying and other commitments outside your university work. It is very easy for a dissertation or project to be continually dropping to the bottom of a long list of priorities. Remember that the whole dissertation from the proposal to submission should take around 300–400 hours of work (proportionately less for a shorter research project). Plan your time accordingly to spread this across the whole year.

The best way to do this is to plan the dissertation in various stages. Think about how long each week you are going to spend researching: finding your sources, reading the material and making notes on the research you are undertaking. Think about how long you will undertake this research phase before beginning to write your individual chapters, and how long you will need to spend writing. Be sure to factor in sufficient time for carrying out additional research and redrafting your work. Finally, be sure that you give yourself sufficient time to print and bind your dissertation before submission, assuming that you are not permitted to submit it electronically.

This process of planning should be carefully considered and should be done with your supervisor's guidance. They will be happy to help you and will be impressed that you recognise the need to plan your work. They may also be willing to book in supervision appointments at this stage, so you have clear dates and stages to work towards.

Dealing with administration

Another important consideration early on is whether you need to complete any paperwork for your law school. If your dissertation involves interviews, questionnaires or other data collection exercises, you will need to complete ethical approval forms and training. This is to ensure that any data collection you undertake is done ethically and that any data is used appropriately.

If you wish to use primary sources such as historical documents or public records, you may need to get forms signed by your supervisor or a letter of introduction. You may also need inter-library loans approved for some specialist secondary material. Your dissertation co-ordinator or your supervisor will be able to give you more information on such requirements.

I WISH I'D KNOWN . . .

'Start working on it from the beginning of the year. Don't leave it till the last minute, this will make you so much more stressed and you will end up with a lower quality of work if you rush it.'

Emily Barrett, University of Bristol, Law with Study in Continental Europe, Year 4

RESEARCH PHASE AND EXAMINING THE LITERATURE

Using your skills

Once you have reconsidered your research aim, refined your research questions and planned your time, you will need to begin the arduous but exciting task of researching your subject. You will have already undertaken an initial sweep of the literature in order to construct your proposal. Now it is time to dive deeper into the literature to gain deeper knowledge and a more critical perspective on the subject.

Utilise all the research skills you have developed through your degree so far, and use all sources available to you:

- Check out what is available in the library;
- Speak to the law librarian;
- Research in your institution's digital resources;
- Engage with internet sources.

Use a wide variety of sources and evidence to identify all the key issues and support your analysis and argument. Pull your materials together, and use your analytical and critical skills (see Chapter 10) to identify connections or disparities, and consider different views, theoretical approaches and practical problems, This may well lead you to the exploration of further material, but don't spend too much time exploring issues of only peripheral relevance. You might want to remind yourself of the discussion on research skills in Chapter 8.

It is during this research phase that you may have to undertake data collection, commence any fieldwork or complete any primary document research. This will have to be undertaken with care, but your supervisor or institution will give you any specific guidance for primary data collection.

Being selective

Everybody's experience of researching is different, but a common problem is trying to cram everything you read into the dissertation. Don't be afraid to discard things if they are not appropriate and relevant. It is better to use a bit less material that is all relevant to your project than include inappropriate or irrelevant sources.

The ability to select only relevant sources is an important skill to demonstrate during the completion of the dissertation. As we've seen before in Chapter 8, choosing and using only relevant resources is a very important skill for a successful law student.

THE WRITING PHASE: PUTTING PEN TO PAPER

Planning the structure

The first stage of writing that you will have to do is planning the structure of your dissertation. You may well have prepared an initial draft plan prior to your main research phase and this is good practice. But even so, you'll need to revise it and add depth to it now.

Planning the structure of a dissertation can be difficult, but all you need to do is think carefully about how you are going to answer your research questions, working through each point logically. It is a good idea to divide your plan by chapters, and then divide these again into subheadings. These will form the bones of your dissertation or project, and you can then expand upon these subheadings with summaries of your arguments and/or research within them.

I WISH I'D KNOWN . . .

'Before you start writing, have a one-page plan on what the structure of your dissertation would look like and discuss this plan with either your academic supervisor or a friend who is studying law.'

Godwin Tan, University College London, LLB Law, Year 3

There is no hard and fast rule for structuring the dissertation or research project, and different types of dissertations may require a different structure. For example a comparative dissertation, which is often a requirement for students on law programmes with a year abroad, will look very different from a data-driven analysis of a national legal issue.

Speak to your supervisor and ask for their guidance, bearing in mind that the clearer and more detailed your plan, the better the supervisor will be able to see your thinking and be able to advise. Many law schools will also allow you access to dissertations submitted in previous years so you can see examples of suitable structures, and appropriate writing styles.

Beginning to write

Once you have a carefully considered structure and a clear plan, the process of writing should be far easier. Some students find writing easier than others—but the hardest bit is always making a start. Many students try to write a certain amount of words every day, others will work for long periods of time then step away for a few days to 'recover'. Whatever your writing habits, just do it—start writing.

INSIDER KNOWLEDGE

'Break it down into bitesize chunks. Set yourself reasonable time for each section. If you become stuck on a certain section do not procrastinate. Move on and come back to it later. Looking at something with fresh eyes always helps.'

Salauoddin Asghar, Strategy and Performance Manager, London Borough of Barking and Dagenham

If you are struggling to start, you may find it useful to sit down and begin typing or writing on a blank piece of paper for 10 minutes without stopping. Don't worry about spelling, punctuation, grammar or formatting. Just write. This is called free writing and it is an excellent tool to start getting your ideas down onto paper. You can always edit it later or even throw it away. If it is useful, type it up and edit it, and build in your evidence and research.

Keep in mind that a dissertation or research project is not an essay, you can't just finish it overnight. You will need to be disciplined in achieving deadlines and submitting chapters for feedback to your supervisor. Setting yourself realistic deadlines for chapters is so important and is the only way to complete this project.

You should also start writing as soon as possible. Many students like to leave writing the whole dissertation until the end, and are nervous about starting to write before they feel absolutely all possible research is completed. However, writing can often trigger ideas to inform your research. And if you delay writing too long you won't have time to undertake additional research that becomes necessary, nor to rewrite chunks of your work if you decide to refocus and adapt your research questions.

I WISH I'D KNOWN . . .

'Start writing early and don't be afraid of exceeding the word limit at the start. You will eventually realise that certain paragraphs are either irrelevant or incorrect and will need to be taken out.'

Godwin Tan, University College London, LLB Law, Year 3

Finally, an obvious but important reminder: be sure to back up all your drafts and notes. Many students have lost substantial amounts of their work from failing to back up. Save it on pen drives, on cloud-based services, and even email it to yourself. Just make sure you have numerous copies. Law schools will not accept technological problems as a valid excuse for late submission or poor performance. You should also save drafts as separate documents as you go along. Not only does this ensure you've got something to fall back on if you ever have a problem saving your work, it is essential should any questions later arise about whether the work is all your own.

Assistance with research and writing—working with your supervisor

Institutions will have different protocols and expectations regarding the level of help that supervisors will provide during the course of your dissertation or project. This will usually be outlined to you at the beginning of the process by the supervisor or the dissertation/project co-ordinator.

Whatever role the supervisor will play, use them! Remember to keep in touch with them and approach them if you need help. All dissertation supervisors will want to help where they can to guide you towards producing the best work, so far as they are able within the guidelines of the particular module.

Remember that supervisors will be far more inclined to help you if they can see that you are working hard, and if they feel you value their time. Be sure to treat your supervisor with respect and always attend booked meetings or notify the supervisor well in advance if you won't be able to attend. Value your supervisor's expertise—both in relation to the subject and in research and writing. Be sure to listen to their comments and address their feedback. They have been in the same position as you and can pass on valuable guidance and information to help you, if you are willing to listen, engage and respond positively.

While not all supervisory relationships run smoothly, most do, and many supervisors and students find these amongst the most rewarding of their many teaching and learning experiences. If you do have any significant problems with your supervisor, speak to the dissertation coordinator or your personal tutor. They will be able to help you resolve any issues.

Writing up and the drafting process

Once you have first drafts of your chapters, they will need redrafting. Depending on your law school's approach, supervisors may be able to give you feedback on individual chapters, and this feedback will need to be incorporated into the next draft. Supervisors' comments will be really valuable in drawing out weaknesses in your argument and writing, making a huge difference to the standard of your completed work. Make sure you allocate enough time to making these changes and redrafting appropriately. Then you will probably need to redraft it again after reading it and making your own comments. This may happen a number of times. This can be frustrating, but it is an important part of the writing process.

As you go through this drafting process, be sure that all of your chapters have a clear and coherent narrative. All of your chapters should contribute to the overall aim of the work, even if each chapter has explored a different aspect or answered a different research question. Your chapters should all work to tell a clear story, to address a clear aim. This is often referred to as the narrative in your work. But this simply means that the work is clearly addressing the research aim throughout, and all your chapters are working towards a coherent goal.

Redrafting also ensures that your arguments are sufficiently critical and analytical, and not overly descriptive. It should ensure that your themes and arguments are coherent and developed throughout the work. Redrafting should also eliminate spelling, punctuation and grammatical errors, while ensuring that your referencing is comprehensive and consistent. If you have struggled with effective redrafting and editing in the past, try reading your work aloud to yourself, and try giving it to a friend to read it through for you. Reading it aloud will allow you to hear errors that you have become blind to, while a critical friend will be able to spot issues with your work that you can easily overlook with project weary eyes.

Remember to proofread all aspects of your work. This is really important for several reasons:

- Check for errors or typographical mistakes that will reduce the overall standard of your work;
- Ensure your work flows and your section headings make sense;
- Check that everything is referenced and attributed to avoid plagiarism (see Chapter 11 for more on referencing, plagiarism and good academic practice);
- Make sure your references are consistent and conform to your law school's preferred style.

COMING TO AN END

Keeping positive

There may be times during the research, writing or drafting processes where you might despair and think that you can't finish it. You may even start to hate the dissertation or research project, and wish you'd never started.

This is all part of the challenge and you must stay positive. If you feel sick of working on it, walk away for a few hours or even a day or two. Go and do something fun that has nothing to do with the project, relax and don't think about it. This will allow you to clear your head, re-energise and then come back to it with fresh perspective. You could also try discussing the subject with a friend or family member, to remind yourself of why you were interested in it in the first place. You can finish it, and you will. You just need to take a break, regroup and come back ready to nail it!

Binding and submission

Many institutions have turned to electronic rather than paper submissions for much assessed work, but it is still more common to require dissertations (and sometimes research projects) to be submitted in traditional bound paper form.

So the final two tasks to complete the dissertation will probably be binding and submission. Most universities have a copy shop or print shop that will both print and bind the work for you and, if not, there will be one in your local town/city. Aim to print your dissertation at least a week before your deadline to make sure you have plenty of time. If you wait till the last day you could be met by queues of other students all trying to do the same thing, and miss your deadline.

Make sure that you have checked your law school's requirements for submission. Some schools will want you to submit your dissertation or project with two copies, and some will have specific requirements for the type of binding. If you check with your school and write down the specific directions, the print shop will take care of it for you. Once it's been printed and bound, it is time to submit—don't get the submission date or time wrong.

Using the dissertation or legal research project in the future

As we discussed earlier, there are many reasons to undertake a dissertation or legal research project: to further your knowledge of a chosen subject, to explore a particular social or political interest, to undertake the challenge of writing a long piece of work, for the sheer thrill of seeing your name on the front of a bound piece of work, or just because it is a requirement of your course. However, these projects can also be very valuable for employability. They can be an excellent opportunity to demonstrate your sophisticated research and writing skills to future employers and evidence a range of transferable skills.

For many careers, including the legal profession, the ability to undertake detailed and comprehensive research is an essential skill. Extended pieces of work like these provide you with tangible evidence of your research ability, which you can show to potential employers during an interview or assessment day.

While completing the dissertation you will have selected, read, critiqued and presented numerous types of legal and non-legal sources, appraised them for their validity, incorporated them effectively, and referenced them appropriately. You will have become adept at locating relevant resources using various digital search engines and hardcopy libraries to find the most suitable sources for your work. You will have had to read sources, summarise and synthesise them, using them appropriately to support your critique of the subject. You will also have been ruthless; discarding irrelevant material and only selecting resources that are most relevant to your work. You may even have undertaken practical fieldwork or data collection. Regardless of whether you have realised it, you will have become a skilled researcher!

The dissertation or research project also shows that you have and can maintain a real and deep interest in the law, by focusing on a particular issue and exploring it in depth. It can provide a valuable talking point and demonstrate your critical, analytical and evaluative abilities, especially if you remain up-to-date with the subject of your dissertation. It gives you the opportunity to demonstrate that you are a reflective person through explaining the experience of undertaking this work, the challenges you faced and how you overcame them. It shows potential employers that you can work under your own initiative, project manage your work, manage your time, deal with pressure, have a constructive relationship with a supervisor, and complete a long project on time and to a good professional standard. Be sure to tell any potential employer exactly what you can do.

SUMMARY—HELP YOURSELF . . .

- **Explore the possibilities**
  - Find out what different research modules are offered, and whether they are compulsory or optional.
  - Think about the benefits a research project can offer you, while reflecting on your own work habits.
  - Speak to those you need to, such as the module co-ordinator and/ or potential supervisors, well in advance of starting your work.
  - Consider possible topics, and check availability of material.

- **Plan carefully**
  - Spend time thinking about the topic, title, research aim and questions.
  - Continually refine and modify to ensure a focused approach.
  - Check all requirements, including any need for permissions etc.
  - Don't skimp on the planning stage—get a clear structure in place, and add to it as your research progresses.

- **Work steadily, methodically and critically**
  - Research broadly and deeply, and keep pursuing relevant material from a variety of sources.
  - Organise your time across the whole period available—make, and stick to, deadlines.
  - Challenge your assumptions, critique the material, question your arguments—write, rewrite and rewrite again.
  - Edit your work to ensure it is the best it can be.
  - Stay positive.

- **Use your supervisor effectively**
  - Take responsibility for your own project, but benefit from your supervisor's experience.
  - Make the most of every meeting by being well prepared, and knowing what you want from the meeting.
  - Act on feedback.

- **Don't forget about your work once it is finished**
  - Reflect on the skills and competencies you have demonstrated.
  - Be proud of your achievements.

15

EXAMS AND REVISION

'N.B.—Do not on any account
attempt to write on both sides
of the paper at once.'

W. C. SELLAR AND R. J. YEATMAN,
1066 and All That: A Memorable History of England

INTRODUCTION

Exams are by far the most common form of assessment in UK law schools, and you will almost inevitably sit quite a few of them during your legal studies. Of course education, including legal education, is about much more than exams, and success is about much more than results. That should be clear throughout this book. Nevertheless a successful law student wants their success reflected in their results—and exams will make up a big part of those results.

By understanding the format of exams, knowing how best to prepare for them, and thinking about effective approaches to them, you can approach exams calmly and be in the best possible position to achieve the results you deserve. This chapter will look at all these things, with hints and tips on things to do and things to avoid in your revision, preparation and exam—some just as practical as the incomparable advice of Sellar and Yeatman that opens this chapter. Many of the general points on assessment covered in Chapter 11 and advice on essays and problem questions in Chapter 12 will also be relevant to exams.

We won't pretend exams aren't important, or stressful, but if you approach them effectively, you'll be in a position to do your best. This chapter will also consider how to deal with the aftermath of exam time, whether the outcome was better or worse than you'd hoped for.

TYPES OF EXAM

'Closed book' and 'open book' exams

The vast majority of law exams are 'closed book' or 'closed note' exams. These are traditional exams where you do not know what topics are going to come up, and are not permitted to take any material into the exam with you.

Even in a 'closed book' exam you may be provided with some selected statutory material in the exam, or be allowed to bring in an approved statute book or specified statutes. (A statute book is simply a collection of relevant statutory materials, such as Blackstone's Statutes series—your tutor may recommend a particular book.) If you are allowed to take in a statute book, or equivalent, it must usually be unannotated, meaning that you cannot write any notes in it at all. You may be allowed to highlight parts or add tabs, but every law school's rules are different—you *must* check your law school's rules to ensure you don't commit an exam offence with potentially very serious consequences.

If you are allowed to bring in statutes, there is no obligation to do so, but you might be at a disadvantage if you don't. This is because the examiner will assume you have that material with you, so won't give you any additional credit for recalling it, and you won't be able to check a provision should you need to.

'Open book' or 'open note' exams usually look very similar to traditional 'closed book' exams, but allow you to bring material into the exam with you. You may be allowed to bring in any material at all, or just a set number of pages of notes, or only some types of material. Make sure you check the rules for your particular exam and stick to them rigidly.

Both closed and open book exams have their advocates. If you are very able but do not have a great memory, you may well find open book exams a much fairer test of your ability. But if you have an excellent memory you might prefer closed book exams where you won't be distracted by having notes with you.

Take-home and seen exams

Much less common are 'take-home exams' or 'seen' or 'open' exams, or similar names. These differ significantly from both closed and open book exams, and may well differ in quite how they operate in different institutions, so check your own rules carefully.

In a take-home exam, you will usually be given exam questions with a set period of time, usually no more than a few days, to work on them in your own time before submitting them, rather than sitting them unseen in an exam environment. In many ways it has more in common with a traditional essay or problem question assessment, but with much less time for research and planning. The time pressure is less acute than in a traditional exam, but more can be expected of you.

A seen or open exam may give you some advance notice as to the topic that you will be tested on or give you particular work or reading in advance, with you then facing a question or questions on that topic during your exam. You may be permitted to bring your prepared work into the exam with you and the exam is often of a longer length than a traditional exam, but this isn't necessarily the case.

Length of exam

Law exams vary in length, but are rarely shorter than one hour, or longer than three hours. If you have specific educational requirements you may be allowed additional time and should discuss this with your personal tutor or student support centre.

Longer exams can initially feel a bit daunting, but you may come to prefer these over shorter exams, as the longer time gives you more flexibility when allocating time for thinking, planning and writing each question. Shorter exams can feel particularly frantic, although it is easier to retain your focus throughout—and they are over more quickly.

Structure of exam

You will normally have some choice over which questions you answer: for example you might have to answer two questions from a choice of four, or three from seven. Quite how many questions you are given, and how many you must answer, will depend on your law school and module.

Sometimes an exam will include one or more compulsory questions, or will require you to pick at least one question from separate parts of the exam paper. It is therefore really important to read and understand the exam rubric (the instructions) before starting work. You should be told what the rubric is well before the exam so you know what to expect, but do check if you have not been told.

Questions may have more than one part—follow the instructions on such questions closely to see whether you should answer all parts, or only some. For example it might say 'Answer both (a) and (b)', or 'Answer either (a) or (b)'—getting it wrong can have a big impact on your mark.

Type of questions

Law exams typically have a mix of essay questions and problem questions, although different modules may favour one over the other. We've looked at these in Chapter 12, and the points there remain relevant, the difference being that you've got much less time to put your response together in an exam. You may have a free choice from both kinds of question, or you may have to choose a certain number of questions of each type. Where there are restrictions the exam paper should be split into sections so it is clear which questions you have to choose from.

Other styles of question are less common in law exams but you may come across multiple choice questions (MCQs), or short-form questions requiring a short explanation, summary or mini-essay. If present in an exam they may well be a compulsory part of a longer exam that also contains traditional essay and problem questions. You may even come across reflective questions in an exam, but this is uncommon, and would normally be made clear to you in advance.

REVISION AND PREPARING FOR EXAMS
Preparation

Exams aim to test how far you have achieved the learning outcomes of the module you have been studying and meet the applicable assessment criteria. So law exams will typically aim to test your knowledge and understanding of a subject, and your ability to analyse and apply relevant law to issues and problems—using, not just reciting, the law. That is what your preparation needs to establish, as illustrated in Figure 15.1.

FIGURE 15.1: Basic requirements for an exam

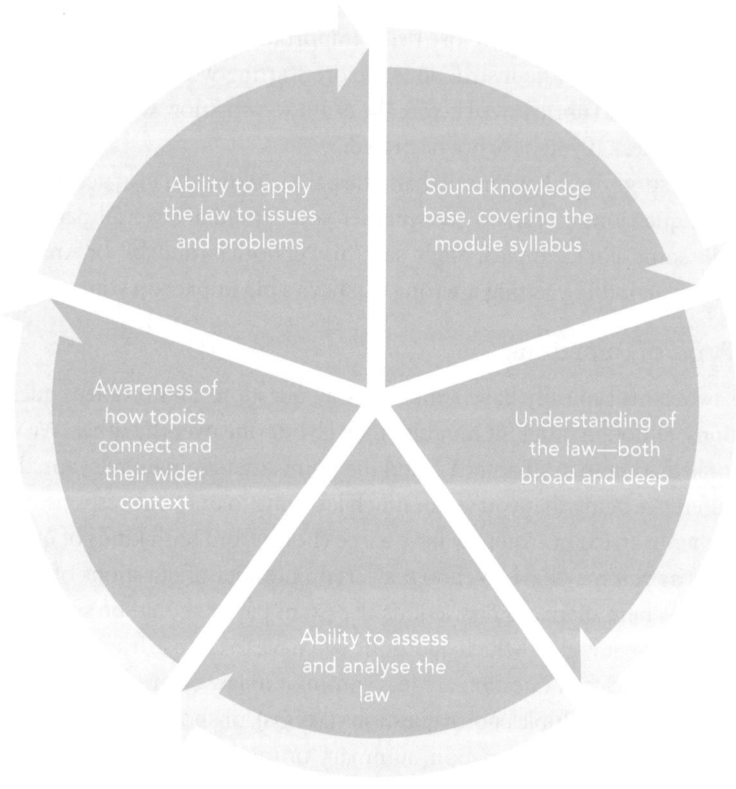

In order to do this, you will also need:

- An awareness of, and ability to use, relevant legal materials;
- The ability to structure your material and argument effectively;
- The ability to write coherently under time pressure.

None of these things can be gained overnight. Preparation for an exam therefore starts as soon as you start studying a module; the more work you put in, the better prepared you will be. The more reading you do, the more formative exercises you undertake, the more you revise and consolidate your knowledge as you go along, the easier you will find the final stages of preparation.

I WISH I'D KNOWN . . .

'I wish I had made notes for subjects throughout the year, rather than trying to rush them at the end as the revision time goes very quickly.'

Charlotte Brown, Bournemouth University, LLB Law, Year 3

So ideally your preparation for an exam is over the long term. This means you can build a solid foundation and begin to stretch yourself. It also enables you to benefit from feedback, both formal and informal, throughout your studies, lifting you to greater heights. (Chapter 13 explores feedback and how to make best use of it.)

While long-term preparation is the ideal, that doesn't mean that all is lost if you have taken a more relaxed approach to your studies during the term. All the things you need to show can be achieved to some degree through end-of-study revision alone, but if you haven't been preparing during the year, you will have a harder task ahead of you.

Revision

Your revision needs to work on all the things you need to demonstrate, not just on storing (and retrieving) information. Figure 15.2 shows the stages of revision.

FIGURE 15.2: Essential stages of revision

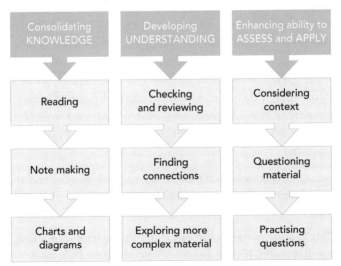

Think too about whether you need to work on the other skills that are essential to do well in law exams. For example, it might be a good idea to practise:

- Incorporating different legal sources effectively within your answer;
- Structuring your answers so that the issues and argument are clear;
- Writing brief but effective introductions and conclusions;
- Communicating clearly, working on your written English language skills if necessary.

I WISH I'D KNOWN . . .

'Revision is what it says it is—looking back at material you have already learnt. You shouldn't be using this time to learn concepts for the first time, rather you should be using it to develop what you already know and gathering more information to be able to deliver a first-class answer in your exam.'

Emily Barrett, University of Bristol, Law with Study in Continental Europe, Year 4

Organising your revision

To achieve all these things your revision needs to be active, not passive. Simply reading material or listening to lecture recordings is ineffective even for consolidating knowledge, let alone the deeper-level learning that is needed to do well in a law exam.

What revision activities work best for you depends to some extent on your own learning style and strengths. We touched on these in Chapter 8. For example, if you have identified strengths in the Read/Write category, you may find making lists most helpful, while a Visual learner might do better with diagrams and plans. It is helpful to use a variety of revision techniques, both to test what works best for you, and to maximise the effectiveness of your revision overall. To revise actively:

- Read actively. Look back at Chapter 8 for tips on how to make the most of your reading, but remember to keep thinking critically (see Chapter 10);
- Refine your notes so you can easily flick through topics at a later stage of revision. Try sub-headings, colour coding, lists, flash

cards and diagrams. There are plenty of apps available to aid your revision, for example iMindMap (https://imindmap.com/) or Evernote (https://evernote.com/);

- Rephrase points rather than copying out textbook definitions—pretend you have to explain a point to a non-expert friend;
- Make a separate list of topics where your understanding is shaky so you can come back to these in depth later;
- Practise answering exam style questions. You can use past papers and tutorial/seminar questions—textbooks too often have sample questions at the end of each chapter. Sometimes just prepare a plan, sometimes prepare an answer and at least some of the time write an answer under time pressure. Evaluate/'mark' your answer afterwards;
- Find a 'study buddy' or start a study group with some friends. Don't just chat about the subject or exam, set yourselves particular tasks such as choosing a past exam question and comparing answers, or selecting some further reading that you then summarise and explain to each other.

I WISH I'D KNOWN . . .

'It may sound obvious, but you wouldn't believe how few of my friends complete timed practice problem questions before their exams. Most of us look at past papers and questions, but very few actually answer them properly under timed conditions.'

Jessica Allen, University of Nottingham, Law with French and French Law, Year 4

Allow yourself enough time for your revision and organise the time you've got. (We looked at time management more generally in Chapter 4.) If your exams are mainly at the end of the academic year then the Easter vacation tends to be the most concentrated time for serious revision. Creating a revision timetable is important to give you focus and ensure you cover everything. It should also reflect other commitments, such as paid work or family, and allow time for exercise and relaxation which are essential to your well-being through this period.

Remember to take account of when you work best—morning, afternoon or evening—giving some of your best time to all of your subjects over the course of your revision. And you shouldn't necessarily allocate equal time for every subject:

- Did you work hard through the year on all modules? If you neglected a module during the year, it will need more time now;

- What is the credit value of the exam? All exams are important, but one with a bigger impact on your grade should get more time;

- How difficult did you find the module? You will need more time for modules you found particularly challenging, but don't neglect your stronger subjects.

You've probably made yourself a revision timetable before, but if you need help creating one there are lots of guides and templates available online—it doesn't need to be complicated. There are also apps, such as MyStudyLife (http://www.mystudylife.com), that can help you organise your time.

I WISH I'D KNOWN . . .

'I wish I'd known how helpful it could have been to create a revision schedule. I also wish I'd known to not plan in revision sessions the night before the exam; it only brings confusion and stress.'

Gabrielle Bargas, University College London, LLB Law with French Law, Year 2

What to revise

What you revise for each module should be guided by the syllabus and learning outcomes: there is little point in revising something that is not being assessed. Coverage of topics in lectures, tutorials and seminars will be a good guide as to what in general terms is most likely to turn up in your exam, but given the importance of independent study, this should not be your sole guide.

Remember that anything on the syllabus could be in the exam, unless you've been told expressly from an authoritative source (that means a lecturer, not a fellow student) that it won't be. Topics covered in formative and other summative assessments can still be included in an exam.

You should also have regard to the type and style of exam you will be taking. If you will be given a choice of questions then you may be able to limit the topics you cover to some extent. If the exam has compulsory questions or very little choice, you sensibly need to cover all topics.

Students sometimes spend lots of time analysing past exam papers, hoping to work out what topics will come up. Past papers can give an indication of likely or particularly favourite topics for a module, but be careful not to over-think. They can be a guide to what your lecturers view as the 'big' topics that will nearly always come up—assuming that neither the lecturers nor the law have changed—and the style of question, but can't do much more than this. After all, if a topic has come up every year for the past three years, does that make it more or less likely it will come up again—will the question-setter follow a habit or think it is time for a change? There is no way of knowing, so don't waste time trying to work it out.

Similarly, where available, examiners' reports from previous years' papers can be helpful. They may give you an idea of areas where other students commonly struggle or omit points in the subject. But never try to 'learn' answers from past exams if you are given examples to look at— not only will they not be answering *your* questions, markers are very alert to this and will give you little or no credit for simply parroting someone else's words.

So while module coverage and past practice is of value in identifying topics that are more likely to come up, it would be very risky to think you can work out what is coming up in detail or with any great certainty. 'Question-spotting', ie revising only for those questions you are expecting to come up, is a dangerous habit to adopt. If you get it wrong you will find yourself woefully underprepared for the exam. Even if you correctly identify a topic that comes up, it could be a narrow question on an element of the topic you are less comfortable with, or in a question format you don't like, or combined with a question on a topic you haven't revised. Targeted revision, ie focusing effort on the main topics and your preferred topics, is generally sensible provided you cover enough topics and in sufficient depth; question-spotting is not.

INSIDER KNOWLEDGE

'Do not leave it to the last minute. Make revision notes weeks in advance so you can return to them at the salient time. Do not, I repeat, do not, gamble on what may or may not come up.'

David McCormick, Barrister, Exchange Chambers

COPING THROUGH REVISION AND EXAMS

Taking control

Coping with a stressful event is easier if you feel in control. That means knowing what is coming, as far as possible, and being prepared. So ensure you check and double-check all the details of your exam—date, time, length, permitted material, number of questions etc. Work through past papers and practise questions during your revision to aid familiarity, but also remember to review your module description and/or handbook in relation to module assessment and revisit any revision lectures and study guidance provided.

Your revision plan should ensure you are as prepared as you can be, covering all you need to from the syllabus. Work through each topic, testing yourself as you go, and create short revision notes for regular quick recaps as well as lengthier notes. Practise writing quickly and effectively in limited time so you know you can.

Staying healthy

The exam and revision period can be intense and stressful and you need to give yourself the best possible chance of success. Your health and well-being are important at all times, but much easier to neglect during the exam period. Don't. As a successful law student you need to look after your own well-being, just as you take personal responsibility for your studies. That doesn't mean that you are alone, any more than you are alone in your studies; there is always help and guidance available. But it does mean you need to reflect on your own position, identify strengths and weaknesses in your approach, attitude and lifestyle, monitor yourself, and take action when you need to, whether alone or with help.

INSIDER KNOWLEDGE

'Go back to basics. Talk to other students who you trust or who seem to be on top of things. Speak to students in the years above and ask how they coped.'

Charlie Shepherd, Company Director

There are simple—and obvious—ways you can help yourself while revising and taking exams. Don't ignore them.

- **Take regular breaks**

  - Allow for regular breaks in your revision schedule and after each exam. It is not effective to keep working for long periods of time at a stretch—your concentration will drop significantly over time and your revision will be much less effective. Breaks also give your brain the chance to process information, making it easier to recall.

  - As a rough guide, 45 minutes of revision with 15 minutes' break per hour seems to work for most people. However some find they work best in shorter bursts, perhaps 20–30 minutes, with a shorter break in between and occasional longer breaks. Others prefer to work for a full hour or even a bit more, before taking a break, but utilising different study techniques within that time to keep focused. See what works best for you.

  - Use your breaks effectively to recharge. Get outside if you can. Build in longer breaks for exercise, whatever form that takes— anything counts. Physical activity and relaxation are essential to your well-being and will contribute to successful study.

- **Eat healthily**

  - However short of time you are, don't rely on takeaways and convenience food, your brain needs all the nutrients it can get. There is lots of advice out there (see for example: http://www.nhs. uk/LiveWell/Goodfood/Pages/goodfoodhome.aspx)—it needn't take more time or money.

  - If you are in shared accommodation, consider sharing meals with a friend during this busy time—it will reduce the overall time you spend cooking and encourage you to take a break while you eat together.

- Get enough sleep

  - Your revision and exam performance will be compromised if you don't get enough sleep. If you keep working through the night when exams are approaching, any benefit will be minimal because you will be too tired to concentrate.

  - Sleep deprivation will impact on your ability to understand the law, retain information, and think and write coherently in the exam

- Keep positive

  - Cultivating a positive mindset helps you cope with revision and exams. If you find yourself feeling overwhelmed, or doubting yourself, change your focus by remembering how far you've already come and how much you do know. Speak to a supportive friend or family member.

  - After a tough exam a low mood is understandable. To keep positive, accept that what is done is done—and is probably not as disastrous as you think. Keeping looking forward, don't dwell on the past.

  - Keep things in perspective—exams are important, but other things such as family and friends are far more so. No bad experience lasts forever, and no academic disaster is as important in the long run as we think it is at the time. It would be hard to find any successful individual who had never had a bad day.

I WISH I'D KNOWN . . .

'Remember to not cut out the rest of your life during exam term—keep on cooking and eating, keep on exercising, make sure you do venture outdoors and speak to people about things other than law.'

Fiona Lin, University of Cambridge, Law, Year 3

Seeking help if you need it

The stress of exams affects people in different ways, and to varying extents. Unfortunately some people find it much harder to cope than others, and may find themselves in a high state of anxiety, whether during revision or exams themselves. This can affect both preparation and performance, which in turn adds to the anxiety and makes things worse.

If you find worry and anxiety are impacting on your ability to do your best in exams, or suspect it will because of past experience, then seek help as soon as you possibly can. All universities offer support services to their students, and are very experienced in getting students through difficult periods. Let your personal tutor know too, so s/he can provide support and advice, and direct you to sources of help. Being stressed or anxious does not stop you from being a successful law student, it makes you human. But you do need to help yourself—and that includes asking others for support and advice when you need it.

INSIDER KNOWLEDGE

'Most people experience modest levels of stress, but try to recognise when stress levels become high or uncomfortable and don't be afraid to seek help from your personal tutor or university wellbeing service.'

Dr Richard Bowyer, Senior Lecturer, University of Exeter

IN THE EXAM ROOM

Staying calm

Staying calm in an exam helps you to do your best. That doesn't mean being entirely without nerves, apprehension or excitement—a bit of adrenalin is good—it just means keeping things under control. If you feel nervous or anxious:

- Don't join in discussions of the law or what might come up in the exam while queuing to enter the exam room;
- Focus on the now: do not dwell on past perceived failures, or future plans which depend on the exam;
- Shut out negative thought patterns: remember that you have worked hard, you have revised and you can do this;
- Breathe slowly, deeply and regularly;
- If you are struggling to focus, slow your reading down and look at each individual element of a question, reassuring yourself that there will be things there that you can deal with;

- Avoid looking at other students—don't worry if they are writing before you, or asking for extra paper or anything else—focus on your own work.

I WISH I'D KNOWN . . .

'If you see a question you have not prepared for when you flip open the exam paper, don't panic! Once you go into panic mode, everything is lost. Take some deep breaths and try to use what knowledge you have to formulate a logical answer.'

Monica Chen, University College London, LLB Law, Year 2

By staying calm you can avoid making the kind of mistakes that could lead to you dropping big marks, as discussed in Chapter 11. In the panic of an exam it is particularly easy to forget to:

- Follow instructions carefully;
- Answer the question, not just the topic;
- Support your points with authority;
- Explain points clearly and directly.

Time management in exams

You need to manage your time in the exam carefully to do your best. It is important to split your time evenly between questions if they are evenly weighted. If you spend much too long on the first question, you will have to do later questions in a rush, and may even run out of time completely by the final question. The negative impact of this on your overall mark will far outweigh any benefit you'd get from doing more on the earlier question. That doesn't mean you should stop mid-sentence, but once your allotted time is up, wrap up quickly and move on.

I WISH I'D KNOWN . . .

'I wish I had known that each exam question deserves the same amount of time and to not spend too much time on one question.'

Glen Joel Sylvester, Bournemouth University, LLB Law, Year 3

Practising answering exam-style questions in limited time will really help you with time management in the exam itself. It will also remind you that you need to use your time wisely—getting to the main issues rather than discussing the law generally.

If you do run out of time then remember that an examiner will give you credit for anything that is possibly credit-worthy, but cannot give you marks for a blank space. A few marks are much better than none when it comes to working out your final grade so get as much down as you can. Even a few bullet points will show the examiner that you did have some relevant knowledge, understood the question and were going to head in the right direction. Obviously, the more detail you can include the better, but at least try to get a few points down.

If you finish writing before the end of the exam please don't leave early, even if you are allowed to. Use the time to check through your answers, adding in any further points or authorities that you have remembered, and clarifying passages that are a bit unclear.

If you've finished with a lot of time to spare then you need to look carefully to see if you have missed a significant issue. If you have, add a paragraph to the essay, indicating with an asterisk where it should go in your answer. Consider whether you have provided enough depth in your answers and if not, add more relevant authorities and discuss the issues a bit further if you can. Make full use of the time you have.

Choosing questions

If you have a choice of questions you need to make your choice fairly quickly, in order to maximise your time planning and writing your answers. You will know what topics you feel most comfortable with and may have a preference for particular types of question, so can probably immediately identify one or two questions you like, and can also rule out a couple. That will bring you pretty close to the number of questions you will have to answer; you can then select the best of the rest to make up your choice. Make at least a provisional choice of questions before starting to write, so you don't spend more time agonising over your choice later on.

As we discussed in Chapter 12, neither essay nor problem questions are intrinsically easier. It is usually best to do a mix of both if you can. You may prefer one over the other, but students aren't always right in their perception of which they are better at, so don't let the style of question influence you too much. Formative assignments may give you an indication of where your strengths lie, but, in any event, you may have little choice if your preferred topics come up in a particular form.

Approaching the questions

Most students choose to start with the question they think is their strongest. This is sensible as it enables you to start positively, and hopefully impress the examiner. There is a risk though that you could spend too much time on the first question if it is your best topic. Accordingly some students start with another question, and do their favourite one second. It makes sense to leave the question you think will be your weakest until last so if you run short of time it has the least impact on your overall mark, but if you split your time sensibly this shouldn't happen.

Read the question really carefully before starting to write. Do not assume that you know what the topic is just because it looks like a question you did in a tutorial, or it is in the same place as a question on that topic in the previous year's exam paper. Read, think and identify the issues, making sure you have the knowledge base you need to deal adequately with all, or nearly all, of them.

Planning your answer before you start writing any question is really important. The plan helps you to structure your answer and arguments so you know how to start and where you are going, and helps you to focus on the question. It gives you the opportunity to note down any points or cases that you immediately recall—you can also add to the plan while you are writing as points occur to you.

You can write your plan in any form that suits you, but keep it brief. Ideally your plan should go in your answer book (unless you are told not to do this) so if you run out of time when writing the essay you might still get a bit of credit for your approach. Chapter 12 provides guidance on planning and structuring essays and problem questions.

How much should I write?

Students sometimes ask how much they need to write in an exam answer. There is no simple answer to this—it will depend on how many questions you have to answer, the time you've got and your writing style. If you have the opportunity to look at sample exam answers, look at what other students have managed to produce in the time you will be given. And of course practise writing under timed conditions to develop your skills in writing efficiently and effectively.

In a standard law exam, with forty-five to sixty minutes per question, most lecturers would say about 1,200 to 1,500 words per question is realistic. But remember that you are not being marked on the length of your answer—your paper is read, not weighed. What matters is what you say.

If you can grasp the issues speedily, and then write quickly and effectively, you will have an undoubted advantage in an exam. Because this enables you to pack in more content—more law, more application, more analysis. But simply writing lots is not the route to a good answer. As we've discussed before (see Chapter 11), your discussion needs to be relevant, focused and thoughtful. You need to be concise and precise. Just writing down everything you know won't get a good mark, however many pages you fill.

But short answers are also not likely to gain high marks. If you can write concisely and effectively, then you can produce a good answer in much less space than many other students might manage. But your answer must contain enough content. You need to address all the issues, explain all the relevant law, deal with complexities and analyse and apply the law. That takes space, however concise you are. If a typical student might write about 1,200–1,500 words, then writing only 600–800 words is going to put you at an obvious disadvantage.

Different considerations for different exams

Closed book exams

Some students worry that in a traditional closed book law exam they won't be able to recall the information they need, or won't be able to identify what a question is about. Effective revision should help you to locate and recall the material you need, while remaining calm, and lots of practice can help you to spot and focus on the important issues.

Remember too that the examiner knows you do not have information with you and are working under pressure: s/he does not expect miracles of recall. In a closed book exam you will get marks for relevant knowledge, as well as for showing your understanding, analysis and ability to apply the law—but better marks always come from moving beyond simple recitation of facts and knowledge. Don't waste time setting out detailed case facts, repeating memorised lecture notes or covering really basic points at length.

You need to refer to relevant material, particularly primary sources, but also important secondary sources such as reform papers and articles. However, the examiner won't expect you to provide full details, such as a complete case name, or article title, or citations—just enough to identify the material. If you are allowed a statute book or equivalent, you mustn't waste time copying out statutory provisions—just use it to jog your memory of a particular provision, or to make accurate reference to a relevant section.

Open book exams

It is tempting to think open book exams are easier than closed book exams, but this is not so: perhaps surprisingly, students often do less well in open book exams. This may partly be because the examiner will give less credit for simple recitation of relevant knowledge (after all, you have the information with you), but is usually because students have not prepared properly.

A common misconception is that you need to do less revision for an open book exam, because you have your notes with you. In fact, the best students revise just as hard for an open book exam as a closed book exam and barely refer to their notes during the exam. Any time you spend looking up information or checking notes is time you are not spending answering the question; so the more you understand and the more you can recall, the better you will do.

Because of this it is really important that you prepare your material effectively. Don't take in piles of notes and textbooks—you'll never be able to find what you want in a hurry. Better to have a manageable selection of material—a few diagrams, checklists and summaries—that enables you to check for issues you might have forgotten or remind yourself of key cases or academic viewpoints. If you don't know the law before you start the exam, you are highly unlikely to grasp it, and be able to explain and apply it, during the exam—you may not even be able to identify the correct issues to begin with.

Another risk in an open note exam is a temptation to copy material. At worst this amounts to plagiarism: you cannot adopt another's work as your own without acknowledgement in an exam, any more than at other times. Make sure you stick to good academic practice at all times (see Chapter 11 for more on this). Even without plagiarism—perhaps you are reciting your own earlier-prepared work, or using another's work but with acknowledgement—copying means you are not directly engaging with and addressing the question. This is not the way to be a successful law student.

AFTER THE EXAM

It's over!

The immediate aftermath of an exam can be a strange time. You may feel exhausted, relieved, hyped-up and excited, despairing, or strangely deflated. This will depend on how you found the exam, your personality, and how sleep-deprived and stressed you have been. It may also depend on whether this is the first of many exams that you will be taking over the next few days or weeks, or a one-off, or your last exam of the year or law programme.

If you have been taking the exam in a room with lots of other law students there will be lots of excited or nervous chatter in groups outside the exam room as students discuss what questions they answered, whether it was difficult or easy and what the examiner was expecting for a particular question. If you find this debrief helps you calm down then that's great, but it doesn't work for everyone. If you find it stressful to think about the exam, or if there is any danger at all that a casual remark will lead you to worry about whether you've got something right or not, then avoid these discussions—head off in another direction as soon as the exam is over, or stick with friends who don't want to discuss the exam.

Take some time to wind down after an exam. A walk can help to clear your head, allowing you to process thoughts more positively than sitting and dwelling on things. Being active is particularly good if you found the exam tough. But anything that distracts you a bit can be good—listening to a favourite piece of music, immersing yourself in a familiar or exciting novel or just going out to a cafe.

When reviewing the exam after your wind down, don't dwell on the subject itself—it is too late to change what you've written. Instead think about your approach to the exam:

- Did you have enough time, or do you need to be more rigorous in your time management?

- Did you manage to direct your writing to the question, or do you need to work on your answer planning?

- Did you stay calm, or should you be trying some relaxation techniques?

- Did your organisation of any permissible material enable you to use it effectively?

By reflecting on your experience you can reduce the chances of repeating any problems. If you are having difficulties in studying or with your exam technique, if you are ill, or if stress or anxiety is becoming a serious problem then seek advice as soon as you can from your personal tutor or student union/guild advisors, or approach any other relevant source of student support provided in your institution.

INSIDER KNOWLEDGE

'I must admit I did get stressed easily. Chilling out after the exams is a must and try not to overthink the questions.'

Liz MacDonald, Trainee Solicitor, Whatley Weston & Fox

Responding to the results

You will be told when and how your exam results will be made available. Your law school may publish a list of results, but more commonly you will receive an email letting you know your results, or will be told the date on which you will be able to access your results online.

How you feel about your result(s) will vary hugely, depending both on the mark you received, and on your own hopes and expectations. Someone receiving a first class mark is likely to feel delighted, but if they knew they'd done well and thought they'd done even better, they may only be reasonably content. Someone who just managed a 2.2 could be a bit disappointed, but if they had really struggled with the subject then they may well be quite happy. Someone who failed is likely to feel disappointed, even distraught, but if they know they didn't do any work, then they may be pretty phlegmatic about it.

You need to be sensitive to those around you when discussing your own, and their, results. If you've done well, enjoy the moment and don't disparage your own achievements, but recognise that others may not be able to share your joy. Similarly, feel free to share your disappointments, but remember that a disappointing mark for you might look like a real achievement for a friend. Someone who has worked extremely hard, and is proud to have achieved a solid 2.2 mark, might find it difficult to deal with a friend who is upset because they've 'only' achieved a 2.1.

Responding to your results requires you to evaluate both what you achieved in an absolute sense, and what you achieved in terms of your own goals. Have you been successful? As we've seen in Chapter 3, true success lies not about achieving absolute ends ('come top of the class', 'get a 2.1'), but in doing the best you can. That is what you need to be reflecting upon.

Taking things forward—maximising the positives

Whatever the result, even if your mark was what you wanted and expected or better, it is important to learn as much as you can from the experience. If you were happy with your mark, you need to know what you were doing right, so you can keep doing it, and how to do even better. If you were unhappy with your mark, particularly if you didn't do as well as you'd expected, you need to find out why you are not achieving what you may be capable of.

Formal feedback on exams can be limited, but increasingly law schools are doing what they can to provide some feedback beyond the mark itself. You may find that your lecturer will post general feedback on the law school's VLE, and you should look through this as soon as it is available. Guidance provided on specific questions should alert you to any issues you'd obviously missed or misunderstood—that may well explain a lower than expected mark. Even more importantly, look at any guidance on common problems relating to technique or approach, even if couched in terms of the particular module, and consider honestly whether some might apply to your own work. These are points to keep in mind as you continue your studies so you keep improving. Take particular notice too of any guidance given on features of really good answers, so you can look to develop these skills yourself.

In some law schools or for some modules, it may be possible to receive some individual feedback on exams. This is far from universal because of the practical difficulties in feeding back individually on exams when student numbers are high and results are announced only at the end of the year after most students have left. Accordingly, if you are offered individual feedback—take it! Not every law student will be nearly so lucky, so make the most of anything on offer, even if it means delaying a trip home. Feedback on exams may initially seem futile—after all the module is now at an end—but what you are looking for is feed *forward* (see Chapter 13) ie guidance on how to improve in the future, focusing on approach, technique and wider legal skills.

Dealing with disappointment

If you have failed the exam or not got the grade you hoped for, it is entirely natural to feel sad, dismayed, frustrated or even angry. Accept how you feel but recognise you need to move on: a successful law student shows resilience. Remember:

- Look at the positives. Focus on the things you've done well, and what you have achieved so far;

- Keep things in perspective. It seems (and is) important now, but in the larger- and longer-term scheme of things, this is not a huge deal. One disappointing grade does not mean you cannot have a successful life and career;

- Identify actions you can take to learn from the situation. A disappointing grade now could be the trigger you need for greater success in the future;

- Remember you are not alone. You are not the first law student to be disappointed in a mark or to fail an exam, and you won't be the last.

A common reaction when you've been disappointed is to blame the marker, or the lecturer, or some other person or event. Perhaps you do have a good reason for this, but it may also be that you need to reflect realistically on your preparation for and performance in the exam.

That means honestly critiquing your approach to study, not in order to blame yourself, but so that you can think about what you need to do differently in the future—that way you can achieve something positive from your disappointment. So, ask yourself some searching questions:

- Did you work hard throughout the module?
- Did you attend all classes?
- Did you do all the reading, above and beyond the textbook?
- Did you complete all the formative exercises and assessments that were set?
- Did you take all opportunities for feedback, and act on them?
- Did you revise thoroughly, including practising questions?
- Did you attend additional skills-based sessions that were offered?

Some of your answers may indicate that you need to focus your efforts differently in the future.

It may be that you did everything you could, but still didn't do as well as you'd hoped. It is essential that you make use of all the feedback that is available, whether general or individual, think about how it applies to you and what you need to do differently.

Particularly if you have failed an assessment, you may be able to ask the marker or your personal tutor to go through your exam script with you so you can see more clearly what went wrong, and see how to improve next time. If you've had disappointment in more than one exam, a tutor may be able to go through all the relevant exam scripts with you to see if there are recurring problems. If you've done well in another exam, then look at any feedback you have access to for that exam, to see what you did differently there. However disappointed you are, and however frustrated you feel, do try to respond constructively to the feedback process and the advice you receive, or it will have limited value.

If, after critiquing your own performance and receiving any feedback you can access, you genuinely believe there has been a mistake in the marking, then your institution will have an appeals process that you can access. However, you need to be aware that this is not about just asking for a higher mark or second opinion.

Marking at university goes through a range of procedures, from internal marking and internal moderation (a checking process to ensure consistency), to checking by independent examiners from another university called 'external examiners', so there has to be a very good reason for revisiting a mark, usually requiring evidence of a failure to follow proper procedures. Your own institution will be able to direct you to their rules if you want to explore whether you have grounds to appeal a mark, but sometimes you may have to accept that you just didn't do as well as you thought you had.

Retaking an exam

If you fail an exam you will normally be given an opportunity to retake it. Such an exam is often called a 'referred' exam, or 'resit', and they usually take place at the end of the summer vacation just before the return to university. It is important you are available during this period so you get that second chance to pass the module.

Usually you will not be credited with full marks on a referred exam—marks are normally capped at the pass mark. This means that however well you perform in the resit, your grade will be officially recorded at the pass mark. It is still worth doing though as failed modules can mean you are not permitted to complete your degree, or have to retake a year (at your expense), or may prevent a degree from being a qualifying law degree.

There may be other reasons why you need to take a 'resit'. If medical or other serious reasons prevented you from sitting the original exam or affected your performance, you may be granted permission to take the resit exam. To have this right, you will have had to make an application in line with your institution's procedures, with evidence, and often within very strict timescales. Here the resit is usually called a 'deferred' exam, and will count for full marks.

Students who have passed an exam, but are disappointed with their mark, sometimes ask if they can retake the exam to try to get a better mark. This isn't possible, which can be a shock for some students. This highlights how important it is to work hard for every exam, and to be resilient and learn from the experience if you are ultimately disappointed.

If you find yourself having to retake an exam, and it is more common that you might expect, particularly in the early stages of your legal studies, then do use any support available to you. Get feedback on the exam, review your work over the year, revise hard and keep practising your exam skills. It might not make for a fun summer vacation but it is essential if you want to pass that exam. Don't make the mistake of assuming that it will be easier at the second attempt—it will only be easier if you have taken steps to act on the problems you had the first time.

Thinking through your options

With any luck a failed exam only signifies that you have struggled with a particular subject, and so need another attempt, using your previous experience to attain a higher mark. There is no shame in this, and it should present no barrier to you going on to achieve your law degree and future success. After all, not many people pass their driving test first time, but pretty much everyone gets there in the end.

Alternatively a failed exam may indicate that your approach to your studies so far has not been sufficiently committed or appropriately focused. In that case, while you might feel a little chastened by the experience, or regretful, there is no doubt it will have been a lesson well learned and you can move on with reasonable confidence. The disappointment may well encourage you to develop more effective study habits, and make you even more determined to succeed.

That said, failing an exam is undoubtedly an indication that all is not entirely well, and more than one failure should certainly be viewed as a warning sign. It may be that you just need a bit longer than some other students, and perhaps a bit more support, to grasp legal concepts and to develop the skills that you need. If you are sufficiently motivated and determined, and prepared to work hard, we would encourage you to keep going. While you might have some tough times ahead of you, there is every reason to suppose you will make it.

However, a failed exam, particularly if this is not the first or only time, may also trigger some reflection on where you are now. Are you prepared to put in the work that is necessary to move on from here? Does law interest you sufficiently to justify the hours of study that are necessary for success? Is it possible that, while you are perfectly capable of higher-level study, you are not particularly suited to the study of law? Do you have other distractions that make the study of law at your chosen institution much harder than you had anticipated?

This is about evaluating honestly where you are, where you want to be and how you feel about what you would need to do to get there. If you decide that law is not for you, or you are not for law, then you may be able to transfer onto a different course. Depending on the programmes your institution offers, that might mean changing from a law degree to a joint honours degree, so with fewer law modules, or from a qualifying law degree to a non-qualifying law degree with less pressure to take and pass particular modules. Or even changing degree entirely, or moving institution.

A change of direction at any stage in your studies is undoubtedly a big decision and may have financial implications if it adds a year or more to your studies. But it can be a positive step if it puts you on a path that ultimately will suit you better. If you do have doubts about whether you should continue as a law student, or your future path more generally, speak to your personal tutor, your careers advisor and any other supportive people who can help you to reach a sensible decision. Whatever you choose to do, remember to take with you all the positive things you have learned so far.

SUMMARY—HELP YOURSELF . . .

- **Be prepared**
  - Make sure you know what type, style and format every exam will be in—and what that means for your approach.
  - Prepare from the start of the course by taking up all learning opportunities.
  - Be aware of your own learning style, strengths and weaknesses.

- **Revise effectively**
  - Be active, not passive.
  - Think carefully about what topics you focus on and the time you spend on different things.
  - Develop your skills, not just your knowledge.

- Vary the ways in which you revise and the activities you do.
- Work with your own strengths and learning style.

- **Look after yourself**
  - Seek help, guidance and support when you need it.
  - Nurture a positive mindset.
  - Keep healthy and active.

- **Work smartly**
  - Follow instructions and choose any questions thoughtfully.
  - Focus on what you need to do—don't get distracted.
  - Make the best use of the limited time you've got.
  - Remember your learning outcomes and assessment criteria.

- **Reflect on your success**
  - Review your experience to identify issues and strengths.
  - Take and act on any feedback you are offered.
  - Keep your options under review if things aren't going well.
  - Aim to continually develop your legal and other skills.

PART 5
SUCCESS OUTSIDE THE CLASSROOM
Making the most of other opportunities

16

STUDY ABROAD

'Why do you go away? So that you can come back.
So that you can see the place you came from
with new eyes and extra colours. And the people
there see you differently, too. Coming back to where
you started is not the same as never leaving.'

TERRY PRATCHETT,
A Hat Full of Sky

INTRODUCTION

Most universities will offer the opportunity to spend some time studying abroad during the course of a law programme. If you know before
applying for a law degree programme that this is what you want to do
then you will need to explore what options are available and which
institutions offer what you are looking for.

But you may also be given the opportunity to switch to a 'year abroad'
programme after you have started a standard programme—to add in the
year abroad and change, for example, from an LLB Law to an LLB Law with
European Study. Or, you may want some experience of studying abroad
without extending your degree programme; if so there may be opportunities for shorter courses that don't interrupt or extend your law degree.

Spending time studying abroad can be, and usually is, an inspiring and valuable experience. It can undoubtedly enhance your study skills, social skills and employability, as well as offering you the chance to immerse yourself in a new place and culture and just do something a little bit different. But studying abroad also brings challenges. This chapter will look at different ways in which you can experience study abroad, and the benefits that commonly accrue from the experience. We'll also examine some of the downsides to help you weigh up your options properly, and to ensure you are fully prepared for both your time abroad, and your return home.

HOME AND HOST INSTITUTIONS

In this chapter, 'home institution' means the university where you are undertaking your primary legal studies, with 'home country' being the UK. 'Host institution' means the university with which you study when abroad, and 'host country' the country in which you are studying. The particular relationship between your home and host institution is unlikely to be of any concern to you—it could be a long-term partnership, a looser arrangement or part of a network of many institutions. Less commonly, your university may have an overseas campus with the chance to study there for part of your time.

Students spending time studying abroad are usually called 'study abroad students'. The term can encompass both students on a UK degree programme who choose to study overseas temporarily, and students on foreign degree programmes who study temporarily in the UK. Study abroad students are distinct from international students who are studying for their full degree in a UK institution. If you are looking up information online or in a prospectus do bear all this in mind so you access the relevant material. You may also hear the term 'Erasmus students', referring to the long-established scheme for study abroad in Europe.

DIFFERENT WAYS OF STUDYING ABROAD

If you are considering studying abroad as part of your law degree, try to investigate what is on offer as soon as possible. Different institutions offer different opportunities—length of study, year of study, locations, qualification requirements, number of available places, etc. This may influence where you choose to study if you are still to select a university. Check with the law school as well as the central university, as not all university schemes are necessarily available to law students, while there may be particular opportunities for law students that are not generally available.

Find out when you need to apply for study abroad opportunities. Does it have to be in your initial application, or can it be during your first or second year of study? Are any particular qualifications needed? Both these questions may depend on what type of study abroad programme you are interested in. Figure 16.1 shows the range of possible options. If you are already studying law at university and think you might like to study abroad, speak to your personal tutor about what options there are and how they fit your own circumstances and ambitions.

FIGURE 16.1: Different study abroad opportunities

Dual law programmes

Probably the most demanding and intensive, but potentially the most rewarding, study abroad programmes are those combining the study of English law with the study of the law in another jurisdiction. Examples are 'Law and French Law' or 'Law with Italian Law'. Quite a number of universities offer such programmes.

In these programmes you usually study the core legal subjects necessary for a qualifying law degree in the UK, but also study the law of the other jurisdiction and some language modules while still at your home institution. You then spend a further year abroad, usually the penultimate or final year of your degree, studying additional legal modules in the host institution. This year of study abroad may lead to a recognised distinct qualification in the host country, depending on the course and options chosen, as well as counting towards your final degree result.

These dual law programmes, more than most, immerse you within two legal cultures, and are unsurprisingly very highly regarded by employers. They are challenging, because you have to get to grips with new subjects in two jurisdictions, all while you are still new both to law and university-level study. They also require very good language skills, which will be a requirement for admission to the programme.

Dual law programmes offer a valuable opportunity to engage deeply with the law in two jurisdictions, as well as with another country, for an extended period. The year abroad is usually particularly rewarding because you will already have some knowledge of the host country's laws and legal system, and will be living and studying for a demanding qualification alongside students from the host nation. It is essential to engage with the country, institution and culture if you are to do well, and impossible to remain an outsider.

Because the year abroad is such an integral part of the programme, it can be very demanding—it is far from being an 'add-on' or mere experience. Often there are high standards and new ways of working that are initially unfamiliar and may be a bit daunting at first.

Dual law programmes tend to accept small numbers of students compared with standard law programmes. This means everyone gets to know each other well, and staff running the programme are often very focused on your progress and experience. You get the benefit of being part of a small, often very motivated group, while engaging with the wider law student body in other modules.

Against this, you won't share all your modules with other law students, so may feel a bit left out sometimes. And your friends on standard law programmes are likely to be graduating while you still have another year to go. However this is not unique to dual law programmes—students increasingly take different paths and timescales to completion—so don't let this put you off. Dual law students will usually find their module options are much reduced because of the need to fit in other law and language modules. This can be frustrating if it prevents you studying subjects you were keen on, but equally other students don't have the advantage of immersion in the laws and legal system of another country, international experience and the possibility of joint qualification.

Law and language programmes

Taking a joint honours programme that combines law with a language—Law and Spanish for example, or Law with German—can be a way of developing your language skills without having to get to grips with another legal jurisdiction. The additional language qualification and time abroad can enhance your employability, deepen your cultural awareness and provide you with a different perspective and another interest.

This is particularly valuable if you think a straight law degree might feel too confining and you have a facility for languages, or if you want to continue with a language you enjoyed at school but also want to gain a law degree. Although your law options will be a little more constrained than other law students as you'll be fitting in compulsory language modules, this should be less of an issue than on dual law programmes.

Joint law/language programmes will usually include a year abroad but you may not have to study law modules during that year. You may not even have to study at a host institution—you may be able to do a work placement or equivalent in the host country instead. The year abroad may be arranged through the language department, or the law school, or jointly, so how it is organised and what it will entail will differ according to your institution. Check that the programme you are interested in does include study abroad, or other travel and work opportunities, and find out what it involves and how it fits around your law studies.

Year abroad programmes

These programmes have names such as 'Law with International Study' or 'European Legal Studies' and are probably the most common way for law students to study abroad. They usually follow the same pattern as a straightforward law degree, but with an additional year (often the penultimate year of study) where you study in a host institution.

Universities typically have a large number of partner institutions across the globe—from the US to Norway, from the Netherlands to Australia. These will include institutions in English-speaking countries and some elsewhere that teach in English. Accordingly unlike dual law or law/language degrees, you are often not required to undertake any language modules as part of your degree. However, if you are going to a non-English speaking country you may need to demonstrate competency in the relevant language, and even if teaching will be in English, learning the host country's language will help you to make the most of the experience.

Year abroad programmes can be an excellent way of experiencing another country as an insider, gaining insight into the law of another country and seeing how legal study differs across the globe, without the pressure of studying formally for an additional legal qualification. As we've seen, depending on where you study you may not have the pressure of learning another language, or you can take the opportunity to develop existing language skills or learn a new language entirely. Programmes often disperse students very widely, reducing the temptation to stick with students from your home institution or country. This encourages you to interact with other students, forming part of a diverse and multi-cultural group of students.

Short programmes: single semester study abroad

Single semester or single term programmes are not a common option in law schools. This is because law modules often run across the academic year, so you would not be able to complete them if you were studying abroad for a semester. If you are interested in a short study abroad programme do check carefully that you can still complete all the modules you need for your degree (bearing in mind the requirements for a qualifying law degree if that is what you are aiming for), and can gain sufficient credits overall.

If available, a single semester study abroad scheme can be a good way to experience life and study somewhere else without being away from home and familiar study for too long. It may also be cheaper and less disruptive than a year away. The disadvantage is that you are less likely to immerse yourself in another country and lifestyle if you know you are not there for long. And you may only just be getting used to new ways of studying and learning when it is time to leave.

Short programmes: summer school

Another way of experiencing life and study abroad is through a summer school. A key advantage of a summer school is that it doesn't disrupt your normal legal studies, but it won't usually contribute to credits for your degree either. A summer school allows you to visit a new place as an insider rather than as a tourist, to experience a different institution, engage deeply with a topic or topics over a relatively short period of time (commonly two to four weeks) and meet a diverse and motivated group of fellow students from across the world.

Summer schools are offered in a wide range of subjects by a great number of universities. They enable you to engage more deeply in aspects of the law and get the perspective of a different jurisdiction, or you could choose to expand your interests into human rights, global affairs, international finance or just about any other subject you fancy.

Summer schools can only provide limited opportunities to get to know another country and learn new subjects and ways of studying. But they are worth considering if other study abroad opportunities do not fit your plans and you don't have work or family commitments over the summer vacation. Bear in mind that summer schools can be expensive even before international travel is taken into account. Some universities offer scholarships and assistance to those who would not otherwise be able to access educational opportunities so do check with both your home and host institution.

ADVANTAGES OF STUDYING ABROAD

Students cite a large variety of reasons why they choose to study abroad. These include:

- Experiencing life abroad;
- Improving/learning a foreign language;
- Meeting new people;
- Wanting to work abroad in the future;
- Developing new skills;
- Challenging myself;
- Experiencing a different university;
- Enhancing my CV/making myself more employable;
- Having a break from normal studies.

INSIDER KNOWLEDGE

'Studying and living in France for a year was the best part of my studies and one of the elements that I recall most fondly about university. The opportunity to connect with fellow Erasmus students has provided me with lifetime friendships.'

Lali Wiratunga, National Manager Davidson Institute at
Westpac Banking Corporation, Australia

Studying abroad can offer a wide range of benefits, from learning new subjects you wouldn't otherwise come across during your law degree, to developing transferable skills and valuable personal attributes. It can also be evidence of an international outlook if you think in the future you might like to work abroad, do further study abroad, or work for a global business or firm.

I WISH I'D KNOWN . . .

'I wish somebody had told me about the academic, as well as cultural benefits. Everyone framed a year abroad as—let's be honest—a huge social opportunity, where the course load is much easier and you have opportunities to travel, make new friends, and culturally develop yourself. However, I was appreciative of the breadth of subjects I could study, far wider than my home institution. I got to spend a year learning international law, human rights, ethics of law, etc—things not on my usual syllabus.'

Rebecca Agliolo, University of Cambridge, Law, Year 4

Many of the benefits of study abroad stem from leaving your comfort zone and immersing yourself in something very different. Various studies, including European Commission reports, have shown a significant advantage in employability amongst students who have studied abroad, and indicate that employers value the skills developed through study abroad even more than the international experience itself.

When studying abroad you open yourself up to a whole range of new experiences. Just as when you start your legal studies at university, you will need to engage with new people, new opportunities and new challenges—but this time in an entirely new environment and culture. Not only will these experiences broaden your horizons, and change your perspective, they will help you develop important skills. Figures 16.2 and 16.3 present some of the many benefits you will obtain from study abroad.

FIGURE 16.2: Benefiting from new experiences

The learning experience	The student experience	The social experience
• Understanding a new jurisdiction • Different legal systems and approaches • New institution and teaching environment • Teaching styles and approach of tutors • Hours of work • Amount of guidance provided • Presenting work in unfamiliar formats • Library and legal research	• Meeting new people of different nationalities • Working in diverse groups with different attitudes to studying • Speaking (and thinking) in a different language • Experiencing being an 'outsider' • Fitting into existing friendship groups and making new ones • Representing your country and institution	• New culture, customs and social expectations • Political/social environment and engagement • Exploring a new town/city/area • Meeting local people and fellow students • Food, drink and entertainment • Sporting, cultural or religious activities

FIGURE 16.3: Developing skills and attributes

Study skills	Transferable skills	Personal attributes
• Trying out different study techniques • Learning in larger or smaller groups • Working with less, or more, direction • Comparative skills – comparing jurisdictions and rules • Working under time pressures • Showing flexibility in approach to study • Critical thinking	• Foreign language proficiency • Oral communication • Written communication • Problem solving • Decision making • Presentational skills • Teamworking • Networking • Planning and organisation	• Openness to and acceptance of change • Coping with new experiences • Adaptability and flexibility • Resilience • Motivation to succeed • Confidence • Tolerance and acceptance of difference • Ability to make friends

I WISH I'D KNOWN . . .

'I wish I'd known how much more independent I'd become. You learn to deal with administrative things like tax or national insurance numbers, registering at the GP, or more practical things like managing your money or cooking for yourself.'

Gabrielle Bargas, University College London, LLB Law with French Law, Year 2

DEALING WITH THE DOWNSIDES

There are very real benefits to study abroad but it isn't always idyllic, nor does it suit everyone. The extent to which you might benefit will depend on your personality and circumstances as well as the experience itself. For example if you know you really struggle to cope with change then you might find your anxiety outweighs the benefits. Or if you have a young family, spending even a few weeks abroad may not be feasible. Reflect on your own circumstances, personality traits and longer-term goals to decide if study abroad is right for you.

Reasons students have given for not studying abroad include:

- Family/personal relationships;
- Cost, or uncertainty about cost;
- Need to keep my job in the UK to finance my studies;
- Didn't realise it would be a good thing to do;
- Unsure about where I'd want to go;
- Missed the deadline for applying;
- Want to get my degree completed as soon as possible.

So study abroad isn't for everyone, although at least some of these problems could have been avoided with good planning. For example, your university could advise you on the financial support available, depending on your home country, institution, preferred host nation and personal circumstances; or put you in touch with those who have studied in different countries.

I WISH I'D KNOWN . . .

'I wish someone had told me about the numerous grants available—I was worried about the expense, but there was funding aplenty.'

Rebecca Agliolo, University of Cambridge, Law, Year 4

Even when study abroad is the right choice, there can be downsides, and we'll look at the most significant now. These can be minimised if they are recognised and planned for, and must be balanced against the very many positives of study abroad.

Extending the period of study

Degree programmes that involve a year abroad mean you take an extra year to complete your degree. This has benefits—you get to be a student for longer!—but it does delay the moment of graduation and the point at which you start your career, and adds to the cost of your education. Most students who have undertaken study abroad would agree though that the benefits are worth both the cost and the extra time. And the additional skills and experience gained through study abroad may mean you can get on and ascend the career ladder more quickly after graduation.

Shorter study abroad programmes will not normally increase your overall study time, but may still cause some disruption. Organising accommodation and planning your time abroad will take time that you might otherwise be spending on your studies, and you need to be sure that you can still cope with the demands of your course. Don't let that put you off, but be aware of the need to manage your time and get organised. Take advantage of all the advice and support your home and host institutions provide.

Change in learning culture

The learning culture at the host institution may be very different to what you're used to. Depending on where you study you may find yourself in much larger or smaller classes of students, with more hands-off, or more interactive ways of teaching. Expectations on student involvement, work load, interaction with lecturers, even presentation of essays will all be different—quite apart from using new legal research tools and unfamiliar legal sources.

The first classes and the first assessment are often the points of greatest stress, so don't worry if you feel a bit overwhelmed at these times. You coped with new experiences when starting your legal studies and will do so again.

Before you leave, find out how classes are usually taught in your host country and institution. Read all the material you are provided with. Ask your home institution to put you in touch with fellow students, ideally other law students, in the year(s) above you who are studying or have studied at the same host institution or in the same country, and speak to them about their experience. You can't expect to know everything before you go, but a few pointers will help you settle in quickly and feel more confident.

When you arrive, go to induction sessions and talk to other students—don't worry if your questions seem basic, it is important to understand how things work and it is a good way to make initial contacts. You may find you don't have support akin to the 'personal tutor' system, but there will certainly be someone whose role it is to provide support and advice to study abroad students. Seek help if you need it. You may be offered a student mentor or buddy while studying abroad—having a friendly and experienced student on hand can be very helpful, particularly in the early days.

Change in wider culture

It is not just the teaching culture that will be different—you are now a resident of a new country, one that you may not have visited before. And you aren't just there to have a good time, you have classes to attend, work to do and assessments to pass. This is an exciting time, but don't expect to feel at home instantly.

While you should throw yourself into the experience whole-heartedly, avoid exhausting yourself in the first week or so. So have a good look around your new town or city—remind yourself why you chose it—but perhaps leave some of the sight-seeing until you've settled in a bit more. When you do get the chance, visit the sights but also start viewing the town/city as a resident and spend time absorbing the atmosphere.

You'll also need to do all the mundane day-to-day things that need doing: food shopping and using a launderette might not be exciting, but they certainly get you close to real life! Find out about social activities within your host institution and locally and get involved: joining a sports club, going to the gym, taking language lessons, singing in a choir or whatever else interests you, will help your new town or city become your home.

I WISH I'D KNOWN . . .

'It can be quite daunting, living in a new country, especially with a foreign language. Communication barriers became a daily occurrence, and even doing the simplest tasks became a challenge. Also, the method of teaching may widely vary from what you are used to: I had numerous group projects and essays, which I've never had to do before—I found it quite challenging.'

Rebecca Agliolo, University of Cambridge, Law, Year 4

Homesickness

It isn't uncommon to feel a bit lonely or homesick at first, although it isn't inevitable. Some students adapt very quickly, are naturally confident and relish the change; others find it harder to settle. Some may even think they've made a mistake and spend their first weeks exploring how to re-join their year-group at home. None of this is really surprising—after all, everything is different—but it isn't a great way to start your experience.

If you do start to doubt your decision, and this might even happen before you leave, it helps to focus on the positives. Keep in mind all the really good reasons why you chose a study abroad programme—they far outweigh any disadvantages.

Homesickness does wear off. And while a semester or year can feel like a long time when it has only just started, it goes very quickly. We've yet to meet a student who has regretted their decision to persevere, even if they felt really miserable at the start. Help yourself by not spending too much time checking on social media what your friends are doing at home, nor by Skyping family or partners at every opportunity.

Keep yourself busy by immersing yourself in your studies, and by attending social events and activities. Force yourself to leave your accommodation and smile, even if you don't feel like it—sitting alone makes things worse. Find fellow study abroad students to explore with and share your experiences, and talk to home students too. It won't be long before you've forgotten ever feeling lonely or homesick—your next problem may be not wanting to come home.

RETURNING TO 'NORMALITY'

Whether you've been looking forward to coming home, or wish you could stay away longer, the return to the familiar offers both rewards and challenges. You have the excitement of seeing friends and family, and telling them all your news and stories in person, but life in the UK may seem a bit dull (and quite probably wet and cold) after the fun and challenges of your time abroad. Hopefully you will feel refreshed and re-motivated as you move into the final stages of your degree, or into work/further study if you have now completed your degree programme. If you do feel a bit apprehensive about the year ahead, this is just because it is, temporarily, unfamiliar—you will settle back in very quickly indeed.

Joining a new year-group

If you have been on a year-long study abroad programme and it was not your final year, you will be joining a new group of students on your return. Your contemporaries may still be studying, albeit a year ahead—if so you can rekindle old friendships and benefit from their experience. If you are returning to your home institution for your final year, most of your former cohort will have graduated. They will still be happy to share their expertise, but won't be around to distract you. Some returning law students find this quite an advantage as they get their heads down for a final push to complete their degree.

In practice, fitting into a new year-group is easier than you might anticipate. Although you might think of the year-group you are joining as a unit which you haven't been part of that is far from the case. The size of law schools now mean that a year-group rarely feels like a coherent whole, while different option choices mean students will usually be in new groups where they may not know anyone. There will also be plenty of other students on different study paths; not just other study abroad students like you, but also those repeating a year, studying part-time, or temporarily studying in the UK from abroad. So don't assume your new classmates all know each other—they don't.

Just as you did when you started your studies, and started your study abroad, make the effort to get to know students in your classes and through social events. Consciously think of yourself as a member of this new group rather than an outsider. By all means spend time with existing friends, and this can be helpful when sorting accommodation for example, but don't neglect to make new ones. They'll still be here when others have moved on.

Re-engaging with your home institution

During your study abroad you will have worked with different teaching and learning styles, and faced new expectations. Having spent the year or semester getting used to a new way of work, it is now time to switch back again. It may take a short while to remember quite what is expected of you in your home institution, but it doesn't take long.

If you have any doubts about what you need to do, (re-)read the module information and student handbook, and ask the relevant person, whether administrator, module co-ordinator, lecturer or personal tutor, if it still isn't clear. Make sure you've got the up-to-date version of any documents as rules and regulations can change from year to year and you might not be told expressly.

Study will inevitably feel different on your return. Your study abroad will have changed you, and you now have different strengths and skills than when you left. Remember that as you progress through your degree, expectations on students increase in any event, so things will feel a bit different for everyone, even those who haven't left the UK.

Using new skills and knowledge

Settling back in and re-engaging with your home institution doesn't mean forgetting about your experience abroad. Reflect on your experience: how you studied, what you studied, and what else you learned:

- What differences did you note in teaching and learning and study techniques? What did you find particularly helpful, or unhelpful? Can you incorporate some of these into your study back home? Has it changed your learning style in any way? By reflecting on your study experience, you can enhance your learning as you progress;

- In what ways did the law you studied differ from the equivalent UK law? What similarities did you note? How did the different political or social background impact on the law? Can you utilise your broader knowledge to aid your critical thinking in work you are doing now? Are there areas you'd like to explore more deeply? Study abroad gives you the insight to make you a much more thoughtful and critical law student, as well as opening avenues for further study or work abroad;

- Reflect too on the 'softer' skills you have developed, the activities you undertook and the challenges you have overcome. Don't think they are obvious or assume you'll remember events when you want to. Update your PDP (personal development plan) and your CV, so you have evidence ready when it is time for job applications.

I WISH I'D KNOWN . . .

'Don't worry about having missed out; all you've got is new experiences and knowledge to bring to the subject.'

Madeleine Burrell, University of Oxford, Law with German Law, Year 3

Another way of gaining value from your study abroad is to share the experience. That doesn't just mean telling all your friends about it— they'll get bored after a while. Offer your experience to those running the study abroad scheme in your home institution; they will usually be delighted to have feedback on the scheme, the host institution and degree programme. They may even ask you to contribute to sessions aimed at new study abroad students. As well as being personally satisfying, this develops new skills and can further enhance your CV.

You can also support and advise new students who are considering study abroad, or who have selected the host institution you attended. Your experience, tips and reassurance may be the key to their own successful experience.

I WISH I'D KNOWN . . .

'It will be the best year of your life. You will develop as a person by being forced out of your comfort zone. Enjoy every moment of it because next year you will spend every moment wishing you were back.'

Emily Barrett, University of Bristol, Law with Study in Continental Europe, Year 4

THE OTHER DIRECTION—WHEN 'ABROAD' IS THE UK

This chapter has focused on study abroad opportunities for law students studying at UK institutions. But lots of law students come in the opposite direction too—students from overseas who spending a year or semester studying with a UK institution and who will face new ways of studying, new student colleagues and a new culture. Much of the advice in this chapter is just as relevant to students from overseas spending some time studying in the UK, as it is to UK students studying abroad.

If you are coming to the UK for temporary study, we would urge you to make sure you attend induction events, so that you can understand what is expected of you, share experiences and meet fellow students and lecturers. But also go to other social events and talk to students in your classes or residence. Gain the benefit of their experience—they have probably been studying law in the institution for a while now—and make friends and valuable contacts. Don't just stick with other students of your own nationality, or you won't get full advantage of your time in the UK.

I WISH I'D KNOWN . . .

'I wish I'd known how many other international students there would be. You can always meet plenty of people from your home country, whether by joining societies or in your course.'

Gabrielle Bargas, University College London, LLB Law with French Law, Year 2

If you are a UK-based student then try to make study abroad/Erasmus students studying alongside you feel welcome. It might be easier to stay with your existing friendship group, but that can leave study abroad students rather isolated. Just as importantly, you miss the chance to learn from different experiences of law and study. The input of overseas students can be really valuable in exploring the law, because they are in a position to compare jurisdictions, so take advantage. The involvement of study abroad students also provides the opportunity to explore other cultures and make friends and contacts for life. It may even inspire you to spend some time studying abroad yourself.

SUMMARY—HELP YOURSELF . . .

- **Consider your options**
  - Identify the various different study abroad options available.
  - Recognise the many and diverse advantages to study abroad.
  - Reflect on your own personality, circumstances and career plans.
  - Get all the information you can, and speak to those who have already studied abroad.

- **Get stuck in**
  - Explore your new environment and start experiencing life as a resident.
  - Investigate how things work in a new institution, where to go and where to find out more information.
  - Immerse yourself in a new way of work—don't constantly compare with what you are more familiar with.
  - Get involved in your new life, joining groups and making friends.

- Speak to other students—both study abroad and home students—and don't stick with those from your home country.

- Remember any confusion, anxiety, homesickness or loneliness will soon pass.

- **Reflect on your experience**
  - Re-engage with your home institution, and make friends within your new year-group.

  - Reflect on how you learned, what you learned and other skills and experiences. Think about how these can help your ongoing study and your career plans.

  - Update your CV and similar documents.

- **Extend a welcoming hand**
  - Guide and support students who are considering study abroad.

  - Give a warm welcome to overseas students who are studying temporarily with your home institution, learn from each other, and encourage diverse study and friendship groups.

  - Keep in touch and create a global network of friends and contacts.

17

EXPANDING LEGAL SKILLS—
MOOTING, NEGOTIATION AND MORE

'Let us never negotiate out of fear.
But let us never fear to negotiate.'

JOHN F. KENNEDY

INTRODUCTION

Much of your study for a law degree relates to the substantive study
of law—whether learning rules, finding and using legal sources, or
critically thinking about law's place in the world. As we've seen (for
example, in Chapter 6) the law degree also helps you develop skills you
need for successful academic study of law that will, in turn, be used in
future employment.

However, your law degree can also provide you with opportunities
to put your knowledge of law and your legal skills into practice, and
further develop skills that are key to legal practice. This is important
if you want to pursue a career as a lawyer of course, but is of much
wider value in developing specific skills to enhance employability
more generally.

A lot of the activities considered in this chapter will be offered as
extra-curricular activities through your law school or student law society. Additionally, more and more law schools are offering modules
covering specific legal skills or are embedding these activities into

standard programmes. Even so, to get the broadest and deepest experience you will need to engage in additional opportunities outside the curriculum.

In this chapter, we will explore the important legal skills-related extra-curricular activities that are commonly available, considering the value of these programmes to the successful law student. This chapter will explain how these activities can further develop skills such as analysis and critical thinking, while also developing transferable skills such as professionalism, teamworking, presentation and timeliness.

LEGAL SKILLS PROGRAMMES AND EXTRA-CURRICULAR ACTIVITIES

There is a strong tradition in law of using extra-curricular activities to teach, develop and practise practical legal skills. Traditionally, this has been co-ordinated by individual members of staff or student law societies. This remains the case for most law schools but, as mentioned above, some of these activities may now also feature within the curriculum.

Figure 17.1 shows the most common legal-skills based opportunities offered by law schools. Engaging in these activities will give you the

FIGURE 17.1: Common opportunities to develop practical legal skills

opportunity to apply your legal learning to practical situations, and develop specific skills.

You are likely to benefit from taking up as many opportunities as you sensibly can over the course of your degree programme. You will undoubtedly have restrictions on your time, and it is unlikely to be possible to do everything. But aim to try at least one of these legal skills activities during your time in law school. Focus on those that best fit your interests and career goals, and think carefully about when you are likely to be best able to fit in the additional commitment.

I WISH I'D KNOWN . . .

'Take more in your first year—it'll look so much better when you're applying for vacation schemes in the first semester of second year. Do clinics and get any practical work experience you can—it really will help pay off in terms of skills. Try and stick to those you think will benefit your career choice and don't over burden yourself.'

Alexandra Townsley, University of Nottingham, LLB Law and American Law, Year 3

There are also individual opportunities to develop skills beyond the curriculum. These include entering law essay competitions (run by various bodies, from The Times newspaper to the Bar Council) or submitting work to student law journals. Your university or student law society may well alert you to some of these opportunities but they do not tend to be organised as extra-curricular activities.

If your law school does not offer a law-related activity that you are interested in, consider starting something yourself. Investigate getting a team together, talk to your lecturers and enter one of the national or international competitions. This would show great initiative and ensure you get the opportunities you want.

INSIDER KNOWLEDGE

'Do as much of this as you can. My university offered limited places for such activities, meaning I was unable to benefit from the practical experience. I feel this left me (and others like me) disadvantaged.'

Jane Alice Murray, Legal Assistant, Local Authority

MOOTING

What is mooting?

In essence mooting is an advocacy competition and training exercise. It has been a traditional method of teaching practical aspects of law for centuries.

Mooting is a simulated court hearing, usually an appeal hearing. It specifically develops skills associated with being a barrister, but solicitors now increasingly act as advocates too, and mooting also develops a number of broader skills that we'll discuss towards the end of this chapter.

If you are mooting, you will usually be paired with another student, given a problem scenario and allocated a side to represent. This will be either the appellant (the individual or group appealing the decision of the lower court) or the respondent (the individual or group replying). Each side will have two representatives, so each moot involves four students. In your pair you will probably need to decide who is senior counsel—who is often the first to speak, and may have a right of reply—and who is junior counsel. Alternatively, you may be told which role you have been given.

The two teams then put forward their arguments about the law based on the factual scenario presented. These scenarios are usually like extended problem questions that you will have to analyse carefully and then research the law around the subject. This will usually be a contentious area of law or an area that is currently undergoing some major changes. To prepare for the moot you will need to:

- Research the topic and particular issues;
- Develop arguments around the facts in the problem;
- Present a written submission outlining your arguments—a skeleton argument;
- Collate the authorities you will rely on—the court bundle.

You then present your arguments orally, dressed in court robes—don't worry, you borrow these—to a 'judge' or a panel of judges. These judges might be your peers, your lecturers, a barrister or even an actual judge. Regardless of who the judge is, mooters must treat him or her with respect and address them properly. This is part of court etiquette and usually makes up part of your score for the moot. It is also good practice for addressing any senior member of the legal profession.

The judge may ask questions or ask you to explain a point further, giving you the opportunity to show you can 'think on your feet'. Understandably some students can find mooting rather nerve-racking, particularly at first. But very few students regret giving it a try, and many really relish the opportunity and rise to the challenge.

Mooting competitions

Most students moot in specific competitions, with different rounds and a final winner or winning team. Most law schools or student law societies run internal competitions and many other organisations run regional, national or international competitions. There may even be a small regional competition between you and a rival law school.

In a mooting competition, each mooter is judged on their performance and given a scorecard outlining their performance according to different criteria. Different competitions may have different criteria, and different rules about the proceedings of the moot, so be sure to read any relevant rule book carefully.

There are many different mooting competitions that cover different areas of law, while individual moots may be based on any legal subject matter. In general mooting competitions, the earlier rounds commonly start off with a problem from an area such as contract law or tort law, but then get more complex, covering anything from property law to intellectual property or human rights law.

Many national and international moots focus on specialist areas of law—the Jessup moot on international law is probably one of the most famous and prestigious international student mooting competitions. These international competitions show how important mooting is to legal education, not just in this country but in other jurisdictions too. Mooting competitions tend to follow the court-hearing format, but other formats are emerging. For example, moots that include arbitration (a less formal form of dispute resolution) are becoming more common, especially in subjects like maritime law, as are mediation and trial advocacy competitions.

I WISH I'D KNOWN . . .

'Extra-curricular legal activities come with many unexpected benefits. For instance, winning mooting competitions may lead to work experience or judicial marshalling experience. Furthermore, employers like to see evidence of achievements in university, and joining such competitions is one of the many ways to build such evidence. Extra-curricular legal activities can also help you in your academic studies of law. For instance, if you mooted on contract law, your in-depth understanding and critical analysis of specific contract law cases will come in handy during the examinations.'

Godwin Tan, University College London, LLB Law, Year 3

Tips for mooting

Preparation

Meet with your partner as soon as the mooting problem is released. You need to make sure that you both understand the issues you are being asked to address. Doing this early will help you ensure that you plan your time properly in the run-up to the moot, as you do not want to be rushing to do a bundle or draft arguments the night before. Make sure that you and your partner can fit your preparation for the moot around your other commitments. This in itself can be a big challenge that will test your time management skills. By beginning to prepare early, you can be sure that you have sufficient time to develop and research your arguments carefully.

Even if the moot is on a subject that you have studied or are quite familiar with, research it afresh. Make sure you re-read the lead cases. Revisit the most relevant statutes. Research more widely to include professional or academic publications. You should have a good survey of the literature before you start to think critically and develop your argument.

As you begin to put your skeleton argument and written submission together, construct your bundle of authorities in parallel. It will help you become familiar with the relevant authorities that you will direct the judges towards as you proceed through your oral submission. It will also save you time later.

Practice

Make sure that you practise your oral submissions. You could do this in front of the mirror or record yourself on your laptop, tablet or phone. Be critical. Are you reading too much straight from your notes? Does it seem natural? Are you following important rules of etiquette?

Also present your submission in front of your partner so that they can question you as you proceed. This will help you become accustomed to interventions, which can throw you off your argument and 'flow'. Finally, if you and your partner wish to undertake a dress rehearsal, try to rope in some friends to act as judges. We find that coffee and cake is usually a valuable incentive to help.

Remember to accept feedback and be reflective. If you get feedback from your partner, colleagues or even a judge, engage with it and adjust your practice accordingly. They are all trying to help you improve.

The moot itself

On the day of the moot, treat it as if you were actually going to court. Make sure you know where you are going and be early. It is always better to be early and have plenty of time to arrange your materials and compose yourself.

It is okay to feel nervous. Use the adrenaline to your advantage. If you get flustered—and most people do at some point—just pause, apologise briefly to the judge and start again from an appropriate place. Moot judges may well be tough in their questioning—to enable you to show off your skills—but will be very understanding of a few nerves.

Remember that although this is a competition, it is important to remain respectful and professional. Treat your fellow mooters with courtesy, be open and honest. Mooting is a test of your advocacy skills, not the ability to 'get one over' on someone else or win at any cost.

NEGOTIATION

What is negotiation?

Negotiation exercises and competitions give you opportunities to develop your skills in non-adversarial approaches to resolving disputes. Negotiation is the most common way for disputes to be settled out of court, and is a process of compromise and agreement to find an acceptable outcome for both clients.

Negotiation in legal practice has a number of advantages over immediate recourse to legal action. It is often cheaper than formal court proceedings, reduces the courts' time, and may better preserve any relationship between the clients. Most judges will expect parties to have gone through some form of negotiation prior to going to court.

The ability to negotiate is fundamental to being a successful solicitor and plays a role in the working lives of other legal professionals too. Negotiation skills are also valuable for many other spheres of employment, as you will always need to compromise and take account of other people's interests. Negotiation develops a whole range of connected skills, as we'll see later on in this chapter.

Negotiation as a student activity

Negotiation exercises and competitions usually involve two teams of two students negotiating to try to find a resolution that benefits their respective clients. Prior to the exercise, each team will be given a set of common information, which will outline the scenario, the problem and the information that is known to both parties. Each team will also be given a set of instructions from their clients about what they are willing to compromise on and what they regard as essential.

You may also be given some confidential information from your client that may help to support your arguments for a particular outcome. You will need to decide when to use this confidential information and when it is best to hold back. This information can be key to turning the tide of a negotiation, but you must assess it carefully as it could be detrimental to an agreement, especially if it is something that will make the other team question your client's ability or willingness to abide by any compromise.

Once you have all the information, which is usually given out about a week before the negotiation, you will have to prepare carefully. You should begin by dissecting the problem, researching the relevant law to support your argument and developing a negotiation strategy and plan.

Some teams will also be asked to write an agenda for the meeting. This agenda should cover the key points that your client wishes to negotiate on. This is a good place to start with your negotiation plan to ensure that you have covered all the major points in the negotiation. But be prepared. The other side may ask to change the agenda at the start of the meeting and while you don't have to oblige, it can throw you off your stride before you even begin.

You will have a set amount of time to try to come to a compromise. This could be fifteen minutes, thirty minutes, an hour or maybe even more, but you may have to bring things to a close early if you are getting nowhere. You must always do what is best for your client based on their instructions. You will need to decide on the best approach for you and your client—are you going to be accommodating or tough, how far will you bend, and when?

Each individual participant will be marked against a number of criteria and you will be given a scorecard at the end which will show where you did well and where you need to improve. The best negotiators may progress individually, with new teams formed in the next round, or scores may be added together so the best team progresses at each stage. This will depend on the rules of the competition, so just as with mooting, make sure you read the rulebook.

There are numerous negotiation competitions you may be able to enter during your time as a law student. These may be internal, regional, national or international competitions and much like mooting they may be based on general areas of law or be subject-specific. We have seen negotiations based on everything from tort law to employment law, and contract law to property law. Many negotiation scenarios will cover a few different areas of law, and some negotiation competition briefs will focus on areas of business practice also.

Tips for negotiation competitions

Preparation

It is important to start preparing well in advance of the negotiation to ensure you have sufficient time in your busy schedule to prepare and do all the research that needs to be done. This aspect of time management may be even more important in negotiation than mooting as you will have numerous different factors of a problem to explore. There will also be different permutations of possible compromises which you will need to consider and evaluate.

You should research the relevant law, just as you would for a moot, but ensure that you also have sufficient knowledge of the subject matter of the problem. This is particularly important in negotiation competitions with a commercial or business flavour. Be sure that you understand every fact and have a wider awareness of the sector you are being asked to assist with.

While you cannot practise a negotiation as such, you can certainly work on ensuring that your communication skills are as clear as possible. Developing a really clear negotiation plan can assist this. You will want to outline the various different strategies and outcomes you want to explore in your negotiation.

Check and practise different negotiation strategies that have been discussed in any legal skills module you have taken, or read up on possible strategies in an appropriate legal skills or specialist negotiation book. It is important to have numerous potential options for your negotiation outcome. By really thinking about what can be sacrificed and what is essential, and working out in advance what any potential compromises might look like, you will be better prepared for the rigours of a difficult negotiation.

INSIDER KNOWLEDGE

'What kind of negotiator you are can depend on your personality and an effective negotiator is not always the same as being aggressive or getting everything that you want. Each negotiation is different, therefore it is important to have a toolkit of skills and techniques that you can draw on and adapt to each negotiation.'

Natasha Bellinger, Barrister, Magdalen Chambers

Remember that the other side will be aiming to get the best possible outcome for their client. You need to do the same. It is good to compromise in a negotiation, but not at the expense of your client's express wishes. Always stick to their wishes and don't be afraid to 'park' an issue and move on if you feel like you are not getting anywhere. Just as for mooting though, remember that negotiation is not about 'winning' whatever the price—act respectfully, honestly and ethically at all times. It is essential to remain professional throughout your negotiation, even if the opposing side is being difficult and appears to be less keen on compromise than you.

CLIENT INTERVIEWING

What is client interviewing?

Client interviewing is important to legal practice and many other areas of employment. It also develops and enhances a varied range of skills that we'll explore later in this chapter.

Interviewing clients carefully, sensitively and appropriately, while obtaining the necessary information to be able to help them, is key to being a good client interviewer. That includes knowing when to take a few moments to let your client collect their thoughts, understanding when to reassure them, and recognising when to press for more relevant information or check something that was unclear or contradictory.

Your interview with a client is the opportunity to explore their legal problem properly. But client interviews throw up particular challenges:

- Clients are rarely legally trained, so are unlikely to provide all the information you need in a clear and concise way;
- Clients are often happy to focus on information that, in a legal sense, is irrelevant or peripheral.

This means that information will arrive much less coherently than in a problem question, negotiation brief or moot scenario. You will need to sort the relevant legal issues and factual information from the irrelevant conversation, and keep things on track. This is often harder than it seems. Client interviewing exercises and competitions allow you to hone these skills and provide ample opportunities to reflect upon your relationship with clients as they sit in front of you.

Client interviewing as a student activity

Generally, a client interviewing exercise or competition will see you paired with another student. You will be given a little factual background on the client's issue, allowing you to research the area of law. However, you will be given far less to go on than in a moot or negotiation, probably only a vague outline of the problem. This means you can undertake some legal research, but most of the preparation work will involve thinking about what the key information is that you want to get from the interview.

You will then be given a set time with your client, usually around thirty to forty-five minutes, to extract the information you need from them. Another student, a lecturer or an actor may play the client, but whoever it is you need to conduct yourself in an appropriately professional manner. This includes:

- Greeting your client appropriately;
- Putting them at ease;
- Ensuring they understand the nature and purpose of the interview;
- If appropriate, explaining costs;
- Explaining confidentiality and what you will do with the information.

Quite what you need to explain may differ according to the client. For example, if you are told this is a business client that your law firm has worked with before, you may just wish to remind them of the purpose of the interview. However, if it is a new client or someone who has never previously had dealings with lawyers, you may need to be more careful in explaining what is going on.

When you question your client about the issue, be sure to let them speak, but don't be afraid to ask further questions based on the information received. Be sure to bring them back politely to the issues at hand if they start to go off the point. You will need to take notes on what is being said and read back the important points to make sure you haven't misunderstood anything critical.

Those playing the 'client' often get fully into the role, and may have instructions to act in a particular way. You may find your client unpredictable, upset or even angry. You will have to decide how best to console an upset client, or calm an angry client. This is a real test of your interpersonal skills and is a vital part of being a successful interviewer. At the end of the interview, you may be expected to deliver some (limited) advice, or you could wrap up by telling the client that you will research their case more thoroughly and get in touch with them at a future date.

Client interviewing may be part of your core learning, an elective module or offered as an optional extra-curricular activity. Local legal practitioners may also come into some law schools to offer client interviewing practice to law students. It is worth remembering that client interviewing is also often an important part of pro bono or law clinic work that you undertake. But many opportunities to undertake client interviewing experiences will be in the form of competitions.

Client interviewing competitions

Some law schools and law societies will offer internal competitions, but most students undertake client interviewing competitions in regional or national competitions. These competitions will have different rules and running orders, so make sure you are familiar with the relevant instructions.

Just like mooting and negotiation competitions, in a client interviewing competition once the interview is completed you will be given a scorecard, marked against specific criteria, to demonstrate where you did well and where you can improve. Then the best client interviewing teams or individual interviewers will progress to future rounds. If the interview is a learning exercise, you will be given feedback on how to develop your skills.

Tips for client interviewing

Preparation

Often there will be very little research you can do in advance of a client interview. You will only have received very basic information. But do what you can with what you've got:

- Double check the information you have already been given;
- Refresh your memory of the basic points of any area of law that is obviously relevant;
- Create a detailed schedule for the interview;
- Make sure you know what you have to do at the beginning of the interview—make a note to ensure that you explain the format of the interview, the fee structure and confidential nature of this information.

The interview

Remember that you must get the information from the client as effectively as possible. You must not lead the client, but be prepared to ask for more information. If you think something is important, press for more. If it is not important, ask them to move on.

Show the client that you are engaged with their story and their information by actively listening. Make sure you acknowledge what they are saying, and focus on the client not on your notes. Recap often, going back through your notes to make sure that the information you have taken is correct and that you have understood clearly the client's issue.

Tailor your style to the client in front of you. Sometimes the client will be familiar with lawyers and will be very clear in their statements. Other times you may need to work much harder to get to the crux of the issue. Remember that your client is a human being with real feelings and may get upset. Use compassion: how would you want to be treated in such a situation?

Treat everyone as an individual and adjust your manner to suit different clients and different problems. A good client interviewer recognises people both as human beings with emotions, and fellow professionals or 'customers' requiring efficient and effective help.

I WISH I'D KNOWN . . .

'I wish I'd known how important it is to get involved in extra-curriculars, especially pro bono work. These help you gain work experience and learn valuable skills.'

Gabrielle Bargas, University College London, LLB Law with French Law, Year 2

DEBATING

You are probably familiar with debating and may have engaged with the activity before coming to law school. Mooting is more common in law schools than debating, with debating more commonly organised by a separate student society or university body. But some law schools and law societies do offer debating competitions directed at law students, and of course there is nothing to stop you joining a debating group outside the law school.

You will also be encouraged to debate issues in an informal way in classes. Debate is a really good way to encourage detailed research, critical thought, the development of arguments and counter-arguments, and public speaking skills. If you aren't provided the opportunity to do this in your law school, do look for a debating society elsewhere in the university.

Debating can take many forms and can be governed by many different rules. Commonly, two teams of two students will be asked to propose and oppose a specific argument—the 'motion'—and will each be given a set time to speak. During their speeches, the other side or the judge (sometimes called the chair) may be permitted to interrupt and ask a question based on the argument being presented.

These questions, sometimes called interventions, are designed to expose the weakness in the speaker's argument or can provide an opportunity to make a counter-argument or contradict a point being made. The other side may also intervene to correct an incorrectly cited fact, statistic or piece of evidence. There may even be interventions from 'the floor', ie those listening to the debate. There are numerous different rules and protocols in debating societies and competitions, so, as always, make sure you check the rulebook for guidance.

As well as debates within your law school and/or institution, there are a number of national and international competitions that you can get involved with. Most of them will not be directly related to law, although of course law impacts on a great number of national, global and social issues. In any event, the wider the range of topics you cover, the more you will show potential employers how adaptable you are and how aware you are of different issues.

DEVELOPING YOUR SKILLS

The activities that we have explored in this chapter all develop a number of valuable skills that will help you both in your legal studies, and in any future career, whether legal or non-legal. While different activities may emphasise particular things, all will develop a range of skills and attributes, often in slightly different ways.

Remember to reflect on your development of these skills and attributes as you participate in these activities, just as you would for skills developed within your formal legal education (see Chapter 6). And include them within any personal development planning you undertake with your personal tutor (see Chapter 4).

Legal analysis and critical thinking

All these activities will develop your skills of legal analysis and critical thinking (see Chapter 10). It is essential that you use your analytical skills to identify the relevant issue or issues in whatever activity you engage with—whether that is to then develop a convincing argument, explore alternative strategies or identify further information you need. You will need to identify the relevant law and quickly become expert in a relatively narrow area. You will need to think critically and creatively about the law and wider context and think quickly to deal with unexpected information.

Research skills

Similarly, these activities can all enhance your research skills (see Chapter 8) as you locate and gain an understanding of the law (or wider issues) in a particular area. This involves not just finding the relevant material, but also selecting between different sources and discarding irrelevant material, and deciding what legal or other information is helpful or unhelpful to your position.

Written communication

While many of these activities focus on oral communication, there are still opportunities to develop your skills in written communication. For example, as part of a mooting competition, you will need to present a written submission and an accompanying bundle of evidence, developing your ability to draft legal documents and collate relevant evidence and encouraging precision in your written work. In negotiation you will have to produce a negotiation plan, while in client interviewing you will need to make coherent notes and may have to summarise your findings or advice in writing.

Oral communication

Mooting and debating are both a great test of your oral ability to put forward a cogent argument. They provide excellent experience in public speaking, speaking eloquently and persuasively, and responding orally to the arguments of others.

Negotiation and client interviewing also develop oral communication skills. A key part of negotiation is ensuring that you can explain clearly what you are trying to achieve and why. You will develop the ability to talk with precision, while also listening carefully to the other side's arguments and positions. You will need to present counter-arguments and deal with the unexpected, formulating arguments quickly.

Client interviewing develops in particular skills of appropriate questioning, active listening and adjusting your presentation of information to the needs of the listener—all essential for good oral communication. It also, more perhaps than the other activities, develops the ability to show rapport and empathy—treating the client as an individual, not just a problem to solve.

Professionalism

All these activities develop your professionalism, and not just though simulating professional activities. Whether adhering to court etiquette or other protocols, responding respectfully to arguments or different perspectives, ensuring precision and accuracy, meeting a high standard in presentation of materials or understanding the requirements of ethical behaviour in all situations—all these are essential to professionalism and professional behaviour.

INSIDER KNOWLEDGE

'I did not undertake any extra-curricular legal activities and looking back on it wished I had. It improves confidence especially when meeting clients and speaking to barristers.'

Liz MacDonald, Trainee Solicitor, Whatley Weston & Fox

Adaptability and quick thinking

You will develop your adaptability, and your ability to 'think on your feet' in all these situations. In mooting this will primarily be in taking account of the other side's points as they flesh out their skeleton arguments in court, and in responding thoughtfully and concisely to questions posed by the moot judge, even on points that may not previously have occurred to you.

Similarly, in debating you will need to respond to the other side's arguments, and possibly to interventions. Negotiations and client interviewing can often take an unexpected turn, requiring you to revisit your plans, deal with new information and make adjustments to your approach.

Teamwork/working with others

Most of these activities involve working in a team, developing skills in effective and constructive teamwork. You will need to discuss issues, agree approaches, develop complementary or alternative arguments, delegate tasks and manage relationships even under tight timescales and significant pressure.

You will also have to work with others beyond immediate team mates. This may be swapping skeleton arguments in a moot, showing respect when listening to or responding to another point of view, developing a level of mutual understanding while remaining assertive in a negotiation, or showing rapport with a client.

Decision making

Your success in all these activities will depend on the decisions you make—from deciding what material to use, to planning an approach or strategy, and when responding to arguments or fresh information. You will develop your skills in decision making as you decide when to take a strict line, when to offer alternatives and when to compromise or deal with sticking points.

Time management

Undertaking any of these activities will use time that you might otherwise have for study or social activities. You will need to be well organised and efficient in order to be able to take on and do your best in extra-curricular activities. Even if the activity is within your programme curriculum you will need to manage your time in order to prepare properly and do your best—balancing research, meeting team members, planning, practising and developing effective approaches to the task.

Reflection

Any activity that develops a skill or skills also provides you with excellent opportunities for developing your reflective abilities. The feedback you receive from engaging in moots, negotiations, debates or client interviewing—whether formal or informal—provides you with valuable information on your performance, skills and attributes. As mentioned earlier, you will need to reflect on this—not just to improve in that activity, but also so that you can use the feedback to enhance your wider learning, and even to guide your future plans.

MAKING FULL USE OF OPPORTUNITIES

Whatever your law school, there will be plenty of opportunities to undertake different activities within, alongside or outside the traditional curriculum to develop your practical legal skills. These will broaden and deepen your legal experience and will often enhance both your appreciation of the subjects you study within the curriculum and the skills you need to succeed in your studies.

I WISH I'D KNOWN . . .

'Try as many of these things as you can manage—I have both participated in and helped organise mooting and legal clinics, and both of them are some of the most rewarding and career-relevant extra-curricular activities I have undertaken whilst at university.'

Fiona Lin, University of Cambridge, Law, Year 3

If you have clear career goals, then use these to direct your efforts towards the most relevant activities, but don't ignore other opportunities. They may spark a new interest or reveal a hidden talent, to say nothing of enhancing your ability to succeed in your legal studies. If you don't yet know what you want to do for a career, engaging with these law-related activities can help to narrow down your choices by giving you a flavour of different work activities.

To enhance the value of every opportunity, reflection is key. Keep brief notes on what you did, how you went about doing it, what skills you learnt or developed while doing it, and think about its value for the future. This isn't just to help you improve your skills, it will help you when the time comes to make applications for jobs or other positions, and when you need to demonstrate your experience in using the skills needed for any future roles (see Chapter 19).

I WISH I'D KNOWN . . .

'I wish I'd known how complementary mooting can be to one's studies. By applying the same technique that I use to analyse a moot problem and write submissions to my problem questions for university, I increased my enjoyment of the classes and grades significantly.'

Alice Munnelly, King's College London, Law with European Legal Studies, Year 3

SUMMARY—HELP YOURSELF . . .

- **Supplement the skills you learn on your degree with the practical skills offered beyond it**
  - Speak to your personal tutor or student law society, or check your law school's website to see what options are available.
  - Research any specific competitions or activities that you want to be involved in.
  - If your school doesn't offer a particular activity, speak to your student union/guild or student law society, or look into setting up the activity yourself.

- **Reflect upon your own experience and goals**
  - Think about your career plans, existing skills, skill gaps and general interests.
  - Decide which general and legal skills you most need or wish to develop.
  - Focus on those activities that more strongly develop the skills you want to concentrate on, bearing in mind that different activities may develop similar skills, but in different ways.
  - Be realistic about what you can manage—aim to get broad experience but don't neglect your studies.
  - Reflect on your skills development and keep records to assist your career pathway.

18

VOLUNTEERING, PAID WORK AND OTHER EXTRA-CURRICULAR OPPORTUNITIES

*'We often miss opportunity because
it's dressed in overalls and
looks like work.'*

THOMAS A. EDISON

INTRODUCTION

Studying law—attending classes, doing your reading, writing essays—is obviously an essential factor in becoming a successful law student. What is more, it will take up a great deal of your time, if you approach it with the seriousness and dedication it deserves. But 'just' studying law, in the sense of completing the strict requirements of your law programme, is rarely enough for success in the longer term.

The extra factor, and what makes your experience as a law student so much more valuable, is extra-curricular activity—the things you do even though there is no obligation to do them for the purposes of your course. In the last chapter we looked at legal skills-based activities, many of which will be extra-curricular, such as mooting and negotiation. In this chapter we will consider extra-curricular opportunities more broadly.

Extra-curricular opportunities range from very law-focused activity, such as working at a law clinic, to things not obviously connected with the law, such as volunteering in your local community, paid work in the student union or bar, or involvement in sports or music. All that you do has value—it will provide personal satisfaction, make your experience as a law student more interesting and enjoyable and make you a more rounded and interesting person.

Just as importantly, all that you do beyond the curriculum will develop new skills and enhance existing ones. It will strengthen your CV and demonstrate to potential employers that you have talents beyond the ability to study, that you can manage your time, and that you would be an interesting person to have around. While legal 'pro bono' work (legal assistance provided 'for the public good' ie voluntarily and without charge) is probably top of the list in terms of its value to law students who want to enhance their legal skills and understanding and pursue a legal career, other opportunities can also provide valuable experience. What matters is that you recognise the worth of all you do, and reflect on the skills and experience you develop as a consequence.

VOLUNTEERING: PRO BONO PROGRAMMES AND BEYOND

Many law students get involved in volunteering during their degree, and for some students it is their first taste of legal practice or even the world of work. Volunteering obviously takes up time, but can be really valuable, both to you as an individual and as a professional-in-training.

The study of law and undertaking voluntary work often go hand in hand. You may have heard people talk about pro bono work at university open days, or even have selected your university based upon what it offers by way of pro bono opportunities. Whether it is a familiar phrase or not, in this section we will explore what the term means, what volunteering can offer the successful law student and the different opportunities (both legal and non-legal) that may present themselves.

Why volunteer?

You may already have volunteering experience, whether working in a charity shop, undertaking a sponsored walk, being a member of a volunteer organisation like St John Ambulance or spending time coaching a sports team. If so you will already be aware of the myriad benefits that volunteering can bring you personally, as well as society more generally.

Being a volunteer can help you develop as a successful law student. Although altruistic, it can also bring personal reward. Firstly, it can give you an excellent sense of individual satisfaction, though contributing and giving back to your community, particularly if using your own skills, or engaging with something you feel passionate about. It demonstrates your social commitment, your commitment to wider society. This is something of interest to employers, particularly as many organisations now have programmes to demonstrate corporate social responsibility (CSR). Volunteering also helps you develop commercial and social awareness, a broader and deeper appreciation of how society and business interact and impact different areas of life.

Voluntary work can also impact directly on your success, in terms of both your degree result and employability, by aiding your overall skills development. Depending on what you choose to do, you may develop a range of skills including:

- Problem solving;
- Project management;
- Leadership;
- Communication;
- Interpersonal skills, including: empathy, understanding and open-mindedness.

And this is recognised by employers. These 'soft' skills often appear within questions on applications for jobs, including training contracts and pupillage applications, and you may be asked about them in interview. If you are aiming for a career in law, then volunteering in the legal sphere can enhance your legal knowledge with practical experience, and further your practical legal skills. Another benefit of volunteering lies in the opportunities it brings for networking and developing contacts outside university, to say nothing of adding to your list of potential referees.

Making the most of volunteering

To get the most personal benefit from volunteering, it is important to reflect on what you do, think about what you have learned, consider what skills you have developed and reflect upon what it has taught you about yourself, others and society. If you do voluntary work, keep a record so you can recall all of these things, as you'll find this useful in the future when you have to conduct skills audits or make job applications.

If this feels selfish, and perhaps alien to the volunteering concept, remember that reflecting on your own skills and experiences enables you to learn and develop your abilities further, which makes you of more use to the organisation with which you work, or in any new positions.

Of course not everyone is in a position to volunteer—sometimes family commitments, time availability, location, finances or all manner of other challenges stand in the way. Or perhaps there simply aren't the opportunities available that you'd be interested in and would find beneficial. But there are all sorts of opportunities out there (both long and short term), and if you can find some time, we would encourage you to consider it. If you've done so already, well done!

I WISH I'D KNOWN . . .

'Don't do so much that it affects your studies. Be selective but make sure you do something.'

Frances Easton, University of Birmingham, Law, Year 3

Opportunities for volunteering

Many universities will have student societies dedicated to volunteering and charity work, most notably RAG (or Rag) societies. These are long-standing student groups that are dedicated to charity work. It is not entirely clear where the term 'rag' came from originally, but in more recent years it has sometimes been referred to as 'Raise and Give'. University Rag societies usually raise money for chosen charities and undertake volunteering work at a variety of organisations, often local to the particular university. They will often hold a 'rag week' dedicated to fundraising: rag weeks at some universities are somewhat notorious for the imaginative, and sometimes hair-raising, ways in which money is raised.

As well as Rag societies, other student societies will undertake volunteering and/or fundraising activities for specific charities. These will range from societies supporting well-known groups such as Amnesty

International, Greenpeace, Barnado's and WWF, to much smaller and local charitable foundations. Other societies, while not directed towards particular charities, will also choose to raise money during the course of the year or provide voluntary assistance. For example, the swimming society may do a swimathon or provide help to support a community sports facility, or the film society may organise a charity film screening.

Of course there is no need to volunteer through a student society, you may want to undertake volunteer work that you can organise yourself. Numerous charities and local organisations rely on help so go out and offer your services, thinking about what particular skills you might be able to offer, and what time you can commit to.

You may wish to focus on a charity that you feel strongly about or have personal experience with, or one that you are interested in knowing more about. Voluntary work may range from offering your services to assist a particular one-off project or providing ongoing support, and you could be offering specific skills or experience, or just your time and willingness to help. Your assistance could range from something specific like helping with a disaster relief appeal after a crisis, or regularly working in a call centre or local charity shop. Whatever you do will be of value to the community and to your personal development.

Legal voluntary work

Your law school may present numerous opportunities for volunteering. Law schools have always been closely linked to volunteering through their pro bono projects. 'Pro bono' comes from the Latin phrase 'pro bono publico' meaning for the public good, which in law generally signifies undertaking legal work without payment. So if a lawyer is acting pro bono, s/he is doing legal work without charge.

Pro bono assistance may be offered to those who would not otherwise be able to afford legal services, or those who have special requirements for legal services that they are unable to access. Many practising lawyers carry out some pro bono work, and some law firms and chambers provide extensive pro bono services or run specific pro bono projects.

University law schools sometimes team up with practising lawyers or charitable institutions to offer pro bono services, or sometimes act on their own. Many have large teams of law students working on different projects that can help both individuals and groups of people. Legal voluntary work while at law school can really help bring the law to life, as well as often providing additional networking opportunities.

Every law school is different and will run different projects so we can't set out all the different opportunities that might be offered, but Figure 18.1 outlines the principal types, and we'll go on to explain some of the most common opportunities.

FIGURE 18.1: Options for legal voluntary work

Before we do so we should note that some law schools are embedding pro bono projects within the curriculum as an elective or compulsory module. These modules, often called clinical legal education or work-based learning and discussed in Chapter 9, mean that you usually undertake specific activities, construct a portfolio of work done and reflect upon your experiences in order to earn credits towards your degree. This is obviously not volunteering in its strictest sense but will still be viewed favourably by employers and will give you skills and experiences that you can draw upon for job applications and interviews.

Law clinics

Most volunteering opportunities offered by law schools are in the form of advisory clinics. These are generally free drop-in sessions for members of the public where law students, under the supervision of a qualified lawyer or other trained individual, help people by offering advice, writing letters, completing forms and other relatively minor legal tasks.

These may be hosted in the law school, in a court, in a law centre in town, in the student union or anywhere else appropriate. Some law schools have really sophisticated law clinics with designated space for meeting clients, while others will be a bit more rough and ready. Whatever the state of the facilities, law clinics offer a really valuable service to their communities. At an even more local level, the law school may help to support a student union advice service, enabling law students to assist other students on matters such as tenancy agreements or welfare benefits.

Volunteering in a law clinic is a really good introduction to legal practice, and gives you the opportunity to practise some of the skills related to law. Generally, a client will come in to see you with a problem. This could potentially concern any area of law: your law clinic might provide guidance on any number of legal areas, perhaps specialising in contract law, family law, refugee and immigration law, employment law, tort law, intellectual property law or property law, or provide a general advice centre.

Being able to identify the issue and the relevant law is of course at the heart of legal study and legal practice. You will have to interview the client to get all the relevant information, research the problem, and help them by drafting a letter or court documents, liaise with qualified lawyers (including your supervisor) and brief the clients on progress. All very valuable skills. You will also develop 'softer' skills such as empathy, active listening, compassion and other interpersonal skills.

The workload you may face in these clinics is likely to be varied, and presents you with a real opportunity to understand what it is like to face a legal problem in practice—while under the careful guidance of a qualified solicitor. Even if you do not intend to practise as a lawyer, it can develop many of the skills you need for success in legal study and beyond.

INSIDER KNOWLEDGE

'Law clinics are often the first opportunity to meet members of the public and provide actual legal advice in relation to genuine legal questions. It is fantastic experience and will enhance any CV or application form.'

Jamie Hill, Barrister

Other opportunities

You may also be able to volunteer in non-client facing pro bono projects during your legal studies. This might involve providing advice to the public or to other students through the design and production of resources, such as leaflets or workshops, that can help specific groups of people. This can be a valuable experience as you will have to take your legal knowledge and convert it into a form that is clear, accurate and can be easily understood by those without legal training.

Other projects might involve you going into local schools to encourage pupils to consider legal problems, develop their critical thinking and problem-solving skills and educate them on their rights. This can be particularly challenging but rewarding. As well as developing valuable skills in presentation, synthesis of material and communication, these kinds of projects can be particularly valuable if you are contemplating teaching or any similar career.

Law schools may also offer opportunities to engage in other legal volunteering programmes. These may be part of international or national networks, with teams of students from different law schools working on combined or individual projects, or may be very local projects designed to help your local community or the population of your university. The nature of the project and the work involved will vary according to your law school and local area, but all will give you the opportunity to meet different groups of people, whether students from other law schools or people from your local community. We can't list all the projects that may be available to you in your own law school but we will look briefly at some of the more widely offered opportunities.

- LawWorks is a charity dedicated to enabling access to justice by providing and facilitating pro bono legal advice. It is a national organisation with headquarters in London and a number of offices around the country. They fund pro bono projects and act as a route of access for people to find pro bono legal services across the country. LawWorks may provide funding or run projects within your law school, or they may pass details of your law clinic to potential clients. They also offer volunteering experience, so keep your eye out for emails, posters and leaflets that may provide you with opportunities outside your school. LawWorks is always under pressure to provide more and more help to those that cannot get legal assistance and is well worth considering if you are looking for volunteering opportunities. More information is available at https://www.lawworks.org.uk/.

- The Law Centres Network is another organisation that is dedicated to providing legal services to those who would otherwise be unable to access help. Law Centres have been a part of the legal landscape for several decades and work within local communities, usually based in towns or cities, offering legal advice and representation to local people, specialising in social welfare law. They offer legal support to individuals and groups on a not-for-profit basis and often work pro bono, relying on both paid lawyers and volunteers. Unsurprisingly they especially like law students! More information can be found at http://www.lawcentres.org.uk/ (or http://www.govanlc.com/salc for law centres in Scotland).

- AdviceUK is the UK's largest support network for free, independent advice centres. While some of what these organisations do is not legally related, much of it is. They provide varied advice on matters such as debt management, addiction, housing and property, and much more. See http://www.adviceuk.org.uk/ for more about what AdviceUK does, and the opportunities there may be for you to offer help.

- Citizens Advice (which supports Citizens Advice Bureaux, or CAB), is a national organisation that you may have heard of, or even used yourself. It provides 'free, independent, confidential and impartial advice to everyone on their rights and responsibilities'. Most towns and cities will have at least one CAB and for many people, the CAB is the first port of call for any issues they face. CAB offer advice on a large number of areas including: benefit rights, employment rights, housing, consumer issues, debt and money matters, tax, discrimination, education and more. As you can imagine, their workload is enormous and they are always looking for volunteers. Many law students give up a number of hours each week to help work through the caseload, with training provided and the guarantee of very varied work. More information is available at https://www.citizensadvice.org.uk/.

You might also choose to get involved with a campaign group or reform society—and there are lots to choose from. Some law schools or student societies will already work with and represent some of these organisations, but even if they don't, there is nothing to stop you getting involved with them or setting up your own society to represent their interests.

- One of the best known of these groups within law schools is the Innocence Project (http://www.innocenceproject.org/). Innocence was founded in 1992 in the USA and is a non-profit organisation committed to clearing the names of wrongfully convicted people across the world. They also campaign for reform within the criminal justice system to prevent future wrongful convictions. The group is also the home of the Innocence Network; a network of law schools, journalism schools and pro bono lawyers across the world that work on their own projects for the release of wrongfully convicted people.

- Amnesty International is another charity that campaigns for the protection of human rights. Many universities have an Amnesty International Society that will hold demonstrations, raise money and seek to educate others on human rights abuses.

- The Howard League for Penal Reform is a well-respected national charity dedicated to improving the standards and treatment of prisoners across the UK. Some universities have Howard League Societies that run events, fundraising activities and demonstrations. All of these can provide you with valuable volunteering experience and the chance to do good for an issue you care about.

You might want to put your legal studies to use in another way by volunteering in a public service. For example, if you are interested in working in the criminal law, or working within the criminal justice system, there are plenty of different opportunities:

- Particularly if you are considering joining the police force, you may want to consider becoming a special constable. Special constables are volunteer police officers from all walks of life who give a minimum of four hours of their time per week to their local police force. Once a special constable has completed their training, they have the same powers as a regular officer and wear a similar uniform.

- The police force also makes much use of Police Support Volunteers (PSV). PSVs are citizen volunteers who perform tasks which complement the duties performed by police officers and staff. Roles range from front counter services and administration to processing crime reports. More information on volunteering in the police service can be obtained from your local police force.

- If you are interested in volunteering in the criminal justice system from a very different perspective you might be interested in becoming an 'appropriate adult'. An appropriate adult is responsible for protecting the rights and welfare of a child or vulnerable adult who is either detained by police or is interviewed under caution voluntarily. More information can be found at http://www.appropriateadult.org.uk/.

- Magistrates are volunteers, hearing cases in local magistrates' courts concerning both criminal and civil matters. Contrary to common perceptions, the magistracy is open to young and old. Being a magistrate does require a significant level of commitment to training and attendance, so do make sure you can meet this without detracting from your studies—in practice it may only be feasible for part-time students: https://www.gov.uk/become-magistrate/can-you-be-a-magistrate.

PAID WORK

Many students will work at some point during their degrees. This may be a necessity to pay for your studies and/or subsistence, or you may be lucky enough that your earnings just help to provide you with a richer social life. You may work for several hours every week in term time and in every vacation, or you may look for a temporary job or do casual labour in the long vacation. Or you may be studying part-time, and working quite extensively alongside your studies. Whichever is true, paid work has many benefits and can help to make you a successful law student.

What work to do?

The work you do, if any, will depend on a number of factors, including:

- What work is available in your area;

- Your experience and/or qualifications;
- Visa restrictions for overseas students;
- Your studies and other commitments.

Studying law successfully will take up a great deal of your time and energy—and should be treated as (almost) equivalent to a full-time job—so take account of this when considering whether to work, and what work to do. This is particularly important for term time work. You can be more flexible during vacation periods, but even then, don't entirely forget your studies, nor the need to take a break. Key amongst the practical matters to consider are:

- **Location and transport**
  - Travelling to work can eat up study time and earnings—stay local. If the job is really good, you need to balance its benefits against those drawbacks.
  - During term time your workplace needs to be close to your law school and accommodation so your attendance doesn't suffer. In vacations, remember to factor in accommodation costs if the job isn't close to home.

- **Flexibility**
  - This is particularly important for term time work, but even in vacations you may need time for pre-reading, interviews and work experience, or revision and resits. Be clear from the start that there will be times during the year when you cannot work or have to reduce your hours.
  - Jobs that allow you to change your hours at fairly short notice are particularly valuable if you are working during the term—such benefits may outweigh a lower wage.

- **Hours of work**
  - Quite aside from flexibility, make sure that you do not take on too much, or your studies and/or your health will suffer. More than fifteen hours a week is likely to put you under real pressure, so don't push yourself too far. While some students may do more, few of these are law students!

I WISH I'D KNOWN . . .

'With a law degree it's a constant struggle to balance [work and study]. Many people have managed to juggle a degree and work but many people have been left behind trying to juggle the two. Advantages are that you have more money, you are building on essential skills (even if you're not in a legal position as there are transferable skills which can be applied to a legal position) and also you're staying active with no time for procrastination. Disadvantages are very little time if any for anything other than work or uni, tiredness, irritability, many students often find themselves depressed by the fact they're constantly working in some way or another and it's obviously harder.'

Sammee Hart, University of East London, LLB Law, Year 2

Practical factors often make employment with the university particularly appealing. Most institutions employ students in different roles, from bar staff to helpdesk support. As employers, universities are obviously familiar with the constraints on your time and tend to be very supportive and flexible. Many universities have a 'JobShop', or your student union/ guild or student helpdesk should be able to direct you to information on what is available.

Other employers located close to a university—particularly those in the hospitality and catering industry—will also be familiar with employing students on both temporary and casual bases. There are websites specialising in student jobs (such as http://www.studentjob.co.uk), but do speak to existing students and the union/guild for inside information on good and bad local employers and agencies.

INSIDER KNOWLEDGE

'Try to get the balance right between working too many hours and not working enough to live on. If you are struggling for money, try reducing the amount of times you go out rather than increasing your working hours as this can be stressful, particularly around exam and assignment times.'

Gavin Teasdale, Solicitor, PGS Law LLP

Another important factor to consider is whether there is work that is relevant, even peripherally, to your career plans or wider interests. There may not be—and if not don't worry because you will still benefit from the work—but it is worth exploring. For example, paid work directly in the law is not easy to obtain, particularly during term time. However, you may still be able to gain experience of the law in action—albeit from a very different perspective—by taking (for example) a temporary or part-time cleaning or catering job at your local court centre or large law firm. There may also be opportunities for those with relevant skills to work as legal secretaries or receptionists in law firms or legal centres. Think imaginatively about the kind of work you might be able to do, on a part-time, temporary or casual basis, and keep an eye out for opportunities.

There are other ways of engaging with the law while earning, but these opportunities are not particularly numerous, nor usually very well paid:

- Large law firms and some other employers may recruit student representatives for your university, often called student ambassadors. These posts can give you great contact with the profession or other areas of business at an early stage in your studies. Your student law society is a good place to ask about opportunities available at your institution;

- Legal publishers use law students to provide feedback on textbooks and other projects—this may be ad hoc (with payment in lunch or books!) or you may get the opportunity to join a student panel providing regular input into developments, for some limited remuneration. Keep an eye out for emails (usually sent via the law school itself) and law publishers' websites;

- Occasionally opportunities come up to assist law school staff with research on particular projects, usually during the summer vacation, but sometimes during the academic year. Such posts are not numerous, but very worthwhile, particularly if you are interested in a research career. If you are interested it might be worth letting your personal tutor know so s/he can put you forward if s/he hears of an opportunity. Some universities will provide formal paid research internships, which will be advertised to their students;

- Your law library may employ students during term time or vacations. These posts will usually be made available through standard university student recruitment channels but you could speak to your law librarian if you are interested.

I WISH I'D KNOWN . . .

'You can be a campus ambassador for an external firm or organisation. This means that you get paid, while having one foot in the door, increasing your chances of securing future employment.'

Godwin Tan, University College London, LLB Law, Year 3

Most students inevitably undertake fairly menial work during their studies, as this is what is most easily available, and tends to be flexible. If you have particular skills or experience you might well be able to make use of them to boost your earning power. For example, students with skills and experience in areas such as IT or secretarial work will be of interest to many employers, including your university, and agencies dealing with temporary work. Or make use of your hobbies by gaining qualifications so you can run or support courses or classes or offer one-to-one tuition. In some areas of work you may be able to offer your services on a self-employed basis. This offers great flexibility, but don't take on too much work, and don't forget you will need to arrange things like insurance. Whatever your work, make sure you understand the tax position by checking with HMRC (Revenue & Customs): https://www.gov.uk/student-jobs-paying-tax.

INSIDER KNOWLEDGE

'I would choose a job you can seek transferrable skills from, the advantages are that you can have money and life experience, but remember that is not your career so don't give 100% to the part-time job, it leaves nothing for your career.'

Danny Smith, Solicitor-Advocate, PCB Solicitors

Benefits of paid work

Work offers many benefits—not just an income and the personal satisfaction of a job well done. Depending on what you do, you will develop a range of skills and attributes—just as with voluntary work—all of which will contribute to making you a successful law student and enhance your employability. Think about the role you play and the tasks you undertake: you will be using and developing a huge range of skills. Figure 18.2 illustrates this.

FIGURE 18.2: Developing skills through work

I WISH I'D KNOWN . . .

'An advantage to having a part-time job whilst studying is that it removes you from the 'bubble' of stress that can sometimes build up when at law school. It's important to develop perspective and real life experience, even if your plan is to get a training contract directly from university. One disadvantage is that it is sometimes necessary to be very flexible at university given that seminar dates and times are not always set in advance. It's difficult to prioritise university if you'll have to miss a shift at work.'

Alice Munnelly, King's College London, Law with European Legal Studies, Year 3

ACTIVITIES AND INTERESTS

Everything we do has value in developing ourselves and building skills. Even hours spent on computer games enhance the gamer's dexterity and reaction speeds! As a successful law student it is sensible to focus on activities and interests that will develop skills that will help your study and/or help to get you the career that you want, whether in law or elsewhere.

Languages and travel

'If you talk to a man in a language he understands, that goes to his head. If you talk to him in his own language, that goes to his heart' (Nelson Mandela). If you are a native English speaker it can be tempting to take advantage of English being spoken so widely across the globe. But the ability to communicate in other languages is valuable for employability and can open up opportunities for work (in the UK and abroad), travel, life and study.

Unsurprisingly, foreign language skills are very highly prized by employers. The 'big' European languages are particularly popular with employers—Spanish, French and German for example—but other languages are also valued, from Punjabi to Polish, and from Mandarin to Malay.

What is more, there is evidence that language learning more generally aids your ability to study. This includes aspects of study particularly relevant to learning the law, such as effective reading, critical thinking and problem solving. So language learning may enhance your chances of success as a law student, quite apart from its relevance to employability.

Language learning could mean taking up a new language, or continuing with one you learned at school or elsewhere. You will usually be able to take a suitable language module as one of your optional subject choices alongside your law modules, and many universities also offer language courses to their students at very favourable rates. It makes sense to take advantage of these opportunities if you can. If you are already fluent (or nearly fluent) in a language, then maintain this with regular conversation with native speakers at the university. And don't just learn the language, get more involved by joining the relevant student association—this will also give you the chance to practise your language skills.

Make the most of any opportunities to travel abroad during your studies. We've looked at the benefits of studying aboard in Chapter 16, but there are plenty of other opportunities too. Law schools and/or student law societies also often run excellent value and sometimes subsidised trips to places such as the European Court of Justice or the International Court of Human Rights. Spending time visiting another country, and engaging actively with its institutions, history and wider culture, shows employers that you take an interest in the world around you and helps to develop an open and flexible attitude.

Sport and the arts

Many law students have a keen interest in one or more sports and/or aspects of the arts and your time at university is an excellent opportunity to indulge your interests and get involved. It is also a great opportunity to try something new, whether that is a development from an existing interest or something fresh. From football to quidditch, and from reading groups to drama, there will be a club or society for just about everything in sport and the arts. And if the university doesn't have one, then look locally, or start one up.

Just doing something is valuable in its own right. Employers like to see an applicant has wider interests, particularly where they demonstrate commitment, determination and resilience. Engaging actively with sports or the arts also helps to provide a release from the pressures of studying law, enabling you to maintain a good sense of perspective and keeping you refreshed.

You can further enhance the value of your sporting and cultural activities by moving beyond participation, and putting something back in. So consider joining a society's committee to help with its organisation, or support those who are beginners, organise tournaments, raise funds for new equipment—anything. Getting more deeply involved can be personally satisfying, and will provide solid evidence of your positive attitude, community engagement and organisational skills to put before employers.

Other interests

Whatever your hobbies or interests, they all say something about you. They make you a more interesting person and your engagement with them develops different skills and competencies. Whether your interest is politics, religion, information technology or something completely different, engage with it meaningfully. Just as we have discussed in relation to sport and the arts, consider getting involved beyond participation. That way you can use your skills and talents to benefit something you love, help others in your area of interest and develop your skills and talents. Everyone wins!

MAKING USE OF ALL YOUR EXTRA-CURRICULAR ACTIVITIES

Whatever you do—whether paid or voluntary, whether fun or a chore, whether related to law or not—you should reflect on what you are doing and learning. Even tasks that appear pretty dull can be more satisfying if you focus on doing them to the best of your ability and explore the range of skills you are developing. Your extra-curricular activity thus has great potential to enhance your success as a law student, both by developing useful skills that will aid your study, and by giving your CV a boost. You may also find that your university has an award scheme to recognise students who are actively engaged in society. This may be linked explicitly to university-led activities, or reward wider community engagement.

I WISH I'D KNOWN . . .

'Extra-curriculars are so important. Not only will they help make your life interesting at university by giving you a wide network of friends, they will become vital when applying for jobs and using your experience as examples of specific skills you have developed.'

Emily Barrett, University of Bristol, Law with Study in Continental Europe, Year 4

Law-focused activities may develop the most obviously relevant skills and competences for a law student. For example working pro bono in a law clinic, or part-time work as a legal secretary, will increase your awareness of law in practice and thus your ability to identify issues, relevant law and practical constraints.

But it is not just law-focused work that can aid your study skills. As we have seen, any experience of work, paid or unpaid, law-focused or not, will develop time management skills. These will help you organise your study, allocate your time effectively and ensure you complete your assessments on time. Similarly, dealing with customers in a bar, organising a dance competition or helping in a charity shop will improve your communication skills so you can explain yourself clearly in different situations and resolve issues constructively. And, underpinning everything you do beyond the curriculum, a willingness to work hard, perseverance, an awareness of the needs of others and the ability to take personal responsibility, all impact positively on your attitude to your legal studies and your eventual success.

Reflect on your extra-curricular activity to further enhance your chances of success. Reflection enables you to understand your skills development (including strengths and weaknesses) and enhances your CV and job applications. We'll look further at these areas in Chapter 19 but don't leave reflection on your extra-curricular activities until the point you apply for positions:

- Reflect on your experiences while they are still fresh in your mind;
- Make notes so you have a reminder and evidence when you need them.

So, if you successfully completed a project at work, write down some brief details, reflecting on the skills you needed, and noteworthy successes or challenges (and how you responded to them). Just as importantly, if you had a bit of a disaster, reflect on your response to that, and what you have learned.

Regular reflection on your extra-curricular activities means that you are continually learning from your experiences—a reflective law student is far more likely to be a successful law student. By making ongoing notes on your experiences and your reflection you will create a valuable resource of evidence relating to your skills, abilities and experience. As we'll see in Chapter 19, that doesn't mean it should all go into a final CV or application; you will need to identify the best evidence to support your case. But the reflective process gives you examples to choose from when the time comes, and enables you to select the most appropriate evidence for different applications. It also means you can give specific examples of events or behaviour to back up statements relating to 'soft' skills that can otherwise appear generic and might therefore be overlooked by an employer.

SUMMARY—HELP YOURSELF . . .

- **Consider volunteering**
  - Explore volunteering opportunities within the law school, the university and beyond.
  - Recognise the many benefits to volunteering, not just to society but to yourself, from personal satisfaction to development of both 'hard' and 'soft' skills.
  - Focus on voluntary work that interests you and/or is relevant to your goals.
  - Legal voluntary work can help develop skills you will use in your legal studies, and in future legal practice or other work, but all voluntary work is valuable.
  - Consider working within a law school clinic or other pro bono project; contact outside institutions who work in areas where you have an interest; explore local community projects and other charities needing help.
  - Remember that volunteering, however valuable, is still 'extra'-curricular—don't neglect your legal studies.

- **Get full value from paid work**
  - Paid work offers much more than just an income, so don't dismiss it as just a chore, or feel aggrieved that you have to work while others don't.
  - Identify skills that your work develops and valuable learning experiences—in whatever form they take; take up any training offered.
  - Be realistic and make sure your work does not impact negatively on your studies.
  - If you can find work that relates to your studies or interests, so much the better.

- **Remember it isn't just work that counts**

  - Maintain existing hobbies and interests, and/or start something new to keep perspective and relieve stress.

  - Hobbies and interests show employers you are a committed individual with a rounded personality.

  - Put something back (and gain skills) by helping out where you can.

- **Make full use of all your extra-curricular experiences**

  - Reflect regularly on what you've been doing and what you've learned.

  - Maintain basic records to help with later personal evaluation and job applications.

  - Explore opportunities, stretch yourself—and enjoy yourself.

PART 6

ENSURING A SUCCESSFUL FUTURE

19

PREPARING TO MOVE ON

'It is always the way of events in this life ... no sooner have you got settled in a pleasant resting place, than a voice calls out to you to rise and move on.'

CHARLOTTE BRONTË,
Jane Eyre

INTRODUCTION

Inevitably, and far more quickly than probably seemed possible at the start, your legal studies will come to an end—it will be time to move on. This chapter looks at what you can do to be prepared for that moment, to increase your chances of success in the next stage of your life and maximise the value of your time as a law student. We'll look in particular at the importance of planning and reflection, sources of support and guidance, preparing CVs and applications and dealing with setbacks. We consider particular career paths more specifically in Chapter 20, as well as the option of postgraduate study.

As you might expect, this chapter is positioned towards the end of this book. But that doesn't mean you should only start thinking about moving on as you reach the end of your legal studies.

Preparing to move on is something to give thought to throughout your legal studies, even if you will naturally focus on it more strongly towards the later stages. You need to apply for many opportunities, such as vacation schemes with law firms, quite early on in your degree—particularly if you want to make full use of the time you have before graduation. So by keeping in mind the next stage, you can make best use of opportunities and put yourself in the strongest possible position when the time comes to move on.

LOOKING FORWARD, LOOKING BACK

Just working hard is rarely sufficient to bring reward in the form of a satisfying career and contented life—you need to take active steps to get there. So going with the flow and seeing what turns up isn't really an option for a successful law student.

Preparing to move on requires thought, planning and reflection, as illustrated in Figure 19.1. This can be time-consuming and challenging, but the process is something you should be familiar with already.

FIGURE 19.1: Thinking about moving on

Looking forward—making plans

We looked at the importance of having (achievable) goals back in Chapter 3, and saw there that 'success' is dependent on, and only meaningful in relation to, your own aims and purposes. So what are your goals in relation to the next stage in your life?

Depending on when you are reading this, and your personality and circumstances, you may have clear plans about your intended career path and life goals. Perhaps you have a childhood ambition that you remain determined to fulfil. Perhaps you've spent your time at university attending lots of talks and doing work experience, and are clear what route you want to take. If so you will have strong motivation for preparing thoroughly and can find out what you need to do to get where you want to be.

But remember that while ambition is important, it is different from having goals. Your goals need to be realistic and achievable, so split your ultimate aim into a series of steps, and remember to couch each goal in terms of an outcome that you can influence and achieve. You might want to revisit the notion of SMART goals that we looked at in Chapter 3. Make sure too that your goals, and ambitions, are truly what *you* want— don't be afraid to revisit and revise your plans, however far down the line you've come on a particular path.

Not every law student has a clear sense of where they are going, or what they want beyond successful completion of their law programme. You may be reading this in the early stages of legal study, and have little idea of your options or what you would like to do after law school. Or perhaps you are now approaching the end of your legal studies, and either still don't know what you want to do, or have found that your initial plans have fallen away as you've discovered more about the opportunities available or your own strengths and interests.

If you don't have a fixed pathway in mind, don't worry—it is not at all uncommon, and there are benefits in being able to respond flexibly to opportunities and new developments. But you still need to be prepared so you are able to respond to what comes up. Spend some time exploring options, and considering your strengths and weaknesses, likes and dislikes.

Looking back—reviewing your experience

Whatever your current plans, or lack of them, you should review and reflect upon your experience as a law student. Looking at your legal studies and your wider activities and experiences, consider:

- What new skills have you developed; what existing skills have you enhanced?
- What experiences have you had—both positive and negative? What have you learned from those experiences?
- What subjects did you particularly enjoy or dislike? Why was this?
- Which study methods did you enjoy, or find particularly helpful or unhelpful? Why do you think this was?
- What is your learning style? Has this changed at all during your period of study?
- Which outside speakers did you find particularly interesting? Why?
- What activities have you been involved with, both within your law school and more widely? Which did you stick with, and why?
- Do you have any regrets? What would you do differently if you had your time again?
- What are you most proud of? Why is this?

It is helpful to reflect like this throughout your studies, so you can modify your activities and behaviour accordingly. But even if you only do this at the end of your law programme, it still has benefits through:

- Pinpointing transferable skills and valuable personal attributes;
- Identifying areas of strength and weakness;
- Clarifying your interests, and what you are likely to find rewarding;
- Locating the positives, and processing the disappointments;
- Identifying gaps in your skills and experiences, and evaluating whether they matter;
- Developing your ability to reflect on and learn from your experiences;
- Providing material for job applications.

Personal development planning

In Chapter 6 we discussed keeping track of your skills development and experiences in a learning journal, 'running CV' or similar resource. These will be very useful to you as you prepare to move on—they will remind you of all you have done, and help you to identify interests, strengths and weaknesses.

You may also have had access to personal development planning (or PDP) platforms or sessions through your university. (They may be called something different, such as a Learning Plan, or Individual Development Plan.)

Student PDP resources are usually online and are designed so you can build up a portfolio of experiences and other information—much like combining a learning journal, running CV and living personal statement, ideally with additional reflection. They can help you to develop your skills and experience as you progress through your study, and will be essential material now as you look back and look forward. PDP resources can be particularly helpful to trigger discussion with your personal tutor and any mentors or advisors as you think about moving on.

But PDP is, or should be, much more than just keeping an online repository up to date with what you've been doing. And planning your own development can, and should, be done whether or not you are encouraged to do so by your institution. PDP should include both aspects of what we've been discussing: reflecting on where you are now *and* where you want to be, as illustrated in Figure 19.2. This will also help you find the important link(s)—how to get from here to there.

FIGURE 19.2: Personal development planning—three stages

SKILLS/EXPERIENCE: WHERE ARE YOU NOW?	• Strengths and weaknesses • Skills/skill gaps • Experiences/gaps in experience
MAKING THE LINK: WHAT DO YOU NEED TO DO?	• Achievable 'SMART' goals, split into distinct tasks • Academic and personal development • Identifying and allocating resources and time
OBJECTIVES: WHERE DO YOU WANT TO BE?	• Ultimate ambitions • Longer-term aims: 3–5 years time • Medium-term aims: next 1–3 years • Short-term aims: next 12 months

By reflecting on your experience, and regularly revisiting your goals and plans, you should be able to identify gaps in your skills and experience. Ideally you will have done a similar exercise before starting your legal studies (see Chapter 3).

What to do about those gaps? You could choose simply to accept any weaknesses, and limit your options accordingly. This might be appropriate for some fundamental things—after all, if you had no sense of smell, there would be little point in aiming to be a perfumer! But for most law students, and most career paths considered by law students, gaps and weaknesses are there to be identified and challenged. So don't limit your options, deal with those gaps:

- To what extent do any gaps/weaknesses impact on your future plans? Are they significant, relevant, peripheral or entirely irrelevant? Place more emphasis on dealing with those that are significant or at least relevant;

- If your plans aren't clear, how far might these gaps/weaknesses limit your future choices? Aim to keep multiple options open;

- What can you do now to fill these gaps? Do you need additional training, further support, different experiences? What other opportunities might be coming up in the near future?

- How can each opportunity be maximised? Could one experience address more than one gap? For example voluntary work overseas could boost teamwork, communication, resilience, language skills etc.

The earlier you address these issues, the more time you have to make use of all the support, advice, guidance and opportunities provided by your law school and institution. You can also use these resources to help you identify the important gaps in the first place.

ADVICE AND NETWORKING

Getting and using help

Whatever stage you are at in preparing to move on from your legal studies, there is plenty of advice and support available, both within and outside your law school. Don't assume advice only has a role to play once you've worked out what you want to do. Figure 19.3 shows various ways in which advice can help you.

FIGURE 19.3: Making full use of available advice

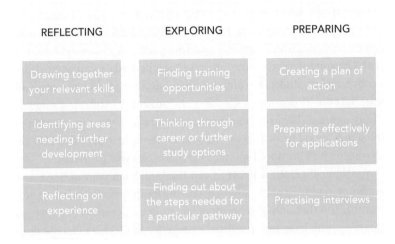

REFLECTING	EXPLORING	PREPARING
Drawing together your relevant skills	Finding training opportunities	Creating a plan of action
Identifying areas needing further development	Thinking through career or further study options	Preparing effectively for applications
Reflecting on experience	Finding out about the steps needed for a particular pathway	Practising interviews

Different sources of advice and support will be able to help you in different ways, so make use of all the help that is out there.

Careers service

Every institution will offer their students a careers service, and this may remain open to you to some extent even after graduation. Take advantage of these expert advisors with years of experience of assisting students. It is usually possible to book a one-to-one meeting with an advisor to explore where you are and where you might go. Take up these opportunities.

Usually the careers service will also have a wide range of material available electronically, including online aptitude tests and similar resources. Don't overlook this great resource: find out what is there, and see where it takes you. It is worth exploring careers resources even if you feel clear about what you want to do. Knowing what is available, and knowing yourself, puts you in a much stronger position as you move on.

The careers service will also arrange talks, meetings and workshops over the course of each academic year. They will usually be advertised centrally rather than through the law school. These can help you find out about different career possibilities, and develop important skills. Keep your options open by attending a range of activities, as you might come across possibilities you hadn't previously contemplated. These events also provide opportunities to make contacts outside the law school, and for networking more generally.

Interestingly, law students sometimes overlook the value of the careers service—perhaps because they see the generalised outlook of a university careers service as insufficiently focused on specific legal career paths. That is a bit misguided. Firstly some careers services have advisors that specialise in advising law students—why wouldn't you want to take advantage of this? But even those without specialist 'law' advisors can offer law students a huge amount. The broad experience of a careers service can offer something that the more focused law school may struggle to provide. After all, moving on isn't just about specific instruction on 'what to do now'.

You'll benefit from support as you think through your options, and guidance in writing applications, preparing for interviews and so on. Remember too that only a minority of law students actually follow a legal career—some have never wanted to practise law, others change their mind whilst studying, while others find there isn't a role for them. With this in mind, keeping an open mind, and benefiting from all the careers service has to offer, is clearly an advantage to the successful law student.

Law school

Your law school will typically offer a great deal of support through specific activities and within existing roles. Make use of what you have. Law school staff work daily with law students, and have watched many hundreds, even thousands, move on in many different directions over the years—as well as having experience of moving on themselves. Unsurprisingly, law students often find the support provided by their law school, or individuals within the law school, to be amongst the most useful in preparing their next steps. But law school staff do tend to focus on specifically legal careers, and won't necessarily have direct experience of different paths, so use other support too.

Law school careers/employability advisor

Some law schools provide their students with access to a specialist advisor. This may be an expert in legal careers, or someone with broader experience of supporting law graduates without necessarily focusing on 'legal' careers. Such specialists should be able to help you think through your options, as well as advising on more practical matters in pursuing a chosen career. You may find the number of times you can access any 'in-house' advisor is restricted, so use your time effectively by thinking in advance about the specific areas you want to address.

Alternatively, or additionally, law schools may offer talks, workshops or one-to-one sessions on specific things such as drafting applications or interview technique. These events are often run by, or with the support of, law alumni (graduates from your law school) or local legal practitioners. Depending on your career path, your law school may also be able to put you in touch with alumni working in your field of interest, to act as mentors or provide advice as you move on.

You may also notice that one of your law school lecturers has an administrative role with a title such as 'director of employability', or 'employment officer'. These individuals are not specialist careers advisors, but have a role in co-ordinating employment activities within the law school and liaising with employers and the careers service. Given their additional experience, they are often a great source of information, and may be willing to see individual students. However individual one-to-one support is more commonly provided by the personal tutor.

Personal tutor

The role of the personal tutor usually includes an element of personal development planning and careers support. This is particularly valuable as your personal tutor gets to know you over a number of years. S/he will have seen how your initial thoughts have been refined, and will have an overview of your skills, abilities and interests.

Your personal tutor won't be an expert in careers and development planning, and so you should not expect them to know everything, nor should you rely on them as a sole source of advice and support. But personal tutors are in a position to signpost other sources of help, and their experience (their own, and from other personal tutees) can provide valuable insights into possibilities and potential problems. Your personal tutor may also be able to put you in touch with a colleague or other contact where appropriate. We looked further at the important role of the personal tutor in Chapter 4.

Student law society

As well as events run by the careers service and the law school itself, the student law society will also usually offer a range of activities that are directly or indirectly connected to employability. These are often organised with particular employers but are rarely just recruitment events—they can range from a talk to a skills workshop, and from a training day to a pub quiz. Most commonly these events are run by large and/or local law firms (solicitors) but even if you don't plan to be a solicitor, they are still valuable for personal development and understanding your options.

The student law society is also a good source of advice more generally. Office-holders in student law societies tend to be keen participants in law school life, and are often very driven, career-focused individuals. They also receive a great deal of information from all sorts of directions—employers, the careers service, the law school etc. So make use of your society, and ask its members for advice and guidance if you need it. Most will be very happy to help and to share their experiences with you.

Employer events, career fairs and law fairs

As we've seen, employers such as law firms will commonly host events of many different forms in conjunction with the student law society, or the law school. Some may offer other opportunities, so keep watch for notices around your university, on law firm websites or on websites such as Lawyer 2B (http://l2b.thelawyer.com/).

Don't wait until the end of your studies before attending talks and events, and don't ignore them just because you don't think you'd want to work for that particular employer or in that particular career. Events like these can highlight new possibilities—they can also help you to decide what you *don't* want to do.

Employers will also attend career fairs. Your university will probably offer a general careers fair, or you may find one run locally in conjunction with several institutions. This can be an excellent opportunity to get a broader view of the range of career options available, and to quiz employers on their interest in law graduate applications. Generalist student career fairs are particularly useful if you are a law student who is not particularly interested in a career directly in law, as law school events naturally focus more on legal careers. Even if you are expecting to follow a legal career path though you should consider attending at least one generalist career fair, to check out other options.

Your law school or student law society may offer a law careers fair, aimed at law students and other students considering a legal career. Law fairs are understandably heavily biased towards legal practice, and solicitors' firms in particular, but many will also have representatives from other employers of law graduates and from barristers' chambers. Law fairs are always worth having a look round, whatever your current career plans. They enable you to see what is on offer without obligation, view the more commercial side of legal practice . . . and pick up a few free pens of course.

Networking

Whatever the event you attend, and whoever you speak to, there is an opportunity for networking. We touched on networking in Chapter 4 as an important skill that you will have been developing from the very start of your legal studies.

Networking is about building professional relationships and so is always valuable for a successful law student. Networking as a law student is not about schmoozing a room and swapping business cards. Neither is it about trying to land yourself a job, there and then. Instead it is about making connections, presenting yourself to best advantage, being memorable (for the right reasons!) and showing interest.

It is often said that good networking is more about giving than getting, and remembering this can help to take the pressure off the experience. Networking is valuable even if you don't currently think you'd be interested in a role that this person represents—you never know when your circumstances might change or you might come across them again.

To make best use of networking opportunities:

- Be prepared to explain a little about yourself and your interests, but be concise and keep things relevant;

- Ask questions and listen—show an interest in the individual's work and own experience. You may even get some valuable insider tips on how to approach your legal studies or job applications;

- Speak clearly and don't use overly casual or inappropriate language, however well you think you are getting on with the other person;

- Dress appropriately for the event. As a law student a conventional approach is safest but you don't need to bury your personality entirely;

- Depending on the occasion, follow up the contact. So making contact wouldn't be appropriate following a quick exchange at a law fair, unless the individual you were speaking to indicated that you should get in touch, but might be if you've had a lengthy conversation about a particular issue, or have been given helpful advice that you are putting into practice.

Another useful tip is to offer your help at events. This shows you are actively engaged, and you are more likely to be noticed than mere attendees. It may also allow longer and more informal contact with those involved, and can take away the embarrassment of approaching people to talk to.

MAKING APPLICATIONS

Moving on rarely, if ever, involves seamlessly moving into a job or other opportunity. Unless you are starting up in business on your own account, or are lucky enough to be heading straight into work with family, it will be necessary to make applications for whatever you want to do, whether that is a job, training or further study.

You already have experience of making applications—at the very least you will have had to apply for your place at law school. You may also have made applications for part-time or temporary jobs, roles such as mentor within your law school or university, or work experience or internships. If you've come to legal study a bit later in life, you've probably made quite a few job applications—or even have experience of sifting through them yourself. Whatever your experience so far, you'll be very aware that your application gives the reader that all important first impression of you—and is essential to get you over the first hurdle.

INSIDER KNOWLEDGE

'Make them interesting, everyone will have a degree, tell us what else you did and what you overcame to get there. Ask yourself what makes me interesting and what can I offer. Don't undersell yourself.'

Danny Smith, Solicitor-Advocate, PCB Solicitors

Being prepared

As a law student, the making of applications often starts a lot earlier than you might expect. Law students can find themselves putting together CVs and making detailed applications long before other students have even thought about visiting the careers service. That is because summer placements and similar opportunities are important if you are aiming (or think you might aim) for a legal career path, while many students will be applying for training positions at law firms during their second year of study.

The timing of applications, how many you have to make and how detailed they need to be, will depend to a great extent on your particular career plans, and how eager you are to push forward. But whatever your chosen route, being prepared well in advance of application deadlines can reduce your workload, and stress, significantly.

I WISH I'D KNOWN . . .

'Start thinking early! In first year, you can go on some internship schemes and open days at law firms or barristers' chambers. You need to stay aware of current affairs and business developments to be prepared for future interviews and assessment days. Don't be disheartened by rejections, and make multiple applications rather than relying solely on a single one succeeding.'

Madeleine Burrell, University of Oxford, Law with German Law, Year 3

The good news is that the successful law student is already well prepared for the application process. Throughout your studies—even in the early stages—you will have been acquiring valuable skills and experience and developing important personal attributes. You will also have been developing the communication skills that will enable you to present all this effectively.

Just as importantly in terms of being prepared, the successful law student has reflected on this development as their studies progressed and made notes on what—and how—they have been learning. Now all that time you spent working on your PDP records, seeing your personal tutor and keeping your CV and personal statement up-to-date really pays off. If you haven't been a reflective learner up till now, and you haven't kept notes of your experience and activities, you will need to do some catching up before you can start putting together your applications. Some of the things you should be able to provide details, and quite possibly reflection, on include:

- Education to date;
- Qualifications;
- Paid work, including part-time or temporary posts;
- Voluntary positions held/charitable activity;
- Other involvement in societies, clubs etc;
- Activities, pastimes and hobbies;
- Additional skills, including languages and information technology;
- Experiences of:
  - completing a project;
  - teamwork;
  - leadership;
  - oral and written communication;
  - problem solving;
  - resilience and/or determination;
  - overcoming adversity;
  - persuading others/negotiating.

CVs and application forms

CV, résumé or application form?

As you'll be aware, CV stands for *curriculum vitae*, translating roughly as 'course of life'. It is a relatively short document, only two to three sides of A4, that summarises your education, qualifications and experiences. A CV is similar to, but not necessarily the same as a *résumé* which is usually shorter, only one to two sides of A4, and is not common in the UK. If a résumé is called for you may be asked also to provide a longer and more detailed CV.

Your CV should be regularly updated to include recent relevant activities. Don't just extend it each time—some earlier or less relevant material will need to be condensed or removed at each update to produce the strongest view of what you offer. There comes a time when school lunch monitor doesn't have quite the impact it might once have done! Quite apart from updating, your CV should be reviewed for every application you make. Even though your qualifications and experience remain the same, you need to check you are including and highlighting those points that are most apposite to the particular role.

Application forms will be provided by the employer or other body to whom you are applying, and can vary hugely, even where the position seems much the same. The form may only ask you for very basic information, relying on your CV for more detail, or may be a lengthy document asking lots of searching questions.

Applications for legal posts are commonly very time-consuming to complete. You need to answer every question thoughtfully and accurately and explain clearly if something isn't relevant—don't just leave a blank. Cutting and pasting from other applications is rarely advisable as questions will differ, even if only subtly, and the position and employer will be different. You may still be able to draw on the same experience, but always rephrase and change the emphasis as necessary.

I WISH I'D KNOWN . . .

'I wish I'd known how vital it is to tailor applications to each firm. It is better to write fewer applications than many sent to as many firms as possible, simply copy and pasted.'

Gabrielle Bargas, University College London, LLB Law with French Law, Year 2

For some roles you will be asked to provide both a CV and a completed application form. Other roles may only require one or the other. Make sure you do as instructed—being able to follow instructions is an important first test of your competence. If, as is sometimes the case, you are given the option of including a CV as well as a completed application form, then it is sensible to include one—other applicants will, and you don't want to be at a disadvantage.

Remember too that a potential employer will want references, and so you will need to provide the names of referees—people who are prepared to comment on your abilities and suitability for the position. For most applications you will need two, and usually one must be from your academic institution. That will usually be your personal tutor, or some other lecturer who knows you well. Ask their permission before you submit your application. Your engagement with your personal tutor, your willingness to participate in class and your involvement with the law school really pays off when it comes to references.

I WISH I'D KNOWN . . .

'When I was working for tutorials, I never considered the fact that it's one's tutorial leaders that are often requested to give references, making it important to build up a relationship from day one.'

Alice Munnelly, King's College London, Law with European Legal Studies, Year 3

Covering letters and personal statements

You may also be asked to include a covering letter and/or a personal statement. These give you the chance to talk more directly to the individual or panel considering your application. Keep it relatively brief (no more than a couple of sides of A4) and highlight:

- **Why you are applying for this role**

  - This is your opportunity to show you know something about the position you are applying for, to convince the reader that you are genuinely interested. So, why this position? Why this company, firm, etc? What makes them stand out, what features of their work or ethos attract you?

- **What makes you right for this role**

  - Here you can pick out particular features from your CV or application that you think are particularly noteworthy, or highlight things that you don't think are fully drawn out elsewhere in the application. But don't just repeat information: try to link together what the role offers with what you offer, and address particular skills or attributes the position demands. What have you got to offer them?

Creating effective CVs and applications

Your careers service will be able to provide you with lots of guidance, and probably one-to-one support, in producing an effective CV and making effective job applications. Your law school or student law society may offer workshops on applications for legal posts. There are also many books and online resources available with detailed guidance and examples of different styles and approaches—a reasonable starting place for some general pointers is https://standout-cv.com/pages/how-to-write-a-cv.

Remember too that your personal tutor may be able to guide you on how best to present *your* material in light of your own situation, and the particular position you are going for. A few key tips for successful CV and application writing, whatever the role, are:

- **Keep it relevant and focused**

  - Think about the post you are applying for, and the people you will be working with. Tailor your CV and/or application form accordingly.

  - Don't simply re-use a CV or application form answers—direct everything clearly to the specific application and questions asked.

  - Make reference to the specific role or employer (etc) but don't just copy material from their website or brochure.

  - Present your material in an appropriate form. For example if you are applying to a law firm, using comic font or patterned paper is not a good idea. Your personality will still be there in what you've done and what you say. As a side note, do not include a photograph unless specifically told to do so.

- **Focus on your strongest points**

  - Emphasise your achievements to give the best overall impression. Focus on your strongest features that are most relevant to the position.

- Don't worry if you haven't done the obvious things, just look for alternative ways of showing achievement. Just because you've never been president of the student law society doesn't mean you haven't developed leadership skills elsewhere.

- Don't ignore weaker points entirely—the reader will notice obvious gaps or omissions—but you don't need to flag them up.

- Find the positives in less obviously favourable things that still have to be mentioned. For example re-taking an A-level can show determination and resilience, or you may have used feedback and learned from experience following a disappointing grade.

- **Show, don't just tell**

  - The reader shouldn't have to guess the point you are trying to make, nor will they necessarily recognise your achievements if you don't spell them out.

  - Give specific examples of things that you are claiming, particularly skills and attributes. So don't simply say you are a good team player, give at least one example of a situation showing just that.

  - Explain what you've learned from experiences, rather than just saying what those experiences were.

- **Don't skimp in preparation**

  - Check instructions carefully and follow them.

  - Think about each answer in an application form. Address questions directly, even if that means having to select and reflect on different experiences from those you've used in other applications.

  - Read through your documents carefully. Make sure they don't contain mistakes such as spelling errors, using the wrong word or typos.

  - If you really aren't that interested in the position then don't bother with a half-hearted application—save yourself, and the reader, time. Focus your efforts on positions you genuinely want.

- **Make it easy for the reader**
  - Present things clearly so they are easy to read. Use a clear font, sensible type size and leave space between sections.
  - Be concise and don't try to squeeze in too much information.
  - Use headed sections to distinguish between different parts and use bullet points where appropriate.
  - Make sure your name is on every page in case pages get separated when printed out.

INSIDER KNOWLEDGE

'Law is about words and so in drafting any document (whether a job application, court application, letter to client etc.), ensure that this is the best that you can do for the type of document involved; this is particularly important in job applications where careless wording may cause the recipient summarily to throw out your application on the spot if you could not be bothered to check that the drafting of the application letter is absolutely correct.'

Peter Bailey, In-house Author at Sweet & Maxwell, and part-time teacher in law at Reading Law School

REAPPRAISING YOUR CAREER GOALS

Persistence and realism

As we've seen, there is much you can do to maximise your chances of success when moving on. But the road to a successful career is rarely smooth and not every law student ultimately obtains the position they initially aspired to. That is true for graduates in every subject, law is not unique. But it is perhaps particularly apparent in law, where the number of law graduates vastly exceeds the numbers of trainee lawyer positions. There are plenty of jobs for law graduates out there, but they won't all be barristers and solicitors, and they won't always be highly remunerated.

Wherever you are heading, you will need to work at it. We are not suggesting you shouldn't aim for the job of your dreams, but you do need to be both persistent and realistic.

INSIDER KNOWLEDGE

'I didn't follow a legal career and it worked out pretty well for me. Law gives you the foundation to move into many different fields.'

Salauoddin Asghar, Strategy and Performance Manager,

London Borough of Barking and Dagenham

Moving on almost always entails hurdles and setbacks. Of course we all know some fortunate individuals who seem to pick up every opportunity and be offered everything they apply for. (Although they are usually not just lucky—they tend to be exceptionally able, hard-working and well-rounded individuals!) But that is a minority. Most law students—and yes, the successful ones too—have to fight a bit to get to where they want to be.

Be prepared to receive knock-backs, and get some rejections. It can hurt, but remember rejection means that you are not quite the right fit for the position, not that there is anything wrong with you personally. Use every setback as the chance for reflection—review your CV, go back through your application and always take up any offer of feedback from a recruitment panel. Every rejection means your next application, or your next interview performance, can be a little stronger.

Persistence is therefore particularly important for a successful law student. You have to keep picking yourself up and trying again. In all likelihood, one day there will be a breakthrough. There is also a need for a healthy dose of realism however. There is no point in throwing yourself against a brick wall for all eternity. If you are getting continuous rejections, particularly if you are never reaching the final selection stages or the feedback is similar each time, something probably needs to be addressed:

- Do you need something more?
- Are you presenting yourself ineffectively?
- Are you appropriately qualified for this position?

Review where you are and what you need. Speak to your personal tutor and careers advisor. This may pinpoint action you can take to improve your chances significantly. Or it may indicate that your particular goal is unlikely to be achievable, at least at present. It can be difficult to come to terms with a long-held ambition being unachievable, but it is important to review your aims and goals in light of changing circumstances. Otherwise you will miss opportunities for which you might be better suited.

I WISH I'D KNOWN . . .

'A law degree is a passport to many different professions. The skills one hones on the course, such as critical thinking and written advocacy, are valued beyond the legal profession.'

Godwin Tan, University College London, LLB Law, Year 3

Taking opportunities, exploring options

Rethinking your options can be tough, particularly if you've always seen yourself in a particular role. You need to view this as a stage in the process of finding the right route for you, rather than a step backwards. While Figure 19.4 is a rather simplistic view of this, it is designed to highlight the importance of reflection and revisiting your plans.

FIGURE 19.4: Finding a new route

So if things are persistently not working out for you, don't get stuck in a rut, or make yourself miserable trying for positions that you aren't (yet) suited for. Take action:

- Take up all opportunities you can find—voluntary work, training, further study, similar jobs in a different field, lower-level jobs within the same field—to get yourself in a stronger position;
- Discuss your situation with other people, such as your personal tutor, careers advisors, mentors, friends and family; work through what really matters to you, and take advice from those who know you and know the job market;
- Make use of any contacts you've made through networking, exploring possibilities and gaining more experience;
- Explore alternatives and keep them in mind.

Don't give up on your dreams too early, but there is no harm in considering other options. Many of your experiences to date—even if they were focused in one particular direction—will still support other career choices with a bit of lateral thinking. And most individuals who were 'forced' into a different career path than the one they'd initially intended have no regrets at all at the turn their lives have taken.

SUMMARY—HELP YOURSELF . . .

- **Know where you are going**
  - Think through your ambitions, goals and short-term tasks.
  - Engage with personal development planning opportunities.
  - Check your goals are realistic and align with your skills and interests.
  - Don't be afraid to revisit your plans and change your goals.

- **Be prepared**
  - Reflect on your skills and experience to date, and as you go along.
  - Keep track using a learning journal, working CV, living personal statement or PDP resource.

- Access, and use, different sources of advice.
- Take up opportunities such as interview practice/CV writing workshops.
- Make full use of networking opportunities.

Ensure your CV and applications are really effective

- Take time to get them right.
- Keep them focused and directed.
- Take advice from the experts.
- Continually update, modify and improve your material.

Look forward to moving on

- Keep positive even when things are uncertain.
- Explore other options and possibilities where needed; don't get fixated on a single route to success.

20

CAREER PATHWAYS

'Are you planning to follow a career in Magical Law,
Miss Granger?' asked Scrimgeour.
'No, I'm not,' retorted Hermione.
'I'm hoping to do some good in the world!'

J. K. ROWLING,
Harry Potter and the Deathly Hallows

INTRODUCTION

Career opportunities for law graduates are many and varied. As well as knowledge and understanding of the law, and a deep and broad understanding of the wider legal and social environment, the law degree also helps you develop valuable skills and attributes.

These are not limited to narrowly 'legal' skills such as using legal search engines or reading cases. The most valuable skills and attributes are transferable, ie of use beyond your degree studies, and beyond legal practice. Law is particularly good at developing these transferable skills, which means that law graduates, or graduates of programmes where law is a significant component, are well suited to a variety of different careers, and are attractive to a range of employers.

This chapter will discuss the valuable, marketable features of a law degree, before moving on to consider particular career pathways. We'll discuss traditional legal pathways—towards a career as a solicitor, barrister or legal executive—and also other careers involving the law. We'll consider other career pathways too; there are many careers that have little to do with the law on a day-to-day basis, but welcome law graduates because of the skills they offer. This chapter will also look at the opportunities for, and merits of, further study.

In a book of this nature we can't cover absolutely everything, nor tell you everything you need to do on any particular path. But we will highlight the breadth of possibilities open to you as a successful law student, and give you some things to consider as you contemplate options and head on to your career pathway.

LAW DEGREE = LEGAL CAREER?

It should already be obvious that studying for, and obtaining, a law degree, doesn't mean you have to become a lawyer, or even work in or with the law at all. Successful law students head in all sorts of different directions after graduation, and have a whole range of different career plans—a successful law student doesn't necessarily become a professional lawyer.

Of course a lot of students who initially embark on a law degree do intend or hope to enter the legal profession, or are considering that alongside other options. Many envisage themselves as a solicitor, others as a barrister, others as working elsewhere in the law.

But not all law students plan to be a lawyer, of whatever sort, so don't be concerned if this is not your ambition. Many students start, and sometimes finish, their law degree with no clear career plans, or may have a career in mind where a law degree isn't essential—perhaps publishing, accountancy or the armed forces. Others plan to use their legal knowledge, but outside the legal professions, perhaps in the civil service, police force or the charitable sector. Yet other students change their mind as they progress through the degree, initially aiming to be a lawyer but then deciding that a legal career is not for them.

I WISH I'D KNOWN . . .

'Law doesn't just mean standing up in court or wearing a wig—hundreds of paths are open to you, and there's no necessity to select one immediately. Do your research, and don't just follow the path everyone else does without checking it's right for you.'

Madeleine Burrell, University of Oxford, Law with German Law, Year 3

There is another group of students too. Some students want to become solicitors or barristers, and work hard towards this goal, but don't make it. We'd rather this wasn't the case, but it is unrealistic to suppose that all law students who want to become professional lawyers can do so. Each year there are vastly more law graduates than there are places for trainee legal professionals, so the numbers just don't add up.

This means that not all law students who initially aimed for a career as a solicitor or barrister will manage to achieve that aim. Even those law schools with a fairly large proportion of their graduates entering the legal profession can't guarantee that all who want that path will make it. If you do want to be a lawyer, don't be too disheartened by this—and make all the efforts you can to make your goal more likely—but do be realistic; be aware of how determined and resilient you may need to be, and keep in mind both alternative careers and the valuable transferable skills you are developing.

I WISH I'D KNOWN . . .

'I wish I'd known how competitive it would be. Not only are you in competition with other law students, but also against others who are completing a GDL.'

Gabrielle Bargas, University College London, LLB Law with French Law, Year 2

THE LAW DEGREE—A (VERY) MARKETABLE COMMODITY

The value of a law degree

Many employers would be keen to add an employee with legal understanding to their team, but the value of the law degree is much more than this. Over the course of this book we have discussed lots of different skills and attributes that you possess, have developed or are developing during your legal studies (see in particular Chapter 6).

It is worth reflecting on these, to understand how far you've come, and your considerable value to employers and society. Doing so makes it easy to see why law graduates are prized by employers outside as well as within the law. The law degree is also valued by employers as a particularly intellectually challenging, rigorous and demanding programme, which is not the universal perception (whether fair or not) of all other degree programmes.

All these factors make the law degree—your law degree—a very marketable commodity. Figure 20.1 provides a reminder of some of the many valuable skills and attributes of a successful law student.

I WISH I'D KNOWN . . .

'A 2:1 in a law degree seems to carry more weight than a 2:1 in something else.'

Alice Munnelly, King's College London, Law with European Legal Studies, Year 3

As well as recognising these many and varied skills and attributes, it is important to reflect on how they fit your career plans—some careers may focus more on particular skills than others and you should seek to develop these more strongly. As always, think about ways in which

FIGURE 20.1: A reminder of skills and attributes

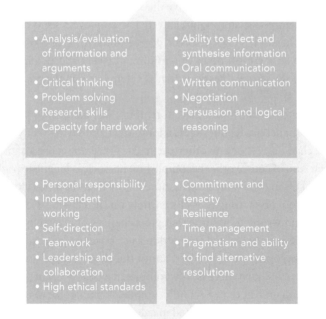

you might be able to increase your skillbase or enhance existing skills, to make you even more marketable.

When considering these skills, think also about both what you *like* doing, and your *aptitude* for particular tasks. This can help you, perhaps with the help of an advisor from your careers service (see Chapter 19), to explore career options that play to your strengths and interests, and ultimately focus on a career pathway that takes you in a direction that best suits you.

The value of *your* law degree

As we've seen, every law degree has value. But that doesn't mean every law graduate is viewed in the same way by potential employers. A big factor in differentiating between applicants will be the additional skills and experience and the extra-curricular activities of an individual—we've thought about those in Chapters 17 and 18 in particular. But other factors may also influence the relative value of your own law degree.

The most obvious of course is the grade of the degree. The higher the classification, the more impressive the achievement is going to look to a potential employer, although relatively few employers seem concerned about applicants having a first class degree. Some roles, or some employers, will have a cut-off point of a minimum level of academic achievement. For the legal professions that is often, but not always, an upper second (2.1).

It is therefore fair to say that more doors will be open to you if you obtain a higher grade. But that is a long way from saying that you need a first class degree, or any other particular grade, to secure a satisfying career. And of course other accomplishments such as languages or leadership skills may be valued much more highly than the grade alone.

So it would be wrong to focus entirely on the classification of your degree, and wrong to assume that your chances of a particular career will necessarily be ruined if you don't get a particular grade. Firstly, not all employers are concerned about the classification—what matters is that you have successfully completed a course of further study, and a law degree at that. Secondly, employers recognise that achievement is not always fully reflected in a degree result, and most will take many other factors into account in considering an application. So they, and you, should view and evaluate your application in the round. If you do feel that less-than-stellar results are holding you back you could consider undertaking a further programme of study to try to enhance your application—the merits of this are considered later in this chapter.

The 'value' of your degree to some employers may also be influenced by where you studied. You've probably heard people discussing whether X is a 'good university' or whether Y is 'good for law'. Perceptions like these mean that some employers may regard law degrees from some institutions more favourably than those from some other institutions. This may be because of the perceived quality of the staff (not necessarily the teaching!), the extra-curricular activities or the rigour of the learning and assessment practices—or all manner of other things. But this effect shouldn't be overstated, and it certainly shouldn't squash your ambitions or put you off applying for the job you really want, wherever you are studying.

For a start, no one would agree completely on which university law schools should go on a list of 'good' ones—and it would constantly change. While there is a tendency to favour the older (pre-1992) and Russell Group universities (a group of highly selective, research-intensive universities), a list of 'good' law schools wouldn't necessarily include all the Russell Group, and would definitely include some other and newer universities. It wouldn't even entirely match the national university league tables. Furthermore, an individual's perceptions of what law schools are particularly good will be influenced by their own experience—where they studied, where their colleagues studied, how engaged the student body there was at a law fair or guest lecture, and so on.

In truth, the classification of your degree, your other skills and achievements, and your extra-curricular activities, are more important than where you studied. While a 'good' law school might help you to achieve all those things, once you've done so, *where* you did so doesn't matter nearly so much. Reflecting this, and to prevent inadvertent discrimination, a number of employers—including law firms—are moving to 'institution-blind' selection, so the recruitment panel won't even know where you studied. So, wherever you are studying, don't be put off from considering all possible career options and employers.

LEGAL PATHWAYS

The legal professions

The term 'lawyer' is often used to encompass all those legally qualified and working in the law, but in this jurisdiction (England & Wales) there is a split profession. The traditional professions of solicitor and barrister are distinct and your pathway to a legal career will differ according to which you are aiming for. (Although the legal system and organisation of the legal professions differs in Scotland, Scotland too has a similarly split legal profession—solicitors and advocates.)

The legal professions also include legal executives, with a role very similar to solicitors, but whose route to qualification is different again. A lot of legal work is now also dealt with by paralegals but we'll say a bit more about these in a bit; for now our focus is on solicitors (and legal executives) and barristers.

While lawyers can share many traits, the different professions tend to require, or at least emphasise, particular—and distinct—skills and competences. This is particularly true of the distinction between solicitors and barristers (there is much more in common between solicitors and legal executives). A precise distinction is difficult because there is huge variety in terms of what individuals do, and how they do it, within each of the professions. And there can be some overlap in terms of what individuals do on a day-to-day basis, and certainly lots of overlap in terms of the areas of law covered. But in essence:

- *Solicitors* are usually the first port of call for someone seeking legal advice. A solicitor provides advice, seeks to find a resolution to the legal issue at hand and represents their client when dealing with other parties. Solicitors usually specialise in a particular area of law (eg family law, crime, corporate law). The role of a *legal executive* is very similar to that of a solicitor, although sometimes working within a narrower area—the difference lies more in the training than the role. On any particular day a solicitor/legal executive might expect to be: getting instructions from a new client, discussing an issue with a client (in person or remotely), writing letters and other documents, holding meetings with colleagues, negotiating an agreement, liaising with courts or other public bodies or drafting instructions to barristers.

- *Barristers* also usually specialise in a particular area of law. They are usually instructed by solicitors/legal executives to provide advice on particular and specific legal issues, and, as specialist advocates, to represent the solicitor's client should a matter go to court. On any particular day a barrister might be: holding a conference (in person or remotely) with a solicitor and/or client, researching a point of law, writing an opinion on a legal matter, drafting legal documents such as a claim, appearing in court or negotiating a settlement.

- The split in the legal profession is sometimes likened to medicine, with solicitors as the GPs, and barristers the consultants/surgeons. There is something in that, but it isn't a great analogy not least because solicitors tend to be specialists as well, just working in a different way, and focusing on different elements of a client's needs.

You can specialise in pretty much any area of law, whichever professional role you favour. The difference is much more about how you work, than the law you do. So think about the kind of work activities you have found an enjoyable challenge, and are particularly good at. What have you really got a buzz out of while studying law?

INSIDER KNOWLEDGE

'Law is a fascinating career. It, generally, presents something different every day. For me this was the biggest draw. If you are going to spend 40/50/60 years doing something, it will be much easier if it interests you.'

David McCormick, Barrister, Exchange Chambers

Also think about your personality and the way you want to live your life, for example do you relish independence or prefer to work within teams, prefer security and stability or constant change and new challenges? Even within a profession there can be a great deal of difference in how you might work and the expectations on you—for example a solicitor in a large City firm will have a very different working life to a solicitor in a high street practice, while a barrister specialising in criminal law will work very differently from one specialising in company law.

So before embarking too far on any particular legal career pathway, do a bit of research on what the job might entail and the different possibilities. Watching TV shows—whether *Silk* or *Suits*—does not give an accurate impression!

Explore the professions' websites, attend careers events and speak to visiting practitioners. Visiting the courts can also help to show you at least one small facet of a professional lawyer's life, and how the roles of solicitor and barrister differ. If you are contemplating the Bar (ie being a barrister—not heading off for a drink) also look at barrister Simon Myerson's reasons why you might want to be a barrister: https://pupillageandhowtogetit.wordpress.com/2008/09/01/why-i-want-to-be-a-barrister/. Once you've found out a little more, and sooner rather than later, you should try to obtain vacation placements (solicitor) and mini-pupillages (barrister) to get a clearer insight into the careers (and the differences between them)—more on this in just a bit.

The pathways

The pathways to become a solicitor, legal executive or barrister are different, not least because the training needs to focus on different competences to reflect the different roles. Although you can transfer between the professions at a later point, or catch up if you don't take the right step at the ideal time, it is obviously easier to follow the right path from the start.

The following section provides some guidance on the basic pathways in England and Wales, assuming you will be starting with a law, or other, degree. (The pathways to qualification are different in Scotland; we will explain the key differences as we go along.) For more detail, and to check the most up-to-date requirements, see the professions' websites:

Solicitors:

> The Law Society: http://www.lawsociety.org.uk/law-careers/ becoming-a-solicitor/
>
> (See also the Solicitors Regulation Authority (SRA): http://www. sra.org.uk/students/students.page)

Barristers:

> The Bar Council: http://www.barcouncil.org.uk/careers/students/

(See also the Bar Standards Board (BSB): https://www.
barstandardsboard.org.uk/qualifying-as-a-barrister/current-
requirements/)

Legal executives:

The Chartered Institute of Legal Executives (CILEx): http://www.
cilex.org.uk/study.

It should also be noted that the legal professions require their members to be of good character. This means that matters such as criminal convictions, county court judgments, bankruptcy, cheating in exams or plagiarism must be disclosed, and may impact on your ability to pursue a legal career.

The solicitor pathway

The pathway for becoming a solicitor is currently in a state of flux. At the time of writing, prospective solicitors need to secure a qualifying law degree (QLD) or Graduate Diploma in Law (GDL), and then undertake the Legal Practice Course (LPC) before moving on to work-based training, a two-year period usually referred to as a training contract. (The LPC is a one-year full-time or two-year part-time course offered by various institutions, covering the skills and knowledge a solicitor needs. It is an expensive course, and does not guarantee you a position as a solicitor.)

A new pathway is expected to be in place from 2020. Those already studying law at that point will have a choice of the old and new pathways.

The new pathway envisages that applicants need no longer have a qualifying law degree or GDL (see Chapter 2) and the LPC will cease to exist. Applicants will still be expected to have a degree, or equivalent, and will have to pass a two-part assessment—the Solicitors Qualifying Exam. A two-year in-work training period will continue to be required. Figure 20.2 (see below) shows the pathway that is expected to apply from 2020, and the elements are explained in more depth afterwards.

The goal for most aspiring solicitors is to become a qualified and practising solicitor, starting as an associate in a law firm and hopefully working in the area of law you find interesting. Before that, as a graduate, you will have had to pass the SQE (the Solicitors Qualifying Exam) and undertake a period of recognised training.

FIGURE 20.2: The solicitor pathway (expected from 2020)

Academic stage	• Complete degree/equivalent level qualification/experience. Although a qualifying law degree/GDL will NOT be a requirement we anticipate that most applicants will continue to have a legal academic qualification • Higher grades (2.1 or above) will ease your route through from here. It isn't impossible to make it with a lower classified degree, but it will be harder
During academic stage	• Undertake vacation placements and/or other work experience • Explore options for preparing for and taking SQE Part 1—your law school and/or careers service will be able to advise you on this • Apply for training contracts
SQE	• Take SQE Part 1, probably prior to commencing your training contract (SQE Part 2 is taken later, during your training contract) • Arrangements for the SQE will become clearer as 2020 approaches—keep an eye on http://www.sra.org.uk and speak to your law school for up-to-date information
Training Contract	• The 'period of recognised training' is often referred to as a 'training contract' • Two-year period of work-based training (usually with a law firm) • SQE Part 2 is taken during this period
Solicitor	• Apply to join the roll of solicitors and obtain a practising certificate • Secure a position at a law firm—in private practice you will usually start as an associate or assistant solicitor

The SQE is an assessment in two parts. The first part, SQE Part 1, will usually be taken before starting your training contract (explained below). It will focus on testing your legal knowledge in areas broadly mapping onto the current Foundations of Legal Knowledge (see Chapter 5). The second part, SQE Part 2, will be taken after your training contract and will be more challenging, testing legal practice-based skills.

The period of recognised training, more commonly called a 'training contract' is an essential part of qualification. Obtaining a training contract is highly competitive, often with detailed and demanding application processes. The basic training contract is a two-year period of work-based training, in which you must experience at least three different areas of practice, with a recognised law firm or other body such as local government or the Crown Prosecution Service. You will put your knowledge and skills into practice, while being supervised and reviewed by experienced solicitors. The new pathway provides more flexibility for this period of training, allowing it to be built up with experience at up to four organisations, and potentially including time spent with a law clinic.

At the end of your training period you may be offered a position as associate or assistant solicitor at the firm at which you've been training. Or you may not—in which case you will need to apply to another firm or elsewhere. (See later on alternative careers for qualified lawyers.)

If you are interested in becoming a solicitor then you should:

- Explore The Law Society's website for more information. The LawCareers.net website is also very useful;
- Keep up to date with the Solicitors Regulation Authority's plans with regard to qualification;
- Speak to your tutor and university careers service;
- Attend lectures and workshops offered by local law firms at your university, and go along to any law careers fairs;
- Speak to your tutor and careers service;
- Apply for vacation placements (see below) at solicitors' firms;
- Consider other work experience opportunities such as marshalling for a judge
- Get relevant skills practice through, for example, negotiation or client-interviewing competitions (see Chapter 17);
- Get involved in pro bono work (see Chapter 18);
- Develop your social and commercial awareness;
- Work hard at your studies and be prepared to persevere.

Vacation placements are periods of structured work experience in a law firm, usually the larger law firms—smaller law firms tend to have less formalised work experience opportunities. They normally last around two weeks, and are often paid. Doing one or more vacation placements isn't absolutely essential but is highly advisable—it enables you to experience what work as a solicitor and in a law firm is like, it gives you the opportunity to make contacts and network, and it shows, for the benefit of future applications, that you are genuinely interested in the law. It also gives the law firm the chance to evaluate you too, which may increase your chances of subsequently getting a training contract there.

Try to gain experience in more than one law firm, working in different areas of the law. Vacation placements are oversubscribed and competitive, so be prepared to make plenty of applications and prepare your applications well, in order to obtain what you need. If you can't get a vacation placement then look for other legal work experience, for example with the local government law department or the courts.

The career pathway for solicitors in Scotland differs a little from that outlined above. Assuming you have a degree (or accelerated degree) in Scots Law, you would then take the Diploma in Professional Legal Practice, the DPL, run by various institutions in Scotland. As in England and Wales, this is then followed by a two-year traineeship with a law firm or other approved organisation. For more information, and details of providers of the DPL, visit the website of the Law Society of Scotland: http://www.lawscot.org.uk/.

The legal executive pathway

Figure 20.3 (see below) illustrates the current pathway to become a legal executive. Always check the CILEx website for up-to-date information on qualification.

Qualification as a legal executive does not require a law degree, or indeed any degree. Instead you study for diplomas at different levels through the Chartered Institute of Legal Executives (CILEx) over several years, usually alongside working in a law firm or other legal environment. However a law degree can provide you with a fast track through CILEx qualification—it is possible to complete the CILEx fast track diploma in

FIGURE 20.3: The current standard legal executive pathway

Academic stage	• Complete qualifying law degree or degree plus graduate diploma in law (GDL) • A qualifying law degree/GDL is NOT a requirement to become a legal executive, but if you don't have one you need to go through the full CILEx study route, rather than the fast track (which is shown here)
Pre-Diploma	• Undertake vacation placements and/or other work experience • Apply for employment with law firm or other legal organisation • Apply for fast track diploma
Fast Track Diploma	• Graduate fast track diploma (CILEx level 6 diploma in legal practice) • Full-time, part-time or distance learning - lasting approx one year part time • Can be done alongside working as a paralegal or trainee legal executive
Qualifying employment	• Complete a three-year period of qualifying employment, eg with a law firm • Can be started before, during or after the diploma • Complete work-based learning logbook and portfolio
Chartered Legal Executive	• Apply to become a fellow of CILEx • Continue in employment where you are, or seek a new position elsewhere

about a year, studying part time. You also need to complete three years of qualifying employment, such as working as a paralegal or trainee legal executive, and if you are working while you study for the diploma this time may count towards that period.

Traditionally, one benefit of qualifying as a legal executive, rather than a solicitor, is that the training has been less expensive, and can be done alongside qualifying employment. That distinction is likely to become a little less clearcut following the changes to qualification for the solicitor profession.

The work of a legal executive is similar to that of a solicitor, although you may not work in quite such a broad range of areas, and you may not be given as much personal responsibility as early on, although this is not always the case. While pay and career prospects are generally better as a solicitor, the gap is beginning to close as the value of legal executives becomes better recognised. Qualifying as a legal executive can also be a step towards subsequent qualification as a solicitor.

Because the role of the legal executive is similar to that of a solicitor, the same kinds of activities we suggested in relation to becoming a solicitor will help to support your applications for employment and ease your pathway. So, for example, use your time at university to gain experience through vacation placements, attending practice-based lectures and workshops and taking up skills-based opportunities.

The barrister pathway

Figure 20.4 (see below) shows the current standard pathway for becoming a barrister. Like the solicitors' profession, the barristers' profession is also looking to create more flexibility in training routes. But for the moment, it seems likely that the BPTC, the Bar Professional Training Course, will remain. Do keep an eye on the profession's websites though, and speak to your law school and careers service about what you need to do.

The goal for most aspiring barristers is tenancy—where a set of chambers accepts you as a member and you start working in earnest on your own account. Before you get that opportunity, the main stages in training for the Bar are the Bar Professional Training Course (or BPTC) and pupillage.

The BPTC, as the name suggests, trains barristers in the professional skills, knowledge and attributes the role requires. It is a one-year full-time course (or two years, part time) and includes things like drafting, advocacy and professional ethics. Before starting the BPTC you will need to (a) pass the Bar Course Aptitude Test (BCAT), and (b) join one of the four Inns of Court.

FIGURE 20.4: The current standard barrister pathway

Academic stage	• Complete qualifying law degree or degree plus graduate diploma in law (GDL) • Higher grades (2.1 or above) will ease your route through from here. It isn't impossible to make it with a lower classified degree, but it will be harder.
Pre-BPTC	• Join an Inn of Court and pass the Bar Course Aptitude Test • Undertake mini-pupillages and/or other work experience • Apply for place on BPTC and pupillages
BPTC	• Bar Professional Training Course • One year (FT) or two years (PT) • Apply for pupillages
Pupillage	• Supervised training with an experienced barrister • At least 12 months, usually split into two six-month periods, with the ability to practise after the first six • Also complete the Advocacy Training and Practice Management courses
Barrister	• Secure a tenancy, ie become a member of chambers • Obtain a full practising certificate • In private practice you will be working on your own account and starting to build a practice

The BCAT tests essential skills such as critical thinking and reasoning, and can be taken at various test centres. The Inns are the ancient institutions governing the Bar, and all barristers must belong to one of them—Gray's Inn, Lincoln's Inn, Inner Temple or Middle Temple. Although you do not need to join an Inn until the May prior to starting the BPTC, it can be worth joining earlier to benefit from your Inn's support, and to have access to scholarship opportunities for the BPTC year.

The BPTC is a very expensive course offered by a range of providers—the full list can be found at the Bar Council's website. Perhaps surprisingly (although less so if you think about the fee income), although the Bar is highly competitive, BPTC providers commonly accept applicants with a lower second class degree. Be warned though—later stages in the pathway, notably pupillage selection, are likely to focus strongly on applicants with higher degree classifications. Be realistic about your chances of obtaining pupillage and tenancy *before* spending time and money on a BPTC.

Pupillage is a minimum twelve-month period of training within a set of chambers, split into two periods of six months. You work with and under the supervision of a pupil supervisor, who will be an experienced barrister, but you will also be given the opportunity to experience work with other barristers in the chambers. Applications for pupillage are made through the Pupillage Gateway, administered by the Bar Council.

Getting pupillage is very competitive—a great number of those who have completed the BPTC won't get pupillage, and even those who secure pupillage won't necessarily secure a tenancy. Such is the attrition rate during the barrister career pathway, it is absolutely essential that you think very clearly about your career goals, and are realistic about your prospects. Speak to tutors, visiting practitioners and alumni—ask your law school to help you get in touch with someone appropriate—to weigh up your own situation. And have a look at Simon Myerson's 'Pupillage and how to get it' blog (noting the editorial/credo): https://pupillageandhowtogetit. wordpress.com).

If you are interested in becoming a barrister then you should:

- Explore The Bar Council's website for more information. The LawCareers.net website is also very useful;
- Speak to your tutor and careers service;
- Attend lectures and workshops offered by barristers at your university;
- Apply for mini-pupillages at barristers' chambers (see below);
- Consider other work experience opportunities, such as marshalling a judge, or working with the Crown Prosecution Service;
- Visit your local courts;

- Experience mooting (see Chapter 17) and get additional skills practice through things like negotiation and debating;
- Get involved in pro bono work (see Chapter 18);
- Develop your social and commercial awareness;
- Work hard at your studies and be prepared to persevere.

Mini-pupillages are periods of usually one or two weeks of work experience at a barristers' chambers. Most mini-pupillages will give you the opportunity to explore different areas of work with different barristers, although the variety you experience will depend on the chambers.

If you want to be a barrister then doing one or more mini-pupillages isn't absolutely essential but is highly advisable. As well as helping you to consider what area you might be interested in working in, it will be much harder to convince someone later that you are genuinely interested in the Bar if you haven't gone to the trouble of getting some experience. If you aren't able to obtain a mini-pupillage then do what you can to find other legal work experience, such as working with an employed barrister, or marshalling (shadowing a judge).

INSIDER KNOWLEDGE

'Get some relevant work experience by doing mini-pupillages but don't fill your summer holiday with those. You will learn as much from doing three or four of them as you will from doing ten. Try to find sets which offer the sort of work in which you think you might be interested, rather than simply an available mini-pupillage, so that you can get a taste of the kind of work you think you might like to do but don't close your mind to different types of work. The life-style of a civil practitioner can be very different from that of a criminal or family practitioner so it is worth thinking about how you might like to work as well as what work you might like to do.'

Anna Vigars QC, Barrister, Guildhall Chambers

In Scotland, the career pathway for advocates initially follows the same route as training to be a solicitor in Scotland—graduation, DPL and then training contract. Those wishing to become advocates must then pass additional examinations set by the Faculty of Advocates, and obtain pupillage, which is commonly known as devilling in Scotland. See the Faculty of Advocate's website for more information: http://www.advocates.org.uk.

Other opportunities for qualified solicitors and barristers

Most qualified solicitors, legal executives and barristers work in private practice. Solicitors and legal executives usually work within a law firm, while barristers are usually self-employed, working in chambers. However not all legal professionals work in private legal practice, and other options include:

- **Crown Prosecution Service**

  - The Crown Prosecution System is central to the criminal justice system as it advises the police in relation to potential prosecutions, and is responsible for prosecuting the majority of criminal cases through the courts. CPS lawyers are therefore involved from an early stage in the process, and have opportunities for advocacy, without the uncertainties and insecurity of private practice. In Scotland the equivalent service is the Crown Office and Procurator Fiscal Service (COPFS).

- **Government legal service**

  - The government legal service employs a number of qualified lawyers (mainly solicitors) to provide legal services and advice to government organisations and departments. The nature of the work can thus vary enormously depending on the department involved.

- **Local government law officer**

  - Local government law officers advise councils on the legal aspects of the various and varied local services provided, from education to noise abatement, and from planning applications to social services.

- **In-house lawyer with a business, institution or charity**

  - Larger business, charities and institutions such as universities will rely on their in-house lawyer or legal team for advice on all manner of things, from employment and pensions, to contracts and planning regulations. Work tends to be varied, requiring a practical, pragmatic and solution-focused approach.

While many of these posts are filled by solicitors, legal executives and barristers who have previously worked in private practice, some are filled by individuals directly from the training stage. Posts like these tend to offer a very different way of life to private practice, and with different pay and career progression opportunities.

Other legal career pathways

There are many ways, quite apart from qualifying as a barrister, solicitor or legal executive, of utilising your law degree in your future career. This section will explain a little more about the more common other legal career opportunities.

Paralegal

Paralegals are increasingly used by law firms to conduct legal and administrative work, supporting solicitors and legal executives. Work can vary from undertaking tasks that a solicitor or legal executive would do, albeit usually under more supervision, to largely menial tasks. It is an excellent way of obtaining more experience in the law and legal practice, making contacts and impressing a particular law firm, all while earning.

A paralegal position can be a valuable stepping stone to a training contract either with the same firm or elsewhere. It is even possible now to qualify as a solicitor through working as a paralegal, but it is more common and straightforward to do so through a training contract.

Legal analyst

Another way of involvement in legal practice is as a legal analyst, but the term may be used for quite disparate roles. This could be a fairly high-level position, often, but not exclusively, filled by qualified solicitors or barristers, overseeing or advising on specialist areas of work. More commonly it is a role akin to a paralegal, perhaps preparing and managing documents, assisting in research, reviewing materials and producing summaries.

Legal academic

As a law student you will have come across many legal academics, from postgraduate teaching assistants to professors, and everything in between. But although you will have seen a lot of the teaching side of the role, you are unlikely to have seen the full picture.

Most academics spend their time with a mix of teaching (lectures, tutorials etc), administrative tasks (from acting as a personal tutor, to monitoring admissions or being Head of Department) and research, usually involving the publication of papers (articles), monographs (books) and reports. The precise mix of responsibilities will depend on the post and the institution. Most academic posts require an excellent academic record, with a postgraduate degree (usually a PhD) or professional experience. Most jobs are advertised on http://www.jobs.ac.uk.

INSIDER KNOWLEDGE

'I've always enjoyed teaching. When I was an undergraduate student I worked with gifted and talented teenagers on university campuses in the USA through Camp America; it was my first taste of engaging students in education. However, I wanted a career where I had flexibility in what I did, engaged with students who really wanted to be there, and, of course, get to call myself Dr. That motivated me to work hard in my undergraduate degree, get funding to do a Masters degree, and progress to do a PhD; all with the aim of teaching university students when I finish.'

Edward Burtonshaw-Gunn, PhD student and Land Law
Tutor, University of Bristol

Legal researcher

Research posts are available within institutions such as the Law Commission (http://www.lawcom.gov.uk/working-for-the-law-commission/) as well as within universities (research-only posts are often called research fellowships, rather than lectureships). Posts are most commonly connected to particular projects, so will be fixed-term contracts, but they can on occasion lead to a more permanent research position. Many research jobs are advertised on http://www.jobs.ac.uk.

Law officer

Roles within legal teams in businesses, charities and institutions may be filled by law graduates or those with other legal training or experience, even if not qualified as a barrister, solicitor or legal executive. Work might include researching issues, working on projects, checking compliance with regulations and drafting legal and other documents.

Court staff

Court staff, such as ushers, do not need to have a law degree as the role does not require legal knowledge, but it can be an interesting post for a law graduate as you will be intimately involved with the legal process. The work includes tasks such as ensuring everyone is in court at the right time, preparing the courtroom and administering the taking of oaths.

Legal secretary

Being a legal secretary is not a graduate role, but law graduates may work as a legal secretary, either temporarily to gain experience and contacts in legal practice, or as a career choice that allows them to be engaged with the law without the pressures and responsibilities of legal practice. Most legal secretaries work in law firms, where they support lawyers, dealing largely with administrative and secretarial matters such as producing legal documents and letters, and liaising with clients.

The type and level of work will depend on the place of work, the seniority of the post and the experience of the individual. Having a law degree can be an advantage when seeking such a position as it indicates you are interested in the law, shows you have knowledge and understanding of a wide range of legal subjects and demonstrates essential skills such as clarity of thought, time management, analysis etc. For more information, see The Institute of Legal Secretaries and PAs' website: https://www.institutelegalsecretaries.com/.

There are lots of other roles that involve some contact with law and regulation, but where it would be a stretch to describe them as 'legal' careers. Accordingly they appear in the next section.

OTHER CAREER PATHWAYS
Looking outside the law

Law students sometimes complain, and often with some justification, that there is too strong a focus during their law degree on legal practice and becoming a lawyer. There are, of course, a great many other interesting and rewarding graduate careers open to law students, and you should keep your options open and explore widely. In fact other than those careers requiring very specific qualifications—medicine, for example—most career opportunities are very much available to law graduates. This includes some careers that are fed by specialist degree programmes—teaching and accountancy, for example—as there are alternative qualifying routes for graduates without these qualifications.

We can't hope to cover all possibilities here—as we mentioned in Chapter 2 our graduates have gone in all sorts of unexpected directions—but have focused on roles for which law graduates are likely to be well suited. We hope to encourage you to think broadly and adventurously about where your legal studies could take you.

Civil Service

Opportunities as a civil servant can be very diverse, with much depending on which part of government you aim for: work in the Government Statistical Office is likely to be very different from work in the Diplomatic Service for example. But all will require a sound sense of public duty and individual responsibility, and will involve communication, dealing effectively with other people, analysis and problem solving—all very much within the successful law student's capabilities.

As a graduate you may be eligible to apply for a Fast Stream scheme, which gives an accelerated route to leadership roles in the Civil Service. More information on working in the Civil Service, including information on the Fast Stream, can be found at: https://www.gov.uk/government/organisations/civil-service/about/recruitment.

INSIDER KNOWLEDGE

'My role gives me a different way to use my legal knowledge; before applying to the Civil Service I had never considered it as a career option, but the Faststream scheme, whilst extremely competitive, provides fantastic opportunities to see a different side to the law in departments such as the Ministry of Justice, Home Office and Department of Health.'

Kate Briden, Director, Royal Courts of Justice Group

Police service

While the police are obviously very much connected with the law, the role of a police officer is very different to that of a practising lawyer! Although a degree is not a requirement to join the police service—and all police officers start on the beat—the skills and knowledge of a law student can be a great asset, and may well assist your progression within the service. Applications are made directly to a specific police force, but general information can be obtained from the College of Policing: http://recruit.college.police.uk/Pages/home.aspx.

Politics

Many well-known politicians have been lawyers, including former Prime Minister Tony Blair. If you have an interest in politics, you are probably already involved with a local or student political organisation—if not, it is probably time to start if you want to take things further. Speak to the party about opportunities and vacancies, but be prepared to do a fair amount of work voluntarily, at least in the early days. If you are more interested in policy than party politics, consider work within a policy institute, which range from independent bodies to those with strong party affiliations.

Business and finance

There are so many roles within this area—from starting your own business, to managing or directing a medium-sized company, accountancy, tax consultancy or joining a major financial institution. Law graduates are often just as highly valued as those who have specialised in business, economics or finance, and it isn't always necessary to undertake further training before making applications or pursuing your own business interests.

While many law graduates go into accountancy and tax work, another role that might be of particular interest to law graduates is that of company secretary. This is an important position in a public company (private companies do not need to have a company secretary) ensuring the company complies with the vast array of relevant legislation and practises good corporate governance. While no specific qualification is required, law graduates are valuable because of their skills and familiarity with legislation and regulation. More information can be found at: https://www.icsa.org.uk/. Explore the myriad options available in business and finance through your careers service and try out various roles through work experience.

Teaching

Teaching, at whatever level, can be very rewarding, and will make excellent use of your communication, resilience and problem-solving skills. Graduate entry into the teaching profession is through a postgraduate certificate in education (PGCE), which combines academic and in-school training. You might also want to consider the 'Teach First' scheme (http://www.teachfirst.org.uk), which is an intensive teaching and leadership scheme over two years designed for top graduates. Teach First graduates may subsequently choose to stay within teaching or use the experience to support their pursuit of other career goals, including legal careers.

Social work

Although lawyers sometimes get a bad press, many law students come to the law because they want to help others, and have a strong interest in injustice and social inequality. For these students a career in social work may be worth considering. The Frontline scheme (http://www.thefrontline.org.uk/) offers top graduates a fast, intensive route into challenging work and leadership.

Administration and management

The variety of roles in administration and management (including areas such as human resources) across a vast array of organisations, industries and institutions, mean that most law graduates would be able to find something to suit their skills and abilities. Many roles in management and administration involve some overlap with law and regulation, as well as a lot of teamwork, problem solving, attention to detail, and communication. Work in this field is often varied, with good career prospects, and jobs at all levels tend to be relatively widely publicised.

FURTHER STUDY

Not every law student intends to move directly into a job, or job-related training, after completing their legal studies, and there are plenty of post-graduate study options available. These vary in length of study, nature of study and subject of study. While the following discussion focuses on law programmes, further study options are not necessarily limited to law—many postgraduate programmes in other subjects are open to law graduates.

Postgraduate study options

Shorter postgraduate degrees, usually lasting one or two years, are known as masters degrees (LLM, MA or MSc). They fall into two broad categories—taught courses, and masters by research—although typically there is at least some class learning and some research in both.

I WISH I'D KNOWN . . .

'I am currently applying, and I think then it is really important to reflect on why you have enjoyed studying law, and why you have succeeded in developing your knowledge in your areas of interest.'

Fiona Lin, University of Cambridge, Law, Year 3

Taught degrees

The majority of students studying law at postgraduate level are on taught masters/LLM programmes. LLM students will usually select between four and eight options (depending on credit value) from a vast array of specialist and advanced taught modules, and will also usually be required to undertake a research project/dissertation. Teaching and assessment methods for a taught masters programme will vary according to the institution and subject, but compared with undergraduate law programmes, there is usually a greater emphasis on seminars and individual presentations rather than lectures, and coursework rather than exams.

Taught law masters programmes may be general, enabling students to select any module they like from those offered. Or they may be specific/branded, such as an LLM in Commercial Law, or LLM in International Law, in which students must select their subjects from a specialist list.

Choosing a specialist masters can help you focus on an area of particular interest to you, either to build on options taken as an undergraduate or to take up new subjects. Undertaking a specialist law masters programme can show future employers that you are really serious about a particular area of the law, and have gained broad and deep knowledge of the area. You might even benefit from a non-law masters programme in a connected area—for example business or finance if you are looking for a corporate post—to gain different perspectives and skills. If you want to continue with your studies but don't have any particular idea of what to specialise in, then a general law masters is likely to be a better bet—particularly if you are still exploring interests and deciding what to do in the future, or will be pursuing a career that does not require expertise in any particular area.

Research degrees

Postgraduate degrees by research will involve some training in research techniques, but otherwise you will mostly be working on your own. It will be for you to develop a research proposal (your current tutors may be happy to discuss this with you), and submit it for consideration. If accepted, you will hone this proposal with a supervisor and engage in your own research (with regular supervision) to produce a thesis.

A masters by research normally lasts a year, giving you the opportunity to immerse yourself in a topic, but probably not become a world expert. If you have a major piece of research in mind, or wish to pursue a research career, you should consider a PhD (or doctorate). This involves working on a significant piece of original research, over a three-year period (if full-time), becoming part of the research community of your institution and probably working towards publishing articles and giving papers at academic conferences over that period.

Given the intensive nature and long timescale of a PhD—and the very demanding nature of the work and assessment—it is important that you think carefully about the topic you want to research, where you want to study, who is available to supervise your research (you will need to identify an appropriate expert) and how to finance your studies and living expenses. You also need to carefully examine your motivation and resilience to ensure you can survive the pressures of researching and writing at this level.

INSIDER KNOWLEDGE

'When approaching a PhD the most important thing you need is discipline. To get to this stage in academia you will have shown a consistent level of understanding and ability but in the PhD you need to apply these skills independently. You can no longer rely on members of staff or handouts to guide your learning. The PhD is a task in time management as well as your ability to self-motivate. Although it sounds easy, to do so consistently over three years or more is the most challenging aspect of a PhD.'

Richard Costidell, PhD Student and Assistant
Teacher, University of Bristol

Why consider postgraduate study?

Reasons why a law student might want to undertake postgraduate study encompass the personal, professional and practical, and vary according to the student. Postgraduate study can benefit a wide range of students. Those who were high-flying undergraduates can push themselves to even greater heights, pursue existing interests and talents or stretch themselves in new areas. Those who found undergraduate study harder may find they flourish as they continue to develop their skills, and experience different study and assessment practices. All students may enjoy exploring new subjects, engaging with issues at a higher level and working with experts on matters of topical interest.

Postgraduate study can enhance a CV and thus career prospects in many ways. But the benefits need to be evaluated in light of your own goals and position. A postgraduate degree is not a requirement for most careers, and won't necessarily make up for a weak undergraduate performance. Reasons for undertaking postgraduate study are many and varied:

- Desire to specialise in a particular field, either through interest or to enhance career prospects;
- Further opportunity to develop academic and broader skills;
- Pursuing an interest started at undergraduate level, perhaps in a dissertation;

- Studying a further and broader selection of law subjects;
- Developing interests into a connected, non-legal, field;
- Opportunity to attend a different or more prestigious university;
- Interest in an academic research/teaching career;
- Wanting further time to think about career options.

Whatever your reasons for considering further study, weigh up your options carefully—both whether to continue in further study, and what (and where) to study. Postgraduate study isn't always the best option for all students in all circumstances. Although it can bring benefits, it adds to the total expense of your education, while simultaneously delaying the point at which you'll start to earn a living. It requires strong academic ability and hard work, and won't necessarily improve your chances of success in all job markets.

Discuss your plans with your tutor and your careers advisor, to see whether further study is likely to assist your longer-term career goals, and if so, what route might be best. Remember too that while a future employer will be interested in your further study, they won't just accept that an applicant with a postgraduate degree is necessarily better than one without. They will expect you to be able to justify your decision— and to have some pretty convincing and positive reasons. Just wanting to be a student for a little longer won't be sufficient!

SUMMARY—HELP YOURSELF . . .

- **Think widely about your career options**
  - Recognise the many skills you can offer, both legal and transferable.
  - Remember that legal careers are much more varied than just the traditional solicitor/barrister choice.
  - Explore non-legal careers as well as legal careers.
  - Visit careers fairs, speak to your careers service, attend talks and workshops from alumni and other guest speakers.

- **Ease your pathway**
  - Make sure you understand the steps you need to take on the pathway to your chosen career, and when things need to be done.
  - Speak to people in your institution, and any contacts in the same profession, for advice and hints on how to approach each step.
  - Check what is needed with relevant professional bodies, and make sure there have been no changes since you last looked.
  - Undertake relevant work experience.
  - Aim to work on the skills, and engage in activities, that are most directly relevant to your chosen career.

- **Consider the possibility of further study**
  - Explore the different options—within and outside law.
  - Carefully weigh up the benefits against the downsides, with a particular focus on your own career plans.
  - Consider your own motivations and willingness to engage in further academic study.

21

A SUCCESSFUL FUTURE

'Jack: You're quite perfect, Miss Fairfax.
Gwendolen: Oh! I hope I am not that.
It would leave no room for developments,
and I intend to develop in many directions.'

OSCAR WILDE,
The Importance of Being Earnest

INTRODUCTION

As we reach the end of this book, we hope we have managed to convey at least some of the very many things that go into making you a successful law student. And while success may be up to you in terms of the things you do, and how you do them—and we have sought to provide guidance on all this—it also depends on your attitude to success, what you choose to do and how you choose to view it.

Of course your success does not end with graduation. In this final short chapter we are going to look forward to a successful future beyond law school. We'll start by considering what may, but needn't, be your last contact with your institution, and then think about ways in which you can use the legal skills and personal attributes that you have developed during your studies in the future. We will end by briefly revisiting the notion of success, to see what that might mean as you move on to a successful future.

LEAVING LAW SCHOOL

By the time you move on you will in all probability have accumulated many years of experience, acquired several life-long friends and many acquaintances, and developed new passions and interests. You'll have become an accomplished legal thinker and writer, and a reflective learner. Your time at law school will have changed you, and you may find it hard to remember the individual who started this process perhaps three, or more, years earlier.

Completing your legal studies and leaving law school is a big moment in any law student's life. You'll say farewell to friends, tutors and quite possibly a well-loved institution and city. You also have the excitement of celebrating achievements—large and small—and looking forward to moving on. Attending a graduation ceremony, if possible, helps to bring your experience to a positive close, marking the end of a significant stage in your life, and the beginnings of the next. It can also bring your wider family together with friends and tutors, so everyone can enjoy your success.

Graduation day is also a good opportunity to say goodbye to your personal tutor and lecturers, as well as your friends. You might be surprised at just how interested your lecturers and tutors have been in your progress, how much they care and how pleased they are with your success.

Graduation need not be a final goodbye. For many students, completing their law degree is the last contact they will have with their law school, other than perhaps the occasional request for a reference! That of course is absolutely fine.

But you may choose to maintain some kind of contact, and law schools welcome ongoing relationships with their alumni. This could be as simple as letting your personal tutor know how you are getting on in the next stage of your life, or attending open lectures to catch up with old contacts. Or, as you work through different elements of your successful, and undoubtedly challenging, life and career, you might want to offer your support through careers guidance, mentoring or even guest lecturing on specialist areas.

Many law graduates find that a meaningful, even if intermittent, relationship with their law school or particular individuals within their law school, is very rewarding. It can both shape and enhance their own careers, and provide a means of engaging with a new generation of successful law students.

MAKING USE OF YOUR SKILLS AND ATTRIBUTES

As a successful law student you have acquired valuable knowledge, essential and transferable skills and admirable personal attributes. These can, and should, be used and continually developed and added to—whether for personal satisfaction, social or community benefit, or career development.

Continuing to develop

Over the course of your legal studies you will have put a huge amount of effort into developing your skills, aided by support, guidance and the obvious incentive of assessment. That support and guidance, as well as the pressure of assessment, will be rather less after graduation, but for a successful future you will still need to continue to develop your skills and attributes. The end of study doesn't mean the end of learning.

Whatever career path you follow, you will have numerous opportunities for training and development. Sometimes they will be compulsory, sometimes optional, and sometimes they have to be hunted out. But take all you can. Once you are working, training can sometimes seem like an unnecessary burden or distraction in a busy life. But skills or wider understandings may come from the most surprising places, if you are prepared to give every learning opportunity a chance.

When attending training sessions—even if they are compulsory and seem pointless—never assume the trainer has nothing worthwhile to teach you, or you have nothing to learn. Try not to view obligations such as the 'continuing professional development' requirements in many professions as an imposition. Quite apart from your personal growth, remember that further training and active engagement with learning can also be a way of distinguishing yourself from other applicants when looking for new positions, as well as providing further opportunities for networking.

As well as directed learning, or training, it is important to maintain wide interests. Continue to take an interest in the world around you, with the benefit of your legal knowledge. While you are unlikely to keep up with all the activities you engaged in at university, try to maintain at least some of your interests, or find new ones.

Don't make excuses—excuses are all too easy to find when you are busy. So squeeze out some time to continue to visit the theatre or sing in a choir; move from playing to coaching as your legs give way; take a weekly rather than daily fitness class; travel for a weekend if you can't find a free week. Successful law students tend to be very hard workers, but work is not everything. Use your time management skills to ensure a reasonable work-life balance whatever the pressures upon you.

Mentoring

Mentoring can be a key part of a successful future, and has a role to play both at the start of your career, and as your career develops. Mentoring provides a mechanism for support and guidance from someone more experienced than you.

If you are fortunate enough to have a mentor allocated to you, or simply have someone who acts informally in that role, then do make full use of that relationship. That doesn't mean doing exactly what they say—a good mentor won't tell you what to do anyway. But it can be very useful to discuss your ideas, ambitions, career plans and challenges with someone with a different perspective and the advantage of a few more years' experience. Many mentors find the relationship equally rewarding and developmental.

INSIDER KNOWLEDGE

'If you can, find a mentor. I have had 3 during my career. All were invaluable to me.'

Jonathan Brew, Senior Partner, Harrison Clark Rickerbys

Don't forget too that you may have a valuable role to play as mentor to someone else. If you are just starting out on a career that might seem a long way off. But it needn't be. You already have the skills and experience to act as mentor—many new law students would welcome the support and advice of someone who has only recently gone through the same experiences they are now facing for the first time. This may be informal. Perhaps you have friends and contacts in lower years of their studies, or just about to go to university. Or it could be more formal. Speak to your law school or student law society about offering support and mentoring from your position of experience.

A broader outlook

This book has naturally focused on what *you* need to do for success. But just as studying law is not about working alone or ignoring the needs of others, neither is a successful future just about what you can do for yourself.

As we've seen, law is pervasive. It both shapes and is shaped by society. Consequently law students benefit from a broad and deep appreciation of the world and society around them, as well as being very well qualified in a range of valuable skills with many valuable attributes. So a law graduate is extremely well placed to benefit their community, whether local, national or global—everyone can make a difference. Caitlin Moran puts it rather well in her recent book, *Moranifesto*:

> All the answers will *never* come in one person. The future is a communal ef-fort—like a patchwork quilt. Everyone interested in forming our society takes a square each—a square they have chosen according to their interests, knowledge and ability—and sews it, and then we join them together to make a fabulous quilt. That's how things get done.

If your future lies in legal practice, then you will be able to put your legal knowledge or experience directly to use for the benefit of society. Take an interest in the many pro bono schemes and advice centres that try to bridge the gaps in the provision of justice. Offer your skills to a charity or political group. Direct your passions towards something you believe in. Even if you have no desire to work with the law, the broad, essential, transferable skills you have developed will be of value in the world around you, and enhance your experience of your successful future. Think about what you can offer your community, to benefit others, and yourself.

I WISH I'D KNOWN . . .

'My definition of success was to make money as I saw the law degree as a money-making degree. Now I have a real appreciation for the way the law impacts our lives as well as the fulfilment that comes from helping others. I think that success now means to help change other people's lives.'

Lul Sheikh-Salah, BPP University, LLB, Year 3

SUCCESS AND THE FUTURE

Whether or not you achieve 'success' of course depends on how you define it. In Chapter 3—and throughout this book—we emphasised that success depends on your goals, and making your best efforts towards them, rather than absolute notions of attainment.

As you move on from law school you will need to decide how you want to approach your future—whether to strive continually for ultimate aims that may not be attainable, or to work towards individual achievable goals and accept and deal with the circumstances you find yourself in. You will probably guess that we think the latter is more likely to result in a successful future in terms of your well-being, and quite probably in terms of career satisfaction too.

INSIDER KNOWLEDGE

'Dream big, hold onto that dream and build on it. Use your legal skills as a force for good and you will be closer to a happy life.'

Lali Wiratunga, National Manager Davidson Institute at
Westpac Banking Corporation, Australia

Whether your plans are ambitious or modest, couched in absolute terms or in terms of effort, it is highly unlikely that your future plans will all run smoothly. Perhaps the most valuable skill of the successful law student is resilience. You will need to be able to process disappointment or unexpected developments, and move on. That includes being sufficiently adaptable to change your plans, even if this means admitting to yourself and others that perhaps you have been following the wrong path for you. Keep your life, goals and ambitions under review, and enjoy a successful future wherever it takes you.

Good luck.

INDEX